AQA A LEVEL
SOCIOLOGY
BOOK ONE
INCLUDING AS LEVEL

Rob Webb
Hal Westergaard
Keith Trobe
Annie Townend

NAPIER PRESS **Sociology**

For Anna Pellizzi

Published by Napier Press Limited
Email: enquiries@napierpress.com
Website: www.napierpress.com

Third Edition © Napier Press 2015

First Edition published in 2004 by Napier Press
Second Edition published in 2008 by Napier Press

ISBN-10: 0-9540079-1-3
ISBN-13: 9780954007911

The authors assert the moral right to be identified as the authors of this work.

British Library Cataloguing in Publication Data
A catalogue record for this book is available from the British Library

Design by HL Studios
Cover design by Promo Design
Printed and bound by Pureprint

The publishers would like to thank the following for permission to reproduce photographs. Alamy Images pages 5, 6, 8, 10, 15, 16, 18, 26, 33, 36, 46, 50, 66, 81, 89, 90, 92, 100, 105, 108, 116, 121, 124, 136, 151, 166, 170, 175, 178, 188, 193, 195, 210, 213, 215, 220, 225, 227, 229, 230, 234, 239, and 245. Corbis pages 73, 76, and 97. Daniel Bridge page 157. Getty Images pages 153, 165, 191, 198, 221, and 224. Johnson Matthey page 39. Mirrorpix page 148. Photofusion pages 24, 43, 53, 59, 61, 132, and 185. Wikipedia page 180.

Every effort has been made to contact the holders of copyright material, but if any have been inadvertently overlooked the publishers will be pleased to make the necessary arrangements at the first opportunity.

Go to www.sociology.uk.net
Online support for Sociology teachers and students using this book.

CONTENTS

Tour of the book's features

Before you start to use the book, we invite you to come on a quick tour to show you the book's features and help you get the most out of it.

▲ Topic pages

Each chapter is divided into manageable sized topics, each covering a separate issue in sociology. The topic page also has a Getting Started activity to get you thinking, and Learning Objectives that spell out what you are going to learn in that topic.

The AQA Specification

The specification is the syllabus produced by the exam board, telling you what you have to study. The AQA specification for Education requires you to examine the following:

● The role and functions of the education system, including its relationship to the economy and to class structure.

● Differential educational achievement of social groups by social class, gender and ethnicity in contemporary society.

● Relationships and processes within schools, with particular reference to teacher/pupil relationships, pupil identities and subcultures, the hidden curriculum, and the organisation of teaching and learning.

▲ The AQA specification

This is the syllabus produced by the exam board that tells you what you are required to study for the exam. It appears at the start of each chapter.

Activity **Research**

Cannibalism as a norm

...go to www.sociology.uk.net

▲ Activities

These develop your knowledge, understanding and skills by giving you a task to carry out, on your own or with your classmates. Some involve research outside class, carrying out small surveys or researching on the internet. Most of the activities can be found at this book's own dedicated website at www.sociology.uk.net.

Analysis and Evaluation

What problems might there be in using evidence such as paintings and diaries, as Ariès does, to understand childhood or family life in the past?

▲ Question panels

In each topic, there are short questions for you to answer on your own or with others. These can be either Application questions or Analysis and Evaluation questions; both types are designed to help you develop your exam skills.

▼ Boxes

These contain extra information, such as examples, details of important sociological ideas or studies, or relevant laws and policies. Some have questions to get you thinking further.

Box 7   Postmodern society and the family

Postmodernists argue that since the late 20th century, society has entered a new 'postmodern' phase. Postmodern society has two key characteristics:

Diversity and fragmentation: Society today is increasingly fragmented, with an ever greater diversity of cultures and lifestyles - more a collection of subcultures than a single culture shared by all. People can 'pick and mix', creating their identities and lifestyles from a wide range of choices. For example, different ethnic and youth subcultures, sexual preferences, and social movements such as environmentalism, all offer sources of identity.

Rapid social change: New technology and the electronic media have dissolved old barriers of time and space, transformed our patterns of work and leisure, and accelerated the pace of change. One effect of this rapid change is to make life less predictable.

Investigating the reproduction of class inequality

The issue of the reproduction of class inequality has certain important **research characteristics** – particular features that may make it easy or difficult to investigate. For example:

- Since schools do not track and record the careers of their ex-pupils, there is no ready-made data for researchers to use.
- Contacting former pupils may be difficult both because any addresses the school still holds for them may be out of date, and because researchers may not be given access to this information anyway.

1 What other research characteristics of the reproduction of class inequality can you think of? You could consider issues of access, ethical concerns etc particular to investigating the reproduction of class inequality.

◄ Investigating education

These special boxes appear in Chapter 2 *Education*. They help you to understand the issues involved in researching topics in education.

Topic summary

Participant observation (PO) involves joining in with a group to gain **insight**, and can be overt or covert. Research goes through three phases: getting in, staying in and getting out. **Covert** PO may produce more **valid** data, but is **ethically** questionable and faces practical problems of maintaining one's cover.

▲ Summaries

Each topic ends with a summary that picks out the most important points. This at-a-glance overview helps you to consolidate what you have learned and revise for the exam.

Box 17 Positivism, interpretivism and experiments

Positivists favour the *laboratory* experiment in principle because it achieves their main goal of reliability:

- Careful control over experimental conditions and experimenter detachment produce reliable data because other researchers can replicate the experiment.

However, positivists nonetheless recognise the shortcomings of laboratory experiments:

- It is often impossible or unethical to control the variables.

For these reasons, positivists sometimes use the *comparative method* instead.

Interpretivists reject the laboratory experiment because it fails to achieve their main goal of validity. It is an artificial situation producing unnatural behaviour. Interpretivists favour more naturalistic *field* experiments, but positivists criticise this method for giving us less control over variables.

See Box 12 on page 94 for more about positivism, interpretivism and research methods.

◄ Theory and methods boxes

These special boxes appear in Chapter 3 *Research methods*. They help you to understand some important theoretical issues linked to the research methods that sociologists use.

METHODS IN CONTEXT
using experiments to investigate education

Sociologists sometimes use experiments to study issues such as:
- Teacher expectations
- Classroom interaction

- One third (the low expectancy group) were told that he was poorly motivated with a low IQ.
- One third were given no information.

Methods in context ▲

A key feature of the AS and A level exams is that you have to apply research methods to topics in education. These special sections in Chapter 3 help you do just that. They also include practice questions and the examiner's advice on how to tackle them.

Questions to try ▶

At the end of each topic, there is a set of practice questions to help you prepare for the exams. At the end of each chapter there is a full set of questions for both AS and A level.

Preparing for the exams

Tackling the AS sociology exam   000

▲ Preparing for the exams

This is a special chapter dedicated to helping you succeed in the exams. It explains what the exam papers cover, the different types of question and how to tackle them. It also includes practice papers for both AS and A level.

▼ QuickCheck Questions

These test-yourself questions come at the end of each topic to test your understanding of what you have read and to reinforce your knowledge of key ideas. You can check your answers at our website.

Key Concepts

The following is an alphabetical list of some of the key concepts you need to know for AS level Sociology. You can

When you look up a concept other terms in the explanation

Key concepts ▲

This is a list of essential terms you need to know, defined briefly and clearly, often with links to other concepts to help you develop your understanding. Use it as a quick reference section to check the meaning of key terms. Also good when revising for the exams!

The examiner's advice ▶

These give you advice and guidance, and help you plan your answers to the essay questions.

CHAPTER 1

What is sociology?

GETTING STARTED

1 Working on your own, using a sheet of A4 paper, draw a picture or diagram of how you see society. You could use stick people, shapes (circles, triangles etc.), signs and symbols or anything else you like. There is no right or wrong answer.

2 Stick your pictures on the wall. Look at everyone's pictures.

   a What similarities are there, if any? Can you group any of them together?

   b What do the pictures tell us about how the people in your class see society?

   c As a class, compare your answers to question b. Did you all reach the same conclusion about how people see society?

What is sociology?

Sociology is the study of society and of people and their behaviour.

Sociologists study a wide range of topics. For example, the AQA AS and A level specifications include topics such as education, families and households, beliefs in society, and crime and deviance.

In studying topics like these, sociologists create **theories** to explain human behaviour and the workings of society. Theories are explanations of the patterns we find in society. For example, we may have a theory as to why there are differences in girls' and boys' achievement levels in school.

Sociology is an **evidence-based** subject. This means it is not just about the sociologist's personal opinion or pet theory – our opinions and theories must be backed up by facts about society. Sociologists therefore collect evidence methodically by carrying out **research** to establish whether their theories are correct. A good theory is one that explains the available evidence.

As well as producing theories about society, sociology has practical applications. For example, if we know the causes of social problems such as educational under-achievement, we may be able to use this knowledge to design **social policies** to improve children's educational opportunities. Governments may use the findings of sociological research to develop more effective policies.

Learning objectives

When you have studied this chapter, you should:

- Know the meaning of key terms: culture, norms, values, socialisation, status and role.
- Understand the importance of culture and socialisation for explaining human behaviour.
- Understand the difference between structural and social action views of society, and between consensus and conflict views of society.
- Understand the differences between traditional, modern and postmodern society.
- Know the main patterns of inequality in today's society.
- Understand that sociologists use a variety of research methods and that these have both strengths and limitations.
- Know what studying AS and A level sociology involves, including the exam papers, assessment objectives and ways of developing your knowledge and skills.

Nature or nurture?

People disagree about whether our behaviour is somehow 'natural' or innate (inborn), or whether it is the result of nurture – that is, our upbringing in society.

Some biologists argue that behaviour is mainly shaped by natural **instincts**. An instinct is an innate, fixed, pre-programmed pattern of behaviour shared by all members of a given species. For example, all blackbirds are 'programmed' to produce the same song patterns, and a blackbird reared in isolation from others will still produce the same song.

In other words, instinctive behaviour doesn't have to be learned. Many instincts are an automatic response to particular stimuli in the environment, such as birds migrating as the seasons change. These behaviours are not learned and the animal apparently has no control over them.

Many biologists argue that, like animal behaviour, our behaviour too is governed by instinct. For example, they claim that humans have natural instincts for reproduction and self-preservation, and that women have a maternal instinct for childbearing and rearing.

However, sociologists question whether human behaviour really is governed by instincts. They point out that on the whole our behaviour is not fixed biologically.

Although we may all possess the same biological urges or drives, the way we act on them varies between individuals and societies. For example:

- Although we all have a sex drive, the way we satisfy it can vary: from promiscuity to monogamy, polygamy etc – or we may choose to remain celibate.
- We have a drive for self-preservation, yet some people choose to commit suicide or risk their lives in war.
- Women are said to have a maternal instinct, yet some choose to abandon or abuse their children – and today over a fifth of all women in Britain choose not to have children at all.

If our behaviour really was determined by instincts, we would not expect to find such enormous variations in behaviour between individuals and societies.

Sociologists argue that the reason for these variations is that our behaviour is **learned** rather than instinctive. Much of this learning occurs in our early years through contact with others and this has an enormous influence on our behaviour and development.

For example, language, knowledge of right and wrong, practical skills such as dressing oneself, table manners and so on all have to be learnt from other members of society. Box 1 shows some of the harmful effects that lack of social contact in our early years can have on human development.

Sociologists therefore argue that biology and instincts cannot explain our behaviour, because most of it is learned not inborn, and because it is not fixed for all members of our species, but varies between societies. As an alternative way of explaining human behaviour, therefore, sociologists use the two related ideas of culture and socialisation.

▲ Much of our learning occurs in our early years.

Culture, norms and values

Sociologists define **culture** as all those things that are learned and shared by a society or group of people and transmitted from generation to generation. Culture includes all the things that a society regards as important, such as customs, traditions, language, skills, knowledge, beliefs, norms and values.

For example, the culture of societies whose way of life is based on hunting will include hunting skills and techniques, knowledge of the habits and movements of game animals and so on. Similarly, such cultures often contain shared beliefs about the spirits of the animals they hunt and how they should be treated.

Members of a society also share norms and values. **Values** are general principles or goals. They tell us what is good and what we should aim for. For example, modern American society places a high value on individual achievement and the accumulation of personal wealth. By contrast, societies such as those of Native American Indians place a high

Box 1 The effects of extreme isolation

Over the years, there have been several cases of 'feral' (wild) children found in forests and elsewhere who had apparently been reared by wolves or other animals. There is no way of knowing for sure if such children really had been nurtured by animals, but it is certain they had had little contact with other humans. One case was that of Shamdev, an Indian boy aged about five found in a forest playing with wolf cubs. When first found:

'Shamdev cowered from people and would only play with dogs. He hated the sun and used to curl up in shadowy places. After dark he grew restless and they had to tie him up to stop him following the jackals which howled around the village at night. If anyone cut themselves, he could smell the scent of blood and would scamper towards it. He caught chickens and ate them alive, including the entrails. Later; when he had evolved a sign language of his own, he would cross his thumbs and flap his hands: this meant "chicken" or "food".' (The Observer, 30 August 1978)

Of course, it is possible that parents abandon children like Shamdev precisely because they are abnormal, and such children may not have developed normally even if they had been raised in human company. However, the case of Isabelle suggests otherwise. Discovered at the age of six, Isabelle was the child of a deaf mute single mother. Both mother and child had been kept shut up by the family in a darkened room for most of the time.

According to Kingsley Davis (1970), 'Her behaviour towards strangers was almost that of a wild animal, manifesting much fear and hostility. In place of speech she made a strange croaking sound. In many ways she acted like an infant... At first it was even hard to tell whether or not she could hear, so unused were her senses.'

She was also unable to walk properly, and at first it was thought she might have severe learning difficulties. However; in two years of intensive training, Isabelle was able to cover the stages of learning that normally take six years and she went on to develop normally. These examples show that basic human social characteristics are not inborn or instinctive. We have to learn to be 'normal human beings' through contact with others in our early years.

Working alone or in small groups:

1 Make a list of all the characteristics of Shamdev and Isabelle that might be described as 'non-human'.

2 What 'human' characteristics, skills and abilities would you expect a normal five or six year old child to possess? Are any of these inborn?

3 What conclusions would you draw about the importance of nurture and nature in human development?

---

value on individuals fulfilling their duties to the group, including the duty to share their wealth rather than keep it for themselves.

While values lay down general principles or guidelines, **norms** are the specific rules that govern behaviour in particular situations. For example, cultures that place a high value on respect for elders usually have specific rules on how they are to be approached or addressed. It may not be

permissible to look directly at them when speaking to them, or openly disobey or disagree with them.

Each culture has detailed rules or norms governing every aspect of behaviour, from food and dress to how we perform our jobs or who we may marry. Some norms, such as written laws or rules, are formal. Other norms are informal, such as table manners.

If we fail to keep to a norm, others may punish us. For example, stealing may result in a fine or imprisonment. Likewise, when we uphold a norm, we may be rewarded. For example, obeying the norm that we should work hard at school may earn us a place at university,

Sociologists use the term **sanctions** to describe anything that encourages people to conform to norms. Rewards are positive sanctions, while punishments are negative sanctions. Sanctions are a form of **social control**. That is, they are a way of ensuring that society's members behave as others expect them to.

Cultures and their norms vary greatly. What one culture considers normal or desirable, another may see as unacceptable. For example, in some cultures it is permitted to have several spouses at the same time (polygamy),

Activity What counts as food?

1 In small groups, discuss whether or not you would find it acceptable to eat the following: cats, dogs, rabbits, guinea pigs, horses, lambs, calves, swans, beefburgers.

2 In your groups, carry out research to find cultures where the following are:

a forbidden as food: beef; pork; shellfish. Explain why they are forbidden.

b acceptable as food: insects (e.g. grubs, grasshoppers); snakes; rats.

3 As well as the type of food that people may eat, many cultures have rules on the slaughtering of animals for food. Find an example of a rule from a particular culture that governs how animals must be slaughtered.

4 Which of your answers to 1, 2 and 3 are examples of formal norms, and which are examples of informal norms?

5 What does this activity as a whole tell us about what counts as food?

Activity Research

Cannibalism as a norm

...go to www.sociology.uk.net

▲ Horsemeat butchers, France

Socialisation

As the examples of feral children show (see Box 1), we are not born knowing right from wrong, how to speak a language or what type of food we should eat. That is, we are not born with a culture – instead we must learn it from other members of society.

Sociologists refer to this process of learning one's culture as socialisation – learning all the things that are necessary for us to be accepted as full members of society. Another way of describing socialisation is to say it is a process of 'internalising' the culture, whereby society 'gets into' and becomes part of us.

Socialisation begins when we are born and continues throughout life. Sociologists distinguish between primary and secondary socialisation:

- **Primary socialisation** takes place in the early years of life and occurs largely within the family, where we learn language, basic skills and norms.
- **Secondary socialisation** takes place later, at school and in wider society.

Through primary socialisation, we learn what is expected of us as members of a family, but secondary socialisation introduces us to the more impersonal adult world. As well as the family and school, there are other agencies of socialisation, including peer groups, the mass media and religion. Each of these plays a part in transmitting the norms, values and skills we need in order to perform our roles in society.

Activity	Gender role socialisation

1 In what ways would you say little boys and little girls are treated differently? What kinds of behaviour are encouraged and discouraged for each gender?
2 The following gender patterns have been found in work roles:
   a Primary school teachers and checkout workers are more likely to be female than male.
   b Secondary school head teachers and engineers are more likely to be male than female.
   Why are certain jobs seen to be more appropriate for men and others more suitable for women?
3 Is there any gender discrimination in the job market? If so, why do you think it exists?

whereas in others only one is allowed (monogamy). Similarly, some cultures have taboos on specific foods, or rules about what foods may be eaten together.

There may also be cultural variations within a society, especially a large complex one such as Britain. Different groups may have their own **subcultures** that vary significantly from the mainstream culture. For example, different religious groups may have different dietary norms as well as different beliefs about the afterlife.

Cultures and their norms and values may change over time. For example, attitudes to a wide range of behaviour, including smoking, homosexuality, married women working, cohabitation and sex before marriage have all changed in the recent past.

Activity	Research

Changing norms about homosexuality

...go to www.sociology.uk.net

Status and role

A **status** is a position in society. We can think of society as made up of lots of different positions or statuses. Some statuses are **ascribed**: based on fixed characteristics that we are born with and cannot normally change, such as our sex or ethnicity. Other statuses are **achieved** through our own efforts, such as getting into university or being promoted at work.

Those who occupy a given status are expected to follow particular norms of behaviour. For example, someone occupying the status of teacher is expected to mark students' work, treat them fairly, start lessons punctually, know their subject and so on. This set of norms together makes up the **role** of teacher.

Activity **Status and role**

Norms are expectations of how those who occupy a role should act. The text gives the example of a teacher.

1 Work in small groups. Each group should take one of the roles below. Compile a set of norms for your particular role. Try to be quite detailed and specific.

   a Gym instructor   **b** Passenger on a bus
   c Doctor   **d** Checkout worker

2 What could you do to disrupt the expectations that others (e.g. bus driver, patient, shopper) have of your role? Based on the norms you have identified, suggest some behaviours that would be unexpected for that role. For example, before the start of the first lesson a teacher might sit at the back of the class as the students enter and not make it clear they were the teacher until long after the lesson was due to start.

3 Share your group work with the rest of the class. What does this activity tell us about the importance of the norms associated with social roles?

Socialisation involves not only learning the general culture of society as a whole, but also the things we need to perform our particular roles within society. For example, boys and girls may be socialised differently to prepare them for different gender roles in adulthood.

Individual and society

So far, we have assumed that individuals are shaped by the socialisation process to ensure that they perform the roles society requires of them. However, this implies we are simply the products of society and have no choice in how we act. How true is this? There are two main views:

- the structural view
- the social action view.

The structural view sees us as entirely shaped by the structure of society (the way society is organised or set up). It sees us as behaving according to society's norms and expectations, which we internalise through the socialisation process.

In this view, society determines our behaviour – we are like puppets on a string, manipulated by society. This is sometimes described as a 'macro' (large-scale) approach because it focuses on how wider society influences us. The emphasis is firmly on the power of society to shape us.

The social action view sees us as having free will and choice. It emphasises the power of individuals to create society through their actions and interactions. This is

sometimes described as a 'micro' approach because it focuses on small-scale, face-to-face interactions between individuals. An example is the study described in Box 2, which shows how the beliefs that we hold about others influence how we interact with them.

In practice, most sociologists accept that individuals do have some degree of choice, as the social action view argues, but that their choices are limited by the structure of society, as the structural view argues.

Activity **Research**

Think about your own educational experiences and choices.

1 In what ways do you have freedom of choice about your education?

2 In what ways are your choices shaped by wider society (e.g. by your parents' views or income, the job market, your school or college)?

Consensus or conflict?

Although structural sociologists agree that society shapes our behaviour, there are disagreements among them about the kind of structure society has. Functionalist sociologists see society as based on value consensus; that is, harmony and agreement among its members about basic values. By contrast, Marxist sociologists see society as based on conflict.

According to **functionalists**, society is held together by a shared culture into which all its members are socialised. Sharing the same culture integrates individuals into society by giving them a sense of solidarity or 'fellow feeling' with others. It enables members of society to agree on goals and how to achieve them and so allows them to cooperate harmoniously.

Functionalists see society as like a biological organism such as the human body. Like a body whose parts (organs, cells etc) fit together and depend on one another, society too is a system of interdependent parts. Each part performs functions that contribute to the well being of society as a whole. For example, the family reproduces the population and performs the function of primary socialisation, while the education system equips us with the knowledge and skills needed for work.

Marxists disagree with the functionalist view. They see society as based on class conflict, not consensus. They argue that society is divided into two social classes:

- **The minority capitalist class, or bourgeoisie,** own the means of production such as the factories, raw materials and land.
- **The majority working class, or proletariat,** own nothing but their own labour, which they have to sell to the bourgeoisie in order to survive.

The bourgeoisie exploit the workers and profit from their labour. This exploitation breeds class conflict, which

▲ Why do the police target some groups more than others?

Karl Marx (1818-83) believed would eventually lead to the working class overthrowing capitalism and creating a classless, equal society. In the Marxist view, all social institutions – such as religion, the media and the education system – serve to maintain capitalism, for example by promoting the idea that inequality is inevitable and fair.

Feminist sociologists agree with Marxists that there are fundamental divisions and conflicts in society, but they see gender rather than class as the most important division.

They regard society and its institutions as male-dominated or *patriarchal*. For example, they see the family as unequal and oppressive, with women doing most of the housework and childcare.

Diversity and identity

According to Marxists and functionalists, in modern society the individual's identity is largely fixed. Marxists see our identity as stemming from our class position, while functionalists see it as the result of being socialised into the shared culture.

However, **postmodernist** sociologists argue that we are now living in a postmodern society (see Box 3). Unlike modern society, where individuals share a common culture or class identity, postmodern society is fragmented (splintered) into a wide variety of different groups.

These groups are based on differences in ethnicity, age, religion, region, nationality, sexuality and so on. This diversity gives individuals greater freedom to 'pick and mix' their identities from a wide variety of sources.

However, critics argue that postmodernists exaggerate how far things have really changed. In particular, postmodernists ignore the continuing importance of social inequality and the ways this limits people's choices and shapes their lives.

> In what ways does poverty limit people's choices and shape their lives?

Box 2	Shoplifting in Chicago

Interactionist sociologists take a social action approach to crime. Rather than seeing crime as caused by 'society', they see it as the outcome of the labels people apply to others in their interactions with them. Mary Cameron's (1964) study of shoplifting in Chicago department stores is a good example of this approach.

Cameron found that stores didn't automatically prosecute everyone they suspected of shoplifting. They were often reluctant to prosecute because of the difficulty of proving the case and the cost of releasing employees to be witnesses. They were inclined to let suspects off with a warning, particularly if they were willing and able to pay for the goods.

However, not everyone was treated in the same way. According to Cameron, store detectives made assumptions about what the 'typical shoplifter' is like. They believed adolescents and black people were more likely to be shoplifters and kept them under surveillance when they were in the store. By contrast, the detectives were unlikely to be suspicious of people they saw as 'respectable'. These people tended to be middle-class and white. Even when the detectives witnessed an offence, they were less likely to report it if the suspect was of a similar background to themselves.

When arrests were made, the stores were more likely to press charges if the suspects were black. For example, only 9% of arrested white women were charged, but 42% of black women. Furthermore, when cases went to court, not only were black women more likely to be found guilty; they were six times more likely to be jailed than white women.

Cameron's study shows how people's beliefs about others influence how they act towards them. In this case, the ideas of the store detectives and others about the 'typical shoplifter' affected which groups they chose to pursue, and this in turn criminalised more blacks than whites.

1 What evidence does Cameron give of suspects being able to negotiate an outcome other than prosecution?
2 Apart from being young and black, what other characteristics do you think store detectives might see as typical of shoplifters?
3 How could you apply Cameron's ideas to explaining the fact that the working class are more likely to be convicted of crimes than the middle class?

Social change and types of society

Sociology as a subject first developed in response to major changes that began to take place in western society from the 18th century onwards. One key change was urbanisation – the shift from a largely rural society where people lived in villages, to an urban society where they lived in towns and cities. The process of urbanisation was paralleled by one of industrialisation, in which the workforce increasingly moved out of agriculture and into factory production.

These changes had an enormous impact on all areas of social life and to understand them, many sociologists made a distinction between two types of society:

- traditional society: a rural-agricultural society where there was little social change, a strong sense of community and religion dominated people's view of the world.

- modern society: an urban-industrial society with social and technological change and a belief in progress and science.

However, some sociologists argue that we now live in a new type of society:

- postmodern society: a post-industrial society in which change is increasingly rapid but uneven, and where people have lost faith in the ability of science to bring about progress.

In postmodern society, information technology and the media play a central role. The world moves towards a single global economy and culture. Sources of individual identity become more diverse.

Critics argue that postmodernists exaggerate this change and that we are still living in the modern rather than a postmodern era. For example, Marxists argue that society is still capitalist and class inequality remains its key feature.

Inequality

Britain remains an unequal society. For example, the richest 10% in Britain own 44% of the nation's total wealth, while the poorest half of the population share only 9% of total wealth.

Sociologists are interested in social stratification – that is, inequalities between groups such as social classes, men and women, ethnic groups and age groups. They use the concept of 'life chances' to describe these inequalities. Life chances refer to the chances of enjoying the 'good things', such as educational success, a long and healthy life, high quality housing, and well-paid, interesting work. Different classes, genders, ethnic groups and age groups tend to have different life chances.

Gender

Although there have been major changes in recent years, such as girls overtaking boys at school, men and women still do not occupy equal positions in society.

- More women than men are in poverty. Most low-paid workers and poor pensioners are women.
- On average, women earn about 15% less than men.
- Women do more housework and childcare than men.

Social class

Sociologists usually define a person's class in terms of their occupation. Those in non-manual jobs such as doctors, teachers and office workers are defined as middle-class, while those in manual jobs such as electricians, bus drivers and street sweepers are defined as working-class. Class has a major effect on many aspects of our lives, as the following examples show:

- Manual workers earn less than non-manual workers and are more likely to become unemployed.

- People in class V (unskilled manual workers such as cleaners) are three times as likely to be smokers and nearly five times as likely to die of lung cancer, compared to people in class I (professionals such as doctors).
- The infant mortality rate (deaths during the first year of life) is nearly twice as high for babies in class V as for those in class I.

Ethnicity

Ethnicity refers to shared culture and identity. An ethnic group is one whose members see themselves as a group with a shared heritage and cultural background, often including the same language and religion. Ethnicity doesn't just refer to minority groups – most societies also have an ethnic majority.

- Unemployment is almost twice as high for ethnic minorities as for whites.
- Minority employees tend to earn less than whites and are more likely to work shifts.
- The infant mortality rate of African Caribbean and Pakistani babies is more than double that of whites.

Age

Age is an important factor affecting a person's status and age stratification is a basic feature of many societies.

- In many traditional societies, the old are accorded high status. By contrast, in today's society, they have a low status.
- Children in today's society are economically dependent on adults and legal restrictions prevent them from working. This is not the case in all societies.
- The old and the young are more likely to be poor, compared with other age groups.

These different forms of inequality often overlap. For example, gender and age inequalities may reinforce one another. Women are likely to have smaller pensions in old age because they have not worked full-time for as long, due to family responsibilities.

1 Suggest two reasons for social class differences in death rates.

2 Suggest two reasons why women earn less than men.

3 Suggest two reasons why members of ethnic minority groups are more likely than whites to be unemployed.

How do sociologists study society?

As we saw earlier, sociologists create theories to explain society and human behaviour. To be of any value, these theories must be based on evidence about the real world.

Sociologists have to collect this evidence. To do so, they carry out research using a variety of methods and sources of evidence. These include:

- **social surveys**, which involve asking a sample of people a series of questions in an interview or a written questionnaire
- **participant observation**, where the sociologist joins in with the group they are studying in order to gain deeper insight into their lives
- **official statistics** compiled by the government (for example on educational achievement, family size, unemployment and crime rates).

When choosing a method of research, sociologists need to be aware that every method has its particular strengths and limitations.

For example, a social survey can usually gather information from a large cross-section of the population, but often the results will lack depth and detail, compared for example with a study using participant observation. However, research that uses participant observation can usually only study small numbers of people.

Summary

Sociology is the study of society and human behaviour. Sociologists construct **theories** – general explanations of social patterns. They conduct research to collect **evidence** to support their theories. Governments may use sociologists' findings to develop **social policies**.

Human behaviour is not instinctive, but **learned** through contact with others, as the examples of feral children show. **Culture** includes all those things learned and shared by a group, including knowledge, beliefs, norms and values. **Values** are general principles. **Norms** are specific rules of behaviour. Complex societies may contain many **subcultures**. **Socialisation** is the process of learning one's culture. Sociologists distinguish between **primary** and **secondary** socialisation.

Society is made up of **statuses**, some of which are **ascribed** (fixed at birth) while others are **achieved**. A **role** is the set of norms that govern how a person in a particular status should act.

The **structural view** sees society as shaping the individual. The **social action view** sees individuals as having choice, creating social reality through their interactions. **Functionalists** see society as based on **value consensus**, with interdependent parts performing functions for the good of the whole. **Marxists** see society as based on **class conflict**, in which the bourgeoisie exploit the proletariat. **Feminists** see society as **patriarchal** or male dominated.

Postmodernists believe we have moved to a more **fragmented** society in which there are diverse sources of identity. Critics argue that they ignore important **class**, **gender**, **ethnic** and **age inequalities**. These have a powerful effect on people's **life chances**.

Sociologists use a variety of **methods** and sources, such as surveys, participant observation and official statistics to gather evidence to test their theories.

QuickCheck Questions

Check your answers at www.sociology.uk.net

1 What do the examples of 'feral' children show about human behaviour?

2 Explain what is meant by:
a culture; b norms; c socialisation.

3 Explain the difference between ascribed status and achieved status.

4 What is the difference between the structural and social action views of society?

5 According to Marxists, what is the cause of class conflict?

6 According to functionalists, what is the advantage of members of society sharing the same culture?

7 Explain what is meant by 'patriarchal society'.

8 What is social stratification?

9 In which types of society (traditional, modern or postmodern) are the following features likely to be found:
a belief in progress; b little social change;
c diverse sources of identity?

10 Suggest one limitation of participant observation as a research method.

What does AS and A level sociology involve?

AS and A level sociology gives you an understanding of important aspects of society, and of how sociologists study and explain people's behaviour. Studying sociology will enable you to discuss social issues in a more informed and systematic way and it will help you to make sense of your own and other people's experiences.

The skills you develop will help you to think logically about the world. AS and A level will give you a firm foundation if you want to study sociology at degree level.

Topics and exams

If you are doing AQA AS sociology or the first year of A level sociology, you will study the following topics: education, families and households, research methods, and methods in context.

If you are taking the AS exams at the end of the year, you will sit two papers:
AS Paper 1 Education plus Methods in Context
AS Paper 2 Families and Households plus Research Methods

If you are taking the A level exams at the end of your second year, you will sit three papers:
A level Paper 1 Education, Methods in Context, and Theory and Methods*.
A level Paper 2 Families and Households plus Beliefs in Society.
A level Paper 3 Crime and Deviance plus Theory and Methods*.
*Theory and Methods includes the topics you have studied under Research Methods in your first year, plus the study of sociological theories.

What the examiners are looking for

When you sit an exam, your work is marked in terms of three aims or 'assessment objectives':

- Assessment Objective 1 (AO1): Knowledge and Understanding
- Assessment Objective 2 (AO2): Application
- Assessment Objective 3 (AO3): Analysis and Evaluation

Knowledge and Understanding means you need to know and understand some of the main ideas and methods sociologists use, and what they have discovered as a result of their studies.

Application involves linking ideas, theories and studies to the set question, clearly showing their relevance to what you have been asked about.

Analysis involves explaining things in detail, showing how ideas fit together, comparing and contrasting, organising answers logically and drawing conclusions.

Evaluation involves judging something, such as the advantages and disadvantages of different research methods, or the arguments for and against a sociologist's views.

For more about the exams and assessment objectives, see Chapter 5.

Developing your knowledge and skills

Developing your knowledge and understanding of sociology and your skills of application, analysis and evaluation is a gradual process and something you will need to work at throughout your course. There is no quick fix. However, here are some pointers that will help you:

Keep up with your course Attend regularly, do the work your teacher sets you, pay attention to the feedback you receive, keep your folder well organised.

Work with others Join in class discussions, form study groups with classmates, discuss sociology topics outside class, revise together, talk to friends who have already done sociology.

When you don't understand, ask your teacher or classmates, or look it up. Don't be shy – you're probably not the only one who doesn't get it.

Use your textbook It contains thorough coverage of the topics you're studying and detailed guidance on exam success.

Apply what you learn Sociology is about the real world, and you'll find lots of examples of sociological ideas all around you – in the news, on the street, at home, in school or college. Use examples in your writing. This will help you with the skill of Application.

Be critical When you come across new information, don't take it at face value. Look for the strengths and weaknesses of ideas; ask what evidence there is for someone's argument. This will help you develop the skill of Evaluation.

Take ideas apart to see how they 'tick'. Try to make comparisons and contrasts between the different ideas, theories and methods you study. This will help you develop the skill of Analysis.

Answer the question When doing written work, keep focused on what you've actually been asked. Make a plan, and keep checking back to it and the question. Make it clear why you're including the material.

CHAPTER 2

Education

with special links to research methods

Key questions about education

Sociologists are interested in four main questions about education.

Firstly, why do some pupils achieve more than others? On average, middle-class pupils do better in education than working-class pupils and girls do better than boys, while there are also differences in the achievements of pupils from different ethnic groups.

To explain these differences, sociologists have studied the impact of processes within schools such as the ways teachers label pupils, as well as factors outside school such as children's home background.

Secondly, sociologists have examined the role of education in society and who benefits from it. For example, functionalists claim that education acts as a way of allocating people to jobs on the basis of ability. By contrast, Marxists see it as a means of providing capitalism with an obedient workforce.

Thirdly, sociologists are interested in how pupils experience schooling. For example, girls and boys often study different subjects, while pupils from minority ethnic groups may face racism in school and girls may experience sexism. Such experiences may affect not only pupils' achievement, but also their identity and self-esteem.

Fourthly, the government makes laws and policies that affect education. Sociologists are interested in their impact. For example, do they produce equal opportunity for all pupils?

The AQA Specification

The specification is the syllabus produced by the exam board, telling you what you have to study. The AQA specification for Education requires you to examine the following:

- The role and functions of the education system, including its relationship to the economy and to class structure.
- Differential educational achievement of social groups by social class, gender and ethnicity in contemporary society.
- Relationships and processes within schools, with particular reference to teacher/pupil relationships, pupil identities and subcultures, the hidden curriculum, and the organisation of teaching and learning.
- The significance of educational policies, including policies of selection, marketisation and privatisation, and policies to achieve greater equality of opportunity or outcome, for an understanding of the structure, role, impact and experience of and access to education; the impact of globalisation and educational policy.
- The application of sociological research methods to the study of education.

For full details of the specification, visit www.aqa.org.uk

Boys at Eton public school: fees are over £34,000 per year.

GETTING STARTED

Study the bar chart and answer the following questions.

Figure 2.1: Percentage of pupils gaining 5 or more A*-C grades at GCSE, by parents' social class

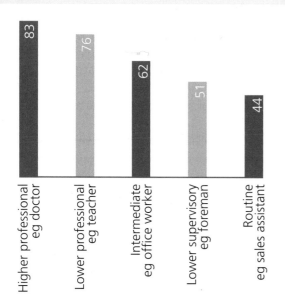

Source: Youth cohort study and longitudinal study of young people in England, 2010

1 What percentage of pupils with parents in **a** the higher professional class and **b** the routine class achieved 5 or more A*-C passes at GCSE?

2 Summarise the relationship between parents' social class and pupils' achievement at GCSE.

3 Make a list of possible reasons why pupils whose parents are higher professionals do better than pupils whose parents are from lower social classes.

Learning objectives

After studying this Topic, you should:

- Be able to describe the pattern of class differences in educational achievement.

- Understand the difference between internal and external factors affecting achievement.

- Understand and be able to evaluate the role of different external factors, including cultural deprivation, material deprivation and cultural capital.

One of the most striking features of education in Britain is the difference in achievement between pupils from different social classes. Despite great improvements in the educational level of the nation as a whole since state education began in 1870, social class differences continue. In this Topic we shall look at the evidence of these differences and at how sociologists have explained them.

When examining social class differences in achievement, the main comparison sociologists make is between working-class and middle-class pupils. Most sociologists use parental occupation to determine a pupil's social class. For example:

- **Middle-class** or non-manual occupations include professionals such as doctors or teachers, together with managers and other 'white collar' office workers and owners of businesses.
- **Working-class** or manual occupations include skilled workers such as plumbers, semi-skilled workers such as lorry drivers, and unskilled or routine workers such as cleaners.

Explaining class differences

Social class background has a powerful influence on a child's chances of success in the education system. Children from middle-class families on average perform better than working-class children, and the class gap in achievement grows wider as children get older. Children of the middle class do better at GCSE (see Figure 2.1), stay longer in full-time education and take the great majority of university places (see Table 2A on page 22).

One popular explanation of class differences in achievement is that better-off parents can afford to send their children to private schools, which many believe provide a higher standard of education. For example, average class sizes are less than half those in state schools. Although these schools educate only 7% of Britain's children, they account for nearly half of all students entering the elite universities of Oxford and Cambridge. According to the Sutton Trust (2011), in a three-year period, one public school alone – Eton – sent 211 pupils to Oxbridge, while over 1,300 state schools sent no pupils at all to these universities.

However, the existence of private education does not account for class differences within *state* education, and most sociological research has focused on why middle-class pupils do better than working-class pupils within the state sector itself.

Internal and external factors

Sociologists are interested in why these class differences in educational achievement exist and they have put forward a number of explanations. We can group these into 'internal' and 'external' explanations or factors – though in reality, of course, these factors are very often linked:

- **Internal factors** – these are factors within schools and the education system, such as interactions between pupils and teachers, and inequalities between schools.
- **External factors** – these are factors outside the education system, such as the influence of home and family background and wider society.

In this Topic, we shall focus on the following external factors that affect pupils' educational achievement: cultural deprivation, material deprivation and cultural capital.

Cultural deprivation

Class differences in children's development and achievement appear very early in life. For example, a nationwide study by the Centre for Longitudinal Studies (2007) found that by the age of three, children from disadvantaged backgrounds are already up to one year behind those from more privileged homes and the gap widens with age.

Some sociologists claim that this is the result of cultural deprivation. They argue that most of us begin to acquire the basic values, attitudes and skills that are needed for educational success through primary socialisation in the family. This basic 'cultural equipment' includes things such as language, self-discipline and reasoning skills.

However, according to cultural deprivation theorists, many working-class families fail to socialise their children adequately. These children grow up 'culturally deprived'. That is, they lack the cultural equipment needed to do well at school and so they underachieve. There are three main aspects of cultural deprivation: language, parents' education and working-class subculture.

Language

Language is an essential part of the process of education and the way in which parents communicate with their children affects their cognitive (intellectual) development and their ability to benefit from the process of schooling.

For example, Hubbs-Tait et al (2002) found that where parents use language that challenges their children to evaluate their own understanding or abilities (for example, 'what do you think?' 'Are you ready for the next step?'), cognitive performance improves. Leon Feinstein (2008) found that educated parents are more likely to use language in this way.

By contrast, less educated parents tend to use language in ways that only require children to make simple descriptive statements (for example, 'what's that animal called?'). This results in lower performance.

Feinstein also found that educated parents are more likely to use praise. This encourages their children to develop a sense of their own competence.

Cultural deprivation theorists see these differences in how parents use language as linked to social class. For example, Carl Bereiter and Siegfried Engelmann (1966) claim that the language used in lower-class homes is deficient. They describe lower-class families as communicating by gestures, single words or disjointed phrases.

As a result, their children fail to develop the necessary language skills. They grow up incapable of abstract thinking and unable to use language to explain, describe, enquire or compare. Because of this, they are unable to take advantage of the opportunities that school offers.

Speech codes

Basil Bernstein (1975) also identifies differences between working-class and middle-class language that influence achievement. He distinguishes between two types of speech code:

- **The restricted code** is the speech code typically used by the working class. It has a limited vocabulary and is based on the use of short, often unfinished, grammatically simple sentences. Speech is predictable and may involve only a single word, or even just a gesture instead. It is descriptive not analytic. The restricted code is context-bound: that is, the speaker assumes that the listener shares the same set of experiences.
- **The elaborated code** is typically used by the middle class. It has a wider vocabulary and is based on longer, grammatically more complex sentences. Speech is more varied and communicates abstract ideas. The elaborated code is context-free: the speaker does not assume that the listener shares the same experiences, and so they use language to spell out their meanings explicitly for the listener. Box 4 gives examples of the two codes.

These differences in speech code give middle-class children an advantage at school and put working-class children at a disadvantage. This is because the elaborated code is the language used by teachers, textbooks and exams. Not only is it taken as the 'correct' way to speak and write, but in Bernstein's view it is also a more effective tool for analysing and reasoning and for expressing thoughts clearly and effectively – essential skills in education.

Early socialisation into the elaborated code means that middle-class children are already fluent users of the code when they start school. Thus they feel 'at home' in school and are more likely to succeed. By contrast, working-class children, lacking the code in which schooling takes place, are likely to feel excluded and to be less successful.

Critics argue that Bernstein is a cultural deprivation theorist because he describes working-class speech as inadequate. However, unlike most cultural deprivation theorists, Bernstein recognises that the school – and not just the home – influences children's achievement. He argues that working-class pupils fail not because they are culturally deprived, but because schools fail to teach them how to use the elaborated code.

Parents' education

Cultural deprivation theorists argue that parents' attitudes to education are a key factor affecting children's achievement. For example, a major early study by Douglas (1964) found that working-class parents placed less value on education. As a result, they were less ambitious for their children, gave them less encouragement and took less interest in their education. They visited schools less often

▲ In what ways are middle-class parents able to give their children a head start?

Box 4   **Restricted and elaborated codes: an illustration**

The difference between speech codes is illustrated by these descriptions given by two five-year-old children, one working-class, the other middle-class, who were each shown the same set of pictures and asked to tell the story:

'They're playing football and he kicks it and it goes through there it breaks the window and they're looking at it and he comes out and shouts at them because they've broken it so they run away and then she looks out and she tells them off.'

'Three boys are playing football and one boy kicks the ball and it goes through the window the ball breaks the window and the boys are looking at it and a man comes out and shouts at them because they've broken the window so they run away and then the lady looks out of her window and she tells the boys off.'

The first child uses the restricted code, where the speech is context-bound. The second child is using the elaborated code, where the speech is context-free.

1 Explain why the first example is context-bound speech and the second is context-free.

2 In what ways might the context-free elaborated code be more useful when writing in an exam or answering questions at an interview for university?

and were less likely to discuss their children's progress with teachers. As a result, their children had lower levels of motivation and achievement.

Leon Feinstein (2008) reaches similar conclusions. He argues that parents' own education is the most important factor affecting children's achievement and, since middle-class parents tend to be better educated, they are able to give their children an advantage by how they socialise them. This occurs in a number of ways:

parenting style

Educated parents' parenting style emphasises consistent discipline and high expectations of their children, and this supports achievement by encouraging active learning and exploration.

By contrast, less educated parents' parenting style is marked by harsh or inconsistent discipline that emphasises 'doing as you're told' and 'behaving yourself'. This prevents the child from learning independence and self-control, leading to poorer motivation at school and problems interacting with teachers.

parents' educational behaviours

Educated parents are more aware of what is needed to assist their children's educational progress. As a result, they engage in behaviour such as:

> "reading to their children, teaching them letters, numbers, songs, poems and nursery rhymes, painting and drawing, helping with homework and being actively involved in their schooling."

Educated parents are also better able to get expert advice on childrearing, more successful in establishing good relationships with teachers and better at guiding their children's interactions with school. These parents also recognise the educational value of activities such as visits to museums and libraries.

use of income

Better educated parents not only tend to have higher incomes. They also spend their income in ways that promote their children's educational success. For example, as Bernstein and Young (1967) found, middle-class mothers are more likely to buy educational toys, books and activities that encourage reasoning skills and stimulate intellectual development. Working-class homes are more likely to lack these resources and this means children from such homes start school without the intellectual skills needed to progress.

Educated parents also have a better understanding of nutrition and its importance in child development and a higher income with which to buy more nutritious food.

class, income and parental education

While better-paid, middle-class parents tend to be better educated than lower-paid, working-class parents, Feinstein notes that parental education has an influence on children's achievement in its own right, regardless of class or income. Thus, even within a given social class, better educated parents tend to have children who are more successful at school. This may help to explain why not all children of working-class parents do equally badly, and why not all children from middle-class families are equally successful.

Working-class subculture

Cultural deprivation theorists argue that lack of parental interest in their children's education reflects the subcultural values of the working class. A subculture is a group whose attitudes and values differ from those of the mainstream culture. According to cultural deprivation theorists, large sections of the working class have different goals, beliefs, attitudes and values from the rest of society and this is why their children fail at school.

Barry Sugarman (1970) takes this view. He argues that working-class subculture has four key features that act as a barrier to educational achievement:

- **Fatalism**: a belief in fate – that 'whatever will be, will be' and there is nothing you can do to change your status. This contrasts with middle-class values, which emphasise that you can change your position through your own efforts.
- **Collectivism**: valuing being part of a group more than succeeding as an individual. This contrasts with the middle-class view that an individual should not be held back by group loyalties.
- **Immediate gratification**: seeking pleasure now rather than making sacrifices in order to get rewards in the future. By contrast, middle-class values emphasise deferred gratification, making sacrifices now for greater rewards later.
- **Present-time orientation**: seeing the present as more important than the future and so not having long-term goals

Investigating parental attitudes to education

The issue of parental attitudes towards education has certain important **research characteristics** – particular features that may make it easy or difficult to investigate. For example:

- Parents with poor personal experiences of education may identify the researcher with the school and refuse to participate.
- Some parents may see questions about parental support for their child's education as 'getting at' them or attempting to portray them as bad parents.
- However, if the researcher can gain parents' trust, they may be more willing to talk because it gives them the opportunity to speak about their feelings towards school.
- Parents are not easily contacted, except through school, so the researcher has to depend on the head's cooperation.
- Another way of contacting parents is through the school's parents' association. However, the middle class are more likely to get involved in such organisations, which may reduce representativeness.
- Issues such as truancy or parental support are sensitive. Parents may be defensive about their role, for example exaggerating the support they give.
- Parents are used to receiving and returning communications from school and may see involvement in the research as a useful aspect of their relationship with the school.
- Some parents have literacy or language problems or may find it difficult to articulate their feelings.

1   What other research characteristics of parental attitudes towards education can you think of? You could consider issues of parental consent, impression management etc particular to investigating this topic.

2   Using the research characteristics listed above and any others you can think of, identify two strengths and two limitations of using **questionnaires** to investigate parental attitudes towards education. You can read more about questionnaires on pages 116–22.

or plans. By contrast, middle-class culture has a future-time orientation that sees planning for the future as important.

Working-class children internalise the beliefs and values of their subculture through the socialisation process and this results in them underachieving at school.

But why do these differences in values exist? Sugarman argues that they stem from the fact that middle-class jobs are secure careers offering prospects for continuous individual advancement. This encourages ambition, long-term planning and a willingness to invest time and effort in gaining qualifications. By contrast, working-class jobs are less secure and have no career structure through which individuals can advance. There are few promotion opportunities and earnings peak at an early age.

Cultural deprivation theorists argue that parents pass on the values of their class to their children through primary socialisation. Middle-class values equip children for success, whereas working-class values fail to do so.

Compensatory education

Compensatory education programmes aim to tackle the problem of cultural deprivation by providing extra resources to schools and communities in deprived areas. They intervene early in the socialisation process to compensate children for the deprivation they experience at home.

The best known example is Operation Head Start in the United States, a multi-billion dollar scheme of pre-school education in poorer areas introduced in the 1960s. Its aim was 'planned enrichment' of the deprived child's environment to develop skills and instil achievement motivation. It included improving parenting skills, setting up nursery classes and home visits by educational psychologists.

The well known TV programme Sesame Street was initially part of Head Start, providing a means of transmitting values, attitudes and skills needed for educational success, such as the importance of punctuality, numeracy and literacy.

In Britain, there have been several compensatory education programmes, such as Educational Priority Areas, Education Action Zones and Sure Start, a nationwide programme aimed at pre-school children and their parents (see Box 5).

The myth of cultural deprivation?

Although it draws our attention to the role of the child's social background, cultural deprivation theory has been widely criticised as an explanation of class differences in achievement.

Nell Keddie (1973) describes cultural deprivation as a 'myth' and sees it as a victim-blaming explanation. She dismisses the idea that failure at school can be blamed on a culturally deprived home background. She points out that a child cannot be deprived of its own culture and argues that working-class children are simply culturally different, not culturally deprived.

They fail because they are put at a disadvantage by an education system that is dominated by middle-class values.

Keddie argues that rather than seeing working-class culture as deficient, schools should recognise and build on its strengths and should challenge teachers' anti-working-class prejudices.

Likewise, Barry Troyna and Jenny Williams (1986) argue that the problem is not the child's language but the school's attitude towards it. Teachers have a 'speech hierarchy': they label middle-class speech highest, followed by working-class speech and finally black speech.

Other critics reject the view that working-class parents are not interested in their children's education. According to Tessa Blackstone and Jo Mortimore (1994), they attend fewer parents' evenings, not because of a lack of interest, but because they work longer or less regular hours or are put off by the school's middle-class atmosphere. They may want to help their child progress but they lack the knowledge and education to do so. There is also evidence that schools with mainly working-class pupils have less effective systems of parent-school contacts. This makes it harder for parents to keep in touch about their children's progress.

Activity Discussion

A child's background can disadvantage their education

...go to www.sociology.uk.net

Material deprivation

Unlike cultural deprivation theorists, who blame educational failure on the inadequacy of working-class subculture, many other sociologists see material deprivation as the main cause of underachievement. The term 'material deprivation' refers to poverty and a lack of material necessities such as adequate housing and income.

Poverty is closely linked to educational underachievement. For example:

- According to the Department for Education (2012), barely a third of pupils eligible for free school meals (FSM) – a widely used measure of child poverty – achieve five or more GCSEs at A*-C including English and maths, as against nearly two thirds of other pupils.
- According to Jan Flaherty (2004), money problems in the family are a significant factor in younger children's non-attendance at school.
- Exclusion and truancy are more likely for children from poorer families. Children excluded from school are unlikely to return to mainstream education, while a third of all persistent truants leave school with no qualifications.
- Nearly 90% of 'failing' schools are located in deprived areas.

There is a close link between poverty and social class. Working-class families are much more likely to have low incomes or inadequate housing. Factors such as these can affect their children's education in several ways.

Housing

Poor housing can affect pupils' achievement both directly and indirectly. For example, overcrowding can have a direct effect by making it harder for the child to study. Overcrowding means less room for educational activities, nowhere to do homework, disturbed sleep from sharing beds or bedrooms and so on.

For young children especially, development can be impaired through lack of space for safe play and exploration. Families living in temporary (bed and breakfast) accommodation may find themselves having to move frequently, resulting in constant changes of school and disrupted education.

Poor housing can also have indirect effects, notably on the child's health and welfare. For example, children in crowded homes run a greater risk of accidents. Cold or damp housing can also cause ill health. Families in temporary accommodation suffer more psychological distress, infections and accidents. Such health problems mean more absences from school.

Diet and health

Marilyn Howard (2001) notes that young people from poorer homes have lower intakes of energy, vitamins and minerals. Poor nutrition affects health, for example by weakening the immune system and lowering children's energy levels. This may result in more absences from school due to illness, and difficulties concentrating in class.

Children from poorer homes are also more likely to have emotional or behavioural problems. According to Richard Wilkinson (1996), among ten year olds, the lower the social class, the higher the rate of hyperactivity, anxiety and conduct disorders, all of which are likely to have a negative effect on the child's education.

Jo Blanden and Stephen Machin (2007) found that children from low income families were more likely to engage in 'externalising' behaviour (such as fighting and temper tantrums), which are likely to disrupt their schooling.

Box 5	Sure Start

Sure Start was a major element in the New Labour government's policies to tackle poverty and social exclusion. By 2010, there were around 3,500 local Sure Start Children's Centres, with all young children in the most disadvantaged areas having access to one. The centres provide integrated education, care, family support, health services and support with parental employment. However, since 2011 there have been significant cuts in funding for Sure Start and many centres have been closed.

The aim of Sure Start is to work with parents to promote the physical, intellectual and social development of babies and young children, particularly those who are disadvantaged, so that they can flourish at home and when they go to school, and thereby break the cycle of disadvantage.

One objective of Sure Start is to improve children's ability to learn, by encouraging high quality environments that promote early learning, provide stimulating and enjoyable play and improve language skills.

> What similarities can you see between Sure Start and Operation Head Start?

Financial support and the costs of education

Lack of financial support means that children from poor families have to do without equipment and miss out on experiences that would enhance their educational achievement. David Bull (1980) refers to this as 'the costs of free schooling'. A study in the Oxford area by Emily Tanner et al (2003) found that the cost of items such as transport, uniforms, books, computers, calculators, and sports, music and art equipment, places a heavy burden on poor families.

As a result, poor children may have to make do with hand-me-downs and cheaper but unfashionable equipment, and this may result in being isolated, stigmatised or bullied by peers. Yet, for many children, suitable clothes are essential for self-esteem and 'fitting in'.

According to Flaherty, fear of stigmatisation may also help to explain why 20% of those eligible for free school meals do not take up their entitlement:

> "I realised when I was in year 7 that the people who got free school meals were teased... I couldn't handle that as I was already getting teased enough, so I don't get free school meals." (Quoted in Ridge 2002)

Teresa Smith and Michael Noble (1995) add that poverty acts as a barrier to learning in other ways, such as inability to afford private schooling or tuition, and poorer quality local schools.

Lack of funds also means that children from low-income families often need to work. Ridge found that children in poverty take on jobs such as baby sitting, cleaning and paper rounds, and that this often had a negative impact on their schoolwork.

Financial support to poorer students staying on in education after 16 that had previously been available through Education Maintenance Allowances (EMAs) was abolished in England by the Coalition government in 2011.

Fear of debt

Going to university usually involves getting into debt to cover the cost of tuition fees, books and living expenses. Attitudes towards debt may deter working-class students from going to university. Using data from a nationwide questionnaire survey of nearly 2,000 prospective students, Claire Callender and Jon Jackson (2005) found that working-class students are more debt averse – that is, they saw debt negatively, as something to be avoided. They also saw more costs than benefits in going to university.

Crucially, Callender and Jackson found that attitude to debt was important in deciding whether to apply to university. The most debt averse students (typically working-class) were over five times less likely to apply than the most debt tolerant students (typically middle-class).

Increases in tuition fees from 2012, to a maximum of £9,000 per year, may mean that the increased debt burden will deter even more working-class students from applying to university. For example, according to UCAS (2012), the number of UK applicants fell by 8.6% in 2012 compared with the previous year.

Furthermore, working-class students who do go to university are likely to receive less financial support from their families. A National Union of Students (2010) online survey of 3,863 university students found that 81% of those from the highest social class received help from home, as against only 43% of those from the lowest class. Fear of debt and more limited financial support help to explain why only about 30% of university students come from working-class backgrounds, despite the fact that this group accounts for about 50% of the population (see also Table 2A).

Financial factors also restrict working-class students' choice of university and chances of success. Diane Reay (2005) found that working-class students were more likely to apply

Table 2A	Percentage of young people entering higher education from the most advantaged and the most disadvantaged areas of England	
	1994/5	2009/10
From the most advantaged areas	50	57
From the most disadvantaged areas	13	19

Source: HEFCE (2010)

to local universities so they could live at home and save on travel costs, but that this gave them less opportunity to go to the highest status universities. They were also more likely to work part-time to fund their studies, making it more difficult for them to gain higher-class degrees.

Dropout rates are also higher for universities with a large proportion of poor students: for example, 16.6% drop out at London Metropolitan, a university with a large working-class intake, but only 1.5% at Oxford, where nearly half the students come from private schools. The National Audit Office (2002) found that working-class students spent twice as much time in paid work to reduce their debts as middle-class students.

Cultural or material factors?

While material factors clearly play a part in achievement, the fact that some children from poor families do succeed suggests that material deprivation is only part of the explanation.

For example, the cultural, religious or political values of the family may play a part in creating and sustaining the child's motivation, even despite poverty. Similarly, Feinstein shows that educated parents make a positive contribution to a child's achievement, regardless of their income level.

Nevertheless, Peter Mortimore and Geoff Whitty (1997) argue that material inequalities have the greatest effect on achievement. For this reason, Peter Robinson (1997) argues that tackling child poverty would be the most effective way to boost achievement.

Cultural capital

Bourdieu: three types of capital

Pierre Bourdieu (1984) argues that both cultural and material factors contribute to educational achievement and are not separate but interrelated. He uses the concept of 'capital' to explain why the middle class are more successful.

The term capital usually refers to wealth but in addition to this economic capital, Bourdieu identifies two further types. These are 'educational capital' or qualifications, and 'cultural capital'. He argues that the middle class generally possess more of all three types of capital.

cultural capital

Bourdieu uses the term cultural capital to refer to the knowledge, attitudes, values, language, tastes and abilities of the middle class. He sees middle-class culture as a type of capital because, like wealth, it gives an advantage to those who possess it. Like Bernstein, he argues that through their socialisation, middle-class children acquire the ability to grasp, analyse and express abstract ideas. They are more likely to develop intellectual interests and an understanding of what the education system requires for success.

This gives middle-class children an advantage in school, where such abilities and interests are highly valued and rewarded with qualifications. This is because the education system is not neutral, but favours and transmits the dominant middle-class culture.

By contrast, working-class children find that school devalues their culture as 'rough' and inferior. Their lack of cultural capital leads to exam failure. Many working-class pupils also 'get the message' that education is not meant for them and respond by truanting, early leaving or just not trying.

Application
Suggest examples of middle-class culture that are transmitted by the education system.

educational and economic capital

Bourdieu argues that educational, economic and cultural capital can be converted into one another.

For example, middle-class children with cultural capital are better equipped to meet the demands of the school curriculum and gain qualifications. Similarly, wealthier parents can convert their economic capital into educational capital by sending their children to private schools and paying for extra tuition. As Dennis Leech and Erick Campos' (2003) study of Coventry shows, middle-class parents are also more likely to be able to afford a house in the catchment area of a school that is highly placed in the exam league tables. This has become known as 'selection by mortgage' because it drives up the cost of houses near to successful schools and excludes working-class families.

▲ Cultural capital includes developing a taste for fine art, classical music and other 'high culture'. What difference might this make to educational achievement?

a test of Bourdieu's ideas

Alice Sullivan (2001) used questionnaires to conduct a survey of 465 pupils in four schools. To assess their cultural capital, she asked them about a range of activities, such as reading and TV viewing habits, and whether they visited art galleries, museums and theatres. She also tested their vocabulary and knowledge of cultural figures.

She found that those who read complex fiction and watched serious TV documentaries developed a wider vocabulary and greater cultural knowledge, indicating greater cultural capital. The pupils with the greatest cultural capital were children of graduates. These pupils were more likely to be successful at GCSE.

However, although successful pupils with greater cultural capital were more likely to be middle-class, Sullivan found that cultural capital only accounted for part of the class difference in achievement. Where pupils of different classes had the same level of cultural capital, middle-class pupils still did better. Sullivan concludes that the greater resources and aspirations of middle-class families explain the remainder of the class gap in achievement.

Activity   Research
Investigating cultural capital

...go to www.sociology.uk.net

Topic summary

Middle-class pupils tend to achieve more than working-class pupils. Some explanations focus on **factors outside school**.

These include **cultural deprivation** – working-class pupils are seen as lacking the right attitudes, values, language and knowledge for success.

Material deprivation means working-class children are more likely to have poorer diets, health and housing, and parents who are less able to meet the hidden costs of schooling.

The middle class have more **cultural capital**. They are better placed to take advantage of the choices offered in the education system.

EXAMINING CLASS DIFFERENCES IN ACHIEVEMENT (1)

QuickCheck Questions

Check your answers at www.sociology.uk.net

1 Identify three ways in which parents' education may influence how they socialise their children.
2 Name two features of working-class subculture described by Sugarman.
3 Identify three characteristics of the elaborated code.
4 What is meant by 'compensatory education'?
5 Suggest three ways in which material deprivation may affect achievement.
6 Identify and define the three types of capital described by Bourdieu.

Questions to try

Whether or not you are taking the AS exams during your A level course, trying the AS questions below is a very good way of testing your knowledge and understanding and practising your skills in preparation for your A level exams.

Item A There are clear social class differences in educational achievement. Some sociologists argue that these are the result of factors outside schools. Some claim that working-class parents place less value on education and so their children see it as less important than do middle-class pupils. Differences in speech codes and in the level of the family's material resources may also have an important impact.

However, others suggest that what happens in school has a greater effect on social class differences in achievement.

Item B In general, middle-class pupils achieve better examination results than working-class pupils, many of whom are in receipt of free school meals. According to Feinstein, as early as 22 months, working-class children are already lagging behind middle-class children in their intellectual development. Many of these children have parents who also underachieved at school.

AS questions

1 Define the term 'immediate gratification'. (2 marks)
2 Using one example, briefly explain how the restricted speech code may lead to underachievement. (2 marks)
3 Outline three ways in which housing may affect achievement. (6 marks)
4 Applying material from Item A and your knowledge, evaluate the view that middle-class pupils' higher levels of achievement are the product of factors outside schools. (20 marks)

A level question

5 Applying material from Item B, analyse two factors outside schools that contribute to working-class underachievement. (10 marks)

The Examiner's Advice

Q4 Spend about 30 minutes on this. Distinguish between cultural and material factors that affect class differences. For material factors, include housing, diet and health, and the cost of education. For cultural factors, include class differences in speech codes, parental attitudes to education, class subcultures and cultural capital. Explain how each factor may affect achievement. Do this by creating a chain of reasoning (see page 248). For example, middle-class parents with cultural capital can use their understanding of the admissions system to get their child into a better school. These pupils are then more likely to achieve because of the better teaching, facilities etc. Use evidence from studies such as Douglas, Bereiter and Engelmann, Bernstein, Hubbs-Tait, Feinstein and Sugarman and develop the points noted in Item A. Evaluate the importance of these factors. Make criticisms of each factor as you go, rather than in a separate section at the end. Identify the connections between external and internal factors (see Topic 2).

Q5 Spend about 15 minutes on this question. Divide your time fairly equally between each factor. You don't need a separate introduction; just start on your first factor. To answer this question, it's essential that you take two points from Item B and show through a chain of reasoning how each one contributes to working-class underachievement. (It is a very good idea to quote from the Item when doing so.) You could use free school meals (FSM), intellectual development or parents' education. For example, only low-income families are eligible for FSM. Such families are less able to afford learning aids. This means pupils will be less well prepared for exams and will underachieve. Use concepts such as material deprivation, restricted code, cultural capital, cultural deprivation, working-class subculture, immediate gratification and debt aversion, and studies such as Bull, Tanner, Flaherty, Ridge, and Callender and Jackson. Include some brief evaluation, e.g. that cultural deprivation explanations blame the victim.

Do teachers' expectations affect pupils' achievements?

GETTING STARTED

1 Write a description of what you think the ideal pupil would be for most teachers.

2 From what you learned in Topic 1, list the factors from a student's home life that might affect how they are viewed by teachers and by other pupils. Include both material and cultural factors.

3 In what ways would each of these factors affect the teacher's view of the student?

4 Do teachers treat all students the same? Give examples to support your answer.

Learning objectives

After studying this Topic, you should:

- Understand the effect on social class differences in educational achievement of the following internal factors: labelling, the self-fulfilling prophecy, streaming, pupil identities and subcultures.

- Be able to evaluate the relative importance of internal and external factors in causing social class differences in educational achievement.

As we saw in Topic 1, external factors (that is, those factors outside the education system) such as cultural deprivation, material deprivation and cultural capital, may play an important part in creating social class differences in educational achievement.

However, we also need to examine the part played by internal factors and processes *within* schools in causing these class differences. Many of these involve the daily face-to-face interactions between teachers and pupils, and among peer groups.

These internal factors and processes include labelling, the self-fulfilling prophecy, pupil subcultures, and how pupils' class identities interact with the school and its values.

This topic explores these factors and their effects upon the educational achievement of pupils from different social class backgrounds.

Labelling

To label someone is to attach a meaning or definition to them. For example, teachers may label a pupil as bright or thick, troublemaker or hardworking.

Studies show that teachers often attach such labels regardless of the pupil's actual ability or attitude. Instead, they label pupils on the basis of stereotyped assumptions about their class background, labelling working-class pupils negatively and middle-class pupils positively.

A number of studies of labelling have been carried out by interactionist sociologists. Interactionists study small-scale, face-to-face interactions between individuals, such as in the classroom or playground. They are interested in how people attach labels to one another, and the effects that this has on those who are labelled.

Howard Becker (1971) carried out an important interactionist study of labelling. Based on interviews with 60 Chicago high school teachers, he found that they judged pupils according to how closely they fitted an image of the 'ideal pupil'.

Pupils' work, conduct and appearance were key factors influencing teachers' judgements. The teachers saw children from middle-class backgrounds as the closest to the ideal, and working-class children as furthest away from it because they regarded them as badly behaved.

However, different teachers may have different notions of the ideal pupil. A more recent study of two English primary schools by Amelia Hempel-Jorgensen (2009) found these notions vary according to the social class make-up of the school:

- In the largely working-class Aspen primary school, where staff said discipline was a major problem, the ideal pupil was defined as quiet, passive and obedient – that is, children were defined in terms of their behaviour, not their ability.
- By contrast, the mainly middle-class Rowan primary school had very few discipline problems and here the ideal pupil was defined instead in terms of personality and academic ability, rather than as being a 'non-misbehaving' pupil, as at Aspen.

Investigating teachers' expectations of pupils

The issue of teachers' expectations of pupils has certain important **research characteristics** – particular features that may make it easy or difficult to investigate. For example:

- Teachers have a professional duty to treat all pupils fairly and may face disciplinary action if they are seen to be doing otherwise – so they are likely to conceal negative expectations from researchers.
- The main way teachers' expectations are transmitted is through classroom interaction and it is relatively easy to see what is going on in such a small social space.
- However, expectations can be transmitted in many other ways. This means that researchers also need to look at setting and streaming, teacher-teacher interaction, written reports, target exam grades, information to parents etc.
- Teachers and pupils may be unaware of how teacher expectations are operating, so directly questioning them may not be effective.
- Some pupils may be unwilling to talk about their perceptions of teacher expectations because they fear getting into trouble if the teacher finds out what they have said.
- Heads may be concerned that the research will create the impression that their school has a problem of negative teacher expectations.

1 What other research characteristics of teachers' expectations of pupils can you think of? You could consider issues of impression management, ethical concerns etc particular to investigating this topic.

2 Using the research characteristics listed above and any others you can think of, identify two strengths and two limitations of using **participant observation** to investigate teachers' expectations of pupils. You can read more about participant observation on pages 136–47.

Labelling in secondary schools

Máiréad Dunne and Louise Gazeley (2008) argue that 'schools persistently produce working-class underachievement' because of the labels and assumptions of teachers.

From interviews in nine English state secondary schools, they found that teachers 'normalised' the underachievement of working-class pupils, seemed unconcerned by it and felt they could do little or nothing about it, whereas they believed they could overcome the underachievement of middle-class pupils.

A major reason for this difference was the teachers' belief in the role of pupils' home backgrounds: they labelled working-class parents as uninterested in their children's education, but labelled middle-class parents as supportive (for example, paying for music lessons or attending parents' evenings).

This led to class differences in how teachers dealt with pupils they perceived as underachieving – setting extension work for underachieving middle-class pupils, but entering working-class pupils for easier exams. Teachers also underestimated working-class pupils' potential and those who were doing well were seen as 'overachieving'.

Dunne and Gazeley conclude that the way teachers explained and dealt with underachievement itself constructed class differences in levels of attainment.

Labelling in primary schools

Labelling occurs from the outset of a child's educational career, as Ray Rist's (1970) study of an American kindergarten shows. He found that the teacher used information about children's home background and appearance to place them in separate groups, seating each group at a different table.

Those the teacher decided were fast learners, whom she labelled the 'tigers', tended to be middle-class and of neat and clean appearance. She seated these at the table nearest to her and showed them greatest encouragement.

The other two groups – whom she labelled the 'cardinals' and the 'clowns' – were seated further away. These groups were more likely to be working-class. They were given lower-level books to read and fewer chances to show their abilities. For example, they had to read as a group, not as individuals.

The self-fulfilling prophecy

A self-fulfilling prophecy is a prediction that comes true simply by virtue of it having been made. Interactionists argue that labelling can affect pupils' achievement by creating a self-fulfilling prophecy, as the following example illustrates:

Step 1: The teacher labels a pupil (e.g. as being very intelligent) and on the basis of this label, makes predictions about him (e.g. he will make outstanding academic progress).

Step 2: The teacher treats the pupil accordingly, acting as if the prediction is already true (e.g. by giving him more attention and expecting a higher standard of work from him).

Step 3: The pupil internalises the teacher's expectation, which becomes part of his self-concept or self-image, so that he now actually becomes the kind of pupil the teacher believed him to be in the first place. He gains confidence, tries harder and is successful. The prediction is fulfilled.

Teachers' expectations

In their study of Oak community school, a California primary school, Robert Rosenthal and Leonora Jacobson (1968) show the self-fulfilling prophecy at work. They told the school that they had a new test specially designed to identify those pupils who would 'spurt' ahead. This was untrue, because the test was in fact simply a standard IQ test. Importantly, however, the teachers believed what they had been told.

The researchers tested all the pupils, but then picked 20% of them purely at random and told the school, again falsely, that the test had identified these children as 'spurters'. On returning to the school a year later, they found that almost half (47%) of those identified as spurters had indeed made significant progress. The effect was greater on younger children.

Analysis and Evaluation
Why do you think the effect was greater on younger children?

Rosenthal and Jacobson suggest that the teachers' beliefs about the pupils had been influenced by the supposed test results. The teachers had then conveyed these beliefs to the pupils through the way they interacted with them – for example, through their body language and the amount of attention and encouragement they gave them.

This demonstrates the self-fulfilling prophecy: simply by accepting the prediction that some children would spurt ahead, the teachers brought it about. The fact that the children were selected at random strongly suggests that if teachers believe a pupil to be of a certain type, they can actually make him or her into that type.

The study's findings illustrate an important interactionist principle: that what people believe to be true will have real effects – even if the belief was not true originally.

The self-fulfilling prophecy can also produce under-achievement. If teachers have low expectations of certain children and communicate these expectations in their interaction, these children may develop a negative self-concept. They may come to see themselves as failures and give up trying, thereby fulfilling the original prophecy.

Streaming

Streaming involves separating children into different ability groups or classes called 'streams'. Each ability group is then taught separately from the others for all subjects. Studies show that the self-fulfilling prophecy is particularly likely to occur when children are streamed.

As Becker shows, teachers do not usually see working-class children as ideal pupils. They tend to see them as lacking ability and have low expectations of them. As a result, working-class children are more likely to find themselves put in a lower stream.

Once streamed, it is usually difficult to move up to a higher stream; children are more or less locked into their teachers' low expectations of them. Children in the lower streams 'get the message' that their teachers have written them off as no-hopers.

This creates a self-fulfilling prophecy in which the pupils live up to their teachers' low expectations by underachieving. For example, Douglas found that children placed in a lower stream at age 8 had suffered a decline in their IQ score by age 11.

By contrast, middle-class pupils tend to benefit from streaming. They are likely to be placed in higher streams, reflecting teachers' view of them as ideal pupils. As a result, they develop a more positive self-concept, gain confidence, work harder and improve their grades. Douglas found that children placed in a higher stream at age 8 had improved their IQ score by age 11.

Streaming and the A-to-C economy

A study of two London secondary schools by David Gillborn and Deborah Youdell (2001) shows how teachers use stereotypical notions of 'ability' to stream pupils. They found that teachers are less likely to see working-class (and black) pupils as having ability. As a result, these pupils are more likely to be placed in lower streams and entered for lower-tier GCSEs. This denies them the knowledge and opportunity needed to gain good grades and widens the class gap in achievement.

Gillborn and Youdell link streaming to the policy of publishing exam league tables. These rank each school

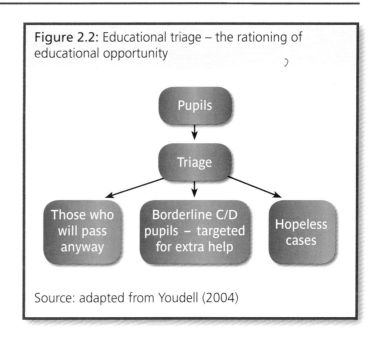

Figure 2.2: Educational triage – the rationing of educational opportunity

Source: adapted from Youdell (2004)

according to its exam performance – for example, in terms of the percentage of pupils gaining five or more GCSE grades A* to C. Schools need to achieve a good league table position if they are to attract pupils and funding.

Publishing league tables creates what Gillborn and Youdell call an 'A-to-C economy' in schools. This is a system in which schools focus their time, effort and resources on those pupils they see as having the potential to get five grade Cs and so boost the school's league table position.

Educational triage

Gillborn and Youdell call this process 'educational triage'. Triage literally means 'sorting'. The term is normally used to describe the process on battlefields or in major disasters whereby medical staff decide who is to be given scarce medical resources. Medics have to sort casualties into three categories: (1) the 'walking wounded', who can be ignored because they will survive; (2) those who will die anyway, who will also be ignored, and (3) those with a chance of survival, who are given treatment in the hope of saving them.

The authors argue that the A-to-C economy produces educational triage. Schools categorise pupils into three types:

- Those who will pass anyway and can be left to get on with it.
- Those with potential, who will be helped to get a grade C or better.
- Hopeless cases, who are doomed to fail.

Teachers do this using a stereotypical view of working-class (and black) pupils as lacking ability. As a result, they are likely to be labelled as 'hopeless cases' and simply 'warehoused' in the bottom sets. This produces a self-fulfilling prophecy and failure.

Thus, the need to gain a good league table position drives educational triage. This becomes the basis for streaming, where teachers' beliefs about the lack of ability of working-class pupils are used to segregate them into lower streams or sets, where they receive less attention, support and resources. This results in lower levels of achievement for working-class pupils.

While Gillborn and Youdell make use of interactionist concepts such as teacher labelling and stereotyping in micro level, face-to-face interactions with pupils, they also put these processes into a broader context. Schools operate within a wider education system whose 'marketisation' policies directly affect these micro level processes to produce class differences in achievement. These policies include the publication of exam league tables. (See Topic 6 for more on the effects of marketisation policies.)

Pupil subcultures

A pupil subculture is a group of pupils who share similar values and behaviour patterns. Pupil subcultures often emerge as a response to the way pupils have been labelled, and in particular as a reaction to streaming.

We can use Colin Lacey's (1970) concepts of differentiation and polarisation to explain how pupil subcultures develop:

- **Differentiation** is the process of teachers categorising pupils according to how they perceive their ability, attitude and/or behaviour. Streaming is a form of differentiation, since it categorises pupils into separate classes. Those that the school deems 'more able' are given high status by being placed in a high stream, whereas those deemed 'less able' and placed in low streams are given an inferior status.
- **Polarisation**, on the other hand, is the process in which pupils respond to streaming by moving towards one of two opposite 'poles' or extremes. In his study of Hightown boys' grammar school, Lacey found that streaming polarised boys into a pro-school and an anti-school subculture.

the pro-school subculture

Pupils placed in high streams (who are largely middle-class) tend to remain committed to the values of the school. They gain their status in the approved manner, through academic success. Their values are those of the school: they tend to form a pro-school subculture.

the anti-school subculture

Those placed in low streams (who tend to be working-class) suffer a loss of self-esteem: the school has undermined their self-worth by placing them in a position of inferior status.

This label of failure pushes them to search for alternative ways of gaining status. Usually this involves inverting (turning upside down) the school's values of hard work, obedience and punctuality. As Lacey says,

'a boy who does badly academically is predisposed to criticise, reject or even sabotage the system where he can, since it places him in an inferior position'.

Such pupils form an anti-school subculture as a means of gaining status among their peers, for example by cheeking a teacher, truanting, not doing homework, smoking etc.

Box 6	Banding and polarisation		
Comparison of top band and middle band year 8 pupils at Beachside Comprehensive			
		Top band	**Middle band**
Percentage of pupils from working-class homes		36	78
Percentage of teachers' time spent maintaining order		1.5	12.5
Average number of detentions, per pupil per year		0.4	3.8
Average number of minutes spent on homework per pupil		47	16
Number of extra-curricular activities, per class		43	10
Percentage of pupils who dislike school		13	48
Views held about each band by pupils in the other band			
Top band pupils saw middle band pupils as thick; rough; boring; simple.			
Middle band pupils saw top band pupils as brainy; unfriendly; stuck-up; arrogant.			
Source: adapted from Ball (1981)			

Investigating anti-school subcultures

The issue of anti-school subcultures has certain important **research characteristics** – particular features that may make them easy or difficult to investigate. For example:

- Members of the subculture are more likely to truant and their absence from school makes it harder for the researcher to maintain contact with them.
- An adult researcher may be seen as an authority figure that pupils with anti-school attitudes may be unwilling to respond to openly.
- However, if the researcher can gain their trust, they may be more willing to talk because it gives them the opportunity to speak about their feelings towards school.
- Operating in an education market where the school's public image is so important, head teachers may refuse permission for research that risks creating the impression that the school has a problem with anti-school subcultures.
- The group nature of pupil subcultures means that peer pressure is much more likely to influence the responses of individual members, making it harder for a researcher to uncover individual variations in attitudes.
- It may be hard to obtain parental consent for the research because parents may not want their children identified as anti-school.

1 What other research characteristics of anti-school subcultures can you think of? You could consider issues of access, streaming etc particular to investigating this topic.

2 Using the research characteristics listed above and any others you can think of, identify two strengths and two limitations of using **group interviews** to investigate anti-school subcultures. You can read more about group interviews on pages 124–34.

Unfortunately, however, although joining an anti-school subculture may solve the problem of lack of status, it creates further problems for such pupils. As Lacey says,

'the boy who takes refuge in such a group because his work is poor finds that the group commits him to a behaviour pattern which means that his work will stay poor – and in fact often gets progressively worse'.

In other words, joining an anti-school subculture is likely to become a self-fulfilling prophecy of educational failure.

David Hargreaves (1967) found a similar response to labelling and streaming in a secondary modern school. From the point of view of the education system, boys in the lower streams were triple failures: they had failed their 11+ exam; they had been placed in low streams; and they had been labelled as 'worthless louts'.

One solution to this status problem was for these pupils to seek each other out and form a group within which high status

went to those who flouted the school's rules. In this way, they formed a delinquent subculture that helped to guarantee their educational failure.

Activity Research

Investigating the impact of setting and streaming

...go to www.sociology.uk.net

---

abolishing streaming

Stephen Ball (1981) takes the analysis a step further in his study of Beachside, a comprehensive that was in the process of abolishing banding (a type of streaming) in favour of teaching mixed-ability groups. As Box 6 shows, banding had produced the kind of polarisation described by Lacey.

Ball found that when the school abolished banding, the basis for pupils to polarise into subcultures was largely removed and the influence of the anti-school subculture declined.

Nevertheless, although pupil polarisation all but disappeared, differentiation continued. Teachers continued to categorise pupils differently and were more likely to label middle-class pupils as cooperative and able.

This positive labelling was reflected in their better exam results, suggesting that a self-fulfilling prophecy had occurred. Ball's study shows that class inequalities can continue as a result of teachers' labelling, even *without* the effect of subcultures or streaming.

Since Ball's study, and especially since the Education Reform Act (1988), there has been a trend towards more streaming and towards a variety of types of school, some of which have a more academic curriculum than others.

This has created new opportunities for schools and teachers to differentiate between pupils on the basis of their class, ethnicity or gender and treat them unequally, as studies such as Gillborn and Youdell (2001) show. (See Topic 3).

the variety of pupil responses

Pro- and anti-school subcultures are two possible responses to labelling and streaming. However, as Peter Woods (1979) argues, other responses are also possible. These include:

- **ingratiation:** being the 'teacher's pet'
- **ritualism:** going through the motions and staying out of trouble
- **retreatism:** daydreaming and mucking about
- **rebellion:** outright rejection of everything the school stands for.

Moreover, as John Furlong (1984) observes, many pupils are not committed permanently to any one response, but may move between different types of response, acting differently in lessons with different teachers.

The theme of pupil subcultures is an important one in several areas of education, and in Topics 3 and 4 there are further examples in relation to ethnicity and gender as well as class.

> **Application**
> What factors *outside* school might lead pupils to group together in pupil subcultures inside school?

Criticisms of labelling theory

Most of the studies we have examined in Topic 2 are influenced by labelling theory. This starts from the idea that under-achievement is the result of pupils being negatively labelled and, often, placed in a lower stream. This creates a self-fulfilling prophecy, with pupils often joining anti-school subcultures that help to guarantee their failure.

These studies are useful in showing that schools are not neutral or fair institutions, as cultural deprivation theorists assume. On the contrary, the interactions within schools can actively create social class inequalities.

However, labelling theory has been accused of determinism. That is, it assumes that pupils who are labelled have no choice but to fulfil the prophecy and will inevitably fail. However, studies such as Mary Fuller's (1984) show that this is not always true. (See Topic 3.)

Marxists also criticise labelling theory for ignoring the wider structures of power within which labelling takes place. Labelling theory tends to blame teachers for labelling pupils, but fails to explain why they do so.

Marxists argue that labels are not merely the result of teachers' individual prejudices, but stem from the fact that teachers work in a system that reproduces class divisions. (See Topic 5 for more about Marxist views of education.)

Pupils' class identities and the school

So far we have focused on how in-school processes such as labelling, streaming and pupil subcultures can shape a pupil's identity and affect their achievement. However, sociologists are also interested in how pupils' class identities that are formed outside school interact with the school and its values to produce educational success and failure.

Louise Archer et al (2010) focus on the interaction between working-class pupils' identities and school, and how this produces underachievement. To understand this relationship, they draw on Bourdieu's (1984) concept of habitus.

Habitus

Habitus refers to the 'dispositions' or learned, taken-for-granted ways of thinking, being and acting that are shared by a particular social class. It includes their tastes and preferences about lifestyles and consumption (such as fashion and leisure pursuits), their outlook on life and their expectations about what is normal or realistic for 'people like us'. A group's habitus is formed as a response to its position in the class structure.

Although one class's habitus is not intrinsically better than another's, the middle class has the power to define its habitus as superior and to impose it on the education system. As a result, the school puts a higher value on middle-class tastes, preferences and so on.

This is linked to Bourdieu's concept of cultural capital (see page 23). Because the school has a middle-class habitus, this gives middle-class pupils an advantage, while working-class culture is regarded as inferior.

Symbolic capital and symbolic violence

Because schools have a middle-class habitus, pupils who have been socialised at home into middle-class tastes and preferences gain 'symbolic capital' or status and recognition from the school and are deemed to have worth or value.

By contrast, the school devalues the working-class habitus, so that working-class pupils' tastes (for example in clothing, appearance and accent) are deemed to be tasteless and worthless.

Bourdieu calls this withholding of symbolic capital 'symbolic violence'. By defining the working class and their tastes and lifestyles as inferior, symbolic violence reproduces the class structure and keeps the lower classes 'in their place'.

Thus there is a clash between working-class pupils' habitus and the school's middle-class habitus. As a result, working-class students may experience the world of education as alien and unnatural.

For example, Archer found that working-class pupils felt that to be educationally successful, they would have to change how they talked and presented themselves. Thus, for working-class students, educational success is often experienced as a process of 'losing yourself'. They felt unable to access 'posh', middle-class spaces such as university and professional careers, which were seen as 'not for the likes of us'.

'Nike' identities

Many pupils were conscious that society and school looked down on them. This symbolic violence led them to seek alternative ways of creating self-worth, status and value. They did so by constructing meaningful class identities for themselves by investing heavily in 'styles', especially through consuming branded clothing such as Nike:

> 'You wouldn't really expect [upper-class] people to come out in Nike tracksuits and stuff, we expect them to have that Gucci designer stuff. But people like us, they're just: we're Nike.' (Sean, Littleton School)

Wearing brands was a way of 'being me': without them they would feel inauthentic. Pupils' identities were also strongly gendered; for example, girls adopted a hyper-heterosexual feminine style (see Topic 4).

Style performances were heavily policed by peer groups and not conforming was 'social suicide'. The right appearance earned symbolic capital and approval from peer groups and brought safety from bullying.

However, at the same time, it led to conflict with the school's dress code. Reflecting the school's middle-class habitus, teachers opposed 'street' styles as showing 'bad taste' or even as a threat. Pupils who adopted street styles risked being labelled as rebels.

Archer argues that the school's middle-class habitus stigmatises working-class pupils' identities. Seen in this light, the pupils' performances of style are a struggle for recognition: while the middle class see their 'Nike' identities as tasteless, to the young people they are a means of generating symbolic capital and self-worth.

Nike styles also play a part in working-class pupils' rejection of higher education, which they saw as both unrealistic and undesirable:

- **Unrealistic** because it was not for 'people like us', but for richer, posher, cleverer people, and they would not fit in. It was also seen as an unaffordable and risky investment.
- **Undesirable** because it would not 'suit' their preferred lifestyle or habitus. For example, they did not want to live on a student loan because they would be unable to afford the street styles that gave them their identity.

According to Archer et al, working-class pupils' investment in 'Nike' identities is not only a cause of their educational marginalisation by the school; it also expresses their positive preference for a particular lifestyle. As a result, working-class pupils may choose self-elimination or self-exclusion from education. In other words, not only do they 'get the message' that education is not for the likes of them, but they actively choose to reject it because it does not fit in with their identity or way of life.

▲ Branded sportswear. A key part of some pupils' identities?

Activity **Webquest**

The habitus of higher education

...go to www.sociology.uk.net

Working-class identity and educational success

Archer's study largely deals with the relationship between working-class identity and educational failure. However, some working-class pupils do succeed. What is the relationship between educational success and working-class identity?

A study by Nicola Ingram (2009) of two groups of working-class Catholic boys from the same highly deprived neighbourhood in Belfast offers an answer to this question. One group had passed their 11-plus exam and gone to grammar school, while the other group had failed and gone to a local secondary school. The grammar school had a strongly middle-class habitus of high expectations and academic achievement, while the secondary school had a habitus of low expectations of its underachieving pupils.

Ingram found that having a working-class identity was inseparable from belonging to a working-class locality. The neighbourhood's dense networks of family and friends were a key part of the boys' habitus. It gave them an intense feeling of belonging. As in Archer's study, street culture and branded sportswear were a key part of the boys' habitus and sense of identity.

However, as Ingram notes, working-class communities place great emphasis on conformity. The boys experienced a great pressure to 'fit in' and this was a particular problem for the grammar school boys, who experienced a tension between the habitus of their working-class neighbourhood and that of their middle-class school.

For example, one boy, Callum, was ridiculed by his classmates for coming to school in a tracksuit on non-uniform day. By opting to 'fit in' with his neighbourhood habitus by wearing his tracksuit, he was made to feel worthless by the school's middle-class habitus. As Ingram puts it, 'the choice is between unworthiness at school for wearing certain clothes and worthlessness at home for not'.

Callum's ridiculing is an example of symbolic violence, in which pupils are forced to abandon their 'worthless' (from the school's point of view) working-class identity if they want to succeed. As the sociologist Meg Maguire (1997) wrote of her own experience of going to grammar school, 'the working-class cultural capital of my childhood counted for nothing in this new setting'.

Class identity and self-exclusion

Despite the class inequalities in education, many more working-class young people now go on to university. Even here, however, the clash between working-class identity and the habitus of higher education is a barrier to success. This is partly due to a process of self-exclusion.

For example, Sarah Evans (2009) studied a group of 21 working-class girls from a south London comprehensive studying for their A-levels. Evans found that they were reluctant to apply to elite universities such as Oxbridge and that the few who did apply felt a sense of hidden barriers and of not fitting in.

According to Bourdieu (1984), many working-class people think of places like Oxbridge as being 'not for the likes of us'. This feeling comes from their habitus, which includes beliefs about what opportunities really exist for them and whether they would 'fit in'. Such thinking becomes part of their identity and leads working-class students to exclude themselves from elite universities.

Like Archer and Ingram, Evans also found that the girls had a strong attachment to their locality. For example, only four of the 21 intended to move away from home to study. As Reay et al (2005) point out, self-exclusion from elite or distant universities narrows the options of many working-class pupils and limits their success. (For more on Evans' study in relation to gender identity, see Topic 4.)

Studies like those of Evans, Ingram and Archer show a consistent pattern of a middle-class education system that devalues the experiences and choices of working-class people as worthless or inappropriate. As a result, working-class pupils are often forced to choose between maintaining their working-class identities, or abandoning them and conforming to the middle-class habitus of education in order to succeed.

The relationship between internal and external factors

The above studies show that to understand class differences in achievement, we cannot look at internal and external factors in isolation from each other, because in reality they are often interrelated. For example:

- Working-class pupils' habitus and identities formed outside school may conflict with the school's middle-class habitus, resulting in symbolic violence and pupils feeling that education is not for the likes of them.

- Working-class pupils using the restricted speech code (an external cultural factor) may be labelled by teachers as less able, leading to a self-fulfilling prophecy (an internal factor).

- As Dunne and Gazeley show, an internal factor – what teachers *believe* about working-class pupils' home backgrounds (an external factor) – actually produces underachievement.

- Poverty – an external material factor – may lead to bullying and stigmatisation by peer groups – an internal process within school. In turn this may lead to truanting and failure.

- Wider external factors outside the individual school may affect processes within it, such as streaming. For example, national educational policies use GCSE league tables to measure schools' performance, allocate funding and even close some schools down as 'failing'. Gillborn and Youdell argue that it is this external factor that drives the A-to-C economy and results in labelling and streaming within schools.

Activity	Discussion

The relationship between internal and external factors

...go to www.sociology.uk.net

Topic summary

Some explanations of class differences in achievement focus on internal factors within school. **Interactionists** argue that schools actively create inequality through **labelling** and the **self-fulfilling prophecy, educational triage, streaming** and polarisation into pro-and **anti-school subcultures**.

Conflicts between the school's **habitus** and pupils' **identities** may lead to **symbolic violence** and **self-exclusion**.

EXAMINING CLASS DIFFERENCES IN ACHIEVEMENT (2)

QuickCheck Questions

Check your answers at www.sociology.uk.net

1 Explain the difference between labelling and the self-fulfilling prophecy.
2 Explain the difference between differentiation and polarisation.
3 Identify two characteristics of a pro-school subculture.

4 Suggest one reason why anti-school subcultures develop.
5 State two criticisms of labelling theory.
6 Explain what is meant by 'habitus'.
7 Explain what is meant by 'symbolic capital'.

Questions to try

Whether or not you are taking the AS exams during your A level course, trying the AS questions below is a very good way of testing your knowledge and understanding and practising your skills in preparation for your A level exams.

Item A   There are major social class differences in educational achievement and some sociologists argue that these are the result of internal factors and processes within schools. These include teacher labelling, the self-fulfilling prophecy, streaming and the creation of pupil subcultures.

However, other sociologists claim that factors outside the school, such as parental attitudes and parental income, are the main causes of working-class underachievement.

AS questions

1 Define the term 'educational triage'. (2 marks)
2 Using one example, briefly explain how pupils' identities may lead to underachievement. (2 marks)
3 Outline three ways in which pupils may respond to labelling and streaming. (6 marks)
4 Applying material from Item A and your knowledge, evaluate the view that social class differences in achievement are the result of what goes on within schools. (20 marks)

A level question

5 Applying material from Item A and your knowledge, evaluate the claim that factors outside the school are the main cause of working-class underachievement. (30 marks)

The Examiner's Advice

Q4 Spend about 30 minutes on this question. Explain a range of factors and processes inside schools. Include teacher labelling, the self-fulfilling prophecy, streaming, pupil identities and subcultures, and the A*-C economy. Explain how each factor may affect achievement. Do this by creating a chain of reasoning (see page 248). For example, the A*-C economy means teachers concentrate on borderline C/D grade students to boost the school's league table position. This means weaker (generally working-class) students receive less help and so underachieve. Use evidence from studies such as Gillborn and Youdell, Becker, Dunne and Gazeley, Archer, Hargreaves and Ball, and develop the points noted in Item A. Evaluate the importance of these factors. For example, labelling theory is too deterministic and also ignores wider external structures of power. You can use external factors such as cultural deprivation but only as criticisms of internal factors.

Q5 Spend about 45 minutes on this question. Note that it focuses on external factors, but you should use internal factors as evaluation (see below). Explain the range of factors outside schools that were covered in Topic 1 (cultural deprivation, material deprivation and cultural capital) and how each one affects achievement. Do this by creating a chain of reasoning. For example, poor diet may make pupils lose concentration and work less effectively. Use evidence from the studies in Topic 1 and develop the points noted in Item A. While you should focus on external factors, you should use internal factors to evaluate external ones. For example, cultural deprivation theory blames pupils' speech codes, but arguably it is teachers' labelling of pupils' speech as inadequate that causes underachievement. Avoid simply listing external and internal factors without linking them.

TOPIC 3

Do teachers treat pupils from different backgrounds unequally?

GETTING STARTED

Using Figure 2.3:

1. Describe the relationship between ethnicity and GCSE performance.

2. Suggest reasons for the differences in achievement between different ethnic groups. (You might find it useful to look back at Topics 1 and 2 on class differences in achievement to give you some ideas.)

Figure 2.3: Percentage of pupils achieving 5 or more GCSE grades A*-C including English and maths, 2013

Source: National Pupil Database

Learning objectives

After studying this Topic, you should:

- Be able to describe the patterns of ethnic differences in educational achievement.

- Understand and be able to evaluate the role of different external factors, including cultural deprivation, material deprivation and racism in wider society.

- Understand and be able to evaluate the role of different internal factors, including labelling, pupil subcultures, the curriculum, institutional racism, and selection and segregation.

ETHNIC DIFFERENCES IN ACHIEVEMENT

In Topics 1 and 2, we saw that social class plays an important part in educational achievement. Just as we can think of everyone as belonging to a class, so too we can see individuals as being part of an ethnic group – whether a minority or a majority group.

Tony Lawson and Joan Garrod (2000) define ethnic groups as 'people who share common history, customs and identity, as well as, in most cases, language and religion, and who see themselves as a distinct unit'. In other words, we are talking about culture – that is, about all those things that are learned, shared and valued by a social group.

One difficulty in studying ethnicity and education is the problem of deciding who to include in an ethnic group. For example, should all 'Asians' be classified together – when this would include people of many different nationalities, religions and languages?

It is a mistake to think of ethnic groups as always being defined by physical features such as skin colour. Although many ethnic minority groups in Britain are non-white, this is not true of all groups. However, it happens that the largest minority groups in Britain are non-white.

Evidence of ethnic differences in achievement

We can see from Figure 2.3 that there are inequalities in the educational achievements of different ethnic groups. For example, whites and Asians on average do better than blacks. However, as Figure 2.3 also shows, there are significant variations among Asians. For example, Indians do better than Pakistanis and Bangladeshis.

There are also important gender and class differences within and between ethnic groups. Among all groups other than Gypsy/Roma and Traveller children, girls do better than boys. Similarly, within each ethnic group, middle-class children do better than working-class children.

White pupils' achievements are very close to the national average – not surprisingly, since whites are by far the largest group, accounting for about four fifths of all pupils. However, when we look more closely, we find major class differences, with many working-class white pupils performing at a lower level than that of other ethnic groups.

For example, according to a DfES (2010) study, only 23% of white boys on free school meals – a common measure of low income – gained five A*-C grades at GCSE. According to Steven Hastings (2006), white pupils make less progress between 11 and 16 than black or Asian pupils, and it is possible that whites may soon become the worst performing ethnic group in the country.

Sociologists are interested in the reasons for these differences in achievement and have put forward a number of explanations. Some of these are similar to the explanations of social class differences in achievement we examined in Topic 1 and Topic 2.

As with class differences, we can separate them into internal and external factors, though these are very often linked.

- **External factors** – factors outside the education system, such as the influence of home and family background and wider society.
- **Internal factors** – factors within schools and the education system, such as interactions between pupils and teachers, and inequalities between schools.

External factors and ethnic differences in achievement

Many sociologists argue that ethnic differences in achievement can best be explained by looking at factors outside the school – in the home, family and culture of the child, and the impact of wider society. The main explanations of this kind are cultural deprivation, material deprivation and class, and racism in wider society.

1 Cultural deprivation

As with explanations of class differences in achievement (see Topic 1), cultural deprivation theory sees the underachievement of some ethnic groups as the result of inadequate socialisation in the home. The explanation has three main aspects:

- intellectual and linguistic skills
- attitudes and values
- family structure and parental support.

Intellectual and linguistic skills

Cultural deprivation theorists see the lack of intellectual and linguistic skills as a major cause of underachievement for many minority children. They argue that many children from low-income black families lack intellectual stimulation and enriching experiences. This leaves them poorly equipped for school because they have not been able to develop reasoning and problem-solving skills.

Similarly, Bereiter and Engelmann (see Topic 1) consider the language spoken by low-income black American families as inadequate for educational success. They see it as ungrammatical, disjointed and incapable of expressing abstract ideas.

There has also been concern that children who do not speak English at home may be held back educationally. However, official statistics show that this is not a major factor. For example, in 2010 pupils with English as their first language were only 3.2 points ahead of those without English as their first language (55.2% to 52.0%) when it came to gaining five GCSE A*-C passes including English and maths. Similarly, David Gillborn and Heidi Safia Mirza (2000) note that Indian pupils do very well despite often not having English as their home language.

Activity | **Webquest**

The school where they speak 20 languages

...go to www.sociology.uk.net

Attitudes and values

Cultural deprivation theorists see lack of motivation as a major cause of the failure of many black children. Most children are socialised into the mainstream culture, which instils ambition, competitiveness and willingness to make the sacrifices necessary to achieve long-term goals. This equips them for success in education. By contrast, cultural deprivation theorists argue, some black children are socialised into a subculture that instils a fatalistic, 'live for today' attitude that does not value education and leaves them unequipped for success.

Family structure and parental support

Cultural deprivation theorists argue that this failure to socialise children adequately is the result of a dysfunctional family structure. For example, Daniel Moynihan (1965) argues that because many black families are headed by a lone mother, their children are deprived of adequate care because she has to struggle financially in the absence of a male breadwinner. The father's absence also means that boys lack an adequate role model of male achievement. Moynihan sees cultural deprivation as a cycle where inadequately socialised children from unstable families go on to fail at school and become inadequate parents themselves.

The New Right put forward similar explanations. For example, Charles Murray (1984) argues that a high rate of lone parenthood and a lack of positive male role models lead to the underachievement of some minorities. Roger Scruton (1986) sees the low achievement levels of some ethnic minorities as resulting from a failure to embrace mainstream British culture.

Ken Pryce (1979) also sees family structure as contributing to the underachievement of black Caribbean pupils in Britain. From a comparison of black and Asian pupils, he claims that Asians are higher achievers because their culture is more resistant to racism and gives them a greater sense of self-worth. By contrast, he argues, black Caribbean culture is less cohesive and less resistant to racism. As a result, many black pupils have low self-esteem and underachieve.

Pryce argues that the difference is the result of the differing impact of colonialism on the two groups. He argues that the experience of slavery was culturally devastating for blacks. Being transported and sold into slavery meant that they lost their language, religion and entire family system. By contrast, Asian family structures, languages and religions were not destroyed by colonial rule.

Sewell: fathers, gangs and culture

Unlike Murray, Tony Sewell (2009) argues that it is not the absence of fathers as role models that leads to black boys underachieving. Instead, Sewell sees the problem as a lack of fatherly nurturing or 'tough love' (firm, fair, respectful and non-abusive discipline). This results in black boys finding it hard to overcome the emotional and behavioural difficulties of adolescence.

In the absence of the restraining influence of a nurturing father, street gangs of other fatherless boys offer black boys 'perverse loyalty and love'. These present boys with a media-inspired role model of anti-school black masculinity, whose ideal Chris Arnot (2004) describes as 'the ultra-tough ghetto superstar, an image constantly reinforced through rap lyrics and MTV videos'.

Many black boys are thus subject to powerful anti-educational peer group pressure: most of the academically successful black boys that Sewell interviewed felt that the greatest barrier to success was pressure from other boys. Speaking in Standard English and doing well at school were often viewed with suspicion by their peers and seen as 'selling out' to the white establishment.

As Sewell says:

> 'The biggest barrier facing black boys is actually black peer pressure. We need to talk about how black students discourage their peers.'

Sewell argues that black students do worse than their Asian counterparts because of cultural differences in socialisation and attitudes to education. As he puts it, while one group is being nurtured by MTV, the other is clocking up the educational hours. Sewell concludes that black children – particularly the boys – need to have greater expectations placed on them to raise their aspirations.

However, critical race theorists such as Gillborn (2008) argue that it is not peer pressure but institutional racism within the education system itself that systematically produces the

▲ Sewell's charity, *Generating Genius,* offers a 'nurturing programme' for students from disadvantaged communities.

failure of large numbers of black boys. (For more on this view, see pages 45–8.)

Asian families

While many black families have absent fathers, in Sewell's view Indian and Chinese pupils benefit from supportive families that have an 'Asian work ethic' and place a high value on education.

Likewise, Ruth Lupton (2004) argues that adult authority in Asian families is similar to the model that operates in schools. She found that respectful behaviour towards adults was expected from children. This had a knock-on effect in school, since parents were more likely to be supportive of school behaviour policies.

white working-class families

Most research has focused on black family structures as possible causes of underachievement. However, as we saw earlier, white working-class pupils often underachieve and have lower aspirations. For example, a survey of 16,000 pupils by Andrew McCulloch (2014) found that ethnic minority pupils are more likely to aspire to go to university than white British pupils.

This low level of aspiration and achievement may be the result of a lack of parental support. For example, Lupton studied four mainly working-class schools – two predominantly white, one serving a largely Pakistani community and the fourth drawing pupils from an ethnically mixed community.

She found that teachers reported poorer levels of behaviour and discipline in the white working-class schools – despite the fact that they had fewer children on free school meals

(a common measure of poverty among pupils). Teachers blamed this on lower levels of parental support and the negative attitude that white working-class parents had towards education. By contrast, ethnic minority parents were more likely to see education as "a way up in society".

Similarly, Gillian Evans (2006) argues that street culture in white working-class areas can be brutal and so young people have to learn how to withstand intimidation and intimidate others. In this context, school can become a place where the power games that young people engage in on the street are played out again, bringing disruption and making it hard for pupils to succeed.

Activity	Discussion

Do cultural differences explain differences in achievement?

...go to www.sociology.uk.net

compensatory education

The main policy that has been adopted to tackle cultural deprivation is compensatory education. For example, the aim of Operation Head Start (see page 20) in the USA was to compensate children for the cultural deficit they are said to suffer because of deprived backgrounds.

Criticisms of cultural deprivation theory

Geoffrey Driver (1977) criticises cultural deprivation theory for ignoring the positive effects of ethnicity on achievement. He shows that the black Caribbean family, far from being dysfunctional, provides girls with positive role models of strong independent women. Driver argues that this is why black girls tend to be more successful in education than black boys.

Errol Lawrence (1982) challenges Pryce's view that black pupils fail because their culture is weak and they lack self esteem. He argues that black pupils under-achieve not because of low self-esteem, but because of racism.

Keddie sees cultural deprivation as a victim-blaming explanation. She argues that ethnic minority children are culturally different, not culturally deprived. They under-achieve because schools are ethnocentric: biased in favour of white culture and against minorities.

These critics oppose compensatory education because they see it as an attempt to impose the dominant white culture on children who already have a coherent culture of their own. They propose two main alternatives:

- **multicultural education:** a policy that recognises and values minority cultures and includes them in the curriculum
- **anti-racist education:** a policy that challenges the prejudice and discrimination that exists in schools and wider society.

Some sociologists argue that material deprivation rather than cultural deprivation is the main cause of under-achievement. We examine their view next.

2 Material deprivation and class

Material deprivation means a lack of those physical necessities that are seen as essential or normal for life in today's society. In general, working-class people are more likely to face poverty and material deprivation.

Material deprivation explanations see educational failure as resulting from factors such as substandard housing and low income. Ethnic minorities are more likely to face these problems. For example, according to Guy Palmer (2012):

- Almost half of all ethnic minority children live in low-income households, as against a quarter of white children.
- Ethnic minorities are almost twice as likely to be unemployed compared with whites.
- Ethnic minority households are around three times as likely to be homeless.
- Almost half of Bangladeshi and Pakistani workers earned under £7 per hour, compared with only a quarter of white British workers.

In addition, ethnic minority workers are more likely to be engaged in shift work, and Bangladeshi and Pakistani women are more likely than others to be engaged in low-paid homeworking.

There are several reasons why some ethnic minorities may be at greater risk of the material deprivation that results from unemployment, low pay and overcrowding:

- Many live in economically depressed areas with high unemployment and low wage rates.
- Cultural factors such as the tradition of purdah in some Muslim households, which prevents women from working outside the home.
- A lack of language skills, and foreign qualifications not being recognised by UK employers. These are more likely to affect recently arrived groups, many of whom are refugees. Most members of established minority groups are fluent in English.
- Asylum seekers may not be allowed to take work.
- Racial discrimination in the labour market and housing market (see the section on 'Racism in wider society' below.)

Analysis and Evaluation

How might (a) parents working shifts and (b) parents engaged in low-paid homeworking affect their children's education?

Such inequalities are reflected in the proportion of children from different ethnic groups who are eligible for free school meals, as Figure 2.4 shows. The material deprivation explanation argues that such class differences explain why Pakistani pupils tend to do worse than Indian and white pupils.

Indian pupils – whose achievements are generally above average – are likely to be from better-off backgrounds. For example, they are the ethnic group most likely to attend private schools – at twice the rate of whites and five times that of blacks.

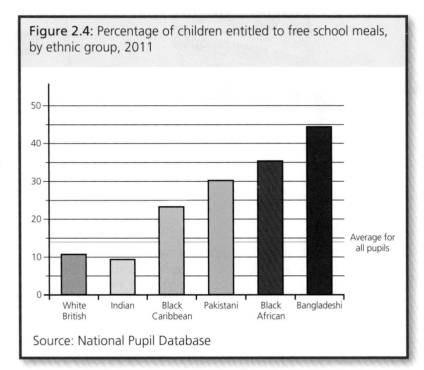

Figure 2.4: Percentage of children entitled to free school meals, by ethnic group, 2011

Source: National Pupil Database

Does class override ethnicity?

Thus if we fail to take the different class positions of ethnic groups into account when we compare their educational achievements, there is a danger that we may over-estimate the effect of cultural deprivation and under-estimate the effect of poverty and material deprivation.

However, even those Indian and Chinese pupils who are materially deprived still do better than most. For example, in 2011, 86% of Chinese girls who received free school meals achieved five or more higher grade GCSEs, compared with only 65% of white girls who were *not* receiving free school meals.

This suggests that material deprivation and social class factors do not completely override the influence of ethnicity. For example, Tariq Modood (2004) found that, while children from low-income families generally did less well, the effects of low income were much less for other ethnic groups than for white pupils.

3 Racism in wider society

While material deprivation and poverty has an impact on the educational achievement of some ethnic minority children, some sociologists argue that poverty is itself the product of another factor – namely, racism. As David Mason (2000) puts it, 'discrimination is a continuing and persistent feature of the experience of Britain's citizens of minority ethnic origin'.

John Rex (1986) shows how racial discrimination leads to social exclusion and how this worsens the poverty faced by ethnic minorities. In housing, for instance, discrimination means that minorities are more likely to be forced into substandard accommodation than white people of the same class.

In employment, too, there is evidence of direct and deliberate discrimination. For example, Wood et al (2010) sent three closely matched job applications to each of almost 1,000 job vacancies. These came from fictitious applicants using names associated with different ethnic groups. For each job, one application appeared to come from a white person and two from members of minority groups. Wood et al found that only one in 16 'ethnic minority' applications were offered an interview, as against one in nine 'white' applications.

This helps to explain why members of ethnic minorities are more likely to face unemployment and low pay, and this in turn has a negative effect on their children's educational prospects.

Internal factors (1) labelling, identities and responses

According to Gillborn and Mirza (2000), in one local education authority, black children were the highest achievers on entry to primary school (20 percentage points above the local average), yet by the time it came to GCSE, they had the worst results of any ethnic group – 21 points *below* the average.

Similarly, Steve Strand's (2010) analysis of the entire national cohort of over 530,000 7-11 year olds shows how quickly many black pupils fall behind after starting school. He found that black Caribbean boys not entitled to free school meals, especially the more able pupils, made significantly less progress than their white peers.

If a group can begin their compulsory schooling as the highest achievers and yet finish it as the lowest achievers, this challenges the assumption made by cultural deprivation theorists that black children enter school unprepared. Instead, it suggests that factors internal to the education system itself may be playing a major part in producing ethnic differences in achievement. These internal factors include labelling and teacher racism, pupil identities, and pupil responses and subcultures.

1 Labelling and teacher racism

To label someone is to attach a meaning or definition to them. For example, teachers may label a pupil as a troublemaker or cooperative, bright or stupid. Interactionist sociologists study the face-to-face interactions in which such labelling occurs.

When looking at ethnic differences in achievement, interactionists focus on the different labels teachers give to children from different ethnic backgrounds. Their studies show that teachers often see black and Asian pupils as being far from the 'ideal pupil'. For example, black pupils are often seen as disruptive and Asians as passive. Negative labels may lead teachers to treat ethnic minority pupils differently. This disadvantages them and may result in their failure.

Black pupils and discipline

A good illustration of the impact of labelling on black pupils comes from studies by Gillborn and Youdell (2000). They found that teachers were quicker to discipline black pupils than others for the same behaviour.

Gillborn and Youdell argue that this is the result of teachers' 'racialised expectations'. They found that teachers expected black pupils to present more discipline problems and misinterpreted their behaviour as threatening or as a challenge to authority. When teachers acted on this misperception, the pupils responded negatively and further conflict resulted. In turn, black pupils felt teachers underestimated their ability and picked on them. Gillborn and Youdell conclude that much of the conflict between white teachers and black pupils stems from the racial stereotypes teachers hold, rather than the pupils' actual behaviour.

This may explain the higher level of exclusions from school of black boys (see Figure 2.5). As Jenny Bourne (1994) found, schools tend to see black boys as a threat and to label them negatively, leading eventually to exclusion. Exclusions affect achievement: only one in five excluded pupils achieves five GCSEs.

According to Osler (2001), in addition to higher rates of official exclusions, black pupils appear more likely to suffer from unrecorded unofficial exclusions and from 'internal exclusions' where they are sent out of class. They are also more likely to be placed in pupil referral units (PRUs) that exclude them from access to the mainstream curriculum.

Black pupils and streaming

As we saw in Topic 2, Gillborn and Youdell found that in the 'A-to-C economy', teachers focus on those students who they believe are most likely to achieve a grade C at GCSE – a process the authors call 'educational triage' or sorting. As a result, negative stereotypes about black pupils' ability that some teachers hold means they are more likely to be placed in lower sets or streams.

Similarly, Peter Foster (1990) found that teachers' stereotypes of black pupils as badly behaved could result in them being placed in lower sets than other pupils of similar ability. Streaming black pupils on the basis of negative stereotypes about their ability or behaviour can result in a self-fulfilling prophecy of underachievement.

Asian pupils

Cecile Wright's (1992) study of a multi-ethnic primary school shows that Asian pupils can also be the victims of teachers' labelling. She found that despite the school's apparent commitment to equal opportunities, teachers held ethnocentric views: that is, they took for granted that British culture and Standard English were superior.

This affected how they related to Asian pupils. For example, teachers assumed they would have a poor grasp of English and left them out of class discussions or used simplistic, childish language when speaking to them.

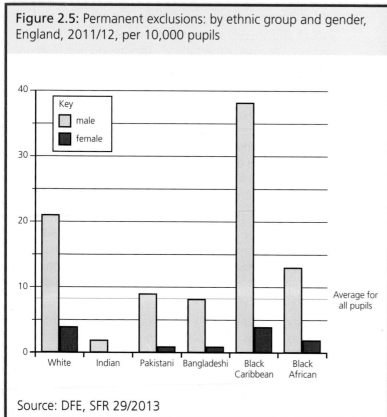

Figure 2.5: Permanent exclusions: by ethnic group and gender, England, 2011/12, per 10,000 pupils

Source: DFE, SFR 29/2013

Asian pupils also felt isolated when teachers expressed disapproval of their customs or mispronounced their names. In general, teachers saw them not as a threat (unlike black pupils), but as a problem they could ignore. The effect was that Asian pupils, especially the girls, were marginalised – pushed to the edges and prevented from participating fully.

2 Pupil identities

Teachers often define pupils as having stereotypical ethnic identities. According to Louise Archer (2008), teachers' dominant discourse (way of seeing something) defines ethnic minority pupils' identities as lacking the favoured identity of the ideal pupil.

Archer describes how the dominant discourse constructs three different pupil identities:

- **The ideal pupil identity** A white, middle-class, masculinised identity, with a normal sexuality. This pupil is seen as achieving in the 'right' way, through natural ability and initiative.
- **The pathologised pupil identity** An Asian, 'deserving poor', feminised identity, either asexual or with an oppressed sexuality. This pupil is seen as a plodding, conformist and culture-bound 'over-achiever', a slogger who succeeds through hard work rather than natural ability.
- **The demonised pupil identity** A black or white, working-class, hyper-sexualised identity. This pupil is seen as an unintelligent, peer-led, culturally deprived under-achiever.

For Archer, ethnic minority pupils are likely to be seen as either demonised or pathologised pupils. For example, from interviews with teachers and students, she shows how black students are demonised as loud, challenging, excessively sexual and with 'unaspirational' home cultures.

In a further study, Archer (2010) found that teachers stereotyped Asian girls as quiet, passive or docile. As Farzana Shain (2003) notes, when Asian girls challenge this stereotype by misbehaving, they are often dealt with more severely than other pupils.

Chinese pupils

Archer argues that even those minority pupils who perform successfully can be pathologised (seen as abnormal). For example, Chinese students were simultaneously praised and viewed negatively by their teachers, who saw them as:

'a homogenous passive, quiet and hardworking mass with Chinese girls as educational automatons, who are too quiet, too passive and too repressed, while the boys tended to be positioned as effeminate and subordinate – and hence not properly masculine – by virtue of their passivity, quietness and hard work.'

While successful, therefore, Chinese students were seen as having achieved success in the 'wrong' way – through hardworking, passive conformism rather than natural individual ability. This meant they could never legitimately occupy the identity of 'ideal pupil'. Archer and Francis (2007) sum up the teachers' view of them as a 'negative positive stereotype'.

Teachers stereotyped Chinese families as 'tight' and 'close' and used this to explain the girls' supposed passivity (similar to the way teachers often see South Asian girls as victims of oppressive family situations). Teachers also tended wrongly to stereotype their Chinese students as middle-class.

The result of the distinctions that Archer identifies is that even the successes of ethnic minority (and female) pupils will only be seen as 'over-achievement' – since 'proper' achievement is seen to be the natural preserve of the privileged, white, middle-class ideal pupil.

3 Pupil responses and subcultures

As we have seen, there is evidence of teacher racism and negative labelling. However, research shows that pupils can respond to this in a variety of ways. For example, they may respond by becoming disruptive or withdrawn. Alternatively, pupils may refuse to accept the label and even decide to prove it wrong by working extra hard. Negative labels do not automatically turn into self-fulfilling prophecies.

Fuller and Mac an Ghaill: rejecting negative labels

A good example of pupils responding by rejecting negative labels is Mary Fuller's (1984) study of a group of black girls in year 11 of a London comprehensive school. The girls were untypical because they were high achievers in a school where most black girls were placed in low streams.

Fuller describes how, instead of accepting negative stereotypes of themselves, the girls channelled their anger about being labelled into the pursuit of educational success. However, unlike other successful pupils, they did not seek the approval of teachers, many of whom they regarded as racist. Nor did they limit their choice of friends to other academic achievers. Instead, they were friends with other black girls from lower streams.

Also unlike other successful pupils, they conformed only as far as the schoolwork itself was concerned. They worked conscientiously, but gave the appearance of not doing so, and they showed a deliberate lack of concern about school routines. They had a positive attitude to academic success but, rather than seeking the approval of teachers, they preferred to rely on their own efforts and the impartiality of external exams.

Fuller sees the girls' behaviour as a way of dealing with the contradictory demands of succeeding at school while remaining friends with black girls in lower streams and avoiding the ridicule of black boys, many of whom were anti-school. They were able to maintain a positive self-image by relying on their own efforts rather than accepting the teachers' negative stereotype of them.

The study highlights two important points. Firstly, pupils may still succeed even when they refuse to conform. Secondly, negative labelling does not always lead to failure. These girls were able to reject the labels placed on them and they remained determined to succeed. There was no self-fulfilling prophecy.

Mairtin Mac an Ghaill's (1992) study of black and Asian 'A' level students at a sixth form college reached similar conclusions. Students who believed teachers had labelled them negatively did not necessarily accept the label. How they responded depended on factors such as their ethnic group and gender and the nature of their former schools. For example, some girls felt that their experience of having attended an all-girls school gave them a greater academic commitment that helped them to overcome negative labels at college. As with Fuller's study, this research shows that a label does not inevitably produce a self-fulfilling prophecy.

▲ A positive attitude to academic success.

Mirza: failed strategies for avoiding racism

Like Fuller, Heidi Safia Mirza (1992) studied ambitious black girls who faced teacher racism. Mirza found that racist teachers discouraged black pupils from being ambitious through the kind of advice they gave them about careers and option choices. For example, teachers discouraged them from aspiring to professional careers.

A large majority of teachers in the study held racist attitudes. Mirza identifies three main types of teacher racism:

- **The colour-blind**: teachers who believe all pupils are equal but in practice allow racism to go unchallenged.
- **The liberal chauvinists**: teachers who believe black pupils are culturally deprived and who have low expectations of them.
- **The overt racists**: teachers who believe blacks are inferior and actively discriminate against them.

Much of the girls' time at school was spent trying to avoid the effects of teachers' negative attitudes. The strategies they employed to do this included being selective about which staff to ask for help; getting on with their own work in lessons without taking part and not choosing certain options so as to avoid teachers with racist attitudes.

However, although the girls had high self-esteem, these strategies put them at a disadvantage by restricting their opportunities. Unlike the girls in Fuller's study, their strategies were unsuccessful.

Sewell: the variety of boys' responses

As we saw earlier, Sewell focuses on the absence of fathers and the influence of peer groups and street culture to explain the underachievement of black boys. However, he also notes that their responses to schooling, including racist stereotyping by teachers, can affect their achievement. He identifies four such responses.

The rebels were the most visible and influential group, but they were only a small minority of black pupils. They were often excluded from school. They rejected both the goals and the rules of the school and expressed their opposition through peer group membership, conforming to the stereotype of the anti-authority, anti-school 'black macho lad'. The rebels believed in their own superiority based on the idea that black masculinity equates with sexual experience and virility. They were contemptuous of white boys, who they saw as effeminate, and dismissive of conformist black boys.

The conformists were the largest group. These boys were keen to succeed, accepted the school's goals and had friends from different ethnic groups. They were not part of a subculture and were anxious to avoid being stereotyped either by teachers or their peers.

The retreatists were a tiny minority of isolated individuals who were disconnected from both school and black subcultures, and were despised by the rebels.

The innovators were the second largest group. Like Fuller's girls, they were pro-education but anti-school. They valued success, but did not seek the approval of teachers and conformed only as far as schoolwork itself was concerned. This distanced them from the conformists and allowed them to maintain credibility with the rebels while remaining positive about academic achievement.

Sewell shows that only a small minority fit the stereotype of the 'black macho lad' (the 'rebels' in Sewell's study). Nevertheless, teachers tend to see all black boys in this way and this contributes to the underachievement of many boys, whatever their attitude to school. Furthermore, many of the boys' negative attitudes are themselves a response to this racism.

Investigating racism in schools

The issue of racism in schools has certain important **research characteristics** – particular features that may make it easy or difficult to investigate. For example:

- Racism is potentially a breach of the law, so teachers, pupils and parents are likely to be particularly careful about displaying racist attitudes to a researcher.
- Teachers are also bound by a code of professional conduct forbidding them from displaying racist attitudes, making it even harder to get behind any public 'front' they may put up.
- Schools are legally required to keep records of any racist incidents and this can provide researchers with relevant statistical data.
- However, there is no easily applicable official definition of a 'racist incident' and some teachers may feel they have had insufficient training to be able to identify one.
- The group nature of some racist behaviour means that peer pressure is likely to influence the responses of individual pupils, making it more difficult for a researcher to uncover individual variations in attitudes.
- It may be hard to obtain parental consent for the research because parents may be unwilling to have their children identified as exhibiting racist behaviour.
- Victims of racism may be unwilling to identify themselves for fear of further abuse for talking to a researcher. Alternatively, victims of racism may welcome an opportunity to share their experiences with a supportive outsider.

1 What other research characteristics of racism in schools can you think of? You could consider issues of confidentiality, stereotyping etc particular to investigating this topic.

2 Using the research characteristics listed above and any others you can think of, identify two strengths and two limitations of using **documents** to investigate racism in schools. You can read more about documents on pages 152–4.

However, while Sewell recognises that teachers' racist stereotyping of black boys disadvantages them and can lead to a self-fulfilling prophecy, he argues that factors external to school, such as the role of peer groups, street culture and the lack of a nurturing father, are more important in producing underachievement.

Evaluation of labelling and pupil responses

Rather than blaming the child's home background, as cultural deprivation theory does, labelling theory shows how teachers' stereotypes can be a cause of failure.

However, there is a danger of seeing these stereotypes as simply the product of individual teachers' prejudices, rather than of racism in the way that the education system as a whole operates. For example, as we saw in Topic 2, Gillborn and Youdell argue that the policy of publishing league tables creates an 'A-to-C economy' and leads to large numbers of black and working-class pupils being placed in lower streams or entered for lower-tier exams.

There is also a danger of assuming that once labelled, pupils automatically fall victim to the self-fulfilling prophecy and fail. Nevertheless, as Mirza shows, although pupils may devise strategies to try to avoid teachers' racism, these too can limit their opportunities.

Internal factors (2) institutional racism

Troyna and Williams (1986) argue that to explain ethnic differences in achievement, we need to go beyond simply examining individual teacher racism. We must also look at how schools and colleges routinely and even unconsciously discriminate against ethnic minorities. They therefore make a distinction between:

- **individual racism** that results from the prejudiced views of individual teachers and others
- **institutional racism** – discrimination that is built into the way institutions such as schools and colleges operate.

Critical race theory

Critical race theory sees racism as an ingrained feature of society. This means that it involves not just the intentional actions of individuals but, more importantly, institutional racism. According to two of the founders of the Black Panther party in the USA, Stokely Carmichael and Charles Hamilton (1967), institutional racism is:

'less overt, more subtle, less identifiable in terms of specific individuals committing the acts... It originates in the operation of established and respected forces in society.'

Locked-in inequality

For critical race theorists such as Daria Roithmayr (2003), institutional racism is a 'locked-in inequality': The scale of historical discrimination is so large that there no longer needs to be any conscious intent to discriminate – the inequality becomes self-perpetuating: it feeds on itself.

Gillborn (2008) applies the concept of locked-in inequality to education. He sees ethnic inequality as "so deep rooted and so large that it is a practically inevitable feature of the education system".

Critical race theorists see the education system as institutionally racist in several ways, which we shall now examine.

Marketisation and segregation

Gillborn (1997) argues that because marketisation gives schools more scope to select pupils, it allows negative stereotypes to influence decisions about school admissions.

Gillborn's view is supported by Moore and Davenport's (1990) American research. They show how selection procedures lead to ethnic segregation, with minority pupils failing to get into better secondary schools due to discrimination. For example, they found that primary school reports were used to screen out pupils with language difficulties, while the application process was difficult for non-English speaking parents to understand.

These procedures favoured white pupils and disadvantaged those from ethnic minority backgrounds. Moore and Davenport thus conclude that selection leads to an ethnically stratified education system.

The Commission for Racial Equality (1993) identified similar biases in Britain. It noted that racism in school admissions procedures means that ethnic minority children are more likely to end up in unpopular schools. The report identifies the following reasons:

- reports from primary schools that stereotype minority pupils
- racist bias in interviews for school places
- lack of information and application forms in minority languages
- ethnic minority parents are often unaware of how the waiting list system works and the importance of deadlines.

The ethnocentric curriculum

The term 'ethnocentric' describes an attitude or policy that gives priority to the culture and viewpoint of one particular ethnic group, while disregarding others. The ethnocentric curriculum is thus a curriculum that reflects the culture of one ethnic group – usually the dominant culture. Many sociologists see the ethnocentric curriculum as a prime example of institutional racism because it builds a racial bias into the everyday workings of schools and colleges. Examples of the ethnocentric curriculum include:

- **Languages, literature and music** Troyna and Williams note the meagre provision for teaching Asian languages as compared with European languages. Miriam David (1993) describes the National Curriculum as a 'specifically British' curriculum that largely ignores non-European languages, literature and music.
- **History** Ball (1994) criticises the National Curriculum for ignoring ethnic diversity and for promoting an attitude of 'little Englandism'. For example, the history curriculum tries to recreate a 'mythical age of empire and past glories', while ignoring the history of black and Asian people.

Bernard Coard (1971; 2005) explains how the ethnocentric curriculum may produce underachievement. For example, in history the British may be presented as bringing civilisation to the 'primitive' peoples they colonised. He argues that this image of black people as inferior undermines black children's self-esteem and leads to their failure.

However, it is not clear what impact the ethnocentric curriculum has. For example, while it may ignore Asian culture, Indian and Chinese pupils' achievement is above the national average. Similarly, Maureen Stone (1981) argues that black children do not in fact suffer from low self-esteem.

Assessment

Gillborn (2008) argues that 'the assessment game' is rigged so as to validate the dominant culture's superiority. If black children succeed as a group, 'the rules will be changed to re-engineer failure'. For example, in the past, primary schools used 'baseline assessments' which tested pupils when they started compulsory schooling. However, these were replaced in 2003 by a new way of measuring pupils' abilities, the foundation stage profile (FSP).

The result of this change was that, overnight, black pupils now appeared to be doing worse than white pupils. For example, in one local authority, where black children in

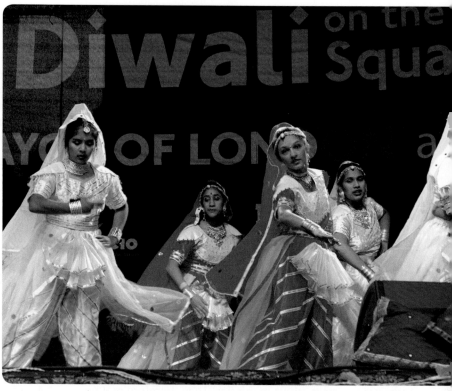

▲ The Hindu festival of Diwali: does the school curriculum ignore minority cultures?

2000 had been the highest achievers on entry to school (20% above the average), by 2003 the new FSP had black children ranked lower than whites across all six developmental areas that it measured. Gillborn concludes:

'And so the old story of Black educational success at age five has been entirely rewritten. The new assessment has established Black failure as, once again, the norm.'

Gillborn explains this reversal as a result of two related institutional factors:

- The FSP is based entirely on teachers' judgments, whereas baseline assessments often used written tests as well.
- A change in the timing: the FSP is completed at the end of reception year, whereas baseline assessments were done at the start of primary school.

Gillborn argues that both these factors increase the risk of teachers' stereotyping affecting the results. For example, a study of GCSE by Sanders and Horn (1995) found that where more weighting was given to tasks assessed by teachers rather than by written exams, the gap between the scores of different ethnic groups widened.

Analysis and Evaluation

Why might a change in the timing of the assessment make it more likely that teachers' stereotypes will affect the results of the assessment?

Access to opportunities

- **The 'Gifted and Talented' programme** was created with the aim of meeting the needs of more able pupils in inner-city schools. While this might seem to benefit bright pupils from minority groups, Gillborn (2008) points out that official statistics show whites are over twice as likely as Black Caribbeans to be identified as gifted and talented, and five times more likely than Black Africans.

- **Exam tiers** Similarly, Tikly et al (2006) found that in 30 schools in the 'Aiming High' initiative to raise Black Caribbean pupils' achievement, blacks were nevertheless more likely than whites to be entered for lower tier GCSE exams. This was often because black pupils had been placed in lower sets. The effect is that they can only gain a grade C at best.

Steve Strand's (2012) analysis of large scale data from the Longitudinal Study of Young People in England (LSYPE) shows a white–black achievement gap in maths and science tests at age 14. He found this to be the result of black pupils being systematically under-represented in entry to higher tier tests. Strand suggests that ethnic differences in entry to test tiers reflect teachers' expectations, leading to a self-fulfilling prophecy.

The 'new IQism'

Access to opportunities such as higher sets or the Gifted and Talented programme depend heavily on teachers' assessments of pupils' ability. This works against black pupils because, as Gillborn notes,

> 'When teachers are asked to judge the 'potential' and/or 'motivation' of their students, they tend to place disproportionate numbers of Black students in low ranked groups.'

Furthermore, teachers place students in sets not only on the basis of prior attainment, but also on disciplinary concerns and perceptions of their 'attitude'. As we saw earlier, Gillborn and Youdell found that teachers had 'racialised expectations' that black pupils would pose more discipline problems.

In what Gillborn calls the new IQism, he argues that teachers and policymakers make false assumptions about the nature of pupils' 'ability' or 'potential'.

They see potential as a fixed quality that can be easily measured – and once a pupil's potential has been measured, they can be put into the 'right' set or stream, onto the Gifted and Talented programme, and so on. Gillborn and Youdell (2001) note that secondary schools are increasingly using old-style intelligence (IQ) tests to allocate pupils to different streams on entry.

For Gillborn, however, there is no genuine measure of 'potential'. All a test can do, is tell us what a person has learnt already or can do now, not what they may be able to do in the future. This is like the driving test; failing it doesn't mean you will never be able to drive – simply that you can't do so now.

From his analysis of school assessment methods, programmes for gifted children, and attempts to measure pupils' potential, Gillborn concludes that the education system is institutionally racist, creating an environment in which ethnic minority pupils are routinely disadvantaged. In his words,

> 'Race inequality is a constant and central feature of the education system. Racism [is] a fundamental defining characteristic of the education system.'

Criticisms of Gillborn

Criticisms of Gillborn's view that ethnic differences in achievement are the result of institutional racism focus on two issues:

- the underachievement of some minority groups such as black boys
- the 'overachievement' of Indian and Chinese pupils.

Black boys' underachievement

As we have seen, critical race theorists such as Gillborn argue that institutional racism is the main cause of under-achievement. They argue that *internal* factors within the education system, such as assessment and setting, systematically produce the failure of large numbers of ethnic minority pupils, especially black boys.

By contrast, sociologists such as Sewell reject this view. Although he does not believe that racism has disappeared from schools, he argues that it is not powerful enough to prevent individuals from succeeding. Rather, in Sewell's view, we need to focus on *external* factors such as boys' anti-school attitudes, the peer group and the nurturing role of the father.

Model minorities: Indian and Chinese achievement

Critics of the idea that the education system is institutionally racist point to the fact that, as well as underachievement of groups such as black boys, there is also 'overachievement' by other, 'model minorities'. For example, Indian and Chinese students perform better than the white majority.

In other words, if these two groups do so well, how then can there be institutional racism in education, as critical race theorists claim?

Gillborn (2008) responds by arguing that the image of Indians and Chinese as hardworking 'model minorities' performs an ideological function. It conceals the fact that the education system is institutionally racist:

- It makes the system appear fair and meritocratic – that Indians and Chinese succeed because they make the effort and take advantage of the opportunities offered to them.
- It justifies the failure of other minorities, such as blacks – that they fail because they are unable or unwilling to make the effort, due to their 'unaspirational' home culture.
- It ignores the fact that 'model minorities' still suffer racism in schools. For example, Chinese students report similar levels of harassment to Black Caribbeans.

Ethnicity, class and gender

Gillian Evans (2006) argues that, to fully understand the relationship between ethnicity and achievement, we need to look at how ethnicity interacts with gender and class. For example, she claims that in examining black children's achievement, sociologists tend to look at their culture and ethnicity, but rarely at their class.

One example of how ethnicity intersects with gender to affect achievement is Paul Connolly's (1998) study of five and six year olds in a multi-ethnic inner-city primary school.

Connolly shows how pupils and teachers construct masculinity differently depending on a child's ethnicity. Teachers saw black boys as disruptive under-achievers and controlled them by punishing them more and by channeling their energies into sport. The boys responded by seeking status in non-academic ways, such as playing kiss-chase and football.

By contrast, teachers saw Asian boys as passive, conformist, keen and academic; when they misbehaved, they were seen as immature rather than threatening. Other boys picked on them to assert their own masculinity and excluded them from playing football. Both teachers and pupils saw Asian boys as more 'feminine', vulnerable and in need of protection from bullying.

Studies such as those by Evans and Connolly show that we cannot consider ethnicity in isolation from gender and class.

For example, Connolly (2006) notes that there is an 'interactions effect': class and gender interact differently with ethnicity depending on which ethnic group we are looking at. For instance, there is a bigger gap between the achievements of white middle-class and white working-class pupils than there is between black middle-class and black working-class pupils.

Activity	Webquest

Do schools disadvantage minority ethnic pupils?

...go to www.sociology.uk.net

Summary

There are achievement **differences between ethnic groups**. For example, Chinese and Indian pupils tend to do better than average, while black pupils do worse. There are class and gender **differences within groups**: e.g. black females do better than black males.

Some explanations focus on **external factors** (outside school), such as **cultural deprivation** due to unstable family structures or inadequate socialisation.

Others argue that the lower **class position** of many minorities, along with **racism in wider society**, leads to material deprivation and lower achievement.

Other explanations focus on **internal factors**. These include the effects of **teachers' racist labelling**, the **identities** they ascribe to pupils and **institutional racism**, e.g. the ethnocentric curriculum and setting.

EXAMINING ETHNIC DIFFERENCES IN ACHIEVEMENT

QuickCheck Questions

Check your answers at www.sociology.uk.net

1 List the following groups in order of achievement at GCSE, highest first: blacks, Chinese, Indians.
2 State one criticism of cultural deprivation theory as an explanation of ethnic differences in achievement.
3 How does Sewell explain the differences in achievement between black boys and Asian pupils?
4 What is meant by the term 'teachers' racialised expectations'?
5 What is meant by the ethnocentric curriculum?
6 Name the three pupil identities described by Archer. Which class and ethnic groups does each identity refer to?

Questions to try

Whether or not you are taking the AS exams during your A level course, trying the AS questions below is a very good way of testing your knowledge and understanding and practising your skills in preparation for your A level exams.

Item A   There are marked ethnic differences in educational achievement. Some minority ethnic groups do much better than others. For example, Indian pupils on average achieve more highly than Pakistanis and Bangladeshis. These differences may be due to factors outside the school. For example, some sociologists suggest that cultural differences have an important influence on achievement. Others claim that it is more to do with the material circumstances of different ethnic groups.

Item B   There are important differences in the experiences of different ethnic groups in the education system, for example in terms of examination entries and allocation to sets or streams. Similarly, studies show that teachers may be quicker to discipline pupils from certain ethnic groups for apparent misbehaviour. These differences can lead to educational failure for some groups.

AS questions
1 Define the term 'model minorities'. (2 marks)
2 Outline three ways in which the ethnocentric curriculum may operate in education. (6 marks)
3 Outline and explain two forms of pupil response to teachers' racism and negative labelling. (10 marks)
4 Applying material from Item A and your knowledge, evaluate the view that ethnic differences in educational achievement are primarily the result of factors outside the school. (20 marks)

A level question
5 Applying material from Item B, analyse two factors inside schools that lead to ethnic differences in educational achievement. (10 marks)

The Examiner's Advice

Q4 Spend about 30 minutes on this question. Avoid lumping all ethnic minority groups together – describe the achievement patterns of specific named groups. Explain a range of factors outside schools that affect ethnic achievement, e.g. linguistic skills, attitudes and values, family structure, cultural deprivation, material deprivation and racism in society. Explain how each may affect achievement. Do this by creating a chain of reasoning (see page 248). For example, the authority model in Asian families mirrors school, so Asian pupils are more respectful towards teachers and work as instructed, leading to educational success. Use evidence from studies such as Murray, Pryce, Driver and Ballard, the Sutton Trust, Evans, Lupton and Sewell, and develop the points noted in Item A. You need to evaluate these factors. Make criticisms of each factor as you go, rather than in a separate section at the end. For example, discuss whether factors inside school, e.g. institutional racism, are more important than external factors in explaining black boys' underachievement.

Q5 Spend about 15 minutes on this question. Divide your time fairly equally between each factor. You don't need a separate introduction; just start on your first factor. To answer this question, it's essential that you take two points from the Item and show through a chain of reasoning how each one leads to ethnic differences in achievement. (It is a very good idea to quote from the Item for each factor.) You could use exam entries, allocation to sets or streams, or disciplining pupils. For example, institutional racism means some minority ethnic pupils are allocated to lower streams than their ability merits. This means their self-esteem is lowered so they cease to try, resulting in underachievement. Use concepts such as teachers' racialised expectations, pupil subcultures, the A*-C economy, model minorities, the new IQism and ideal/pathologised/demonised pupil identities, and studies such as Gillborn and Youdell, Sewell, Mirza, Archer and Francis, and Bourne. Include some brief evaluation.

A growing gender gap in educational achievement.

GETTING STARTED

Look at Figure 2.6. Some sociologists argue that girls achieve better results because they are more conscientious and better organised than boys. Use the following questionnaire to test this claim. You might want to add some additional questions of your own.

Give the questionnaire out in your school/college. Try to ask an equal number of boys and girls to fill it in.

1. What is your gender?   Male   Female
2. What age are you?
3. How much time do you spend on average on homework per week?
   Less than 1 hour   1-2 hours   3-4 hours   5-6 hours   more than 6 hours
4. Do you take pride in your schoolwork?
   Never   rarely   sometimes   often   always
5. How often do you read a book for pleasure?
   Never   rarely   sometimes   often   always
6. How often are you late for school?
   Never   rarely   sometimes   often   always
7. How often do you miss school without a good reason?
   Never   rarely   sometimes   often   always
8. Do you mess about in class?
   Never   rarely   sometimes   often   always

a. Collate your results as a class. What do your class results tell you about the behaviour and attitudes of boys and girls?
b. If there are gender differences, how do you think these may affect achievement in education?
c. Write a paragraph to summarise your findings.

Learning objectives

After studying this Topic, you should:

- Be able to describe the patterns of gender differences in educational achievement.

- Understand and be able to evaluate the explanations for these differences.

- Understand and be able to evaluate the explanations for gender differences in subject choice.

- Understand the effect of school experiences in shaping gender identities.

Along with social class and ethnicity, gender has a major impact on our experience of education. In recent years, there have been some important changes in this area. In particular, while both sexes have raised their level of achievement, girls have now overtaken boys.

On the other hand, one area where gender patterns have been slower to change is in subject choice, with boys and girls often opting to study traditional 'sex-typed' subjects and courses. Similarly, there is also evidence that schooling continues to reinforce differences in gender identity between boys and girls.

The main questions that interest sociologists in the study of gender differences in education are:

- Why do girls now generally achieve better results than boys?
- Why do girls and boys opt to study different subjects?
- How does schooling help to reinforce gender identities?

This Topic examines some of the answers that sociologists have given to these questions.

The gender gap in achievement

Official statistics provide evidence of differences in the achievements of girls and boys at several important stages of their education:

- **On starting school** In 2013, teacher assessments of pupils at the end of year one showed girls ahead of boys by between 7 and 17 percentage points in all seven areas of learning assessed (including literacy, language, maths, and personal, social and emotional development). Girls were also better than boys at concentrating. A DfE (2013) study found that in state primary schools, boys were two and a half times more likely than girls to have statements of special educational needs.
- **At Key Stages 1 to 3,** girls do consistently better than boys. This is especially so in English, where the gender gap steadily widens with age. In science and maths the gap is much narrower, but girls still do better.
- **At GCSE,** as Figure 2.6 shows, the gender gap stands at around 10 percentage points.
- **At AS and A-level** girls are more likely to sit, pass and get higher grades than boys, though the gap is much narrower than at GCSE. In 2013, for example, 46.8% of girls gained A or B grades at A-level, but only 42.2% of boys. Even in so-called 'boys" subjects such as maths and physics, girls were more likely than boys to get grades A to C.
- **On vocational courses** preparing students for a career, results show a similar pattern. A larger proportion of girls achieve distinctions in every subject, including those such as engineering and construction where girls are a tiny minority of the students.

Although results for both sexes have improved at all levels over the years, the girls' rate of improvement has been more rapid and a significant gap has opened up, particularly at GCSE.

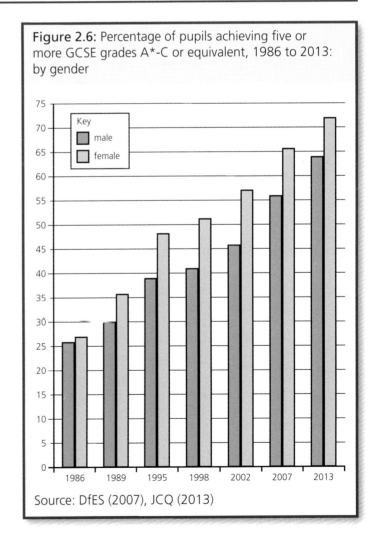

Figure 2.6: Percentage of pupils achieving five or more GCSE grades A*-C or equivalent, 1986 to 2013: by gender

Source: DfES (2007), JCQ (2013)

External factors and gender differences in achievement

There are a number of reasons for gender differences in achievement. As with explanations of class and ethnic differences in achievement, we can divide them into external and internal factors:

- **External factors** – factors outside the education system, such as home and family background, and wider society
- **Internal factors** – factors within schools and the education system, such as the effect of schools' equal opportunities policies.

Many sociologists argue that gender differences in achievement, and especially the more rapid improvement in girls' results, can best be explained by changes that have occurred in factors outside the school, such as the impact of feminism, changes in the family, changes in women's employment, and girls' changing perceptions and ambitions.

1 The impact of feminism

Feminism is a social movement that strives for equal rights for women in all areas of life. Since the 1960s, the feminist movement has challenged the traditional stereotype of a woman's role as solely that of mother and housewife in a patriarchal nuclear family and inferior to men outside the home, in work, education and the law.

Although feminists argue that we have not yet achieved full equality between the sexes, the feminist movement has had considerable success in improving women's rights and opportunities through changes in the law. More broadly, feminism has raised women's expectations and self-esteem.

These changes are partly reflected in media images and messages. A good illustration of this comes from Angela McRobbie's (1994) study of girls' magazines. In the 1970s, they emphasised the importance of getting married and not being 'left on the shelf', whereas nowadays, they contain images of assertive, independent women.

As we shall see, the changes encouraged by feminism may affect girls' self-image and ambitions with regard to the family and careers. In turn, this may explain improvements in their educational achievement.

2 Changes in the family

There have been major changes in the family since the 1970s. These include:

- an increase in the divorce rate
- an increase in cohabitation and a decrease in the number of first marriages
- an increase in the number of lone-parent families
- smaller families.

These changes are affecting girls' attitudes towards education in a number of ways. For example, increased numbers of female-headed lone-parent families may mean more women need to take on a breadwinner role. This in turn creates a new adult role model for girls – the financially independent woman. To achieve this independence, women need well-paid jobs and therefore good qualifications. Likewise, increases in the divorce rate may suggest to girls that it is unwise to rely on a husband to be their provider. Again, this may encourage girls to look to themselves and their own qualifications to make a living.

3 Changes in women's employment

There have been important changes in women's employment in recent decades. These include the following:

- The 1970 Equal Pay Act makes it illegal to pay women less than men for work of equal value, and the 1975 Sex Discrimination Act outlaws discrimination at work.
- Since 1975, the pay gap between men and women has halved from 30% to 15%.
- The proportion of women in employment has risen from 53% in 1971 to 67% in 2013. The growth of the service sector and flexible part-time work has offered opportunities for women.
- Some women are now breaking through the 'glass ceiling' – the invisible barrier that keeps them out of high-level professional and managerial jobs.

These changes have encouraged girls to see their future in terms of paid work rather than as housewives. Greater career opportunities and better pay for women, and the role models that successful career women offer, provide an incentive for girls to gain qualifications.

4 Girls' changing ambitions

The view that changes in the family and employment are producing changes in girls' ambitions is supported by evidence from research. For example, Sue Sharpe's (1994) interviews with girls in the 1970s and 1990s show a major shift in the way girls see their future.

In 1974, the girls had low aspirations; they believed educational success was unfeminine and that appearing to be ambitious would be considered unattractive. They gave their priorities as 'love, marriage, husbands, children, jobs and careers, more or less in that order'.

By the 1990s, girls' ambitions had changed and they had a different order of priorities – careers and being able to support themselves. Sharpe found that girls were now more likely

▲ What policies might encourage more girls to pursue a career in construction?

to see their future as an independent woman with a career rather than as dependent on their husband and his income.

Likewise, O'Connor's (2006) study of 14–17 year olds found that marriage and children were not a major part of their life plans.

Beck and Beck-Gernsheim (2001) link this to the trend towards individualisation in modern society, where independence is valued much more strongly than in the past. A career has become part of a woman's life project because it promises recognition and economic self-sufficiency.

In order to achieve independence and self-sufficiency, many girls now recognise that they need a good education. For some girls in Carol Fuller's (2011) study, educational success was a central aspect of their identity. They saw themselves as creators of their own future and had an individualised notion of self. They believed in meritocracy (equal opportunity for every individual to achieve) and aimed for a professional career that would enable them to support themselves. Clearly, these aspirations require educational qualifications, whereas those of the 1970s girls did not.

class, gender and ambition

However, there are class differences in how far girls' ambitions have changed. Some working-class girls continue to have gender-stereotyped aspirations for marriage and children and expect to go into traditional low paid women's work.

As Diane Reay (1998) argues, this reflects the reality of the girls' class position. Their limited aspirations reflect the limited job opportunities they perceive as being available to them. By contrast, a traditional gender identity (especially being part of a couple) is both attainable and offers them a source of status.

Similarly, Biggart (2002) found that working-class girls are more likely to face a precarious position in the labour market and to see motherhood as the only viable option for their futures. Hence they see less point in achieving in education. For example, most of the low-aspiring working-class girls in Fuller's study were not interested in staying on at school and expressed a desire for low-level jobs.

Activity Research

Investigating pupils' aspirations

...go to www.sociology.uk.net

Internal factors and gender differences in achievement

While factors outside school may play an important part in explaining gender differences in achievement, factors within the education system itself are also important. These include equal opportunities policies, positive role models in schools, GCSE and coursework, teacher attention and classroom interaction, challenging stereotypes in the curriculum, and selection and league tables.

1 Equal opportunities policies

Feminist ideas have had a major impact on the education system. Policymakers are now much more aware of gender issues and teachers are more sensitive to the need to avoid stereotyping. The belief that boys and girls are entitled to the same opportunities is now part of mainstream thinking and it influences educational policies.

For example, policies such as GIST (Girls into science and technology) and WISE (Women into science and engineering) encourage girls to pursue careers in these non-traditional areas. Female scientists have visited schools, acting as role models; efforts have been made to raise science teachers' awareness of gender issues; non-sexist careers advice has been provided and learning materials in science reflecting girls' interests have been developed.

Similarly, the introduction of the National Curriculum in 1988 removed one source of gender inequality by making girls and boys study mostly the same subjects, which was often not the case previously.

Jo Boaler (1998) sees the impact of equal opportunities policies as a key reason for the changes in girls' achievement. Many of the barriers have been removed and schooling has become more meritocratic (based on equal opportunities) – so that girls, who generally work harder than boys, achieve more.

2 Positive role models in schools

As Table 2B shows, there has been an increase in the proportion of female teachers and heads. These women in senior positions may act as role models for girls, showing them women can achieve positions of importance and giving them non-traditional goals to aim for.

Women teachers are likely to be particularly important role models as far as girls' educational achievement is concerned since, to become a teacher, the individual must undertake a lengthy and successful education herself.

3 GCSE and coursework

Some sociologists argue that changes in the way pupils are assessed have favoured girls and disadvantaged boys. For example, Stephen Gorard (2005) found that the gender gap in achievement was fairly constant from 1975 until 1989, when it increased sharply. This was the year in which GCSE was introduced, bringing with it coursework as a major part of nearly all subjects. Gorard concludes that the gender gap in achievement is a "product of the changed system of assessment rather than any more general failing of boys".

Eirene Mitsos and Ken Browne (1998) support this view. They conclude that girls are more successful in coursework because they are more conscientious and better organised than boys. Girls:

- spend more time on their work
- take more care with the way it is presented
- are better at meeting deadlines
- bring the right equipment and materials to lessons.

Mitsos and Browne argue that these factors have helped girls to benefit from the introduction of coursework in GCSE, AS and A level.

Along with GCSE has come the greater use of oral exams. This is also said to benefit girls because of their generally better developed language skills.

Sociologists argue that these characteristics and skills are the result of early gender role socialisation in the family. For example, girls are more likely to be encouraged to be neat, tidy and patient. These qualities become an advantage in today's assessment system, helping girls achieve greater success than boys.

However, Jannette Elwood (2005) argues that although coursework has some influence, it is unlikely to be the only cause of the gender gap because exams have much more influence than coursework on final grades.

4 Teacher attention

The way teachers interact with boys and girls differs. When Jane and Peter French (1993) analysed classroom interaction, they found that boys received more attention because they attracted more reprimands. Becky Francis (2001) also found that while boys got more attention, they were disciplined more harshly and felt picked on by teachers, who tended to have lower expectations of them.

Swann (1998) also found gender differences in communication styles. Boys dominate in whole-class discussion, whereas girls prefer pair-work and group-work and are better at listening and cooperating. When working in groups, girls' speech involves turn taking, and not the hostile interruptions that often characterise boys' speech.

This may explain why teachers respond more positively to girls, whom they see as cooperative, than to boys, whom they see as potentially disruptive. This may lead to a self-fulfilling prophecy in which successful interactions with teachers promote girls' self-esteem and raise their achievement levels.

Table 2B	Percentage of teachers and head teachers who are women, 1992 and 2012			
	Nursery and primary schools		Secondary schools	
	1992	2012	1992	2012
Head teachers	50	71	22	37
Teachers	81	86	49	61

Source: House of Commons Library (2013)

1. Approximately how many times more male than female secondary head teachers were there in 2012?
2. Suggest reasons why there are bigger proportions of female teachers and female heads in primary schools than in secondary schools.

5 Challenging stereotypes in the curriculum

Some sociologists argue that the removal of gender stereotypes from textbooks, reading schemes and other learning materials in recent years has removed a barrier to girls' achievement. Research in the 1970s and 80s found that reading schemes portrayed women mainly as housewives and mothers, that physics books showed them as frightened by science, and that maths books depicted boys as more inventive.

Gaby Weiner (1995) argues that since the 1980s, teachers have challenged such stereotypes. Also, in general, sexist images have been removed from learning materials. This may have helped to raise girls' achievement by presenting them with more positive images of what women can do.

6 Selection and league tables

Marketisation policies (see Topic 6) have created a more competitive climate in which schools see girls as desirable recruits because they achieve better exam results.

David Jackson (1998) notes that the introduction of exam league tables has improved opportunities for girls: high-achieving girls are attractive to schools, whereas low-achieving boys are not. This tends to create a self-fulfilling prophecy – because girls are more likely to be recruited by good schools, they are more likely to do well.

Roger Slee (1998) argues that boys are less attractive to schools because they are more likely to suffer from behavioural difficulties and are four times more likely to be excluded.

As a result, boys may be seen as 'liability students' – obstacles to the school improving its league table scores.

They give the school a 'rough, tough' image that deters high-achieving girls from applying.

Two views of girls' achievement

While there have clearly been changes in gender and educational achievement, sociologists differ in their interpretation of the importance of these changes.

Liberal feminists celebrate the progress made so far in improving achievement. They believe that further progress will be made by the continuing development of equal opportunities policies, encouraging positive role models and overcoming sexist attitudes and stereotypes.

This is similar to the functionalist view that education is a *meritocracy* where all individuals, regardless of gender, ethnicity or class, are given an equal opportunity to achieve (see Topic 5).

Radical feminists take a more critical view. While they recognise that girls are achieving more, they emphasise that the system remains patriarchal (male-dominated) and conveys the clear message that it is still a man's world. For example:

- Sexual harassment of girls continues at school.
- Education still limits girls' subject choices and career options.
- Although there are now more female head teachers, male teachers are still more likely to become heads of secondary schools.
- Women are under-represented in many areas of the curriculum. For example, their contribution to history is largely ignored. Weiner (1993) describes the secondary school history curriculum as a 'woman-free zone'.

Identity, class and girls' achievement

While girls on average now achieve more highly than in the past, this does not mean that all girls are successful. In particular, there are social class differences in girls' achievement. For example, in 2013, only 40.6% of girls from poorer families (those eligible for free school meals) achieved five A*-C GCSEs, whereas over two-thirds (67.5%) of those not on free school meals did so.

Symbolic capital

According to feminists such as Louise Archer et al (2010), one reason for these differences is the conflict between working-class girls' feminine identities and the values and ethos of the school. In her study of working-class girls,

Archer uses the concept of 'symbolic capital' to understand this conflict. Symbolic capital refers to the status, recognition and sense of worth that we are able to obtain from others.

Archer found that by performing their working-class feminine identities, the girls gained symbolic capital from their peers. However, this brought them into conflict with school, preventing them from acquiring educational capital (qualifications) and economic capital (middle-class careers).

Archer identifies several strategies that the girls followed for creating a valued sense of self. These included adopting a hyper-heterosexual feminine identity, having a boyfriend and being 'loud'.

Hyper-heterosexual feminine identities

Many of the girls invested considerable time, effort and money in constructing 'desirable' and 'glamorous' hyper-heterosexual, feminine identities. For example, one girl spent all of the £40 a week she earned from babysitting on her appearance. They constructed identities that combined black urban American styles with unisex sportswear and 'sexy' clothes, make-up and hairstyles.

The girls' performance of this feminine identity brought status from their female peer group and avoided them being ridiculed or called a 'tramp' for wearing the wrong brand.

However, it also brought them into conflict with school. For example, they were often punished for having the wrong appearance: too much jewellery, the wrong clothing or makeup and so on. Teachers saw the girls' preoccupation with appearance as a distraction that prevented them engaging with education.

This led to the school 'othering' the girls – defining them as 'not one of us', incapable of educational success and thus less worthy of respect. Bourdieu describes this process as symbolic violence. Symbolic violence is the harm done by denying someone symbolic capital, for example by defining their culture as worthless.

According to Archer, from the school's point of view, the 'ideal female pupil' identity is a de-sexualised and middle-class one that excludes many working-class girls.

Boyfriends

While having a boyfriend brought symbolic capital, it got in the way of schoolwork and lowered girls' aspirations. This included losing interest in going to university, in studying 'masculine' subjects such as science or in gaining a professional career. Instead these girls aspired to 'settle down', have children and work locally in working-class feminine jobs such as childcare. One girl had to drop out of school after becoming pregnant.

Being 'loud'

Some working-class girls adopted 'loud' feminine identities that often led them to be outspoken, independent and assertive, for example questioning teachers' authority. This failed to conform to the school's stereotype of the ideal female pupil identity as passive and submissive to authority and brought conflict with teachers, who interpreted their behaviour as aggressive rather than assertive.

Working-class girls' dilemma

Working-class girls are thus faced with a dilemma:

- **Either gaining symbolic capital** from their peers by conforming to a hyper-heterosexual feminine identity
- **Or gaining educational capital** by rejecting their working-class identity and conforming to the school's middle-class notions of a respectable, ideal female pupil.

Some girls tried to cope with this dilemma by defining themselves as 'good underneath' (despite the teachers' negative views of them). This 'good underneath' self-image reflects the girls' struggle to achieve a sense of self-worth within an education system that devalues their working-class feminine identities.

Thus, Archer argues that working-class feminine identities and educational success conflict with one another. Working-class girls' investments in their feminine identities are a major cause of their underachievement.

'Successful' working-class girls

Although working-class girls in general are likely to underachieve, some do succeed and go on to higher education (HE). However, even they may be disadvantaged by their gender and class identities, as Sarah Evans (2009) shows in her study of 21 working-class sixth form girls in a south London comprehensive school.

She found that the girls wanted to go to university to increase their earning power. However, this was not for themselves, but to help their families. As one girl said, "The one thing I want to do is just give something back to my family really, that's the most important thing to me, and helping my Nan and all".

The girls' motivation reflected their working-class feminine identities. As Skeggs (1997) notes, 'caring' is a crucial part of this identity, and the girls in Evans' study wished to remain at home and to contribute to their families.

Economic necessity was a further reason for living at home. Cost and fear of getting into debt are major issues for many working-class students in deciding which universities to apply to. However, while living at home made HE more affordable, it also limited their choice of university and the market value of their degree.

But living at home was not just an economic necessity. It was also a positive choice and an aspect of their working-class identities. As Archer (2010) shows, a preference for the local is a key feature of working-class habitus (the ways of seeing, thinking and acting shared by members of a class). The girls showed a strong preference for the local and familiar over the distant.

Thus, as we have seen, the gender identity of working-class girls may play a significant part in their relative lack of success compared with middle-class girls. As Archer shows, a hyper-heterosexual feminine identity puts working-class girls at odds with the school. Evans demonstrates that, even for more successful working-class girls, the 'caring' aspect of working-class feminine identity produces a desire to live at home with their families while studying. This results in their self-exclusion from elite universities further afield and places a limit on their success.

Boys and achievement

We have focused so far on the thing that appears to have changed most – girls' performance. Recently, however, the gender gap in achievement has given rise to concern about boys falling behind.

Several possible factors may be responsible for this. These include external factors (outside the education system) such as boys' poorer literacy skills and the decline of traditional men's jobs, as well as internal factors (within the education system), such as the feminisation of education, the shortage of male primary school teachers and 'laddish' subcultures.

Boys and literacy

According to the DCSF (2007), the gender gap is mainly the result of boys' poorer literacy and language skills. One reason for this may be that parents spend less time reading to their sons. Another may be that it is mothers who do most of the reading to young children, who thus come to see reading as a feminine activity.

In addition, boys' leisure pursuits, such as football, do little to help develop their language and communication skills. By contrast, girls tend to have a 'bedroom culture' centred on staying in and talking with friends.

Poor language and literacy skills are likely to affect boys' performance across a wide range of subjects. In response to this problem, government has introduced a range of policies to improve boys' skills. (See Box 7.)

Globalisation and the decline of traditional men's jobs

Since the 1980s, there has been a significant decline in heavy industries such as iron and steel, shipbuilding, mining and engineering. This has been partly the result of the globalisation of the economy, which has led to much manufacturing industry relocating to developing countries such as China to take advantage of cheap labour.

Traditionally, these sectors of the economy mainly employed men. Mitsos and Browne claim that this decline in male employment opportunities has led to an 'identity crisis for men'. Many boys now believe that they have little prospect of getting a proper job. This undermines their motivation and self-esteem and so they give up trying to get qualifications.

While there may be some truth in this claim, we should note that the decline has largely been in manual working-class jobs that require few if any qualifications. Thus it seems unlikely that the disappearance of such jobs would have much impact on boys' motivation to obtain qualifications.

Feminisation of education

Tony Sewell is reported as claiming that boys fall behind because education has become 'feminised' (BBC, 2006). That is, schools do not nurture 'masculine' traits such as competitiveness and leadership. Instead, they celebrate qualities more closely associated with girls, such as methodical working and attentiveness in class.

Sewell sees coursework as a major cause of gender differences in achievement. He argues that some coursework should be replaced with final exams and a greater emphasis placed on outdoor adventure in the curriculum. He argues: "We have challenged the 1950s patriarchy and rightly said this is not a man's world. But we have thrown the boy out with the bath water."

Shortage of male primary school teachers

The lack of male role models both at home and at school is said to be a cause of boys' underachievement. For example, large numbers of boys are being brought up in the 1.5 million female-headed lone parent families in the UK.

Similarly, only 14% of primary school teachers are male and according to Yougov (2007), 39% of 8-11 year old boys have no lessons whatsoever with a male teacher. Yet most boys surveyed said the presence of a male teacher made them behave better and 42% said it made them work harder.

Some commentators argue that this is because the culture of the primary school has become feminised as a result of being staffed by female teachers, who are unable to control boys' behaviour. In this view, male teachers are better able to impose the strict discipline boys need in order to concentrate. If this view is correct, it would suggest that primary schools need more male teachers.

Box 7	Policies to raise boys' achievement

Government has introduced a range of policies to improve boys' achievement:

- The *Raising Boys Achievement* project involves a range of teaching strategies, including single-sex teaching.
- The *National Literacy Strategy* includes a focus on improving boys' reading.
- The *Reading Champions* scheme uses male role models celebrating their own reading interests.
- *Playing for Success* uses football and other sports to boost learning skills and motivation among boys.
- The *Dads and Sons* campaign encourages fathers to be more involved with their sons' education.

Are more male teachers really needed?

However, research suggests that the absence of male teachers may not be a major factor in boys' underachievement. For example, Becky Francis (2006) found that two-thirds of 7-8 year olds believed the gender of teachers does not matter.

Barbara Read (2008) is also critical of the claims that the culture of primary schools is becoming feminised and that only male teachers can exert the firm discipline that boys need to achieve.

To test these claims, Read studied the type of language teachers use to express criticism or disapproval of pupils' work and behaviour. She identifies two types of language or 'discourse':

- **A disciplinarian discourse:** the teacher's authority is made explicit and visible, for example, through shouting, an 'exasperated' tone of voice or sarcasm.
- **A liberal discourse:** the teacher's authority is implicit and invisible. This child-centred discourse involves 'pseudo-adultification': the teacher speaks to the pupil as if they were an adult and expects them to be kind, sensible and respectful of the teacher.

The disciplinarian discourse is usually associated with masculinity and the liberal discourse with femininity. However, in her study of 51 primary school teachers (25 male and 26 female), Read found that most teachers, female as well as male, used a supposedly 'masculine' disciplinarian discourse to control pupils' behaviour.

Read draws two conclusions from her findings:

1 The fact that most teachers favoured a 'masculine', disciplinarian discourse of control disproves the claim that the culture of the primary school has become feminised, as Sewell and others argue.

2 The fact that female teachers were just as likely as males to use a 'masculine' discourse to control pupils' behaviour disproves the claim that only male teachers can provide the stricter classroom culture in which boys are said to thrive.

Malcolm Haase (2008) echoes Read's first conclusion when he says that although women make up the majority of primary teachers, it is better to think of primary schools as a male-dominated or 'masculinised educational structure that is numerically dominated by women'. For example, as Jones (2006) notes, male teachers in the UK have a one in four chance of gaining a headship; women only one in 13.

'Laddish' subcultures

Some sociologists argue that the growth of 'laddish' subcultures has contributed to boys' underachievement. Debbie Epstein (1998) examined the way masculinity is constructed within school. She found that working-class boys are likely to be harassed, labelled as sissies and subjected to homophobic (anti-gay) verbal abuse if they appear to be 'swots'.

This supports Francis' (2001) finding that boys were more concerned than girls about being labelled by peers as swots, because this label is more of a threat to their masculinity than it is to girls' femininity.

This is because in working-class culture, masculinity is equated with being tough and doing manual work. Non-manual work, and by extension schoolwork, is seen as effeminate and inferior. As a result, working-class boys tend to reject schoolwork to avoid being called 'gay'. As Epstein observes, 'real boys don't work' – and if they do they get bullied. She notes that:

> 'The main demand on boys within their peer group, but also sometimes from teachers, is to appear to do little or no work, to be heavily competitive at sports and hetero-sex, to be rough, tough and dangerous to know.'

Epstein's findings parallel those of Mac an Ghaill and Willis (see pages 63 and 73).

According to Francis, laddish culture is becoming increasingly widespread. She argues that this is because, as girls move into traditional masculine areas such as careers, boys respond by "becoming increasingly laddish in their effort to construct themselves as non-feminine".

The moral panic about boys

Critics of feminism argue that policies to promote girls' education are no longer needed. These critics speak of 'girl power', of girls today 'having it all' and of women taking men's jobs. They believe girls have succeeded at the expense of boys, who are the new disadvantaged.

According to feminists such as Jessica Ringrose (2013), these views have contributed to a moral panic about 'failing boys'. This moral panic reflects a fear that underachieving working-class boys will grow up to become a dangerous, unemployable underclass that threatens social stability.

Ringrose argues that this moral panic has caused a major shift in educational policy, which is now preoccupied with raising boys' achievements. This policy shift has had two negative effects:

1 By narrowing equal opportunities policy down simply to 'failing boys', it ignores the problem of disadvantaged working-class and minority ethnic pupils.

2 By narrowing gender policy down solely to the issue of achievement gaps, it ignores other problems faced by girls in school. These include sexual harassment and bullying, self-esteem and identity issues, and stereotyped subject choices.

Similarly, Audrey Osler (2006) notes that the focus on underachieving boys has led to a neglect of girls. This is partly because girls often disengage from school quietly. By contrast, boys' disengagement often takes the form of public displays of 'laddish' masculinity that attract attention from teachers and policymakers.

Osler gives the example of mentoring schemes aimed at reducing school exclusions among black boys. She points out that these ignore the problem of exclusions among girls, which are increasing more rapidly. Furthermore, girls who are excluded are less likely to obtain places in pupil referral units. Official exclusion rates also mask a wider, hidden problem of exclusion among girls, including self-exclusion (truancy) and internal exclusion (removal from class).

Activity	Discussion

Is the education system biased in favour of boys?

...go to www.sociology.uk.net

Gender, class and ethnicity

However, it would be wrong to conclude that boys are a 'lost cause'. In fact, as Figure 2.6 shows, the performance of both sexes has actually improved considerably in recent years. Boys may now be lagging behind girls, but boys today are achieving more than they did in the past.

Furthermore, as Tracey McVeigh (2001) notes, the similarities in girls' and boys' achievement are far greater than the differences, especially when compared with class or ethnic differences. For example, the class gap in achievement at GCSE is three times wider than the gender gap.

As a result, girls and boys of the same social class tend to achieve fairly similar results. For example, at GCSE in a typical year, the gender gap *within* any given social class is rarely greater than 12 percentage points. By contrast, pupils of the same gender but different social classes achieve widely different results. For example, girls from the highest social class can be as much as 44 points ahead of girls from the lowest class. These figures show that class is a more important influence on a pupil's achievement than gender.

▲ Eighty-nine per cent of all hairdressing apprentices are girls.

Also, the extent to which gender influences achievement itself varies depending on a pupil's class and ethnic group.

For example, the gender gap among black Caribbean pupils is greater than among other ethnic groups. As Fuller shows, many black girls are successful at school because they define their femininity in terms of educational achievement and independence. By contrast, as Sewell found, some black boys fail at school because they define their masculinity in opposition to education, which they see as effeminate.

These examples show that we need to take the interplay of class, gender and ethnicity into account in order to gain a better understanding of differences in achievement. As Connolly (2006) suggests, certain combinations of gender, class and ethnicity have more effect than others. For example, being female raises performance more when 'added to' being black Caribbean than it does when 'added to' being white.

Gender and subject choice

There continues to be a fairly traditional pattern of 'boys' subjects' and 'girls' subjects'. Boys still tend to opt for subjects such as maths and physics, while girls are more likely to choose modern languages, for example.

The National Curriculum gives pupils little freedom to choose or drop subjects by making most subjects compulsory until 16.

However, where choice is possible, both in the National Curriculum and much more so after 16, boys and girls tend to follow different 'gender routes' through the education system. This is shown in National Curriculum options, AS and A levels, and vocational courses.

National Curriculum options

Where there is a choice in the National Curriculum, girls and boys choose differently. For example, although design and technology is a compulsory subject, girls tend to choose the food technology option whereas boys choose graphics and resistant materials.

AS and A levels

Gendered subject choices become more noticeable after 16, when students have more choice. For example, there are big gender differences in entries for A level subjects (see Table 2C), with boys opting for maths and physics and girls choosing subjects such as sociology, English and languages. These differences are mirrored in subject choices at university.

These patterns are not new. For example, the Institute of Physics (2012) found that the proportion of A-level physics students who are girls has been "stubbornly consistent", at around 20%, for over 20 years.

This calls into question the effectiveness of policies such as WISE and GIST aimed at encouraging girls to take up subjects such as physics.

vocational courses

Vocational courses prepare students for particular careers. As Table 2D shows, gender segregation is a very noticeable feature of vocational training. For example, only one in 100 childcare apprentices is a boy.

Explanations of gender differences in subject choice

Why do boys and girls tend to choose different subjects? Sociologists have put forward a number of explanations.

1 Gender role socialisation

Gender role socialisation is the process of learning the behaviour expected of males and females in society.

Early socialisation shapes children's gender identity. As Fiona Norman (1988) notes, from an early age, boys and girls are dressed differently, given different toys and encouraged to take part in different activities.

Schools also play an important part. Eileen Byrne (1979) shows that teachers encourage boys to be tough and show initiative and not be weak or behave like sissies. Girls on the other hand are expected to be quiet, helpful, clean and tidy.

As a result of differences in socialisation, boys and girls develop different tastes in reading. Patricia Murphy and Jannette Elwood (1998) show how these lead to different subject choices. Boys read hobby books and information texts, while girls are more likely to read stories about people.

Table 2C	Candidates sitting GCE A level exams: by gender and subject, UK, 2013	
	% male	% female
Computing	93	7
Physics	79	21
Further Maths	71	29
Mathematics	61	39
History	48	52
Biology	42	58
French	31	69
Drama	31	69
English	28	72
Sociology	25	75
All subjects	46	54

Source: adapted from Joint Council for Qualifications (2013)

Table 2D	Apprenticeships in selected areas, by gender, UK, 2012	
	% male	% female
Children's care	1	99
Health & social care	17	83
Beauty therapy	18	82
Customer service	37	63
IT & telecoms professionals	90	10
Engineering	97	3
Construction	98	2
Vehicle maintenance & repair	98	2
All apprenticeships	47	53

Source: House of Commons Business, Innovation & Skills Committee (2013)

This helps to explain why boys prefer science subjects and why girls prefer subjects such as English.

gender domains

Naima Browne and Carol Ross (1991) argue that children's beliefs about 'gender domains' are shaped by their early experiences and the expectations of adults. By gender domains, they mean the tasks and activities that boys and girls see as male or female 'territory' and therefore as relevant to themselves. For example, mending a car is seen as falling within the male gender domain, but looking after a sick child is not.

Children are more confident when engaging in tasks that they see as part of their own gender domain. For example, when they are set the same mathematical task, girls are more confident in tackling it when it is presented as being about food and nutrition, whereas boys are more confident if it is about cars.

Similarly, Patricia Murphy (1991) found that boys and girls pay attention to different details even when tackling the

▲ Sex-typing of jobs influences boys' and girls' choice of vocational courses.

same task. In general, girls focus more on how people feel, whereas boys focus on how things are made and work. This helps to explain why girls choose humanities and arts subjects, while boys choose science.

2 Gendered subject images

The gender image of a subject affects who will want to choose it. Sociologists have tried to explain why some subjects are seen as boys' or girls' subjects in the first place. For example, Kelly argues that science is seen as a boys' subject for several reasons:

- Science teachers are more likely to be men.
- The examples teachers use, and those in textbooks, often draw on boys' rather than girls' interests.
- In science lessons, boys monopolise the apparatus and dominate the laboratory, acting as if it is 'theirs'.

Similarly, Anne Colley (1998) notes that computer studies is seen as a masculine subject for two reasons:

- It involves working with machines – part of the male gender domain.
- The way it is taught is off-putting to females. Tasks tend to be abstract and teaching styles formal, with few opportunities for group work, which girls favour.

single-sex schooling

Interestingly, pupils who attend single-sex schools tend to hold less stereotyped subject images and make less traditional subject choices. Analysing data on 13,000

Investigating gender and subject choice

The issue of gender and subject choice has certain important **research characteristics** – particular features that may make it easy or difficult to investigate. For example:

- 'Subject choice' and 'gender' are relatively straightforward concepts to operationalise (define and measure) – there are only two genders and subjects are easily identifiable.
- Schools record subject choices by gender through a simple count of who does what subjects that is difficult for schools to falsify.
- Unlike some educational issues, subject choice and gender is not viewed as particularly sensitive and access to information about it is unlikely to be restricted.
- As all schools collect data on gender and subject choice, researchers are able to carry out large-scale studies relatively easily.
- However, schools do not collect data about the reasons behind different patterns of subject choice.
- Teachers wish to maintain a professional image of treating boys and girls equally and so are unlikely to acknowledge that they may channel pupils into gendered subject choices.
- The process of making subject choices is not one that can easily be observed.

1 What other research characteristics of gender and subject choice can you think of? You could consider issues of peer pressure, subject image etc particular to investigating this topic.

2 Using the research characteristics listed above and any others you can think of, identify two strengths and two limitations of using **structured interviews** to investigate gender and subject choice. You can read more about structured interviews on pages 124–35.

individuals, Diana Leonard (2006) found that, compared to pupils in mixed schools, girls in girls' schools were more likely to take maths and science A levels, while boys in boys' schools were more likely to take English and languages. Girls from single-sex schools were also more likely to study male-dominated subjects at university.

Leonard's findings are supported by the Institute of Physics study, which found that girls in single-sex state schools were 2.4 times more likely to take A-level physics than those in mixed schools. The same study found that perceptions of physics are formed outside as well as inside the classroom, for example by the lack of female physicists on television.

Application

Suggest reasons why, in single-sex schools, girls are more likely to choose science and boys are more likely to choose languages.

3 Gender identity and peer pressure

Subject choice can be influenced by peer pressure. Other boys and girls may apply pressure to an individual if they disapprove of his or her choice. For example, boys tend to opt out of music and dance because such activities fall outside their gender domain and so are likely to attract a negative response from peers.

Carrie Paechter (1998) found that because pupils see sport as mainly within the male gender domain, girls who are 'sporty' have to cope with an image that contradicts the conventional female stereotype. This may explain why girls are more likely than boys to opt out of sport.

Similarly, a study of American college students by Alison Dewar (1990) found that male students would call girls 'lesbian' or 'butch' if they appeared to be interested in sport.

The same may be true of some science subjects, especially in mixed schools. For example, as the Institute of Physics found, "There is something about doing physics as a girl in a mixed setting that is particularly off-putting." Peer pressure is a powerful influence on gender identity and how pupils see themselves in relation to particular subjects. In mixed schools, peers police one another's subject choices so that girls and boys adopt an appropriate gender identity, with girls pressured to avoid subjects such as physics.

By contrast, an absence of peer pressure from the opposite sex may explain why girls in single-sex schools are more likely to choose traditional boys' subjects. The absence of boys may mean there is less pressure on girls to conform to restrictive stereotypes of what subjects they can study.

4 Gendered career opportunities

An important reason for differences in subject choice is the fact that employment is highly gendered: jobs tend to be sex-typed as 'men's' or 'women's'. Women's jobs often involve work similar to that performed by housewives, such as childcare and nursing. Women are concentrated in a narrow range of occupations. Over half of all women's employment falls within only four categories: clerical, secretarial, personal services and occupations such as cleaning.

This sex-typing of occupations affects boys' and girls' ideas about what kinds of job are possible or acceptable. Thus for example, if boys get the message that nursery nurses are female, they will be less likely to opt for a course in childcare.

This also helps to explain why vocational courses are much more gender-specific than academic courses, since vocational studies are by definition more closely linked to students' career plans.

Gender, vocational choice and class

There is a social class dimension to choice of vocational course. Working-class pupils in particular may make decisions about vocational courses that are based on a traditional sense of gender identity. For example, most of the working-class girls studied by Carol Fuller (2011) had ambitions to go into jobs such as child care or hair and beauty. This reflected their working-class habitus – their sense of what is a realistic expectation for 'people like us'.

These ambitions may arise out of work experience placements, which are often gendered and classed. For example, Fuller found that placements in feminine, working-class jobs such as nursery nursing and retail work were overwhelmingly the norm for the girls in her study. Fuller concludes that the school was implicitly steering girls towards certain types of job – and hence certain types of vocational course – through the work experience placements it offered them.

Activity   **Research**

Gender and subject choice

...go to www.sociology.uk.net

Pupils' sexual and gender identities

We have seen how socialisation into a gender identity strongly influences pupils' achievements and their subject preferences. Here we examine some of the different ways in which pupils' experiences in school help to construct and reinforce their gender and sexual identities.

These experiences may all contribute to reinforcing what Bob Connell (1995) calls 'hegemonic masculinity' – the dominance of heterosexual masculine identity and the subordination of female and gay identities.

1 Double standards

A double standard exists when we apply one set of moral standards to one group but a different set to another group. In the case of gender identity, Sue Lees (1993) identifies a double standard of sexual morality in which boys boast about their own sexual exploits, but call a girl a 'slag' if she doesn't have a steady boyfriend or if she dresses and speaks in a certain way. Sexual conquest is approved of and given status by male peers and ignored by male teachers, but 'promiscuity' among girls attracts negative labels.

Feminists see these double standards as an example of a patriarchal ideology that justifies male power and devalues women. Double standards can be seen as a form of social control that reinforces gender inequality by keeping females subordinate to males.

2 Verbal abuse

What Connell calls "a rich vocabulary of abuse" is one of the ways in which dominant gender and sexual identities are reinforced. For example, boys use name-calling to put girls down if they behave or dress in certain ways. Lees (1986) found that boys called girls 'slags' if they appeared to be sexually available – and 'drags' if they didn't.

Similarly, Paechter sees name-calling as helping to shape gender identity and maintain male power. The use of negative labels such as 'gay', 'queer' and 'lezzie' are ways in which pupils police each other's sexual identities.

For example, Andrew Parker (1996) found that boys were labelled gay simply for being friendly with girls or female teachers. Both Lees and Paechter note that these labels often bear no relation to pupils' actual sexual behaviour. Their function is simply to reinforce gender norms and identities.

3 The male gaze

There is also a visual aspect to the way pupils control each other's identities. Mac an Ghaill refers to this as the 'male gaze': the way male pupils and teachers look girls up and down, seeing them as sexual objects and making judgements about their appearance.

Mac an Ghaill sees the male gaze as a form of surveillance through which dominant heterosexual masculinity is reinforced and femininity devalued. It is one of the ways boys prove their masculinity to their friends and is often combined with constant telling and retelling of stories about sexual conquests. Boys who do not display their heterosexuality in this way run the risk of being labelled gay.

4 Male peer groups

Male peer groups also use verbal abuse to reinforce their definitions of masculinity. For example, as studies by Epstein and Willis show, boys in anti-school subcultures often accuse boys who want to do well at school of being gay or effeminate.

Similarly, Mairtin Mac an Ghaill's (1994) study of Parnell School examines how peer groups reproduce a range of different class-based masculine gender identities. For example, the working-class 'macho lads' were dismissive of other working-class boys who worked hard and aspired to middle-class careers, referring to them as the 'dickhead

achievers'. By contrast, middle-class 'real Englishmen' projected an image of 'effortless achievement' – of succeeding without trying (though in some cases actually working hard 'on the quiet').

Interestingly, Redman and Mac an Ghaill (1997) found that the dominant definition of masculine identity changes from that of the macho lads in the lower school to that of the real Englishmen in the sixth form.

This represents a shift away from a working-class definition based on toughness to a middle-class one based on intellectual ability. This reflects the more middle-class composition and atmosphere of the sixth form.

Investigating how schooling reinforces gender identities

The issue of how schooling reinforces gender identities has certain important **research characteristics** – particular features that may make it easy or difficult to investigate. For example:

- The gender of the researcher is likely to play a particularly important part. Male pupils and even male teachers may 'play up to' or patronise a female researcher, while female pupils may feel intimidated by a male researcher.

- Some cases of gender identity reinforcement, such as verbal abuse, are explicit, direct and easy to identify and investigate. Others are more subtle and indirect, leaving them open to different interpretations.

- Some head teachers and governors may feel that researching this issue could lead to increased gender stereotyping by drawing attention to it. As a result, they may refuse the researcher access.

- Peer group pressure is an important part of the process of reinforcing gender identities. This creates difficulties for the researcher, who will have to find ways to uncover individual variations in attitudes within the peer group.

- Those involved in the process of reinforcing gender identities may not be aware of what they are doing, so there may be little point in a researcher asking them about the issue.

1 What other research characteristics of how schooling reinforces gender identities can you think of? You could consider issues of access, gender stereotyping etc particular to investigating this topic.

2 Using the research characteristics listed above and any others you can think of, identify two strengths and two limitations of using **unstructured interviews** to investigate how schooling reinforces gender identities. You can read more about unstructured interviews on pages 127–34.

5 Female peer groups: policing identity

As we have seen, Archer shows how working-class girls gain symbolic capital (status and popularity) from their female peers by performing a hyper-heterosexual feminine identity. This involves constructing a glamorous or 'sexy' Nike appearance using particular brands and styles. Female peers police this identity and girls risk making themselves unpopular and being called a 'tramp' if they fail to conform.

Jessica Ringrose's (2013) small-scale study of 13–14 year old working-class girls' peer groups in a South Wales school found that being popular was crucial to the girls' identity. As the girls made a transition from a girls' friendship culture into a heterosexual dating culture, they faced a tension between:

- **An idealised feminine identity** of showing loyalty to the female peer group, being non-competitive and getting along with everybody in the friendship culture.
- **A sexualised identity** that involved competing for boys in the dating culture.

Thus as Currie et al (2007) argue, while relationships with boys can confer symbolic capital, this is a high risk game. This is because girls are forced to perform a balancing act between these two identities:

- Girls who are too competitive and/or think themselves better than their peers risk 'slut shaming' – being labelled as sluts and excluded from the friendship culture.
- On the other hand, girls who don't compete for boyfriends may face 'frigid shaming' by the other girls.

Shaming is thus a social control device by which schoolgirls police, regulate and discipline each other's identities.

A 'boffin' identity Girls who want to be successful educationally may feel the need to conform to the school's notion of the ideal feminine pupil identity. As Reay (2001) found, this involved the girls having to perform an asexual identity, presenting themselves as lacking any interest in boyfriends or popular fashion.

As a result, they risk being given the identity of 'boffin' and excluded by other girls (as well as boys). However, as Francis (2010) found, middle-class female boffins may respond in kind by defining other, working-class, girls as 'chavs'.

6 Teachers and discipline

Research shows that teachers also play a part in reinforcing dominant definitions of gender identity. Chris Haywood and Mairtin Mac an Ghaill (1996) found that male teachers told boys off for 'behaving like girls' and teased them when they gained lower marks in tests than girls. Teachers tended to ignore boys' verbal abuse of girls and even blamed girls for attracting it.

Sue Askew and Carol Ross (1988) show how male teachers' behaviour can subtly reinforce messages about gender. For example, male teachers often have a protective attitude towards female colleagues, coming into their classes to 'rescue' them by threatening pupils who are being disruptive. However, this reinforces the idea that women cannot cope alone.

Topic summary

Girls now do better than boys at all stages of education. Some explanations focus on **external factors** outside the education system – changes in the family, more employment opportunities for women, the impact of feminist ideas and changes in girls' ambitions.

Others focus on **changes within education**, such as the influence of feminist ideas via equal opportunities policies and challenges to stereotyping in the curriculum, more female teachers, coursework and exam league tables.

There are gender differences in **subject choice**. Choices are influenced by early socialisation into gender identities, the image subjects have, peer pressure and career opportunities. Gender differences are more noticeable on **vocational** than on academic courses.

Education also **reinforces gender and sexual identities** and hierarchies e.g. through verbal abuse, peer groups, the male gaze, school discipline and double standards of sexual morality.

EXAMINING GENDER DIFFERENCES IN EDUCATION

QuickCheck Questions

Check your answers at www.sociology.uk.net

1 Identify two changes in wider society that may have improved girls' achievement.
2 Identify three changes within the education system that may have improved girls' achievement.
3 Suggest reasons why shortage of male teachers may *not* explain boys' underachievement.

4 How might working-class girls' identities result in their underachievement?
5 Suggest two reasons for gender differences in choice of vocational courses.
6 Suggest one way in which peer groups may reinforce pupils' gender identities.

Questions to try

Whether or not you are taking the AS exams during your A level course, trying the AS questions below is a very good way of testing your knowledge and understanding and practising your skills in preparation for your A level exams.

Item A   Although achievement levels for both sexes have risen, boys' examination performance has fallen behind that of girls since the 1980s. At the same time, there have been a number of major changes in wider society. These include the decline of traditional jobs in manufacturing industries, a big increase in divorce and more women in paid employment.

Item B   Sociologists have investigated a number of aspects of gender and education. Although it is clear that in most subjects, girls achieve better examination results than boys, girls' experience of schooling in other respects may be less positive. For example, there is evidence that schooling reinforces traditional gender identities. Some sociologists argue that this disadvantages girls.

AS level questions

1 Define the term 'gender domains'.   (2 marks)
2 Using one example, briefly explain how the 'male gaze' may affect pupils' experience of schooling.   (2 marks)
3 Outline three reasons why girls generally achieve more highly than boys in education.   (6 marks)
4 Outline and explain two reasons why girls and boys often choose to study different subjects.   (10 marks)

A level questions

5 Applying material from Item A, analyse two reasons for boys' underachievement compared with girls.   (10 marks)
6 Applying material from Item B and your knowledge, evaluate the claim that although girls outperform boys in terms of achievement, the experience of schooling reinforces traditional gender identities.   (30 marks)

The Examiner's Advice

Q4 Possible reasons include early socialisation, gender domains, subject image, peer pressure, and gendered career opportunities. Describe in some detail each reason, explaining how it leads to a gendered choice of subjects. Do this by creating a chain of reasoning (see page 248). Use concepts such as gender role socialisation, sex-typing, role models, pupils' gender identities and subcultures, and studies such as Byrne, Murphy and Elwood, Browne and Ross, Colley and Paechter.

Q5 To answer this question, it's essential you take points from the Item and show through a chain of reasoning how each results in boys' underachievement. You could use decline of manufacturing jobs, increased divorce or more women in employment. Use concepts such as globalisation, pupils' aspirations, parental role models, lone-parent families and laddish subcultures, and studies such as Francis, Sharpe, Sewell, Carol Fuller and O'Connor. Include some brief evaluation, e.g. most manufacturing jobs required few qualifications, so their decline could not have affected boys' attitudes.

Q6 Spend about 45 minutes on this question. Begin by separating out the two issues in the question. Identify gender patterns in achievement and consider a range of explanations of them, including both internal and external factors. For the second part of the question, use material on subject choice, verbal abuse, peer groups, the male gaze and double standards, explaining how these may reinforce traditional identities. For example, peer groups police pupils' gender identities and punish non-conformity by bullying, ostracising etc. This means pupils are more likely to perform traditional gender identities. Use evidence from studies such as Sharpe, Archer, Gorard, Elwood, Francis, Weiner, Slee on achievement, and Archer, Mac an Ghaill, Paechter, Connell, Lees, Ringrose on identity, and develop points noted in Item A. Develop evaluation, e.g. in relation to achievement, not all girls do well (consider class differences here). In relation to other aspects of education, consider how far schools reproduce patriarchy through reinforcing gender identities.

There are winners and losers in education – but does everyone face the same hurdles?

GETTING STARTED

The picture illustrates the fact that there are winners and losers in education. In pairs or small groups, answer the following:

1 Previous Topics show that schools and teachers may treat pupils unfairly e.g. by negative labelling. Can you list some of the ways the education system treats pupils *fairly*?

2 Make a list of things you have learned in school that you feel will help you succeed in working life, e.g. particular knowledge, skills, attitudes or behaviours. Give reasons for your answers.

Learning objectives

After studying this Topic, you should:

- Know the functions of education that functionalists identify.
- Understand the neoliberal and New Right views of the role of the market in education.
- Understand different Marxist views of the role of education, particularly the reproduction and legitimation of class inequality.
- Be able to evaluate the functionalist, neoliberal and New Right, and Marxist views of education.

When studying the role of education in society, sociologists are interested in questions such as:

- How far does education provide all individuals with equal opportunities for achievement?
- How far does education recreate existing social class inequalities?
- In what ways does education serve the needs of the economy?
- What kinds of knowledge, skills, attitudes and values does education transmit?

As we shall see, sociologists hold conflicting views on these questions. Often, this is because they have different sociological perspectives or viewpoints that see society differently. In this Topic, we focus on the following perspectives or theories of the role of education in society:

- **Functionalism** – a consensus approach
- **Neoliberalism and the New Right** – a conservative, free market approach
- **Marxism** – a class conflict approach.

The functionalist perspective on education

Functionalism is based on the view that society is a system of interdependent parts held together by a shared culture or value consensus – an agreement among society's members about what values are important. Each part of society, such as the family, economy or education system, performs functions that help to maintain society as a whole. When studying education, functionalists seek to discover what functions it performs – that is, what does it do to help meet society's needs?

Durkheim: solidarity and skills

The French sociologist Emile Durkheim (1903), the founder of functionalist sociology, identified two main functions of education: creating social solidarity and teaching specialist skills.

Social solidarity

Durkheim argues that society needs a sense of solidarity; that is, its individual members must feel themselves to be part of a single 'body' or community. He argues that without social solidarity, social life and cooperation would be impossible because each individual would pursue their own selfish desires.

The education system helps to create social solidarity by transmitting society's culture – its shared beliefs and values – from one generation to the next. For example, Durkheim argues that the teaching of a country's history instils in children a sense of a shared heritage and a commitment to the wider social group.

School also acts as a 'society in miniature', preparing us for life in wider society. For example, both in school and at work we have to cooperate with people who are neither family nor friends – teachers and pupils at school, colleagues and customers at work. Similarly, both in school and at work we have to interact with others according to a set of impersonal rules that apply to everyone.

Specialist skills

Modern industrial economies have a complex division of labour, where the production of even a single item usually involves the cooperation of many different specialists. This cooperation promotes social solidarity but, for it to be successful, each person must have the necessary specialist knowledge and skills to perform their role. Durkheim argues that education teaches individuals the specialist knowledge and skills that they need to play their part in the social division of labour.

Parsons: meritocracy

The American functionalist Talcott Parsons (1961) draws on many of Durkheim's ideas. Parsons sees the school as the 'focal socialising agency' in modern society, acting as a bridge between the family and wider society. This bridge is needed because family and society operate on different principles, so children need to learn a new way of living if they are to cope with the wider world.

Within the family, the child is judged by particularistic standards; that is, rules that apply only to that particular child. Similarly, in the family, the child's status is ascribed; that is, fixed by birth. For example, an elder son and a younger daughter may be given different rights or duties because of differences of age and sex.

By contrast, both school and wider society judge us all by the same universalistic and impersonal standards. For example, in society, the same laws apply to everyone. Similarly, in school each pupil is judged against the same standards (for example, they all sit the same exam and the pass mark is the same for everyone).

Likewise, in both school and wider society, a person's status is largely achieved, not ascribed. For example, at work we gain promotion or get the sack on the strength of how good we are at our job, while at school we pass or fail through our own individual efforts.

Parsons sees school as preparing us to move from the family to wider society because school and society are both based on meritocratic principles. In a meritocracy, everyone is given an equal opportunity, and individuals achieve rewards through their own effort and ability.

Davis and Moore: role allocation

Functionalists argue that schools also perform the function of selecting and allocating pupils to their future work roles. By assessing individuals' aptitudes and abilities, schools help to match them to the job they are best suited to.

Kingsley Davis and Wilbert Moore (1945) see education as a device for selection and role allocation. They focus on the relationship between education and social inequality.

Investigating meritocracy in education

The issue of meritocracy in education has certain important **research characteristics** – particular features that may make it easy or difficult to investigate. For example:

- Schools wish to project an image of offering equal opportunities to all their students. Head teachers are unlikely to welcome research that might undermine this image.
- Teachers may feel unable to reveal anything about their school that contradicts its meritocratic image.
- The state education system produces a great deal of statistical data about examination results, pupils on free school meals, gender and ethnicity. This information is highly relevant to the study of meritocracy.
- However, much of this official data does not relate directly to investigating meritocracy. For example, it does not specifically reveal links between parents' social class and their children's educational and employment outcomes.
- Furthermore, similar data from the private education sector is less readily available.
- Some important groups within education, parents and pupils in particular, may not be aware of the degree of inequality in their educational experiences, so it may be pointless questioning them about it.

1 What other research characteristics of meritocracy in education can you think of? You could consider issues of access to results data, ethical concerns etc particular to investigating this topic.
2 Using the research characteristics listed above and any others you can think of, identify two strengths and two limitations of using **official statistics** to investigate meritocracy in education. You can read more about official statistics on pages 149–59.

They argue that inequality is necessary to ensure that the most important roles in society are filled by the most talented people. For example, it would be inefficient and dangerous to have less able people performing roles such as surgeon or airline pilot. Not everyone is equally talented, so society has to offer higher rewards for these jobs. This will encourage everyone to compete for them and society can then select the most talented individuals to fill these positions.

Education plays a key part in this process, since it acts as a proving ground for ability. Put simply, education is where individuals show what they can do. It 'sifts and sorts' us according to our ability. The most able gain the highest qualifications, which then gives them entry to the most important and highly rewarded positions.

Human capital Similarly, Peter Blau and Otis Duncan (1978) argue that a modern economy depends for its prosperity on using its 'human capital' – its workers' skills. They argue that a meritocratic education system does this best, since it enables each person to be allocated to the job best suited to their abilities. This will make most effective use of their talents and maximise their productivity.

Evaluation of the functionalist perspective

- The education system does not teach specialised skills adequately, as Durkheim claims. For example, the Wolf review of vocational education (2011) claims that high-quality apprenticeships are rare and up to a third of 16–19 year olds are on courses that do not lead to higher education or good jobs.
- As Topics 1–4 show, there is ample evidence that equal opportunity in education does not exist. For example, achievement is greatly influenced by class background rather than ability.
- Melvin Tumin (1953) criticises Davis and Moore for putting forward a circular argument: How do we know that a job is important? Answer: because it's highly rewarded. Why are some jobs more highly rewarded? Answer: because they are more important!
- Functionalists see education as a process that instils the shared values of society as a whole, but Marxists argue that education in capitalist society only transmits the ideology of a minority – the ruling class.
- The interactionist Dennis Wrong (1961) argues that functionalists have an 'over-socialised view' of people as mere puppets of society. Functionalists wrongly imply that pupils passively accept all they are taught and never reject the school's values.
- Neoliberals and the New Right argue that the state education system fails to prepare young people adequately for work. We deal with their view next.

Neoliberalism and the New Right perspective on education

Neoliberalism is an economic doctrine that has had a major influence on education policy. Neoliberals argue that the state should not provide services such as education, health and welfare. Neoliberal ideas have influenced all governments since 1979 – whether Conservative, Labour or Coalition.

Neoliberalism is based on the idea that the state must not dictate to individuals how to dispose of their own property, and should not try to regulate a free-market economy. So governments should encourage competition, privatise state-run businesses and deregulate markets.

Neoliberals argue that the value of education lies in how well it enables the country to compete in the global marketplace. They claim that this can only be achieved if schools become more like businesses, empowering parents and pupils as consumers and using competition between schools to drive up standards.

The New Right

The New Right is a conservative political view that incorporates neoliberal economic ideas. A central principle of New Right thinking is the belief that the state cannot meet people's needs and that people are best left to meet their own needs through the free market. For this reason, the New Right favour the marketisation of education (see Topic 6).

There are similarities between the New Right and functionalist views:

- Both believe that some people are naturally more talented than others.
- Both favour an education system run on meritocratic principles of open competition, and one that serves the needs of the economy by preparing young people for work.
- Both believe that education should socialise pupils into shared values, such as competition, and instil a sense of national identity.

However, a key difference with functionalism is that the New Right do not believe that the current education system is achieving these goals. The reason for its failure, in their view, is that it is run by the state.

The New Right argue that state education systems take a 'one size fits all' approach, imposing uniformity and disregarding local needs. The local consumers who use the schools – pupils, parents and employers – have no say. State education systems are therefore unresponsive and inefficient. Schools that waste money or get poor results are not answerable to their consumers. This means lower standards of achievement for pupils, a less qualified workforce and a less prosperous economy.

The New Right's solution to these problems is the marketisation of education – creating an 'education market'. They believe that competition between schools and empowering consumers will bring greater diversity, choice and efficiency to schools and increase schools' ability to meet the needs of pupils, parents and employers.

Chubb and Moe: consumer choice

A good example of the New Right perspective on education comes from the work of the Americans, John Chubb and Terry Moe (1990). They argue that state-run education in the United States has failed because:

- It has not created equal opportunity and has failed the needs of disadvantaged groups.
- It is inefficient because it fails to produce pupils with the skills needed by the economy.
- Private schools deliver higher quality education because, unlike state schools, they are answerable to paying consumers – the parents.

Chubb and Moe base their arguments on a comparison of the achievements of 60,000 pupils from low-income families in 1,015 state and private high schools, together with the findings of a parent survey and case studies of 'failing' schools apparently being 'turned around'. Their evidence shows that pupils from low-income families consistently do about 5% better in private than in state schools.

Based on these findings, Chubb and Moe call for the introduction of a market system in state education that would put control in the hands of the consumers (parents and local communities). They argue that this would allow consumers to shape schools to meet their own needs and would improve quality and efficiency.

To introduce a market into state education, Chubb and Moe propose a system in which each family would be given a voucher to spend on buying education from a school of their choice. This would force schools to become more responsive to parents' wishes, since the vouchers would be the school's main source of income. Like private businesses, schools would have to compete to attract 'customers' by improving their 'product'.

These principles are already at work in the private education sector. In Chubb and Moe's view, educational standards would be greatly improved by introducing the same market forces into the state sector.

> **Analysis and Evaluation**
> In what ways might a voucher system increase class inequalities in education?

Two roles for the state

However, while the New Right stress the importance of market forces in education, this does not mean they see no role at all for the state. In the New Right view, there remain two important roles for the state.

- Firstly, the state imposes a framework on schools within which they have to compete. For example, by publishing Ofsted inspection reports and league tables of schools' exam results, the state gives parents information with which to make a more informed choice between schools.
- Secondly, the state ensures that schools transmit a shared culture. By imposing a single National Curriculum, it seeks to guarantee that schools socialise pupils into a single cultural heritage.

The New Right believe that education should affirm the national identity. For example, the curriculum should emphasise Britain's positive role in world history and teach British literature, and there should be a Christian act of worship in school each day because Christianity is Britain's main religion. The aim is to integrate pupils into a single set of traditions and cultural values. For this reason, the New Right also oppose multicultural education that reflects the cultures of the different minority groups in Britain.

Evaluation of the New Right perspective

- Gewirtz (1995) and Ball (1994) both argue that competition between schools benefits the middle class, who can use their cultural and economic capital to gain access to more desirable schools.
- Critics argue that the real cause of low educational standards is not state control but social inequality and inadequate funding of state schools.
- There is a contradiction between the New Right's support for parental choice on the one hand and the state imposing a compulsory national curriculum on all its schools on the other.
- Marxists argue that education does not impose a shared national culture, as the New Right claim, but imposes the culture of a dominant minority ruling class and devalues the culture of the working class and ethnic minorities.

Activity **Discussion**

Does introducing the market into education benefit everyone?

...go to www.sociology.uk.net

The Marxist perspective on education

Where functionalists see society and education as based on value consensus, Marxists see it as based on class division and capitalist exploitation. Karl Marx (1818–83) described capitalism as a two-class system:

- **The capitalist class** or bourgeoisie are the minority class. They are the employers who own the means of production (land, factories, machinery, offices etc). They make their profits by exploiting the labour of the majority – the proletariat or working class.
- **The working class** are forced to sell their labour power to the capitalists since they own no means of production of their own and so have no other source of income. As a result, work under capitalism is poorly paid, alienating, unsatisfying, and something over which workers have no real control.

This creates the potential for class conflict. For example, if workers realise they are being exploited, they may demand higher wages, better working conditions or even the abolition of capitalism itself. Marx believed that ultimately the proletariat would unite to overthrow the capitalist system and create a classless, equal society.

However, despite this potential for revolution that capitalism contains, it is able to continue because the bourgeoisie also control the state. A key component of the state is the education system, and Marxists see education as functioning to prevent revolution and maintain capitalism.

Althusser: the ideological state apparatus

Marxists see the state as the means by which the capitalist ruling class maintain their dominant position. According to Louis Althusser (1971), the state consists of two elements or 'apparatuses', both of which serve to keep the bourgeoisie in power:

- **The repressive state apparatuses** (RSAs), which maintain the rule of the bourgeoisie by force or the threat of it. The RSAs include the police, courts and army. When necessary, they use physical coercion (force) to repress the working class.
- **The ideological state apparatuses** (ISAs), which maintain the rule of the bourgeoisie by controlling people's ideas, values and beliefs. The ISAs include religion, the media and the education system.

In Althusser's view, the education system is an important ISA. He argues that it performs two functions:

- Education **reproduces** class inequality by transmitting it from generation to generation, by failing each successive generation of working-class pupils in turn.
- Education **legitimates** (justifies) class inequality by producing ideologies (sets of ideas and beliefs) that disguise its true cause. The function of ideology is to persuade workers to accept that inequality is inevitable and that they deserve their subordinate position in society. If they accept these ideas, they are less likely to challenge or threaten capitalism.

Bowles and Gintis: schooling in capitalist America

The American Marxists Samuel Bowles and Herbert Gintis (1976) develop these ideas further. They argue that capitalism requires a workforce with the kind of attitudes, behaviour and personality-type suited to their role as alienated and exploited workers willing to accept hard work, low pay and orders from above. In the view of Bowles and Gintis, this is the role of the education system in capitalist society – to reproduce an obedient workforce that will accept inequality as inevitable.

From their own study of 237 New York high school students and the findings of other studies, Bowles and Gintis conclude that schools reward precisely the kind of personality traits that make for a submissive, compliant worker. For instance, they found that students who showed independence and creativity tended to gain low grades, while those who showed characteristics linked to obedience and discipline (such as punctuality) tended to gain high grades.

Bowles and Gintis conclude from this evidence that schooling helps to produce the obedient workers that capitalism needs. They do not believe that education fosters personal development. Rather, it stunts and distorts students' development.

The correspondence principle and the hidden curriculum

Bowles and Gintis argue that there are close parallels between schooling and work in capitalist society. Both schools and workplaces are hierarchies, with head teachers or bosses at the top making decisions and giving orders, and workers or pupils at the bottom obeying. Box 8 shows some other ways in which school mirrors the workplace. As Bowles and Gintis put it, schooling takes place in 'the long shadow of work'.

Bowles and Gintis refer to these parallels between school and workplace as examples of the 'correspondence principle'. The relationships and structures found in education mirror or correspond to those of work.

Bowles and Gintis argue that the correspondence principle operates through the hidden curriculum – that is, all the 'lessons' that are learnt in school without being directly taught. For example, simply through the everyday workings of the school, pupils become accustomed to accepting hierarchy and competition, working for extrinsic rewards and so on.

In this way, schooling prepares working-class pupils for their role as the exploited workers of the future, reproducing the workforce capitalism needs and perpetuating class inequality from generation to generation.

For example, Phil Cohen (1984) argues that youth training schemes serve capitalism by teaching young workers not genuine job skills, but rather the attitudes and values needed in a subordinate labour force. It lowers their aspirations so that they will accept low paid work.

Investigating the reproduction of class inequality

The issue of the reproduction of class inequality has certain important **research characteristics** – particular features that may make it easy or difficult to investigate. For example:

- Since schools do not track and record the careers of their ex-pupils, there is no ready-made data for researchers to use.
- Contacting former pupils may be difficult both because any addresses the school still holds for them may be out of date, and because researchers may not be given access to this information anyway.
- But fee-paying schools often have old boys/girls associations through which contact with former pupils could be made.
- Former pupils now in working-class jobs may feel they are being viewed as a failure or patronised by a middle-class researcher.
- Schools may be defensive about the occupational futures of their pupils for fear of being seen as having failed them.
- Former pupils may not know the reasons why they get working-class jobs or may see them in very simple terms such as 'I didn't work hard at school'.

1 What other research characteristics of the reproduction of class inequality can you think of? You could consider issues of gatekeepers, ethical concerns etc particular to investigating this topic.

2 Using the research characteristics listed above and any others you can think of, identify two strengths and two limitations of using **questionnaires** to investigate the reproduction of class inequality. You can read more about questionnaires on pages 116–123.

Application

Bowles and Gintis claim that schooling prepares pupils for their future work roles. How might it also prepare them for their future *gender* roles?.

The myth of meritocracy: the legitimation of class inequality

Because capitalist society is based on inequality, there is always a danger that the poor will feel that this inequality is undeserved and unfair, and that they will rebel against the system responsible for it. In Bowles and Gintis' view, the education system helps to prevent this from happening, by legitimating class inequalities. It does this by producing ideologies that serve to explain and justify why inequality is fair, natural and inevitable.

Bowles and Gintis describe the education system as 'a giant myth-making machine'. A key myth that education promotes is the 'myth of meritocracy'. Meritocracy means that everyone has an equal opportunity to achieve, that rewards are based on ability and effort, and that those who gain the highest rewards deserve them because they are the most able and hardworking.

Unlike functionalists such as Parsons, Bowles and Gintis argue that meritocracy does not in fact exist. Evidence shows that the main factor determining whether or not someone has a high income is their family and class background, not their ability or educational achievement.

By disguising this fact, the myth of meritocracy serves to justify the privileges of the higher classes, making it seem that they gained them through succeeding in open and fair competition at school. This helps persuade the working class to accept inequality as legitimate, and makes it less likely that they will seek to overthrow capitalism.

The education system also justifies poverty, through what Bowles and Gintis describe as the 'poor-are-dumb' theory of failure. It does so by blaming poverty on the individual, rather than blaming capitalism ('I'm poor because I wasn't clever enough/didn't work hard enough at school'). It therefore plays an important part in reconciling workers to their exploited position, making them less likely to rebel against the system.

Activity	Media

Fordism and the correspondence principle

...go to www.sociology.uk.net

Willis: learning to labour

All Marxists agree that capitalism cannot function without a workforce that is willing to accept exploitation. Likewise, all Marxists see education as reproducing and legitimating class inequality. That is, it ensures that working-class pupils are slotted into and learn to accept jobs that are poorly paid and alienating.

However, whereas Bowles and Gintis see education as a fairly straightforward process of indoctrination into the myth of meritocracy, Paul Willis' (1977) study shows that working-class pupils can resist such attempts to indoctrinate them.

As a Marxist, Willis is interested in the way schooling serves capitalism. However, he combines this with an interactionist approach that focuses on the meanings pupils give to their situation and how these enable them to resist indoctrination.

Box 8	The correspondence principle

School in capitalist society	reflects	work in capitalist society
Hierarchy of authority among teachers (e.g. head – deputy – classroom teacher) and between teachers and students	reflects	hierarchy of authority in the workplace (e.g. managers – supervisors – workers).
Alienation through students' lack of control over education (e.g. over what to study, timetabling)	reflects	alienation through workers' lack of control over production (e.g. managers decide what, how, when and where to produce).
Extrinsic satisfaction (rewards external to the work itself), e.g. from grades, rather than from interest in the subjects studied	reflects	extrinsic satisfaction, e.g. from pay, rather than from doing the job itself.
Fragmentation and compartmentalisation of knowledge into unconnected subjects	reflects	fragmentation of work through the division of labour into small, meaningless tasks.
Competition and divisions among students, e.g. to come top of class; to be in a higher stream	reflects	competition and divisions among the workforce, e.g. through differences in status and pay.
Levels of education (streams, year groups) • lower levels: few choices; close supervision • higher levels: trusted to get on with work; self-directed learning	reflects	levels of the occupational structure • lower levels: workers closely supervised; given orders. • higher levels: workers internalise company's goals; self-supervision.

The lads' counter-culture

Using qualitative research methods including participant observation and unstructured interviews, Willis studied the counter-school culture of 'the lads' – a group of 12 working-class boys – as they make the transition from school to work.

The lads form a distinct counter-culture opposed to the school. They are scornful of the conformist boys who they call the 'ear'oles' (so called because, unlike the lads, they listen to what the teachers tell them). The lads have their own brand of intimidatory humour, 'taking the piss' out of the ear'oles and girls.

The lads find school boring and meaningless and they flout its rules and values, for example by smoking and drinking, disrupting classes and playing truant. For the lads, such acts of defiance are ways of resisting the school. They reject as a 'con' the school's meritocratic ideology that working-class pupils can achieve middle-class jobs through hard work.

Willis notes the similarity between the lads' anti-school counter-culture and the shopfloor culture of male manual workers. Both cultures see manual work as superior and intellectual work as inferior and effeminate. The lads identify strongly with male manual work and this explains why they see themselves as superior both to girls and to the 'effeminate' ear'oles who aspire to non-manual jobs.

However, it also explains why the lads' counter-culture of resistance to school helps them to slot into the very jobs – inferior in terms of skill, pay and conditions – that capitalism needs someone to perform. For example:

- Having been accustomed to boredom and to finding ways of amusing themselves in school, they don't expect satisfaction from work and are good at finding diversions to cope with the tedium of unskilled labour.
- Their acts of rebellion guarantee that they will end up in unskilled jobs, by ensuring their failure to gain worthwhile qualifications.

For Willis, the irony is that by helping them resist the school's ideology, the lads' counter-culture ensures that they are destined for the unskilled work that capitalism needs someone to perform.

Evaluation of Marxist approaches

Marxist approaches are useful in exposing the 'myth of meritocracy'. They show the role that education plays as an ideological state apparatus, serving the interests of capitalism by reproducing and legitimating class inequality.

However, as Box 9 shows, postmodernists criticise Bowles and Gintis' correspondence principle on the grounds that today's post-Fordist economy requires schools to produce a

▲ Fordism: assembly line mass production at the Ford plant in Detroit, Michigan, 1940. How typical is this of industry today?

very different kind of labour force from the one described by Marxists. Postmodernists argue that education now reproduces diversity, not inequality.

Marxists disagree with one another about how reproduction and legitimation take place. Bowles and Gintis take a deterministic view. That is, they assume that pupils have no free will and passively accept indoctrination. This approach fails to explain why many pupils reject the school's values.

By contrast, Willis rejects the view that school simply 'brainwashes' pupils into passively accepting their fate. By combining Marxist and interactionist approaches, he shows how pupils may resist the school and yet how this still leads them into working-class jobs.

However, critics argue that Willis' account of the 'lads' romanticises them, portraying them as working-class heroes despite their anti-social behaviour and sexist attitudes. His small-scale study of only 12 boys in one school is also unlikely to be representative of other pupils' experience and it would be risky to generalise his findings.

Critical modernists such as Raymond Morrow and Carlos Torres (1998) criticise Marxists for taking a 'class first' approach that sees class as the key inequality and ignores all other kinds.

Instead, like postmodernists, Morrow and Torres argue that society is now more diverse. They see non-class inequalities, such as ethnicity, gender and sexuality, as equally important. They argue that sociologists must explain how education reproduces and legitimates all forms of inequality, not just class, and how the different forms of inequality are inter-related.

Feminists make a similar point. For example, as Madeleine MacDonald (1980) argues, Bowles and Gintis ignore the fact that schools reproduce not only capitalism, but patriarchy too. Similarly, as Angela McRobbie (1978) points out, females are largely absent from Willis' study.

However, Willis' work has stimulated a great deal of research into how education reproduces and legitimates other inequalities. For example, Paul Connolly (1998) explores how education reproduces both ethnic and gender inequalities. Other studies of the inter-relationships between different forms of inequality include Sewell, Evans and Mac an Ghaill (see pages 38, 56 and 63).

Box 9	Post-Fordism and postmodernism

The correspondence principle states that school mirrors the workplace. Capitalism requires low-skilled workers willing to put up with alienating work on mass production assembly lines. This system is often called Fordism because the Ford Motor Company was the first to introduce it. Bowles and Gintis see the education system as preparing pupils to accept this work.

However, postmodernists argue that the Marxist view is outdated. They claim that society has entered a postmodern phase where class divisions are no longer important. Society is now much more diverse and fragmented, and the economy is now based on 'flexible specialisation', where production is customised for small specialist markets. This post-Fordist system requires a skilled, adaptable workforce able to use advanced technology.

Post-Fordism therefore calls for a different kind of education system that encourages self-motivation and creativity. It must also provide lifelong retraining, because rapid technological change makes existing skills obsolete.

As a result, postmodernists argue, education has become more diverse and responsive to the needs of different individuals. In their view, the correspondence principle no longer operates. Unlike Marxists, postmodernists argue that education reproduces diversity, not inequality.

1 Explain the difference between Fordist and post-Fordist production systems.

2 Why do postmodernists argue that post-Fordism needs a different type of education system from that described by the correspondence principle?

Activity Discussion

Which side are you on?

...go to www.sociology.uk.net

Topic summary

Functionalists take a **consensus** view. They see education as performing three important functions – **socialisation into the shared culture**, equipping individuals with **specialist work skills** for the division of labour, and **selection for work roles**. Education is organised on **meritocratic** principles.

The **New Right and neoliberals** take a **conservative** view. They believe education can only perform its role effectively if it is organised on **market** principles rather than run by the state.

Marxists take a **class conflict** approach. They see education as serving the **needs of capitalism**. Education is an **ideological state apparatus** that **reproduces** and **legitimates class inequality** through the **correspondence principle** and **myth of meritocracy**. Although pupils may **resist** indoctrination, their counter-school culture may actually prepare them for unskilled labour.

Postmodernists argue that the economy has become **post-Fordist** and education is becoming more **diverse** and **flexible**.

EXAMINING THE ROLE OF EDUCATION IN SOCIETY

QuickCheck Questions

Check your answers at www.sociology.uk.net

1 Explain the term 'ascribed status'.
2 Explain what is meant by 'particularistic standards'.
3 Identify two ways in which New Right ideas are similar to those of functionalists.
4 Explain the difference between the reproduction of class inequality and the legitimation of class inequality.

5 Explain what Bowles and Gintis mean by the correspondence principle.
6 Explain what is meant by 'post-Fordism'.
7 How does the critical modernist view of education differ from the Marxist view?
8 Suggest two criticisms of Willis' study.

Questions to try

Whether or not you're taking the AS exams during your A level course, trying the AS questions below is a very good way of testing your knowledge and understanding and practising your skills in preparation for your A level exams.

Item A Some sociologists claim that education reproduces and legitimates social class inequality. They argue that it operates in the interests of the ruling class, preparing working-class pupils for working-class jobs and justifying this outcome as fair.

Other sociologists disagree. They claim that education offers all pupils an equal opportunity to succeed.

Item B Functionalist and Marxist sociologists are interested in similar aspects of the role of the education system. For example, both examine the relationship between education and work. Both perspectives also look at how norms and values are transmitted through education. However, while Marxists and functionalists focus on similar issues, they reach very different conclusions about the role of education.

AS level questions

1 Define the term 'myth of meritocracy'. (2 marks)
2 Outline three ways in which the correspondence principle operates within school. (6 marks)
3 Outline and explain two roles that education fulfils according to functionalists. (10 marks)
4 Applying material from Item A and your knowledge, evaluate the view that 'education reproduces and legitimates social class inequality'. (20 marks)

A level question

5 Applying material from Item B and your knowledge, evaluate the view that 'while Marxist and functionalist approaches focus on similar issues, they reach very different conclusions about the role of education'. (30 marks)

The Examiner's Advice

Q4 Spend about 30 minutes on this question. Identify the view as a Marxist one and define reproduction and legitimation. Explain how each contributes to social class inequality. Do this by creating a chain of reasoning (see page 248). For example, education produces sets of ideas that disguise the real cause of class inequality. Working-class pupils are taught to accept that their subordinate position is the result of a meritocratic system in which they had an equal chance to succeed. This means they are less likely to challenge the capitalist system afterwards in work. Use evidence from studies such as Althusser, Bowles and Gintis, and Willis, and develop the points noted in Item A.

Evaluate the view, making criticisms of each argument as you go along rather than putting them in a separate section at the end. For example, what Marxists see as ruling-class ideology, functionalists see as shared values.

Q5 Spend about 45 minutes on this question. The most effective way to tackle it is to use the 'similar issues' and 'different conclusions' wording in the question to organise your answer. First identify the similar issues Marxists and functionalists focus on. These include the teaching of values, preparation for work, role allocation and unequal educational outcomes. Present a 'Marxist versus functionalist' account of each issue in turn. This will build a strongly evaluative answer. Do this by creating a chain of reasoning. For example, both perspectives see education as important in establishing a person's status. For functionalists, we achieve status through our individual efforts within a meritocracy, whereas for Marxists, our class background determines our status. Use evidence from studies such as Durkheim, Parsons, Davis and Moore, Althusser, Bowles and Gintis and Willis, and develop the points in Item B. Remember also to evaluate the view as a whole at the end, e.g. by considering their similarities (e.g. the education system as a structure) and their differences (e.g. consensus versus conflict views).

Working-class pupils, Walsgrove Colliery School, Coventry, 1952

GETTING STARTED

The following points highlight some key phases of education policy in the UK.

In pairs, discuss these and make notes on whether you think each one would have a positive or negative effect on the education of pupils. Would the effect be the same for all pupils regardless of social class, gender or ethnicity? Give reasons for your answers.

1 Having to pass an exam at age 11 to get into a particular secondary school.

2 All students in one area having to go to the same local school.

3 Schools competing to attract the best students.

4 Parents being able to choose which school their child attends.

Feed back your responses to the rest of the class. Does everyone agree?

Learning objectives

After studying this Topic, you should:

● Know the main features of important educational policies, including the tripartite system, comprehensivisation, marketisation, privatisation and globalisation, and policies relating to gender and ethnicity.

● Be able to apply sociological perspectives to educational policies.

● Be able to evaluate the impact of educational policies on inequality of achievement.

EDUCATIONAL POLICY AND INEQUALITY

'Educational policy' refers to the plans and strategies for education introduced by government, for example through Acts of Parliament, together with instructions and recommendations to schools and local authorities. Examples of educational policy include the 2010 Academies Act, which made it possible for all state schools to become academies.

Most educational policy is a response to the following issues:

Equal opportunities How far do government policies help to achieve equal opportunities for all pupils? How far do they actually make the inequalities greater?

Selection and choice What types of school should we have? Should schools be able to select their pupils? Should parents be able to choose which school their children attend?

Control of education Who should control schools and what they teach? How much influence should central government, local councils, schools themselves, businesses, teachers, parents and pupils have?

Marketisation and privatisation Should state schools operate like businesses within an 'education market'? Should they be given to private companies to run?

Many educational policies have contributed to maintaining and justifying inequality between classes, genders and ethnic groups. However, certain policies have had some success in reducing inequality. This Topic examines the relationship between inequality and educational policy.

Educational policy in Britain before 1988

Before the industrial revolution in the late 18th and early 19th centuries, there were no state schools. Education was available only to a minority of the population. It was provided by fee-paying schools for the well off, or by the churches and charities for a few of the poor. Before 1833, the state spent no public money on education.

Industrialisation increased the need for an educated workforce, and from the late 19th century the state began to become more involved in education. Reflecting the growing importance of education, the state made schooling compulsory from the ages of 5 to 13 in 1880.

In this period, the type of education children received depended on their class background. Schooling did little to change pupils' ascribed status (the position they were born into). Middle-class pupils were given an academic curriculum to prepare them for careers in the professions or office work.

By contrast, working-class pupils were given a schooling to equip them with the basic numeracy and literacy skills needed for routine factory work and to instil in them an obedient attitude to their superiors.

Selection: the tripartite system

From 1944, education began to be influenced by the idea of meritocracy – that individuals should achieve their status in life through their own efforts and abilities, rather than it being ascribed at birth by their class background.

The 1944 Education Act brought in the tripartite system, so called because children were to be selected and allocated to one of three different types of secondary school, supposedly according to their aptitudes and abilities. These were to be identified by the eleven plus (11+) exam.

- **Grammar schools** offered an academic curriculum and access to non-manual jobs and higher education. They were for pupils with academic ability who passed the 11+. These pupils were mainly middle-class.
- **Secondary modern schools** offered a non-academic, 'practical' curriculum and access to manual work for pupils who failed the 11+. These pupils were mainly working-class.

(The third type, technical schools, existed in a few areas only, so in practice it was more a bipartite than a tripartite system.)

Thus, rather than promoting meritocracy, the tripartite system and 11+ *reproduced* class inequality by channelling the two social classes into two different types of school that offered unequal opportunities. The system also reproduced gender inequality by requiring girls to gain higher marks than boys in the 11+ to obtain a grammar school place.

The tripartite system also *legitimated* (justified) inequality through the ideology that ability is inborn. It was thus argued that ability could be measured early on in life, through the 11+. However, in reality children's environment greatly affects their chances of success.

The comprehensive school system

The comprehensive system was introduced in many areas from 1965 onwards. It aimed to overcome the class divide of the tripartite system and make education more meritocratic. The 11+ was to be abolished along with grammars and secondary moderns, to be replaced by comprehensive schools that all pupils within the area would attend.

However, it was left to the local education authority to decide whether to 'go comprehensive' and not all did so. As a result, the grammar-secondary modern divide still exists in many areas.

Two theories of the role of comprehensives

As Topic 5 showed, Marxists and functionalists see the role of education very differently. Functionalists see it as fulfilling essential functions such as social integration and meritocratic selection for future work roles. By contrast, Marxists see education as serving the interests of capitalism by reproducing and legitimating class inequality. We can apply these theories to the role of comprehensive schooling.

Functionalists argue that comprehensives promote social integration by bringing children of different social classes together in one school. However, an early study by Julienne Ford (1969) found little social mixing between working-class and middle-class pupils, largely because of streaming.

Functionalists also see the comprehensive system as more meritocratic because it gives pupils a longer period in which to develop and show their abilities, unlike the tripartite system, which sought to select the most able pupils at the age of eleven.

However, Marxists argue that comprehensives are not meritocratic. Rather, they reproduce class inequality from one generation to the next through the continuation of the practice of streaming and labelling. These continue to deny working-class children equal opportunity.

Yet by not selecting children at eleven, comprehensives may appear to offer equal chances to all. This 'myth of meritocracy' legitimates (justifies) class inequality by making unequal achievement seem fair and just, because failure looks like it is the fault of the individual rather than the system.

Marketisation

Marketisation refers to the process of introducing market forces of consumer choice and competition between suppliers into areas run by the state, such as education. Marketisation has created an 'education market' by

- reducing direct state control over education
- increasing both competition between schools and parental choice of school.

Marketisation has become a central theme of government education policy since the 1988 Education Reform Act (ERA), introduced by the Conservative government of Margaret Thatcher.

From 1997, the New Labour governments of Tony Blair and Gordon Brown followed similar policies, emphasising standards, diversity and choice. From 2010, the Conservative-Liberal Democrat coalition government took marketisation even further, for example by creating academies and free schools.

As we saw in Topic 5, neoliberals and the New Right favour marketisation. They argue that marketisation means that schools have to attract customers (parents) by competing with each other in the market. Schools that provide customers with what they want – such as success in exams – will thrive, and those that don't will 'go out of business'.

parentocracy

Policies to promote marketisation include:

- Publication of league tables and Ofsted inspection reports that rank each school according to its exam performance and give parents the information they need to choose the right school.

- Business sponsorship of schools.
- Open enrolment, allowing successful schools to recruit more pupils.
- Specialist schools, specialising in IT, languages etc, to widen parental choice.
- Formula funding, where schools receive the same amount of funding for each pupil.
- Schools being allowed to opt out of local authority control, e.g. to become academies.
- Schools having to compete to attract pupils.
- Introduction of tuition fees for higher education.
- Allowing parents and others to set up free schools.

Miriam David (1993) describes marketised education as a 'parentocracy' (literally, 'rule by parents'). Supporters of marketisation argue that in an education market, power shifts away from the producers (teachers and schools) to the consumers (parents). They claim that this encourages diversity among schools, gives parents more choice and raises standards.

The reproduction of inequality

However, despite the claimed benefits of marketisation, its critics argue that it has increased inequalities. For example, Stephen Ball (1994) and Geoff Whitty (1998) note how marketisation policies such as exam league tables and the funding formula reproduce class inequalities by creating inequalities between schools.

league tables and cream-skimming

The policy of publishing each school's exam results in a league table ensures that schools that achieve good results

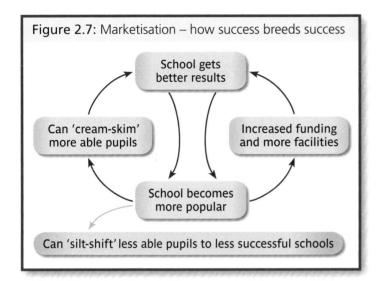

Figure 2.7: Marketisation – how success breeds success

- School gets better results
- Increased funding and more facilities
- School becomes more popular
- Can 'silt-shift' less able pupils to less successful schools
- Can 'cream-skim' more able pupils

are more in demand, because parents are attracted to those with good league table rankings. As Will Bartlett (1993) notes, this encourages:

- **cream-skimming** 'Good' schools can be more selective, choose their own customers and recruit high achieving, mainly middle-class pupils. As a result, these pupils gain an advantage. (See Figure 2.7.)
- **silt-shifting** 'Good' schools can avoid taking less able pupils who are likely to get poor results and damage the school's league table position.

For schools with poor league table positions, the opposite applies: they cannot afford to be selective and have to take less able, mainly working-class pupils, so their results are poorer and they remain unattractive to middle-class parents. The overall effect of league tables is thus to produce unequal schools that reproduce social class inequalities.

Activity **Webquest**

Marketisation and selection

...go to www.sociology.uk.net

the funding formula

Schools are allocated funds by a formula based on how many pupils they attract. As a result, popular schools get more funds and so can afford better-qualified teachers and better facilities. Again, their popularity allows them to be more selective and attracts more able or ambitious, generally middle-class applicants.

On the other hand, unpopular schools lose income and find it difficult to match the teacher skills and facilities of their more successful rivals. Thus, popular schools with good results and middle-class pupils thrive; unpopular schools fail to attract pupils and their funding is further reduced.

A study of international patterns of educational inequality by the Institute for Public Policy Research (2012) found that competition-oriented education systems such as Britain's produce more segregation between children of different social backgrounds.

Gewirtz: parental choice

Not only do marketisation policies benefit the middle class by creating inequalities between schools. By increasing parental choice, marketisation also advantages middle-class parents, whose economic and cultural capital (see page 23) puts them in a better position to choose 'good' schools for their children.

This is shown in Sharon Gewirtz's (1995) study of 14 London secondary schools. Gewirtz found that differences in parents' economic and cultural capital lead to class differences in how far they can exercise choice of secondary school. She identifies three main types of parents, whom she calls privileged-skilled choosers, disconnected-local choosers and semi-skilled choosers.

Privileged-skilled choosers These were mainly professional middle-class parents who used their economic and cultural capital to gain educational capital for their children. Being prosperous, confident and well educated, they were able to take full advantage of the choices open to them.

These parents possessed cultural capital. They knew how school admissions systems work, for example the importance of putting a particular school as first choice. They had the time to visit schools and the skills to research the options available.

Their economic capital also meant they could afford to move their children around the education system to get the best deal out of it, for example by paying extra travel costs so that their children could attend 'better' schools out of their area.

Disconnected-local choosers These were working-class parents whose choices were restricted by their lack of economic and cultural capital.

They found it difficult to understand school admissions procedures. They were less confident in their dealings with schools, less aware of the choices open to them, and less able to manipulate the system to their own advantage. Many of them attached more importance to safety and the quality of school facilities than to league tables or long-term ambitions.

Distance and cost of travel were major restrictions on their choice of school. Their funds were limited and a place at the nearest school was often their only realistic option for their children.

> **Analysis and Evaluation**
> Suggest reasons why working-class parents might be less able to manipulate the education system to their advantage.

Semi-skilled choosers These parents were also mainly working-class, but unlike the disconnected-local choosers, they were ambitious for their children. However, they too lacked cultural capital and found it difficult to make sense of the education market, often having to rely on other people's opinions about schools. They were often frustrated at their inability to get their children into the schools they wanted.

Thus, although in theory the education market gives everyone greater choice, Gewirtz concludes that in practice middle-class parents possess cultural and economic capital and have more choice than working-class parents.

The myth of parentocracy

Not only does marketisation reproduce inequality; it also *legitimates* it by concealing its true causes and by justifying its existence.

Ball believes that marketisation gives the appearance of a 'parentocracy'. That is, the education system seems as if it is based on parents having a free choice of school. However, Ball argues that parentocracy is a myth, not a reality. It makes it appear that all parents have the same freedom to choose which school to send their children to.

In reality, however, as Gewirtz shows, middle-class parents are better able to take advantage of the choices available. For example, as Leech and Campos show in Topic 1, they can afford to move into the catchment areas of more desirable schools.

By disguising the fact that schooling continues to reproduce class inequality in this way, the myth of parentocracy makes inequality in education appear fair and inevitable.

Application

1 Explain the difference between the 'myth of parentocracy' and Bowles and Gintis' 'myth of meritocracy'.

2 What similarity is there between these two 'myths'?

New Labour and inequality

While marketisation policies have tended to increase inequality, the New Labour governments of 1997 to 2010 also introduced a number of policies aimed at reducing it. These included:

- Designating some deprived areas as Education Action Zones and providing them with additional resources.
- The Aim Higher programme to raise the aspirations of groups who are under-represented in higher education.
- Education Maintenance Allowances (EMAs): payments to students from low-income backgrounds to encourage them to stay on after 16 to gain better qualifications.

- Introduction of the National Literacy Strategy, literacy and numeracy hours, and reducing primary school class sizes. It is claimed these policies are of greater benefit to disadvantaged groups and so help to reduce inequality.
- City academies were created to give a fresh start to struggling inner-city schools with mainly working-class pupils.
- Increased funding for state education.

However, critics such as Melissa Benn (2012) see a contradiction between Labour's policies to tackle inequality and its commitment to marketisation – something she calls the 'New Labour paradox'.

For example, despite introducing EMAs to encourage poorer students to stay in education, Labour also introduced tuition fees for higher education that may deter them from going to university.

Investigating how middle-class parents 'play the system'

The issue of how middle-class parents 'play the system' has certain important **research characteristics** – particular features that may make it easy or difficult to investigate. For example:

- Some of the ways in which middle-class parents 'play the system' verge on illegality – for example giving a false address so as to be in the preferred school's catchment area. Parents are unlikely to trust a researcher sufficiently to disclose such wrongdoing.
- Pupils may have little awareness of how their parents succeeded or failed in getting them into a particular school, so there may be little point in asking them.
- Some of the ways in which middle-class parents 'play the system' may be hidden from public view, for example having friends in the teaching profession who can give them advice on admissions. It may be difficult for researchers to uncover these hidden processes.
- This is an ill-defined idea – for example, is middle-class parents buying a house near a 'good' school 'playing the system' or simply a sensible family decision?
- Most schools wish to represent themselves as having fair admissions policies and as welcoming all applicants, so they may not welcome research that suggests otherwise.

1 What other research characteristics of how middle-class parents 'play the system' can you think of? You could consider issues of cultural capital, confidentiality etc particular to investigating this topic.

2 Using the research characteristics listed above and any others you can think of, identify two strengths and two limitations of using **unstructured interviews** to investigate how middle-class parents 'play the system'. You can read more about unstructured interviews on pages 127–34.

Furthermore, New Labour governments neither abolished fee-paying private schools nor removed their charitable status (estimated to be worth over £165 million per year).

Conservative government policies from 2010

The Conservative-led Coalition government (2010-2015) and the Conservative government from 2015 accelerated the move away from an education system based largely on comprehensive schools run by local authorities. Its policies have been strongly influenced by neoliberal and New Right ideas about reducing the role of the state in the provision of education through marketisation and privatisation. (See Box 10.)

David Cameron (Prime Minister, 2010-15) stated that the aim of the Coalition's education policy was to encourage 'excellence, competition and innovation', by freeing schools from the 'dead hand of the state', through policies such as academies and free schools. Furthermore, cuts were made to the education budget, as part of the government's general policy of reducing state spending.

Academies

From 2010, all schools were encouraged to leave local authority control and become academies. Funding was taken from local authority budgets and given directly to academies by central government, and academies were given control over their curriculum.

By 2017, over 68% of all secondary schools had converted to academy status. Some academies are run by private educational businesses and funded directly by the state.

However, whereas Labour's original city academies targeted disadvantaged schools and areas, the Coalition government, by allowing any school to become an academy, removed the focus on reducing inequality.

Free schools

Although funded directly by the state, free schools are set up and run by parents, teachers, faith organisations or businesses rather than the local authority.

Supporters of free schools claim that they improve educational standards by taking control away from the state and giving power to parents. Free schools, it is claimed, give parents and teachers the opportunity to create a new school if they are unhappy with the state schools in their local area.

However, Rebecca Allen (2010) argues that research from Sweden, where 20% of schools are free schools, shows that they only benefit children from highly educated families. Other critics claim that free schools are socially divisive and that they lower standards – Sweden's international educational ranking has fallen since their introduction. Charter schools in the USA (which are similar to free schools) have also been criticised for appearing to raise standards but only doing so by strict pupil selection and exclusion policies.

In England, evidence shows that free schools take fewer disadvantaged pupils than nearby schools. For example, in 2011 only 6.4% of pupils at Bristol Free School were eligible for free school meals, compared with 22.5% of pupils across the city as a whole (DoE 2012).

Analysis and Evaluation

Why might free schools be more likely to attract pupils from better-off backgrounds?

▲ Selection by mortgage? Not all parents can afford to move into the catchment area of a popular school.

Fragmented centralisation

Ball (2011) argues that promoting academies and free schools has led to both increased fragmentation and increased centralisation of control over educational provision in England.

- **Fragmentation** The comprehensive system is being replaced by a patchwork of diverse provision, much of it involving private providers, that leads to greater inequality in opportunities.
- **Centralisation of control** Central government alone has the power to allow or require schools to become academies or allow free schools to be set up. These schools are funded directly by central government. Their rapid growth has greatly reduced the role of elected local authorities in education.

Policies to reduce inequality

While the Conservative-led coalition's marketisation policies are said to have increased inequality, they also introduced policies aimed at reducing it. These included:

- **Free school meals** for all children in reception, year one and year two.
- **The Pupil Premium** – money that schools receive for each pupil from a disadvantaged background.

However, Ofsted (2012) found that in many cases the Pupil Premium is not spent on those it is supposed to help. Only one in ten head teachers said that it had significantly changed how they supported pupils from disadvantaged backgrounds.

Furthermore, as part of the Conservative government's 'austerity' programme, spending on many areas of education has been cut: spending on school buildings was cut by 60%, many Sure Start centres were closed, the Education Maintenance Allowance (EMA) was abolished and university tuition fees tripled to £9,000 a year.

Critics argue that cutting Sure Start and the EMA has reduced opportunities for working-class pupils. Similarly, increased university fees may discourage them from entering higher education (see Topic 1).

The privatisation of education

Privatisation involves the transfer of public assets such as schools to private companies. In recent years, there has been a trend towards the privatisation of important aspects of education, both in the UK and globally. In the process, education becomes a source of profit for capitalists in what Ball calls the 'education services industry' or ESI.

Private companies in the ESI are involved in an ever increasing range of activities in education, including building schools; providing supply teachers, work-based learning, careers advice and Ofsted inspection services; and even running entire local education authorities.

Large-scale school building projects often involve public-private partnerships (PPPs), in which private sector companies provide capital to design, build, finance and operate educational services. Typically, such contracts last for 25 years or more, during which time the local council pays a monthly lease and a management fee out of public funds.

Many of these activities are very profitable. According to Ball (2007), companies involved in such work expect to make up to ten times as much profit as they do on other contracts. However, local authorities are often obliged to enter into these agreements as the only way of building new schools because of a lack of funding by central government.

Activity Media

Sponsored academies — a public-private partnership

...go to www.sociology.uk.net

Blurring the public/private boundary

Many senior officials in the public sector, such as directors of local authorities and head teachers, now leave to set up or work for private sector education businesses. These companies then bid for contracts to provide services to schools and local authorities. For example, two companies set up in this way hold four of the five national contracts for school inspection services.

As Allyson Pollack (2004) notes, this flow of personnel allows companies to buy 'insider knowledge' to help win contracts, as well as side-stepping local authority democracy.

Privatisation and the globalisation of education policy

Many private companies in the education services industry are foreign-owned. The exam board Edexcel is owned by the US educational publishing and testing giant Pearson, and according to Ball some Pearson GCSE exam answers are now marked in Sydney and Iowa.

Similarly, according to Buckingham and Scanlon (2005), the UK's four leading educational software companies are all owned by global multinationals (Disney, the US toy companies Mattel and Hambro, and French media corporation Vivendi). Many contracts for educational services in the UK are sold on by the original company to others such as banks and investment funds. In a globalised world, these are often bought by overseas companies.

Conversely, some UK edu-businesses work overseas. For example, Prospects has worked in China, Macedonia and Finland. Often, private companies are exporting UK education policy to other countries (for example, Ofsted-type inspections) and then providing the services to deliver the policies. As a result, nation-states are becoming less important in policymaking, which is shifting to a global level and which is also often privatised.

The cola-isation of schools

The private sector is also penetrating education indirectly, for example through vending machines on school premises and the development of brand loyalty through displays of logos and sponsorships. This process has been called the 'cola-isation' of schools.

According to Molnar (2005), schools are targeted by private companies because 'schools by their nature carry enormous goodwill and can thus confer legitimacy on anything associated with them'. In other words, they are a kind of product endorsement.

However, the benefits to schools and pupils of this private sector involvement are often very limited. For example, according to Ball, a Cadbury's sports equipment promotion was scrapped after it was revealed that pupils would have to eat 5,440 chocolate bars just to qualify for a set of volleyball posts. According to Sharon Beder (2009), UK families spent £110,000 in Tesco supermarkets in return for a single computer for schools.

Education as a commodity

Ball concludes that a fundamental change is taking place in which privatisation is becoming the key factor shaping educational policy. Policy is increasingly focused on moving educational services out of the public sector controlled by the nation-state, to be provided by private companies instead. In the process, education is being turned into a 'legitimate object of private profit-making', a commodity to be bought and sold in an education market.

As Box 10 shows, privatisation means that the state is losing its role as the provider of educational services. For Ball, the overall effect is that:

'More and more areas of education are now subject to business practices and financial logics, and bought and sold as assets and made part of investment portfolios. The possibilities of privatisation continually expand, and the ratcheting up of policy over time opens up more education services for profit.'

Similarly, Marxists such as Stuart Hall (2011) see Conservative government policies as part of the 'long march of the neoliberal revolution'. Hall sees academies as an example of handing over public services to private capitalists, such as educational businesses. In the Marxist view, the neoliberal claim that privatisation and competition drive up standards is a myth used to legitimate the turning of education into a source of private profit.

| **Box 10** | **Neoliberalism and privatisation** |

Neoliberal and New Right approaches largely share the functionalists' view that education must be meritocratic and must promote social integration. However, unlike functionalists, they are critical of the role of the state in performing these functions. They argue that the state's involvement leads to bureaucratic self-interest, the stifling of initiative and low standards. To overcome these problems, the education system must be marketised. In their view, competition will make schools more responsive and raise educational standards. We can identify two types of marketisation:

Type 1: an internal market within the state education system

This was established by the 1988 Education Reform Act, which directed state schools to act more like private businesses, e.g. competing for pupils. However, schooling was still largely delivered by the state, mainly through local authority schools.

Type 2: the privatisation of state education

In a privatised system, the state ceases to be the actual provider of educational services. Instead, private companies or voluntary organisations deliver education and the state is reduced to two roles:

- It commissions educational services, putting them up for contract and deciding which private bidder gets the contract.
- It acts as regulator, setting targets and monitoring performance to ensure that the private providers meet certain standards, e.g. through Ofsted inspections.

This form of marketisation began in the late 1980s in a fairly limited way but the trend has steadily accelerated as more areas of the education system have been opened up to private businesses.

Policies on gender and ethnicity

So far we have focused largely on policies affecting class differences in achievement. However, policies can also have an impact on other differences in achievement, such as gender and ethnicity.

Gender

In the 19th century, females were largely excluded from higher education. More recently, under the tripartite system, girls often had to achieve a higher mark than boys in the 11+ in order to obtain a grammar school place.

Since the 1970s, however, policies such as GIST have been introduced to try to reduce gender differences in subject choice. For more about policies on gender, see Topic 4.

Ethnicity

Policies aimed at raising the achievements of children from minority ethnic backgrounds have gone through several phases:

Assimilation policies in the 1960s and 70s focused on the need for pupils from minority ethnic groups to assimilate into mainstream British culture as a way of raising their achievement, especially by helping those for whom English was not their first language. A related policy is that of compensatory education (see Topic 3).

However, critics argue that some minority groups who are at risk of underachieving, such as African Caribbean pupils, already speak English and that the real cause of their under-achievement lies in poverty or racism.

Multicultural education (MCE) policies through the 1980s and into the 1990s aimed to promote the achievements of children from minority ethnic groups by valuing all cultures in the school curriculum, thereby raising minority pupils' self-esteem and achievements.

However, MCE has been criticised on several grounds:

- Maureen Stone (1981) argues that black pupils do not fail for lack of self-esteem, so MCE is misguided.
- Critical race theorists argue that MCE is mere tokenism. It picks out stereotypical features of minority cultures for inclusion in the curriculum, but fails to tackle institutional racism.
- The New Right criticise MCE for perpetuating cultural divisions. They take the view that education should promote a shared national culture and identity into which minorities should be assimilated.

Social inclusion of pupils from minority ethnic groups, and policies to raise their achievement, became the focus in the late 1990s. Policies include:

- Detailed monitoring of exam results by ethnicity.
- Amending the Race Relations Act to place a legal duty on schools to promote racial equality.
- Help for voluntary 'Saturday schools' in the black community.
- English as an Additional Language programmes.

However, Heidi Safia Mirza (2005) sees little genuine change in policy. She argues that, instead of tackling the structural causes of ethnic inequality such as poverty and racism, educational policy still takes a 'soft' approach that focuses on culture, behaviour and the home.

Similarly, Gillborn argues that institutionally racist policies in relation to the ethnocentric curriculum, assessment and streaming continue to disadvantage minority ethnic group pupils (see Topic 3).

Topic summary

Policies can have important effects on **inequalities** within the education system. Policy has gone through three main phases since 1944.

The first was the **tripartite system**, with selection at 11+ (based on the idea of innate ability) for either grammar or secondary modern school. **Comprehensivisation** from 1965 abolished the 11+; all children went to comprehensive schools, but **streaming** continued.

Marketisation from 1988 aimed to create an education market, with parental choice and competition between schools. More recently, there has been some **privatisation**.

Some sociologists see most policies as **reproducing and legitimating inequality**. Some policies have aimed to deal with **gender** and **ethnic** differences in achievement.

While marketisation has been the dominant policy since 1988, some **policies to reduce inequality** have also been introduced.

EXAMINING EDUCATIONAL POLICY AND INEQUALITY

QuickCheck Questions

Check your answers at www.sociology.uk.net

1   In what way did the tripartite system reproduce class inequality?
2   Identify two reasons why comprehensivisation did not end educational inequality.
3   Explain how the idea that there is a 'parentocracy' legitimates inequality.
4   Explain why an education market might raise educational standards.

5   Identify two policies that have helped to create an education market.
6   In what ways might the education system be a source of profits for private companies?
7   Explain what is meant by 'assimilation' policies in relation to ethnicity and education.
8   Suggest two criticisms of multicultural education policies.

Questions to try

Whether or not you are taking the AS exams during your A level course, trying the AS questions below is a very good way of testing your knowledge and understanding and practising your skills in preparation for your A level exams.

Item A   Until the 1980s, most education was provided by elected local education authorities, directed and funded by central government. However, the 1988 Education Reform Act began the marketisation of education, aimed at raising standards by increasing parental choice and competition between schools. After 2010, there was a substantial move towards the privatisation of education through policies such as the growth of chains of academies run by private businesses.

Some sociologists claim that the main impact of marketisation and privatisation policies has not been to raise standards, but to increase educational inequality.

AS level questions

1   Define the term 'reproduction of social inequality'.   (2 marks)
2   Using one example, briefly explain how 'multicultural education' may reduce ethnic differences in achievement.   (2 marks)
3   Outline and explain the effects of two marketisation policies.   (10 marks)

A level questions

4   Outline two criticisms of the comprehensive school system.   (4 marks)
5   Applying material from Item A and your knowledge, evaluate the claim that marketisation and privatisation policies have increased educational inequality.   (30 marks)

The Examiner's Advice

Q3 Spend about 15 minutes on this question. Divide your time fairly equally between each policy. You don't need a separate introduction; just start on your first policy. Possible policies include exam league tables, parental choice, specialist schools, free schools, Ofsted inspections, the funding formula, open enrolment, academies, the National Curriculum. Describe in some detail each policy. Explain the effect of each of the two policies. Do this by creating a chain of reasoning (see page 248). For example, exam league tables give parents the information to identify and choose the best schools, as in a market. This means that the middle class, who possess more cultural and economic capital with which to make choices, gain advantage. Use concepts such as parentocracy, myth of parentocracy, fragmented centralisation, reproduction and legitimation of inequality, competition, selection by mortgage, economic and cultural capital, and studies such as David, Ball, Whitty and Gewirtz.

Q5 Spend about 45 minutes on this question. First explain what marketisation and privatisation mean, and how they differ; e.g. privatisation goes beyond marketisation by taking state-funded education out of state control and placing it in private hands. Identify and explain policies firstly that create an education market, and secondly policies that move control of education away from the state. Do this by creating a chain of reasoning. For example, formula funding means schools get funds based on how many pupils they attract. This puts pressure on schools to improve results so as to gain more funding by attracting more pupils. These well-resourced, popular schools can then select successful middle-class pupils. Meanwhile, working-class pupils are more likely to end up in schools with more limited funding and underachieve. Use evidence from studies such as Ball, Whitty, David, Gewirtz, Allen, Pollack, Molnar, Beder and Hall, and develop the points noted in Item A. Evaluate the impact of individual policies as you go along, as well as the claim as a whole in your conclusion.

CHAPTER 2

EXAMINING EDUCATION

AS questions

Item A   Some sociologists see differences in achievement as resulting from factors internal to the education system. Processes within schools that can cause these differences include labelling, streaming and the various ways pupils respond to being treated differently. In many cases, these factors link together to create substantial inequalities in educational experiences and outcomes.
By contrast, other sociologists claim that home and community background exerts a greater influence on achievement.

1   Define the term 'legitimation' of inequality.   (2 marks)
2   Using one example, explain how education may reinforce social solidarity.   (2 marks)
3   Outline three policies that may reduce inequality in education.   (6 marks)
4   Outline and explain two factors external to the education system that may cause gender differences in achievement.   (10 marks)
5   Applying material from Item A and your knowledge, evaluate the view that factors internal to the education system are the main cause of differences in achievement between social groups.   (20 marks)

A level questions

Item A   There are clear differences in achievement based on ethnicity. Some sociologists point to the role of parents and family in affecting educational outcomes. How far educational success is valued within the family and community is potentially very influential. Other sociologists argue that economic disadvantage is a crucial factor in influencing educational success and failure.

Item B   Some commentators argue that education policies in the last 30 years have raised achievement for all through creating a market in the state education system. They argue that reducing state control over education and increasing parental choice means that schools have to be more business-like and compete with each other for pupils by raising their standards of teaching.
However, some sociologists argue that one effect of these marketisation policies has been to increase inequality between pupils from different social classes and ethnic backgrounds.

1   Outline two factors within the education system that may cause gender differences in subject choice.   (4 marks)
2   Outline three material factors that may cause class differences in achievement.   (6 marks)
3   Applying material from Item A, analyse two processes external to the education system that may cause differences in achievement between ethnic groups.   (10 marks)
4   Applying material from Item B and your knowledge, evaluate the claim that 'education policies in the last 30 years have raised achievement for all through creating a market in the state education system'.   (30 marks)

The examiner's advice for AS questions 4 and 5, and for A level question 3, are on page 256.

For A level question 4, see the answer on the next page along with the examiner's comments and mark.

Answer by Elaine

A level question 4: Applying material from Item B and your knowledge, evaluate the claim that 'education policies in the last 30 years have raised achievement for all through creating a market in the state education system'.

Government policies over the past 25-30 years have introduced a market in education. The Conservative government began this with the 1988 Education Reform Act (ERA). New Labour continued it from 1997 to 2010, while the Conservative-Liberal Democrat coalition took it even further. However, New Labour also brought in policies that tried to directly help the most disadvantaged groups as well. All governments since the 1980s have been strongly influenced by neoliberal ideas which argue that establishing a market is the best way to improve education.

> Puts marketisation in historical and theoretical context.Good point about non-marketisation policies – but needs developing further with examples.

ERA brought in several marketisation policies. SATs at different ages and GCSEs enabled schools' performance to be compared by producing league tables that show which schools are doing best in terms of exam results. However, this is a problem because a school could be doing well just because it has a middle-class intake, not because of better teaching etc. Later versions of league tables took students on free school meals into account in drawing up the tables..

> Some relevant policies identified. Some good understanding and evaluation of league tables.

League tables are linked to parental choice. Before ERA, schools had catchment areas and children just went to the local school. Now parents can choose which school to apply to and they can use league tables to find out the best performing schools and try to send their children there. This turns parents and pupils into consumers of education – one side of the education market. This 'parentocracy' has been criticised by Ball, who claims this is all appearance and no substance. Gewirtz also argues that middle-class parents use their greater economic and cultural capital to 'play the system' and get their children into the top schools.

> Good analysis shown in explaining role of league tables within the education market. Some reference to relevant studies, but should develop these further.

The other side of the market is the way schools have to operate like businesses who have to compete to attract consumers. The main way this has been done is through formula funding, whereby schools get funded according to how many pupils they attract. The better performing the school, the more pupils they attract and the more money they get – just like a business. However, this has been criticised for being unfair to schools with working-class pupils. They do less well in exams so the image of the school drops. Parents send their children elsewhere and the school loses money. The school becomes a sink school and the pupils who are still there lose out. This is unlikely to raise standards in those schools.

> Strongly analytical and evaluative – first explains the role of formula funding in the education market and then criticises it.

More recently, policies giving schools more freedom to act in ways they think will bring in more pupils have been introduced. These include schools becoming academies, which takes them out of local council control. This is not just marketisation, but the privatisation of state education. In what Ball sees as 'fragmented centralisation', the growth of academies and also of free schools marks a major change of direction.

> Introduces some more recent policies, but doesn't develop them very far. Needs to discuss impact on inequality and clearer explanation of privatisation.

The way the education system now works is a long way from the old comprehensive system where schools had catchment areas and everyone went there. Whether or not these changes have raised standards is another question. The claimed intention of all policies is to raise standards but the evidence on standards is incomplete and difficult to estimate.

> Makes some general points but not really getting to the point of the question.

> The question asks if policies have raised achievement for all through creating a market, so you need to discuss the impact of marketisation policies on achievement.
>
> This answer does well on the policies to create a market but it is limited in several ways. The policies referred to are mainly pre-2010, with only a brief reference to more recent policies near the end; these need further development. Secondly, there is only passing reference to policies supporting groups who are failing within the education system. The answer would also benefit from some development of the theoretical context – neoliberal ideas about privatisation versus critics. Finally, it needs more focus on the issue of how marketisation policies may or may not have raised achievement.

21/30

CHAPTER 3

Research Methods

with special application to education

In the previous chapter we looked at what sociologists have discovered in studying education. But how exactly do sociologists study the topics they are interested in? In this chapter, we examine how sociologists go about investigating society.

The purpose of sociology is to answer questions about social life and the social world. For example, why do middle-class children generally achieve better exam results than working-class children? What causes divorce? How far do the media influence people's behaviour?

To answer questions like these, sociologists develop **theories**. A theory is a general explanation of how or why social life follows the patterns it does.

A good theory is one that explains these patterns. That is, it explains all the available evidence that can be found about the topic being investigated. If a theory does not explain the **evidence** that we or others have gathered about the topic, we need to replace it with one that does.

Sociologists therefore try to ensure that their theories are based on sound evidence. To do otherwise would risk their work being discredited by other sociologists.

We thus need good, sound evidence to test our theories. But what **methods** can we use to obtain it? This chapter is concerned with the different methods sociologists use for collecting information about society, and with the issues we need to think about when deciding which methods to use.

The AQA Specification

The specification is the syllabus produced by the exam board, telling you what you have to study. The AQA specification for Research Methods and Methods in Context requires you to examine the following:

- Quantitative and qualitative methods of research; research design.

- Sources of data, including questionnaires, interviews, participant and non-participant observation, experiments, documents and official statistics.

- The distinction between primary and secondary data, and between quantitative and qualitative data.

- The relationship between positivism, interpretivism and sociological methods; the nature of 'social facts'.

- The theoretical, practical and ethical considerations influencing choice of topic, choice of method(s) and the conduct of research.

- The application of sociological research methods to the study of education.

For full details of the specification, visit www.aqa.org.uk

TOPIC 1

What personal skills and characteristics might be useful for a researcher studying this group?

GETTING STARTED

A Look at the photograph above of some members of the religious sect, Hare Krishna. As a sociologist, this might be a group that you want to study. On your own or in pairs, answer the following:

  1 What kinds of things would you want to know about the sect?

  2 What ways could you use to find these things out?

  3 Why might your own beliefs affect the success or otherwise of your research? What other personal characteristics of yours might make a difference and why?

  4 What prior knowledge or training might you need in order to research this sect successfully?

B Imagine you wanted to study gender and educational achievement. One way would be to look at official statistics collected by the government, such as those on page 51.

  1 What do these statistics tell us about gender and achievement?

  2 What kinds of things *don't* the statistics tell us that we might want to know?

C To understand gender and achievement better, you might seek more in-depth information by carrying out research yourself, rather than just using existing statistics. For example, you could talk to boys and girls in detail about their experiences of education.

  1 What would be the advantages of carrying out your own research on this topic rather than just relying on government statistics?

  2 What problems might you have in analysing the detailed information that you would gain from an in-depth conversation?

Learning objectives

After studying this Topic, you should:

- Know what the main types of data are and what research methods sociologists use.

- Understand the practical, ethical and theoretical factors influencing choice of method and topic, and be able to assess their relative importance.

- Understand the difference between positivist and interpretivist approaches to research.

CHOOSING A RESEARCH METHOD

Sociologists use a wide variety of different methods and sources to obtain data (information or evidence) about society. To make sense of this variety, we can classify them into:

- Primary and secondary sources of data.
- Quantitative and qualitative data.

Primary and secondary sources of data

Primary data is information collected by sociologists themselves for their own purposes. These purposes may be to obtain a first-hand 'picture' of a group or society, or to test a hypothesis (an untested theory).

Methods for gathering primary data include:

- **Social surveys**: these involve asking people questions in a written questionnaire or an interview.
- **Participant observation**: the sociologist joins in with the activities of the group he or she is studying.
- **Experiments**: sociologists rarely use laboratory experiments, but they sometimes use field experiments and the comparative method.

A big advantage of using primary data is that sociologists may be able to gather precisely the information they need to test their hypotheses. However, doing so can often be costly and time consuming.

Secondary data is information that has been collected or created by someone else for their own purposes, but which the sociologist can then use.

Sources of secondary data include:

- **Official statistics** produced by government on a wide range of issues, such as education, crime, divorce and unemployment, as well as other statistics produced by charities, businesses, churches and other organisations.
- **Documents** such as letters, emails, diaries, photographs, official reports, novels, newspapers, the internet and television broadcasts.

Using secondary data can be a quick and cheap way of doing research, since someone else has already produced the information. However, those who produce it may not be interested in the same questions as sociologists, and so secondary sources may not provide exactly the information that sociologists need.

Quantitative and qualitative data

Sociologists make use of two different kinds of data in their research: quantitative data and qualitative data.

Quantitative data refers to information in a numerical form. Examples of quantitative data include official statistics on how many girls passed five or more GCSEs, the percentage of marriages ending in divorce or the number of people who are unemployed.

Similarly, information collected by opinion polls and market research surveys often comes in the form of quantitative data – for example, on the proportion of the electorate intending to vote for a particular party or how many people take holidays abroad.

Qualitative data, by contrast, gives a 'feel' for what something is like – for example, what it feels like to get good GCSE results, or for one's marriage to end in divorce.

Evidence gathered by using participant observation aims to give us a sense of what it feels like to be a member of a particular group.

Similarly, in-depth interviews that probe deeply into a person's views can give us an insight into what it is like to be in that person's 'shoes'. These methods can provide rich descriptions of people's feelings and experiences.

Box 11	Some examples of types of data	
	Quantitative data	Qualitative data
Primary sources	Questionnaires Structured interviews	Participant observation Unstructured interviews
Secondary sources	Official statistics	Letters Newspaper articles

Application

Which of the four categories above does each of the following sources of data belong in?

- **a** field experiments
- **b** paintings
- **c** exam league tables
- **d** school reports
- **e** divorce statistics.

Factors influencing choice of methods

Given the wide range of methods available, how do we select the right one for our research? Different methods and sources of data have different strengths and limitations and we need to be able to evaluate these when selecting which to use.

We can look at these strengths and limitations in terms of a number of practical, ethical (moral) and theoretical issues.

Practical issues

Different methods present different practical problems. These include:

time and money

Different methods require different amounts of time and money and this may influence the sociologist's choice.

For example, large-scale surveys may employ dozens of interviewers and data-inputting staff and cost a great deal of money. By contrast, a small-scale project involving a lone researcher using participant observation may be cheaper to carry out, but it can take several years to complete.

The researcher's access to resources can be a major factor in determining which methods they employ. A well-known professor will probably have access to more research funds than a young student, for example.

requirements of funding bodies

Research institutes, businesses and other organisations that provide the funding for research may require the results to be in a particular form. For example, a government department funding research into educational achievement may have targets for pass rates and so require quantitative data to see whether these targets are being achieved. This means the sociologist will have to use a method capable of producing such data, such as questionnaires or structured interviews.

personal skills and characteristics

Each sociologist possesses different personal skills and this may affect their ability to use different methods. For example, participant observation usually requires the ability to mix easily with others as well as good powers of observation and recall, while depth interviews call for an ability to establish a rapport (relationship of empathy and trust) with the interviewee. Not all sociologists have these qualities and so some may have difficulty using these methods.

subject matter

It may be much harder to study a particular group or subject by one method than by another. For example, it might prove difficult for a male sociologist to study an all-female group by means of participant observation, while written questionnaires may be useless for studying those who cannot read or write.

research opportunity

Sometimes the opportunity to carry out research occurs unexpectedly and this means that it may not be possible to use structured methods such as questionnaires, which take longer to prepare. For example, a Glasgow gang leader offered the sociologist James Patrick (1973) the chance 'out of the blue' to spend time with his gang. With little time to prepare, Patrick had no option but to use participant observation. In other circumstances, the researcher might have been able to set up the research opportunity carefully beforehand and have plenty of time to select their methods.

▲ Using secondary data from the Census saves sociologists time and money, but may not provide exactly the information they need

Ethical issues

Ethics refers to moral issues of right and wrong. Methods that sociologists use to study people may raise a range of ethical questions. The British Sociological Association sets out ethical guidelines for the conduct of research, including the following principles.

informed consent

Research participants (the people being studied) should be offered the right to refuse to be involved. The researcher should also tell them about all relevant aspects of the research so that they can make a fully informed decision. Consent should be obtained before research begins and, if the study is lengthy, again at intervals throughout the process.

confidentiality and privacy

Researchers should keep the identity of research participants secret in order to help to prevent possible negative effects on them. Researchers should also respect their privacy. Personal information concerning research participants should be kept confidential.

harm to research participants

Researchers need to be aware of the possible effects of their work on those they study. These could include police intervention, harm to employment prospects, social exclusion and psychological damage. Wherever possible, researchers should anticipate and prevent such harm.

vulnerable groups

Special care should be taken where research participants are particularly vulnerable because of their age, disability, or physical or mental health. For example, when studying children in schools, researchers should have regard for issues of child protection. They should obtain the consent of both the child and the parent, and they should provide information in language that the child can understand.

covert research

Covert research is when the researcher's identity and research purpose are hidden from the people being studied. This can create serious ethical problems, such as deceiving or lying to people in order to win their trust or obtain information. Clearly, it is impossible to gain informed consent while at the same time keeping the research or its purpose secret.

However, some sociologists argue that the use of covert methods may be justified in certain circumstances. These may include gaining access to secretive, dangerous or powerful groups.

Activity	Discussion

Should research always be ethical?

...go to www.sociology.uk.net

Theoretical issues

This refers to questions about what we think society is like and whether we can obtain an accurate, truthful picture of it. Our views on these issues will affect the kinds of methods we favour using.

validity

A valid method is one that produces a true or genuine picture of what something is really like. It allows the researcher to get closer to the truth.

Many sociologists argue that qualitative methods such as participant observation give us a more valid or truthful account of what it is like to be a member of a group than quantitative methods such as questionnaires. This is because participant observation can give us a deeper insight through first hand experience.

reliability

Another word for reliability is replicability. A replica is an exact copy of something, so a reliable method is one which, when repeated by another researcher, gives the same results.

For example, in physics or chemistry, different researchers can repeat the same experiment and obtain the same results every time. In sociology, quantitative methods such as written questionnaires tend to produce more reliable results than qualitative methods such as unstructured interviews.

Application

Read the following statements and decide which one is an example of reliability and which of validity:

1 My mum had the flu. She told me how she was hot, tired and aching all over. When she had finished describing her symptoms in detail, I really knew what it must feel like to be so ill.

2 We took my mum's temperature and it was 102 degrees. She decided to go to the doctor, who took her temperature too and it came out as 102 degrees. She checked it again when she got home and it was still 102.

representativeness

Representativeness refers to whether or not the people we study are a typical cross-section of the group we are interested in. Imagine for example that we want to know about the effects of divorce on children. It would take a great deal of time and money to study every child of divorced parents, and we might only be able to afford to study a sample of, say, 100 such children.

However, if we ensure our sample is representative or typical of the wider population, we can use our findings to make generalisations about all children of divorced parents, without actually having to study them all.

Large-scale quantitative surveys that use sophisticated sampling techniques to select their sample are more likely to produce representative data.

methodological perspective

Sociologists' choice of method is also influenced by their methodological perspective – their view of what society is like and how we should study it. There are two contrasting perspectives on the choice of methods: positivism and interpretivism.

Positivists prefer quantitative data, seek to discover patterns of behaviour and see sociology as a science.

Interpretivists prefer qualitative data, seek to understand social actors' meanings and reject the view that sociology can model itself on the natural sciences.

Box 12 explains why positivists and interpretivists prefer different types of methods and data.

Functionalists and Marxists often take a positivist approach. They see society as a large-scale (macro-level) structure that shapes our behaviour. By contrast, interactionists favour an interpretivist approach. They take a micro-level view of society, focusing on small-scale, face-to-face interactions.

conclusion

The sociologist's theoretical perspective is usually the most important factor when choosing which method to use. Whenever possible, they will want to obtain the type of data – quantitative or qualitative – that their perspective views as most appropriate.

However, practical and ethical factors usually limit the choice. Just because a sociologist *prefers* a particular kind of method, doesn't mean that they can simply go ahead and use it. Time, resources, access, consent, privacy and so on are all constraints on their choice.

Finally, even sheer chance may determine the method used. For example, David Tuckett (2001) describes how one postgraduate sociology student found himself taken ill with tuberculosis and confined to a hospital ward, so he used this as an opportunity to conduct a participant observation study.

Box 12	Why do positivists and interpretivists prefer different types of data?

Positivists and interpretivists collect and use different types of data: positivists prefer quantitative data, while interpretivists prefer qualitative. This is because they make different assumptions about the nature of society and how we should study it.

- Positivists assume that society has an objective factual reality – it exists 'out there', just like the physical world of nature.

  ↓

- Society exerts an influence over its members, systematically shaping their behaviour patterns.

  ↓

- Positivist research uses quantitative data to uncover and measure these patterns of behaviour.

  ↓

- By analysing quantitative data, positivists seek to discover the objective scientific laws of cause and effect that determine behaviour.

  ↓

- Positivists thus prefer questionnaires, structured interviews, experiments and official statistics. These produce data that is both reliable and representative.

- Interpretivists reject the idea of an objective social reality – we construct reality through the meanings we create in our interactions with others.

  ↓

- Our actions are based on the meanings we give to situations; they are not the product of external forces.

  ↓

- Interpretivist research uses qualitative data to uncover and describe the social actor's 'universe of meaning'.

  ↓

- By interpreting qualitative data, interpretivists seek to gain a subjective understanding of actors' meanings and 'life worlds'.

  ↓

- Interpretivists thus prefer participant observation, unstructured interviews and personal documents. These produce data that is valid.

Factors influencing choice of topic

Before choosing which method to use, sociologists need to decide what topic they wish to study. Several factors influence their choice.

the sociologist's perspective

The sociologist's theoretical perspective is a major influence on their choice of research topic. For example, a New Right researcher may study the effects of welfare benefits on the growth of lone-parent families, since the idea of welfare dependency is central to their standpoint. By contrast, a feminist researcher is more likely to choose to study domestic violence, as opposition to gender oppression lies at the heart of the feminist perspective.

society's values

Sociologists themselves are part of the society they study and thus are influenced by its values. As these values change, so does the focus of research. The rise of feminism in the 1960s led to a focus on gender inequality and today's environmentalist concerns have generated interest in 'green crimes' such as toxic waste dumping.

practical factors

Practical factors, such as the inaccessibility of certain situations to the researcher, may also restrict what topic they are able to study. For example, although sociologists may wish to study the ways in which global corporations make their decisions, this may not be possible because these are made in secret.

funding bodies

Most research requires funding from an external body. These bodies include government agencies, the Economic and Social Research Council (ESRC), charities and businesses. As the funding body is paying for the research, it will determine the topic to be investigated.

Activity	Research
Perspective and choice of method	
...go to www.sociology.uk.net	

Box 13	Triangulation

In practice, sociologists often use a combination of methods. For example, they may begin with a limited number of in-depth, unstructured interviews to gain insights; these can then be used to develop questions for a questionnaire given to a larger sample.

This process is called 'triangulation'. It involves using two or more sources or methods to obtain a more rounded picture by studying the same thing from more than one viewpoint.

The idea is that different methods can complement each other – the strengths of one counter the weaknesses of the other. Combining them gives us the best of both worlds: reliable and representative quantitative data covering large numbers of cases, as favoured by positivists, and valid qualitative data looking at a smaller number in depth, as preferred by interpretivists.

The process of research

Once we have chosen a topic for research and a method for investigating it, there are a number of further steps we need to go through. The first of these is to formulate an aim or hypothesis for the research.

Formulating an aim or hypothesis

Most studies either have a general aim or a specific hypothesis. A hypothesis is a possible explanation that can be tested by collecting evidence to prove it true or false.

For example, we may suspect that family size affects educational achievement. If so, we can formulate a specific hypothesis as a cause-and-effect statement, such as: 'differences in family size cause differences in achievement'. We can then collect evidence to test whether or not this is true. If the hypothesis turns out to be false, we must discard it.

Discarding a hypothesis might seem like a bad thing, but in fact it means we have made some progress. For example, if our research reveals no link with family size, we have learned something new and so we can now turn our attention to another possible cause instead – perhaps parental attitudes, or income? We simply formulate a new hypothesis and set out to test it.

The advantage of a hypothesis is that it gives direction to our research. It will give a focus to our questions, since their purpose is to gather information that will either confirm or refute (disprove) our hypothesis.

Positivists favour a hypothesis as the starting point for research. This is because they seek to discover cause-and-effect relationships – e.g. that large family size causes underachievement. Using quantitative methods such as questionnaires, they formulate questions designed to discover whether and why these factors are linked.

While a hypothesis is a statement about a specific relationship ('A causes B'), an aim is more general. It identifies what we intend to study and hope to achieve through the research. Often it will simply be to collect data on a particular topic, such as the way of life of a subculture.

The advantage of an aim is that it is more open-ended. We are not tied to trying to prove a particular hypothesis; instead we can gather data on anything that appears interesting about a situation. This can be very useful at the start of our research, when we know very little about the topic – since by definition, in this situation we would have no real idea about what hypothesis we wanted to test.

Interpretivists often favour a broad aim rather than a hypothesis, since they are interested in understanding actors' meanings, so the task is to find out what the actors themselves think is important, rather than to impose the researcher's own possible explanations in the form of a hypothesis.

Operationalising concepts

Suppose our hypothesis is that working-class pupils achieve lower qualifications because of lower parental income. Before we can test it, we need a working or 'operational' definition of our key ideas – in this case, social class. The reason is simple: without a working definition, we won't be able to count the numbers of working-class pupils who have or don't have qualifications.

Now, 'social class' is a fairly abstract concept, so we need a way of *measuring* what class each pupil belongs to. Most sociologists would probably use parental occupation as an indicator of a pupil's social class. This process of converting a sociological concept (such as class) into something we can measure is called 'operationalisation'.

Once we have operationalised our concept, we can start devising questions that measure it. For example, we might ask parents, 'what is your job?' This will allow us to see what social class each pupil belongs to. We can then correlate this with information we collect about their qualifications to find out whether our hypothesis is true or false.

Operationalising a concept may seem straightforward, but a problem can arise when different sociologists operationalise the same concept differently. For example, we might disagree about whether a routine office worker is working-class or middle-class. This can make it hard to compare the findings of different pieces of research.

Application
Write an operational definition of the following concepts that would allow you to measure them in a survey: (a) material deprivation; (b) anti-school subculture; (c) educational underachievement.

Positivists are concerned to operationalise concepts because of the importance they place on creating and testing hypotheses. By contrast, interpretivists put less emphasis on operationalising concepts. This is because they are more interested in actors' own definitions and understandings of ideas such as 'class', 'achievement' etc, than in imposing their own definitions of these concepts.

The pilot study

Sociologists who use social surveys (questionnaires and structured interviews) often carry out a pilot study before conducting their main survey. This involves trying out a draft version of the questionnaire or interview schedule (the list of interview questions) on a small sample.

The basic aim of the pilot study is to iron out any problems, refine or clarify questions and their wording and give interviewers practice, so that the actual survey goes as smoothly as possible.

For example, Young and Willmott (1962) carried out just over 100 pilot interviews to help them decide on the design of their study, the questions to ask and how to word them.

A pilot study may reveal that some questions are badly worded and hard to understand, or that the answers are difficult to analyse. After carrying out the pilot study, it should be possible to finalise the questionnaire or interview schedule.

Samples and sampling

Sociologists often aim to produce generalisations that apply to all cases of the topic they are interested in. For example, if we were interested in educational achievement, we would ideally want our theory to explain the achievement levels of *all* pupils, not just the ones who were in our study.

Obviously, however, we do not have the time or money to include every pupil in the UK in our study, so we have to choose a *sample* of pupils to include. A sample is a smaller sub-group drawn from the wider group that we are interested in. The process of creating or selecting a sample is called *sampling*.

The basic purpose of sampling is usually to ensure that those people we have chosen to include in the study (such as pupils) are representative or typical of the research population, including all the people we have *not* been able to include in the study. (The research population refers to the whole group that we are interested in – all pupils, in this case.)

So long as our sample is representative, we should be able to generalise our findings to the whole research population. This is particularly attractive to positivist sociologists, who wish to make general, law-like statements about the wider social structure.

The sampling frame

To choose a sample, we first need a sampling frame. This is a list of all the members of the population we are interested in studying. For example, Young and Willmott used the electoral register (the list of people entitled to vote) as their sampling frame. It is important that the list we use as a sampling frame is as complete and accurate as possible. It should also be up to date and without duplications – otherwise the sample chosen from it may not be truly representative of the population.

Once we have obtained our sampling frame, we can choose our sample from it. In selecting the sample, we need to ensure it is representative of the wider population we are interested in (see Figure 3.1).

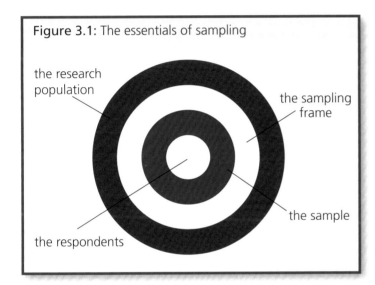

Figure 3.1: The essentials of sampling

the research population

the sampling frame

the sample

the respondents

Sampling techniques

Sociologists use various sampling techniques to obtain a representative sample:

- **Random sampling** is the simplest technique, where the sample is selected purely by chance. For example, names may be drawn out of a hat. Everyone has an equal chance of being selected. A large enough random sample should reflect the characteristics (e.g. gender, class etc.) of the whole research population. However, not all random samples are large enough to ensure this happens.
- **Quasi-random or systematic sampling** is where every nth person in the sampling frame is selected. Young and Willmott used every thirty-sixth name on the electoral register for their sample.
- **Stratified random sampling** The researcher first stratifies (breaks down) the population in the sampling frame by age, class, gender etc. The sample is then created in the same proportions, e.g. if 20% of the population are under 18, then 20% of the sample also have to be under 18.
- **Quota sampling** The population is stratified as above, and then each interviewer is given a quota of say, twenty females and twenty males, which they have to fill with respondents who fit these characteristics. The interviewer keeps at this task until their quota is filled.

Non-representative sampling

As we have seen, the purpose of sampling is usually to ensure that the people we include in our study are representative of the research population. However, for both practical and theoretical reasons, not all studies use representative sampling techniques.

Box 14   **The biggest blunder in survey history?**

The biggest blunder in survey history was probably the 1936 poll on voting intentions carried out by an American magazine, the Literary Digest. The poll asked respondents how they would vote in the forthcoming election: for Landon, the Republican Party candidate, or for Roosevelt, the Democratic Party candidate. Two million people responded to the poll. The great majority surveyed said they would vote for Landon and the magazine predicted a Republican victory. Yet when the election came, Roosevelt won by a landslide. How could the magazine have got it so wrong?

The answer lies in the sampling frame used for the questionnaire. The magazine had used the telephone directory, wrongly assuming it would be a reasonably good list of all those who were entitled to vote. However, in 1936, telephones were still something of a luxury; many poorer voters were not telephone subscribers and did not appear in the directory. Since in America, poorer voters have tended to be Democrats and richer voters Republicans, using the directory to draw the sample was bound to over-represent the intentions of rich Republican voters and under-represent those of poor Democrats.

▲ Roosevelt (left) celebrating his election victory

practical reasons

There are several practical reasons why it may not be possible to create a representative sample.

- The social characteristics of the research population, such as age, gender and class, may not be known. It would thus be impossible to create a sample that was an exact cross-section of the research population.
- It may be impossible to find or create a sampling frame for that particular research population. For example, not all criminals are convicted, so there is no complete list available from which to select a sample.
- Potential respondents may refuse to participate. For example, some criminals may refuse for fear that their responses may be passed to the police.

Where it is not possible to obtain a representative sample, sociologists sometimes use snowball or opportunity samples.

- **Snowball sampling** involves collecting a sample by contacting a number of key individuals, who are asked to suggest others who might be interviewed, and so on, adding to the sample 'snowball' fashion, until enough data has been collected. Although not representative, this can be a useful way to contact a sample of people who might otherwise be difficult to find or persuade to take part, such as criminals.
- **Opportunity sampling**, sometimes called convenience sampling, involves choosing from those individuals who are easiest to access. Examples include selecting from passers-by in the street or from a captive audience such as a class of pupils. In neither case is the sample likely to be representative of the target research population.

theoretical reasons

Even where it is possible to create a representative sample, some researchers may not choose to do so, because of their methodological perspective (see Box 12). Interpretivists believe that it is more important to obtain valid data and an authentic understanding of social actors' meanings than to discover general laws of behaviour. Because interpretivists are less concerned to make generalisations, they have less need for representative samples.

Once we have selected the sample, we can begin to collect data about the topic using a suitable research method.

Box 15	Case studies

A case study involves the detailed examination of a single case (or a few cases at most), such as a school, family, workplace or even just one individual. As such, they are not representative and we cannot generalise from them. Nevertheless, they have several uses:

- To suggest hypotheses at the start of research: looking closely at one case may give us ideas we can test on a larger group.
- To provide a detailed insight into a particular group. Participant observation studies are usually case studies.
- To study exceptional cases. An example is Weber's (1905) study of the role of the Calvinist religion in the rise of capitalism, which he saw as unique.
- In a large-scale quantitative study, they can illustrate general points in more detail and give the study a qualitative dimension.

Topic summary

Sociologists test their theories using **quantitative** or **qualitative** data. Sociologists obtain **primary** data themselves, using methods including questionnaires, interviews and observation. **Secondary** data is produced by others but used by sociologists.

In choosing a method, sociologists take several issues into account. **Practical** issues include time and funding. **Ethical** issues include the researcher deceiving the subjects. **Theoretical** issues include validity, reliability and representativeness.

Perspective also affects choice of method. **Positivists** prefer **quantitative** data; **interpretivists** favour **qualitative** data. **Choice of topic** is also affected by society's values and funding bodies.

Before conducting research, the researcher needs a **hypothesis** (a testable statement) or aim, and concepts need to be **operationalised**. A **pilot study** may be used to iron out problems. A **representative sample** is essential if findings are to be generalised.

EXAMINING CHOICE OF RESEARCH METHODS

QuickCheck Questions

Check your answers at www.sociology.uk.net

1 Give one example of (a) a qualitative primary method; (b) a quantitative secondary source.
2 What practical issues might affect a sociologist's choice of research method?
3 Identify three ethical issues that sociologists face.
4 What does 'reliability' mean?
5 True or false? If a method produces valid data, then when another sociologist uses it they should get the same results.

6 True or false? Interpretivists (a) see sociology as a science; (b) prefer qualitative data.
7 Suggest two research methods that (a) positivists and (b) interpretivists might prefer to use.
8 What is a hypothesis?
9 What measure might you use to operationalise the idea of 'social class'?
10 Define the following terms: (a) research population; (b) sample; (c) sampling frame.

Questions to try

Whether or not you're taking the AS exams during your A level course, trying the AS questions below is a very good way of testing your knowledge and understanding and practising your skills in preparation for your A level exams.

AS questions

1 Outline two reasons why it may not be possible for sociologists to create a representative sample. (4 marks)
2 Evaluate how far different factors may affect sociologists' choice of research methods. (16 marks)

A level question

Please see the A level question and student answer by Viola on page 160, along with the Examiner's comments and marks.

The Examiner's Advice

Q2 You need to deal with practical, ethical and theoretical factors. You might find it useful to organise your answer by starting with theoretical factors, especially the positivist-interpretivist debate, and how these influence sociologists' preferred method. Then go on to look at how practical and ethical factors may restrict their choice.

Theoretical factors include reliability, representativeness and validity. Explain these terms and apply them to particular methods – e.g. quantitative methods like structured interviews are usually more reliable and representative than qualitative methods like unstructured interviews, but less valid.

Practical factors include time, cost, access to the group you wish to study, funding bodies' requirements, the researcher's personal skills and characteristics, and research opportunity (including pure chance). Give some examples of these from different methods – e.g. government funding agencies often want quantitative data so researchers may need to use questionnaires.

Ethical factors include confidentiality and privacy, harmful effects (especially in relation to vulnerable groups), anonymity. Some methods have special ethical problems – e.g. covert observation involves deceit and lack of informed consent.

Link the different practical, theoretical and ethical factors rather than just dealing with each one separately. For example, covert participant observation may produce valid data, but it involves deceit and it may also be difficult to maintain one's cover. Compare different methods in terms of theoretical, practical or ethical factors – e.g. questionnaires are quicker to conduct than participant observation. Use examples from studies employing different methods and sources.

A captive population – but the researcher may find it difficult to gain access.

GETTING STARTED

A Imagine you are going to conduct research into bullying in a school.

1 Whose permission would you need to carry out your research?

2 How is the school day organised? What restrictions and opportunities might this create for your research?

3 In what ways could the age of the pupils affect your research?

4 How might teachers feel about a researcher being in their classroom or staffroom? How might this affect your research?

5 Given that you are researching bullying, do you think parents would be willing to let you carry out research with their children? Give your reasons.

6 Do you think the parents themselves would be likely to participate in your research? Give your reasons.

B What problems might you face in trying to study pupils when they are not in a school setting?

Learning objectives

After studying this Topic, you should:

- Know the main characteristics of education as a context for sociological research.

- Understand some of the problems and opportunities that researching educational issues presents for sociologists.

- Be aware of some of the research strategies sociologists use to investigate education.

Going on a school trip.

EDUCATION: THE RESEARCH CONTEXT

As we saw in Chapter 2, sociologists study many different issues in education, such as classroom interaction, pupil subcultures, teacher labelling, parental choice and so on.

In studying educational issues such as these, sociologists need to be aware of the particular characteristics of education, since these will affect their choice of research method and its effectiveness. For example:

- In studying pupil subcultures, there might be problems using covert participant observation, simply because it would prove very difficult for a researcher to pass themselves off as a pupil.
- Similarly, in studying parental attitudes to schooling, there may be difficulties in using written questionnaires to discover the opinions of parents who are illiterate.

In this Topic, we examine some of the key features or research characteristics of education as an area of investigation for sociologists and we look at the kinds of opportunities and problems that these research characteristics can present for the sociologist.

From this, you will be able to see the kinds of issues that you need to take account of when using different methods to research educational topics.

This will help you prepare for the *Methods in Context* questions in the AS and A level exams, where you are required to apply a given research method to a particular issue in education, such as gender and subject choice, racism in schools, material deprivation and underachievement, and so on.

Research characteristics

Throughout the rest of this chapter, we will be applying each of the different research methods that we look at to the study of education. We will deal with this in the special *Methods in Context* sections at the end of Topics 3 to 7.

We can identify five main groups and settings in education whose distinctive characteristics may make them easy or difficult to study.

1 Pupils
2 Teachers
3 Parents
4 Classrooms
5 Schools

Each of these presents particular problems and opportunities for the sociologist in choosing a suitable method to use. We shall examine each of these groups and settings in turn.

We also need to take into account the researcher's own personal characteristics, such as their own experience of education, which may make researching certain educational topics easier or more difficult.

1 Researching pupils

In education, many of the people that sociologists study are children and young people – pupils and students. Malcolm Hill (2005) suggests that there are three major differences between studying young people and studying adults:

- power and status
- ability and understanding
- vulnerability.

These differences raise particular practical, ethical and theoretical issues that researchers need to take into account when researching pupils. We shall now examine each of the three differences identified by Hill, together with the laws and guidelines that affect research with pupils.

power and status

Children and young people generally have less power and status than adults. This makes it more difficult for them to state their attitudes and views openly, especially if they challenge those of adults.

This is particularly true of schools, because they are hierarchical institutions that give teachers higher status and power over pupils. Teachers may sometimes even be able to use this power to influence which pupils are selected for research, for example in order to promote a good image of themselves or the school.

Formal research methods such as structured interviews or questionnaires tend to reinforce power differences. This is because it is the researcher and not the young person who determines what questions are asked and how answers should be formulated.

Sociologists therefore need to consider ways in which they can overcome the power and status differences between adult researchers and young participants. For example, group interviews rather than formal one-to-one interviews may be a good way of doing this. However, it is likely that whatever research methods are used, some power and status differences between researchers and pupils will remain.

Pupils' attitudes towards the power and status differences between themselves and their teachers are also likely to affect how they relate to the researcher. For example, pupils who resent the power of teachers over them may be less likely to cooperate with research. On the other hand, such pupils may feel empowered by participating in the research and express their true feelings about school.

Analysis and Evaluation

1 Why might members of an anti-school subculture be unwilling to cooperate with a researcher who wants to interview them?

2 How could you overcome this problem?

---

ability and understanding

Pupils' vocabulary, powers of self-expression, thinking skills and confidence are likely to be more limited than those of adults – particularly when trying to express abstract ideas.

Given that abstract concepts are a central part of sociological investigation, this poses problems for researchers. For example, the sociologist will need to take particular care in how they word their questions so as to make sure they are understood clearly by their young respondents.

Limitations in pupils' understanding also make it more difficult to gain their informed consent. This is because the sociologist may not be able to explain the nature of the research in words that young pupils can clearly understand.

Young people use language in different ways from adults, which makes the construction of appropriately worded questions particularly demanding. Younger children in particular are also likely to require more time than adults to understand questions.

A young person's memory is less developed than that of an adult, so they may be unable to recall in detail relevant material when asked to do so by the researcher.

However, we should remember that pupils are not a homogeneous group – they are not all the same. Class, age, gender and ethnicity all create differences between pupils that a researcher will have to take into account. For example, there are age, class and ethnic variations in the kinds of language that pupils use, such as differences in speech codes. It may therefore be important to match the gender and ethnicity of the young person and the researcher.

vulnerability and ethical issues

As a result of their more limited power and ability, young people are often more vulnerable to physical and psychological harm than adults. This raises special ethical issues for the researcher. The sociologist should therefore first consider whether the participation of young people in the research is actually necessary and whether they stand to benefit from it.

It is not enough simply to obtain the informed consent of parents or teachers. Most research guidelines emphasise that the young person too should be aware of what the research entails. However, it may be difficult to explain this to a child, and they may not yet be mature enough to decide whether to participate.

Given the vulnerability of school-age pupils, child protection issues are very important. For example, personal data should not be kept unless it is vital to the research.

The researcher should also consider what form the participation will take and any stress that may result. For example, questioning young children for long periods of time would be considered inappropriate.

The greater vulnerability of young people means that there are more 'gatekeepers' controlling access to pupils than there are for most other social groups. These include parents, heads, teachers, local authorities and schools' boards of governors. Generally, the more gatekeepers who are involved, the more difficult it is likely to be to carry out sustained research.

laws and guidelines

In addition, child protection laws such as the Safeguarding Vulnerable Groups Act, 2006, operate a vetting and barring scheme on adults working in schools, which requires researchers to have Disclosure and Barring Service (DBS) checks. This may delay or prevent researchers from carrying out their research.

As a result of ethical concerns, organisations such as Unicef, Barnardo's and the National Children's Bureau have developed special codes of practice for researching young people. These take the British Sociological Association's ethical research guidelines (see page 93) even further in terms of protecting the rights of children involved in research (see Box 16).

Box 16   **Ethical research practice and children**

In its statement of ethical research practice involving children and young people, the children's charity Barnardo's emphasises the core principle of informed consent.

The statement also stresses the need to resist any coercion or pressure upon children to participate in research, for example from teachers, parents or carers.

Special care should be taken when researching at risk or particularly vulnerable children and young people, such as those with special needs.

Researchers should refer participants to relevant support services where appropriate, provide debriefing after participation, and explain the limits to confidentiality (for example where participants disclose abuse, researchers must explain that they cannot keep this secret but must report it).

One advantage of studying pupils is that, because they are legally required to attend school, sociologists will know where to find their target research group – unlike with some other social groups they might study. On the other hand, this is not necessarily the case if the target group is pupils with anti-school attitudes, many of whom may truant regularly from school. Also, of course, pupils are normally in school only during the school day and in term time.

2 Researching teachers

Teachers often feel over-worked and may be less than fully cooperative, even when they want to be helpful. This may mean that interviews and questionnaires need to be kept short, and this will restrict the amount of data that can be gathered. On the other hand, as professionals, teachers are likely to be sympathetic to educational research.

power and status

Power relationships in the school are not equal. Teachers have more power and status because of their age, experience and responsibility within the school. They also have legal responsibilities and a duty of care towards the young people they teach.

The nature of the classroom reinforces the power of the teacher. Teachers often see it as 'my classroom', in which the researcher may be viewed as a trespasser. However, teachers are not fully independent, even in 'their' classroom. Heads, governors, parents and pupils all constrain what teachers may do.

Researchers will need to develop a 'cover' if they intend to carry out covert investigations and this may mean representing themselves as a supply teacher or classroom assistant, for example. Although this gives researchers access, these groups have a lower status within school and other teachers may not treat them as equals.

impression management

Teachers are used to being observed and scrutinised, for example in Ofsted inspections. As a result, they may well be more willing to be observed by a researcher since it is something they are accustomed to experiencing.

However, because a major part of the teacher's role is to 'put on an act' for pupils and others, teachers are often highly skilled at what Erving Goffman (1969) calls 'impression management' – manipulating the impression that other people have of us. The researcher may therefore have to find ways to get behind the public face that teachers put on.

Goffman also analyses how, as social actors, we behave differently when we are acting out a role 'front stage' as opposed to when we are back stage. Some researchers study teachers in their backstage setting – usually the staffroom.

Application

1 How might teachers' front stage and back stage behaviour differ?

2 How might you research their back stage behaviour?

However, getting backstage with teachers poses particular problems. The staffroom is a relatively small social space and, because teaching staff are generally known to each other, a newcomer will stand out and may be treated with some suspicion.

Teachers will be aware that any critical comments they make about the school where they work could affect their career prospects. As a result, they may be reluctant to answer certain questions honestly. However, the researcher may be able to overcome this problem by using observational methods rather than methods that involve asking direct questions, such as interviews or questionnaires.

Head teachers may try to influence which staff are selected to be involved in the research and these may not be fully representative of all teachers in the school. For example, a head may hand pick teachers who will convey a favourable image of the school – another example of impression management.

3 Researching classrooms

The classroom is unusual in being a closed social setting with clear physical and social boundaries. Although not as closed as a prison or psychiatric ward, for example, the classroom is less open than many other settings, such as leisure centres or shops.

The classroom is also a highly controlled setting. For example, the teacher and the school control classroom layout and access, as well as pupils' time, activities, noise levels, dress and language while they are in the classroom. Young people rarely experience this level of surveillance and control in other areas of their lives.

As a result, the classroom behaviour that the researcher observes may not accurately reflect what those involved really think and feel. Furthermore, in classroom interactions, teachers and pupils are very experienced at concealing their real thoughts and feelings from each other – another example of impression management – and they may conceal them from the researcher too.

Application

What motives might pupils have for concealing their real thoughts and feelings from the researcher?

The classroom is a fairly small, confined social space with room for perhaps thirty or so people. Classrooms are also comparatively simple social settings: in most cases there are just two social roles in the classroom – teacher and pupil. All this makes classroom interaction relatively straightforward to observe and analyse.

gatekeepers

Unlike many other social environments, access to classrooms is controlled by a wide range of gatekeepers. These include head teachers, teachers and child protection laws. Generally speaking, the more gatekeepers there are to a particular research setting, the more difficult it is for researcher to obtain and maintain access.

peer groups

Young people may be insecure about their identity and status. Therefore, when in school-based groups such as classes and friendship groups, they may be more sensitive to peer pressure and the need to conform. This may affect the way they respond to being researched.

It may therefore be necessary for example to supervise pupils when they are filling in questionnaires, especially if this is done in class, in order to prevent peers from influencing one another's answers. Similarly, in group interviews, the true attitudes of individual pupils may be hidden behind the dominant attitudes of the peer group.

4 Researching schools

There are tens of thousands of schools of many different kinds in the UK. If the sociologist uses observational methods, they are unlikely to have the time to investigate more than a very few and their research risks being unrepresentative.

Using large-scale surveys or official statistics instead may overcome this problem – though here they may lose the insight that can be gained from the detailed observation of a single school.

The researcher studying schools would need only a few minutes to identify their research population – for example, all the schools in a particular area. This is because the state publishes lists of schools, where they are located and what type of school they are.

schools' own data

What goes on in education is closely scrutinised by the media, parents and politicians. The education system is also highly marketised, with parental choice and competition between schools at its heart.

Partly as a result, there is a great deal of secondary data publicly available about schools, often produced by the schools themselves. This includes exam results and league tables; figures on truancy and subject choices; Ofsted

reports; government inquiries and school policy documents. Schools also produce personal documents, such as reports on individual students.

Schools are therefore 'data-rich' places and sociologists may be able to make use of some of these secondary sources in their research. However, school records are confidential and so researchers may not be able to gain access to them.

Other school data may pose particular difficulties. For example, schools with a truancy problem may falsify their attendance figures in order to present a good image and not deter applications. Similarly, although schools have a legal duty to record all racist incidents, there may be a tendency to downplay such incidents so as to maintain a positive public image.

Official statistics on examination performance should be treated with care. Schools may make changes in the curriculum in order to improve their results (for instance by entering pupils for easier qualifications) and create the image that the school is improving when in reality there may have been little or no change.

Activity | **Research**

Using school documents

...go to www.sociology.uk.net

the law

The law in effect requires young people to attend school in order to be educated. The only other major institution whose inmates are legally compelled to be there is the prison system.

Having such a 'captive population' to study has both advantages and disadvantages. For example, the researcher will know where everyone is – or at least, where they should be – at any given moment. On the other hand, since the school's primary role is to educate pupils, heads and teachers may see involvement in research as interfering with the school's most important function.

Schools operate within a particular legal framework. For example, the law requires them to collect information on pupils' attendance, achievement and so on, and this may be useful to sociologists. On the other hand, the legal duty of care that schools have towards their pupils may mean that researchers' access is restricted.

gatekeepers

Head teachers and governors are gatekeepers who have the power to refuse the researcher access to the school. They may do so if they believe that the research will interfere with the work of the school or undermine teachers' authority.

According to Roland Meighan and Clive Harber (2007), heads sometimes view research negatively. For example, heads' reactions to a research project that Meighan wanted to carry out on consulting pupils about teaching included the following views:

- It is dangerous to involve pupils in commenting on their teachers.
- Discipline would be adversely affected.
- It would be bad for classroom relationships.
- Children are not competent to judge teachers.

Some situations and school settings may be 'off limits' to a researcher – for example, head teachers' interviews with parents. Beynon and Atkinson (1984) note that gatekeepers such as heads often steer the researcher away from sensitive situations, such as classes where the teacher has poor classroom control.

school organisation

Schools are formal organisations with rules and hierarchies. Researchers may come to be seen as part of the hierarchy. For example, students may see them as teachers, while teachers may see them as inspectors. In schools where there is conflict, for example between students and teachers, researchers may even be seen as 'the enemy'.

Application

1 What other occupations are you likely to find in a school apart from teachers and heads?
2 What kinds of things could they tell a researcher about the workings of the school that teachers might not be willing or able to?

Unlike most other organisations in today's society, many schools are single-sex. This may pose problems where the researcher is of a different gender from that of the pupils. For example, the sociologist may become the focus of attention when they might prefer to keep a low profile, for example when conducting participant observation.

Schools are relatively large-scale, complex, highly organised social institutions. They have daily and yearly timetables, management structures, meetings schedules and so on, and these may all affect when and how a study can be carried out. For example, school holidays and exam periods may severely limit the sociologist's research activities.

Furthermore, the size and complexity of schools can cause difficulties for researchers, who often comment that it takes them months to work out where everything is and who does what in a particular school.

▲ A closed institution. What are the similarities and the differences between prisons and schools? How may these affect research?

5 Researching parents

While it is obviously important to study pupils, teachers, classrooms and schools if we want to understand education, parents also play an important part in the educational process.

Parents can influence what goes on in education, for example:

- By how they bring up their children.
- By their involvement in school through parent-teacher contacts, parent governors, attendance at parents' evenings and so on.
- Marketisation policies encourage parents to see themselves as consumers, for example in choice of school.

However, parents are not necessarily an easy group to study. For example, they are not a single homogeneous group. Their class, gender and ethnicity may all affect how willing or able they are to participate in research.

For example, pro-school middle-class parents may be more likely than working-class parents to return questionnaires about their children's education and this will make the research findings unrepresentative.

Parental permission is required for many forms of research with pupils. How likely parents are to give their permission may depend on the sensitivity of the research issue and on whether they can see their children benefiting from being involved. In general, the more sensitive an issue appears to be for parents, the less likely they are to consent to their children participating in research.

Parents may engage in impression management, presenting themselves to researchers in a positive light by exaggerating their involvement in their children's education. For example, they may lie about whether they attend parents' evenings or how often they read to their children. If so, this will result in invalid data being gathered.

access to parents

Many sociologists see parents as playing a vital role in children's education. However, most parent-child interaction takes place in the home. As a private setting often closed to researchers, this presents particular difficulties. For example, while classroom interactions between teachers and pupils can often be observed easily, there are few opportunities to observe whether parents help children with their homework.

Unlike most other important groups within education, parents are unusual in that they are for the most part physically located outside the school. This may make them more difficult to contact and research.

Although lists of parents' names and addresses exist in school records, a school would not normally release such information to researchers. However, the school might well be happy to help a researcher contact parents by using the usual method of sending letters or questionnaires home with pupils. However, this would not necessarily guarantee that parents received them or that pupils always returned the questionnaires that their parents had completed.

The researcher's own experience of education

Virtually everyone – including researchers – has had experience of education. Researchers can draw on their own experience of education, for example when formulating their hypotheses or interpreting data.

However, sociologists' personal experience and familiarity with classrooms and schools can dull their awareness of just how different educational environments are from other social settings. Because sociologists have spent years in school and university, these places may seem 'natural' to them. Thus, when carrying out research, sociologists need to be aware of their taken-for-granted assumptions about schools and classrooms, teachers and pupils.

Likewise, the researcher has probably been quite successful in education and this may make it difficult for them to empathise with students in an underachieving, anti-school subculture. Similarly, class, gender or ethnic differences between researcher and pupils may hinder the research.

Education is also a prominent political issue, with different political parties, pressure groups and individuals holding conflicting opinions about what should happen in schools. Research into educational issues takes place in this political context and the researcher has to be aware that their investigations can become part of a wider political and media debate.

Activity | **Research**

Characteristics of groups and settings in education

...go to www.sociology.uk.net

Topic summary

Education is a research context with many distinctive characteristics. For example, the need to protect **pupils** poses ethical problems.

Classrooms are highly controlled settings and this may make it difficult to uncover real attitudes.

Teachers are accustomed to being observed and may 'put on a show' when being studied.

Schools are closed, hierarchical organisations and this may make access difficult.

Parents may be hard to contact without the school's cooperation.

Researchers need to be aware that their personal characteristics and their own experience of education can influence their research.

EXAMINING EDUCATION: THE RESEARCH CONTEXT

QuickCheck Questions

Check your answers at www.sociology.uk.net

1 Identify three reasons why children and young people may be more difficult to study than adults.

2 What is 'impression management'? Why might teachers be particularly good at impression management?

3 In what ways can a classroom be described as a highly controlled setting?

4 Why might classroom interaction be relatively straightforward to observe?

5 What kinds of (a) statistics and (b) documents might a sociologist use in studying schools?

6 In what ways might the law affect the sociologist's research on schools?

7 Why might head teachers be unwilling to allow a researcher access to their school?

8 Suggest reasons why some kinds of parents may be more willing or able than others to participate in research.

9 Why might a sociologist's own educational experiences be a disadvantage when they come to study education?

The Examiner's Advice

In both the AS and the A level exams, there is a compulsory 20-mark Methods in Context question. For this, you must apply your knowledge of a given method to the study of the particular education issue specified in the question. For example, you might be asked to assess the strengths and limitations of using non-participant observation to investigate truancy from school.

To answer the Methods in Context question successfully, firstly you need to know the main strengths and limitations of the method. However, you must also link some of these strengths and limitations to the research characteristics of the particular education issue, such as truancy. That is, you must link features of the method to the kinds of things that might make the issue (truancy) particularly easy or difficult to study if using that method.

An example

The Topic you have just studied is a very useful place to start if you want to link the strengths and limitations of a method to the research characteristics of a particular education issue. Let's take an example and see how you can use some of the research characteristics of teachers, schools, classrooms etc mentioned in this Topic.

Education issue The study of pupil-teacher interaction in classrooms.

Method Non-participant observation.

Here are some ways you could make the links:

Research characteristic Teachers are used to being observed in the classroom by Ofsted, senior teachers and pupils.
Application of the method Because teachers are familiar with being observed, they may be willing to be studied in this way, especially as the researcher will not be participating in the lesson and so won't be a distraction to learning.

Research characteristic However, 'putting on an act' is part of the teacher's professional role when interacting with pupils, so the observer may find it hard to get behind the public face of the teacher's impression management.
Application of the method This is particularly problematic with non-participant observation because the researcher is unable to ask any probing questions of the teacher.

Research characteristic As a result of their age, pupils are more vulnerable than most groups in society.
Application of the method They may find it strange and unsettling if a new adult in the classroom is not participating in classroom activities. For example, this may mean pupils behave differently from normal, resulting in invalid data.

Research characteristic One of the benefits of studying interaction in classrooms is that the classroom is a relatively small social space.
Application of the method Therefore an observer can see much of what is happening. This is particularly so because they are not participating in classroom activities and so they can give their full attention to what they are observing.

Scientists use laboratory experiments to discover causes. But can we study society in a laboratory?

GETTING STARTED

Scientists often use experiments to test a hypothesis, usually in a laboratory where they can control the experiment. This is possible in the natural sciences due to the nature of the subject matter, such as chemicals, bacteria etc.

A Imagine you are conducting an experiment to test the hypothesis that heating water to a temperature of 100°C causes it to boil.

  1 What factors would you need to control when carrying out this experiment?

  2 Will you be able to measure the results of the experiment accurately?

  3 If another researcher were to carry out the same experiment, why might we expect them to get the same result?

B Imagine you are conducting a laboratory experiment in sociology to investigate the effects of violent video games on children's behaviour.

  1 In what ways might being studied in a laboratory affect the children's behaviour?

  2 What problems could there be in trying to measure their behaviour?

  3 What ethical issues might you face in carrying out experiments on children?

C Using your answers to A and B, briefly summarise the problems of using laboratory experiments in sociological research. Do such experiments have any advantages?

Learning objectives

After studying this Topic, you should:

- Know the similarities and differences between different types of experiments.
- Be able to evaluate the strengths and limitations of experiments.
- Be able to apply your understanding of experiments to the study of education.

EXPERIMENTS

In the natural sciences such as chemistry and physics, scientists set out to discover scientific laws of cause and effect. For example, physicists have discovered that an increase in the temperature of a gas will cause it to expand. The method favoured by natural scientists for discovering these laws is the laboratory experiment.

Sociologists have occasionally used the laboratory experiment as a way of studying human behaviour. In fact, however, this is just one of three different types of experimental method that sociologists sometimes use. The others are field experiments and the comparative method.

Laboratory experiments

An example will help to illustrate the basic principle of the experimental method. Suppose we want to discover what causes plants to grow. One way would be to take a set of identical plants and randomly divide them into two groups – an experimental group and a control group. We then treat them differently, as follows:

- **The experimental group:** with this group, we might vary the quantity of nutrients that they received, carefully measuring and recording any changes in the plants' size that we observe.
- **The control group:** with this group, we would keep the quantity of nutrients constant, also measuring and recording any changes in the size of the plants.

On comparing the results, we notice that the plants in the experimental group have grown more rapidly than the plants in the control group after receiving extra nutrients. In other words, we may have discovered a cause-and-effect relationship: nutrients cause growth.

In scientific terms, the nutrient is the independent variable (the causal factor) and the resulting growth is the effect or dependent variable (since it depends on the first variable, nutrition).

The logic of the experimental method is that the scientist manipulates (alters) the variables in which they are interested, in order to discover what effect they have. By following this method, the scientist can establish a cause-and-effect relationship. In turn, this will allow them to predict accurately what will happen in the future under specified conditions. In our example, the scientist will be able to predict what will happen when a certain quantity of nutrient is given to the plants.

Application
In an experiment to see whether mice develop cancer when exposed to cigarette smoke, is the smoke the dependent variable or the independent variable?

Reliability

Once an experiment has been conducted, other scientists can then replicate it. That is, they can repeat it exactly in every detail. The laboratory experiment is therefore highly reliable, producing the same results each time. There are two reasons for this:

- The original experimenter can specify precisely what steps were followed in the original experiment so other researchers can repeat these in future.
- It is a very detached method: the researcher merely manipulates the variables and records the results. The scientist's personal feelings and opinions have no effect on the conduct or outcome of the experiment.

The laboratory experiment therefore has major advantages as the method used to identify cause-and-effect relationships in the natural sciences. For this reason, we might expect positivist sociologists to use laboratory experiments, since they favour a scientific approach. Despite this, however, there are several reasons why such experiments are rarely used in sociology, even by positivists.

Practical problems

Society is a very complex phenomenon. In practice, it would be impossible to identify, let alone control, all the possible variables that might exert an influence on, say, a child's educational achievement or a worker's attitude to work.

Another practical problem is that the laboratory experiment cannot be used to study the past, since by definition it is impossible to control variables that were acting in the past rather than the present.

In addition, laboratory experiments usually only study small samples. This makes it very difficult to investigate large-scale social phenomena such as religions or voting patterns. The small-scale nature of laboratory experiments also reduces their representativeness.

Ethical problems

There are ethical (moral) objections to conducting experiments on human beings, at least under certain circumstances. These include lack of informed consent, deception and harm to the participants.

Lack of informed consent As a general principle, the researcher needs the informed consent of the research participants. However, this may be difficult to obtain from groups such as children or people with learning difficulties who may be unable to understand the nature and purpose of the experiment.

Deception It is also generally considered wrong to mislead people as to the nature of the experiment, as Stanley Milgram (1974) did in his famous studies of obedience to authority. Milgram lied to his research participants about the purpose of the research, telling them that they were assisting in an experiment on learning, in which they were ordered by the researcher to administer electric shocks when the learner failed to answer questions correctly.

In reality, however, the purpose of the experiment was to test people's willingness to obey orders to inflict pain. Unbeknown to Milgram's research participants, no electric shocks were actually used. Milgram found that 65 per cent of them were prepared to administer shocks of 450 volts.

Harm The experiment may also harm the participants. In Milgram's experiments, many research participants were observed to "sweat, stutter, tremble, groan, bite their lips and dig their nails into their flesh. Full-blown, uncontrollable seizures were observed for three subjects."

However, supporters of Milgram argue that his experiments can be justified ethically because they alert us to the dangers of blindly obeying authority figures. Moreover, the great majority of his participants (74 per cent) said afterwards that they had learned something of lasting value.

The Hawthorne Effect

A laboratory is not a normal or natural environment. It is thus likely that any behaviour in these conditions is also unnatural or artificial. If people do not behave in true-to-life ways, the experiment will not produce valid results.

If people know they are being studied, they may behave differently; for example, by trying to second-guess what the researcher wants them to do and acting accordingly. This will ruin the experiment, which depends on the subjects responding to the variables that the researcher introduces into the situation, not to the fact that they are being observed.

This problem has become known as the 'Hawthorne Effect' or 'experimental effect'. In 1927, Elton Mayo began research into factors affecting workers' productivity at the Western Electric Company's Hawthorne plant.

Working with five female volunteer workers who knew he was conducting an experiment, Mayo altered different variables such as lighting, heating, rest breaks and so on to see what effect they had on the volunteers' output.

Surprisingly, not only did output go up when he improved their working conditions, but it continued to rise even when conditions were worsened. Mayo concluded that the workers were not responding to the changes he was making in the experimental variables (such as the lighting), but simply to the fact that they were being studied and wished to please the experimenter.

> **Analysis and Evaluation**
> Explain why the Hawthorne Effect may lead to invalid data.

Free will

Interpretivist sociologists argue that humans are fundamentally different from plants, rocks and other phenomena studied by natural scientists. Unlike these objects, we have free will, consciousness and choice.

This means our behaviour cannot be explained in terms of cause and effect. Instead, it can only be understood in terms of the choices we freely make. In this view, the experimental method, with its search for causes, is therefore not an appropriate method for studying human beings.

Given these problems, sociologists have two alternatives to laboratory experiments. These are field experiments and the comparative method or 'thought experiment'.

Box 17	Positivism, interpretivism and experiments

Positivists favour the *laboratory* experiment in principle because it achieves their main goal of reliability:

- Careful control over experimental conditions and experimenter detachment produce reliable data because other researchers can replicate the experiment.
- It allows the researcher to identify and measure behaviour patterns quantitatively and to manipulate variables to establish cause-and-effect relationships.

However, positivists nonetheless recognise the shortcomings of laboratory experiments:

- It is often impossible or unethical to control the variables.
- Their small scale means that results may not be representative or generalisable.

For these reasons, positivists sometimes use the *comparative method* instead.

Interpretivists reject the laboratory experiment because it fails to achieve their main goal of validity. It is an artificial situation producing unnatural behaviour. Interpretivists favour more naturalistic *field* experiments, but positivists criticise this method for giving us less control over variables.

See Box 12 on page 94 for more about positivism, interpretivism and research methods.

Field experiments

A field experiment has two features that distinguish it from a laboratory experiment:

- It takes place in the subject's natural surroundings rather than in an artificial laboratory environment.
- Those involved are generally not aware that they are the subjects of an experiment, in which case there is no Hawthorne Effect.

The researcher manipulates one or more of the variables in the situation to see what effect it has on the unwitting subjects of the experiment. For example, in Rosenhan's (1973) 'pseudopatient' experiment, researchers presented themselves at 12 California mental hospitals, saying they had been hearing voices. Each was admitted and diagnosed as schizophrenic.

Once in hospital, they ceased to complain of hearing voices and acted normally. Nevertheless, hospital staff treated them all as if they were mentally ill. None was found out.

This suggests that it was not the patients' behaviour that led to them being treated as sick, but the label 'schizophrenic' itself that led staff to treat them in this way.

Evaluation Rosenhan's study shows the value of field experiments. They are more 'natural', valid and realistic, and they avoid the artificiality of laboratory experiments. However, the more realistic we make the situation, the less control we have over the variables that might be operating. If so, we cannot be certain that the causes we have identified are the correct ones.

Some critics also argue that field experiments are unethical, since they involve carrying out an experiment on their subjects without their knowledge or consent.

Activity   Research

Carrying out a field experiment

...go to www.sociology.uk.net

The comparative method

Unlike other experiments, the comparative method is carried out only in the mind of the sociologist. It is a 'thought experiment' and it does not involve the researcher actually experimenting on real people at all. However, like laboratory and field experiments, it too is designed to discover cause-and-effect relationships. It works as follows:

- Step 1: Identify two groups of people that are alike in all major respects except for the one variable we are interested in.
- Step 2: Then compare the two groups to see if this one difference between them has any effect.

Durkheim's study of suicide

An example of the comparative method is Emile Durkheim's (1897) classic study of suicide. Durkheim's hypothesis was that low levels of integration of individuals into social groups caused high rates of suicide. He argued that Catholicism produced higher levels of integration than Protestantism. From this, he therefore predicted that Protestants would have a higher suicide rate than Catholics.

Durkheim then tested his prediction by comparing the suicide rates of Catholics and Protestants who were similar in all other important respects (e.g., in terms of where they lived, whether they were married or single etc). His prediction was supported by the official statistics, which showed Catholics to have lower suicide rates.

Evaluation In seeking to discover cause-and-effect relationships, the comparative method has three advantages: it avoids artificiality; it can be used to study past events and it poses no ethical problems, such as harming subjects.

However, the comparative method gives the researcher even less control over variables than do field experiments, so we can be even less certain whether a thought experiment really has discovered the cause of something.

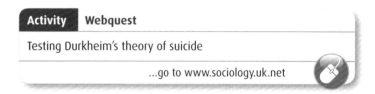

Activity   Webquest

Testing Durkheim's theory of suicide

...go to www.sociology.uk.net

Topic summary

In **laboratory** experiments, scientists manipulate variables to discover **laws** of cause and effect. Although they produce **reliable** data, experiments suffer from **practical** problems (e.g. they cannot be used to study the past), **ethical** problems of experimenting on humans, and are prone to the **Hawthorne Effect**. **Field experiments** and the **comparative method** are used as alternatives.

EXAMINING EXPERIMENTS

QuickCheck Questions

Check your answers at www.sociology.uk.net

1 In an experiment, is the independent variable the cause or the effect?
2 In a laboratory experiment, why is it important to have a control group?
3 Give two reasons why laboratory experiments may produce reliable data.
4 Why might it be necessary to deceive the subjects of an experiment in order for the experiment to work?
5 What ethical justification did supporters of Milgram give for deceiving his subjects?
6 Why do interpretivists argue that the experimental method is not appropriate for studying human beings?
7 Suggest two criticisms of field experiments.
8 Name one study that has used (a) a laboratory experiment; (b) a field experiment; (c) the comparative method.
9 Identify two advantages that the comparative method has over laboratory experiments.
10 Suggest two disadvantages of using the comparative method.

Questions to try

Whether or not you're taking the AS exams during your A level course, trying the AS questions below is a very good way of testing your knowledge and understanding and practising your skills in preparation for your A level exams.

AS questions

1 Outline two advantages of using the comparative method.   (4 marks)
2 Evaluate the practical, ethical and theoretical problems faced by sociologists when using laboratory experiments.   (16 marks)

A level question

3 Outline and explain two reasons why experiments are often associated with the positivist approach in sociology.   (10 marks)

The Examiner's Advice

Q2 Spend about 25 minutes on this question. Focus specifically on *laboratory* experiments. Deal with all three types of problem specified in the question.. Discuss practical problems such as identifying and controlling all potential variables, the small-scale nature of experiments, their artificiality and inability to study the past. Consider ethical problems including informed consent, right to withdraw, misleading participants, and risk of psychological and other damage (especially to vulnerable groups). Examine theoretical problems including validity, reliability and representativeness. Use evidence from studies such as Milgram. Explain why interpretivists reject the laboratory experiment as a research method. Evaluate these problems as you go through each problem rather than offering a list of strengths of laboratory experiments in a separate section at the end. For example, evaluate the ethical problem of misleading participants by arguing that this may be necessary and justifiable in order to prevent the Hawthorne Effect from distorting the results of the experiment.

Q3 Spend about 15 minutes on this question. Divide your time fairly equally between each reason. Don't write a separate introduction; just start on your first reason. Possible reasons include that experiments generate quantitative data, cause-and-effect relationships, hypothesis testing, reliability, objectivity and detachment, manipulation of variables etc. Describe each reason in some detail, explaining how it links to positivism. Do this by creating a chain of reasoning (see page 248). For example, in laboratory experiments the researcher can identify and manipulate variables that affect behaviour. The researcher can measure the effect that a particular variable has and establish a cause-and-effect relationship. Use concepts and issues such as those above.

METHODS IN CONTEXT
using experiments to investigate education

Sociologists sometimes use experiments to study issues such as:

- Teacher expectations
- Classroom interaction
- Labelling
- Pupils' self-concepts
- The self-fulfilling prophecy.

> Before reading this section, re-visit Topic 2 to refresh your understanding of what is special about researching education.

We shall focus here on the use of experiments to study the nature and impact of teacher expectations. Many sociologists claim that teachers' expectations of different groups of pupils have important effects, leading to labelling, the self-fulfilling prophecy and unequal achievement. Both field and laboratory experiments can be used to investigate these 'expectancy effects'. These effects can be positive or negative.

Laboratory experiments and teacher expectations

Several researchers have used laboratory experiments to investigate teacher expectations. For example, Harvey and Slatin (1976) examined whether teachers had preconceived ideas about pupils of different social classes.

Harvey and Slatin used a sample of 96 teachers. Each teacher was shown 18 photographs of children from different social class backgrounds. To control other variables, the photographs were equally divided in terms of gender and ethnicity. The teachers were asked to rate the children on their performance, parental attitudes to education, aspirations and so on.

Harvey and Slatin found that lower-class children were rated less favourably, especially by more experienced teachers. Teachers based their ratings on the similarities they perceived between the children in the photographs and pupils they had taught. This study indicates that teachers label pupils from different social classes and use these labels to pre-judge pupils' potential.

Such expectations may be passed on to pupils through non-verbal communication. Charkin et al (1975) used a sample of 48 university students who each taught a lesson to a ten-year-old boy.

- One third (the high expectancy group) were told that the boy was highly motivated and intelligent.

- One third (the low expectancy group) were told that he was poorly motivated with a low IQ.
- One third were given no information.

Charkin et al videoed the lessons and found that those in the high expectancy group made more eye contact and gave out more encouraging body language than the low expectancy group.

Mason (1973) looked at whether negative or positive expectations had the greater effect. Teachers were given positive, negative or neutral reports on a pupil. The teachers then observed video recordings of the pupil taking a test, watching to see if any errors were made. Finally, they were asked to predict the pupil's end of year attainment. Mason found that the negative reports had a much greater impact than the positive ones on the teachers' expectations.

ethical problems

Laboratory experiments that do not involve real pupils have fewer ethical problems than those that do. Neither Mason nor Harvey and Slatin used real pupils, so no child suffered any negative effects.

However, others, such as Charkin et al, have used real pupils and this raises ethical concerns. Young people's vulnerability and their more limited ability to understand what is happening mean that there are greater problems of deception, lack of informed consent and psychological damage. These ethical concerns are a major reason why laboratory experiments play only a limited role in educational research.

narrow focus

Laboratory experiments usually only examine one specific aspect of teacher expectations, such as body language for example. This can be useful because it allows the researcher to isolate and examine this variable more thoroughly.

However, this means that teacher expectations are not seen within the wider process of labelling and the self-fulfilling prophecy. For example, although Charkin et al identified the existence of positive and negative body language, they did not examine how it might then affect pupils' performance.

practical problems

There are practical problems in conducting experiments on teachers' expectations in schools. Schools are large, complex institutions in which many variables may affect teacher expectations.

For example, their expectations may be influenced by a wide range of variables such as class size, streaming, type of school and so on. In practice, it is impossible even to identify, let alone control, all the variables that might exert an influence on teachers' expectations.

Sociologists are often interested in the role of large-scale social factors and processes such as the impact of government policies on educational achievement, which cannot be studied in small-scale laboratory settings.

> **Analysis and Evaluation**
> Explain how you might use the comparative method as a way of researching the effect of a change in government policy on educational achievement levels.

artificiality

The artificiality of laboratory experiments may mean that they tell us little about the real world of education. For example:

- Charkin used university students rather than teachers.
- Harvey and Slatin used photographs of pupils rather than real pupils.

It is unlikely that university students behave in the same way as experienced teachers, and teachers' expectations are based on more than just pupils' appearance. For example, behaviour, accent and impressions of parents may all play a part.

Field experiments and teacher expectations

Concerns about laboratory experiments have led some sociologists to use field experiments located in real educational settings instead. However, these too have their limitations. Rosenthal and Jacobson's (1968) *'Pygmalion in the Classroom'* illustrates the difficulties of using field experiments to study teacher expectations.

They carried out their research in a California primary school they called 'Oak School'. Pupils were given an IQ test and teachers were told that this had enabled the researchers to identify the 20 per cent of pupils who were likely to 'spurt' in the next year. In reality, the test did no such thing and the pupils were, in fact, selected at random.

Rosenthal and Jacobson had two aims:

- Firstly, to plant in the minds of the teachers a particular set of expectations about their pupils.
- Secondly, to see if this had any effect on pupil performance.

Because the 'spurters' were selected at random, there was no reason to expect their performance would be any different to others in the class unless teacher expectations had an influence. 'Teacher expectations' was therefore identified as the independent variable in their experiment.

All the pupils were re-tested eight months later and then again after a further year. Over the first eight months, pupils gained on average eight IQ points, but the 'spurters' gained 12 points.

When this was broken down by age, the greatest improvement in performance was found in the youngest children, those aged 6-8. However, after a further year, this 'expectancy advantage' only seemed to have an effect among 10-11 year olds.

ethical problems

Field experiments in educational settings pose major ethical problems. The potential impact of the Oak School experiment on pupils is substantial. For example, while the 'spurters' benefited from the study, the remaining 80 per cent of pupils did not. Some may even have been held back educationally because they received less attention and encouragement from teachers.

Children have more rights today than in the 1960s and the legal duty of care that schools have today means that such an experiment is unlikely to be carried out now.

Field experiments work best when those involved are unaware that they are in an experiment. Yet this requires deception – in this case, Rosenthal and Jacobson had to deceive the teachers. Had they known the true nature of the IQ test and the purpose of the research, it would have been impossible to plant expectations in their minds and the experiment would have failed in its purpose.

reliability

Rosenthal and Jacobson's research design was relatively simple and therefore easy to repeat. Within five years of the original study, it had been repeated no less than 242 times. However, given all the many differences between school classes, for example in terms of the age of the pupils, teaching styles and so on, it is unlikely that the original could be replicated exactly.

validity

Rosenthal and Jacobson claimed that teachers' expectations were passed on through differences in the way they interacted with pupils. However, the researchers did not carry out any observation of classroom interaction, so they had no data to support this claim. Later studies that did use observation, such as Claiborn (1969), found no evidence of teacher expectations being passed on through classroom interaction.

broader focus

However, Rosenthal and Jacobson did look at the whole labelling process from teacher expectations through to their effect on pupils, rather than just examining single elements in isolation. Their study was also longitudinal, which allowed them to identify trends over time.

EXAMINING EXPERIMENTS IN CONTEXT

Question to try

For both the AS and the A level exams, you must answer a Methods in Context question.

Item A

Investigating teachers' labelling of pupils

Some sociologists argue that even though teachers have a professional duty to treat all pupils fairly, they often give negative labels to pupils based on the pupils' social class, gender and ethnicity. Pupils may respond to these labels in a variety of ways, including forming anti-school subcultures.

Sociologists may use experiments to investigate teachers' labelling of pupils. One problem is that laboratory experiments are not naturalistic and this can affect the way teachers and pupils act. With covert field experiments, however, the real purpose of the research is not known and this may help to overcome the Hawthorne Effect. Another issue is whether a particular statement or action on the part of a teacher is actually an example of unfairly attaching a label to a pupil. This is very much open to interpretation by researchers.

AS and A level question

1   Applying material from Item A and your knowledge of research methods, evaluate the strengths and limitations of experiments for the study of teachers' labelling of pupils.

(20 marks)

The Examiner's Advice

Q1 Spend about 30 minutes on this. The question requires you to apply your knowledge of experiments to the study of the particular issue of teachers' labelling of pupils. It is not enough simply to discuss the strengths and limitations of experiments in general. Use Item A to help you. For example, it suggests that one research characteristic of teachers' labelling of pupils is that teachers have a professional duty to treat pupils fairly and, since labelling involves judging pupils on their social rather than their educational characteristics, this could be seen as unprofessional. Therefore, teachers are unlikely to label pupils within sight or hearing of a researcher unless they are being studied

covertly, so in this respect covert field experiments could be very effective. You should link other research characteristics of teachers' labelling of pupils to the strengths and limitations of different kinds of experiments. For example, the impact of labelling on a pupil's self-esteem is something that builds up over a period of time and a 'one-off' lab experiment may therefore not be a realistic indicator. Other research characteristics include greater vulnerability of negatively labelled pupils, problems of isolating variables, access to schools and pupils etc. You should link these characteristics to particular strengths or limitations of the method.

An example

In your answer you should connect the strengths and limitations of experiments to the research characteristics of teacher expectations. Here's an example paragraph.

'Item A suggests that whether or not a particular action by a teacher is an example of negative or positive labelling is open to interpretation. A field experiment is particularly useful here because the researcher can observe first-hand the body language as well as the verbal interaction of both teacher and pupil. On the other hand, it would be very difficult to re-create the dynamics of a classroom in an artificial laboratory setting, where teachers may be on their best behaviour because they are aware of being studied, so an experiment of this kind would lack validity.'

Questionnaires can reach large numbers of people.

GETTING STARTED

A Complete the following questionnaire on social class and educational achievement:

1 What is your father's occupation?

  a Higher professional

  b Lower professional

  c Intermediate

  d Lower supervisory

  e Routine or semi-routine

  f Unemployed/not classified

2 What sort of house do you live in?

  a Detached

  b Semi-detached

  c Terraced

3 How many bedrooms are there in your house?

  a 1   **b** 2

  c 3   **d** 4 or more

4 Did your parents go to university?

  a Yes   **b** No

5 Don't you agree that everyone ought to go to university?

  a Yes   **b** No

B Now answer the following questions.

1 How easy did you find it to answer the questions – did it take long?

2 Did you answer honestly? Would everybody? If not, why not?

3 Note any problems you can find with the way the questions are worded.

4 Why might someone answer the same question differently if asked face-to-face rather than in a written questionnaire?

C Using your answers to questions B1 to B4, briefly summarise the positive and negative points about questionnaires.

Learning objectives

After studying this Topic, you should:

- Know the different types of question used in questionnaires and the different methods of administering them.

- Be able to evaluate the strengths and limitations of questionnaires.

- Be able to apply your understanding of questionnaires to the study of education.

QUESTIONNAIRES

An obvious way of gathering data about people is to ask them questions, for example by using written (or self-completion) questionnaires. These can be distributed to people at home and returned by post or in person, e-mailed or completed and collected on the spot. Questionnaires ask respondents (the people who complete them) to provide answers to pre-set questions. There are two types of question:

Closed-ended Respondents must choose from a limited range of possible answers that the researcher has decided in advance, such as 'Yes', 'No' or 'Don't know', rather like multiple-choice questions in an exam.

Each possible answer is given a code, enabling researchers to quantify (count) the number of respondents choosing each of the available answers.

Open-ended questions Respondents are free to give whatever answer they wish, in their own words, and without any pre-selected choices being offered by the researcher.

Advantages of questionnaires

The popularity of questionnaires is undoubtedly due to the considerable range of advantages they offer to researchers.

1 Practical advantages

Questionnaires offer several major practical advantages:

- They are a quick and cheap means of gathering large amounts of data from large numbers of people, widely spread geographically, especially if a postal or online questionnaire is used. For example, Helen Connor and Sara Dewson (2001) posted nearly 4,000 questionnaires to students at 14 higher education institutions around the country in their study of the factors influencing the decisions of working-class students to go to university.
- There is no need to recruit and train interviewers or observers to collect the data, because respondents complete and return the questionnaires themselves.
- The data is usually easy to quantify, particularly where pre-coded, closed-ended questions are used, and can be processed quickly by computer to reveal the relationships between different variables.

2 Reliability

Questionnaires are seen as a reliable method of collecting data. That is, if repeated by another researcher, the questionnaire should give similar results to those gained by the first researcher. There are two reasons for this:

- When the research is repeated, a questionnaire identical to the original one is used, so new respondents are asked exactly the same questions, in the same order, with the same choice of answers, as the original respondents.
- With postal or online questionnaires, unlike with interviews, there is no researcher present to influence the respondent's answers (different researchers might influence respondents to give different answers).

In other words, the questionnaire is a fixed yardstick that can be used by any researcher to obtain the same results (provided that later researchers use a similar sample). This means one researcher's study can easily be repeated and checked by another.

The reliability of questionnaires also means that if we do find differences in the answers that respondents give, we can assume that these are the result of real differences between the respondents and not simply the result of different questions.

A related advantage is that they allow comparisons, both over time and between different societies. By asking the same questions, we can compare the results obtained in two different societies or at two different times.

3 Hypothesis testing

Questionnaires are particularly useful for testing hypotheses about cause-and-effect relationships between different variables. For instance, using the example of educational achievement, analysis of respondents' answers could show whether there is a correlation between children's achievement levels and family size. We might find, for example, that most low achievers come from large families.

From this analysis, we can make statements about the possible causes of low achievement and predictions about which children are most likely to underachieve.

Because questionnaires enable us to identify possible causes, they are very attractive to positivist sociologists, who take a scientific approach and seek to discover laws of cause and effect (see Box 18).

4 Detachment and objectivity

Positivists also favour questionnaires because they are a detached and objective (unbiased) method, where the sociologist's personal involvement with their respondents is kept to a minimum. For example, postal questionnaires are completed at a distance and involve little or no personal contact with respondents. For this reason, positivists see them as a good way of maintaining detachment and objectivity.

5 Representativeness

Because questionnaires can collect information from a large number of people, the results stand a better chance of being truly representative of the wider population than with other methods that study only very small numbers of people.

In addition, researchers who use questionnaires tend to pay more attention to the need to obtain a representative sample. For these reasons, the findings of questionnaires are more likely to allow us to make accurate generalisations about the wider population from which the sample was drawn.

6 Ethical issues

Questionnaires pose fewer ethical problems than most other research methods. Although questionnaires may ask intrusive or sensitive questions, respondents are generally under no obligation to answer them.

Nevertheless, researchers should gain respondents' informed consent, guarantee their anonymity and make it clear that they have a right not to answer any of the questions that they do not wish to.

Disadvantages of questionnaires

Despite their advantages, questionnaires have been subject to some sharp criticisms, especially in relation to the validity of the data they produce.

1 Practical problems

The data from questionnaires tends to be limited and superficial. This is because they need to be fairly brief, since most respondents are unlikely to complete and return a long, time-consuming questionnaire. This limits the amount of information that can be gathered from each respondent.

Similarly, although questionnaires are a relatively cheap means of gathering data, it may sometimes be necessary to offer incentives – such as entry into a prize draw – to persuade respondents to complete the form. This will add to the cost.

With postal and online questionnaires, there are two additional problems. The researcher cannot be sure:

- Whether the potential respondent has actually received the questionnaire.
- Whether a returned questionnaire was actually completed by the person to whom it was addressed.

2 Low response rate

Although questionnaires have the potential to collect data from large, representative samples, very low response rates can be a major problem, especially with postal questionnaires. This is because few of those who receive a questionnaire bother to complete and return it. For example, Shere Hite's (1991) study of 'love, passion and emotional violence' in America sent out 100,000 questionnaires, but only 4.5 per cent of them were returned.

A higher response rate can be obtained if follow-up questionnaires are sent and if questionnaires are collected by hand. However, this adds to the cost and time.

The problem of non-response is sometimes caused by faulty questionnaire design. For example, a questionnaire that

uses complex language may only be completed by the well educated.

The danger with a low response rate is that those who return their questionnaires may be different from those who don't. For example, busy people in full-time work may fail to respond, whereas the unemployed or socially isolated with time on their hands may be more likely to fill in their questionnaires. Similarly, those with strong views on a subject are more likely to respond than those who have little knowledge or interest in it. If the respondents are different from the non-respondents, this will produce distorted and unrepresentative results, from which no accurate generalisations can be made.

> **Analysis and Evaluation**
>
> 1 Why should a sociologist be concerned if their questionnaire had as low a response rate as Hite's?
>
> 2 Websites sometimes contain questionnaires that readers are invited to complete and return. Why might the responses that the website receives be unrepresentative of the general population?

3 Inflexibility

Questionnaires are a very inflexible method. Once the questionnaire has been finalised, the researcher is stuck with the questions they have decided to ask and cannot explore any new areas of interest should they come up during the research.

This contrasts with more flexible methods such as unstructured interviews, where the researcher can simply ask new questions if they seem relevant.

4 Questionnaires as snapshots

Questionnaires are snapshots. They give a picture of social reality at only one moment in time: the moment when the respondent answers the questions.

Questionnaires therefore fail to produce a fully valid picture because they do not capture the way people's attitudes and behaviour change. This snapshot contrasts with the moving image of social life that participant observation can provide.

5 Detachment

Interpretivists such as Cicourel (1968) argue that data from questionnaires lacks validity and does not give a true picture of what has been studied. They argue that we can only gain a valid picture by using methods that allow us to get close to the subjects of the study and share their meanings. Ideally, the method should enable us to put ourselves in the subject's place and see the world through their eyes.

Questionnaires fail to do this because they are the most detached of all primary methods. For example, postal questionnaires involve no direct contact between researcher and respondent.

This lack of contact means there is no way to clarify what the questions mean to the respondent or to deal with misunderstandings. There is no way of knowing whether the respondent and researcher both interpret the questions or the answers in the same way.

6 Lying, forgetting and 'right answerism'

All methods that gather data by asking questions depend ultimately on their respondents' willingness and ability to provide full and accurate answers. Problems of validity are created when respondents give answers that are not full or frank.

For example, respondents may lie, forget, not know, not understand (and not wish to admit that they don't understand), or try to please or second-guess the researcher. Some may give 'respectable' answers they feel they ought to give, rather than tell the truth.

Box 18	Positivism, interpretivism and questionnaires

Positivists favour questionnaires because they achieve the main positivist goals of reliability, generalisability and representativeness:

- Standardised questions and answers produce reliable data because other researchers can replicate the questionnaire.
- Pre-coded responses allow us to produce quantitative data, identify and measure behaviour patterns, and establish cause-and-effect relationships.
- Questionnaires are often large scale and thus more representative.

Interpretivists reject the use of questionnaires because they impose the researcher's framework of ideas on respondents. This tells us little about the meanings held by social actors. Questionnaires fail to achieve the main interpretivist goal of validity.

See Box 12 on page 94 for more about positivism, interpretivism and research methods.

These problems put questionnaires at a disadvantage when compared with observational methods, since the observer can see for himself or herself what the subjects actually do, rather than what they *say* they do.

7 Imposing the researcher's meanings

A valid method is one that gives a truthful picture of people's meanings and experiences. Yet interpretivists argue that questionnaires are more likely to impose the researcher's own meanings than to reveal those of the respondent.

- By choosing which questions to ask, the researcher, not the respondent, has already decided what is important.
- If we use closed-ended questions, respondents then have to try to fit their views into the ones on offer. If they feel some other answer to be important, they have no opportunity of giving it, thus producing an invalid picture of their reality.
- On the other hand, if we use open-ended questions, respondents are free to answer as they please, but when the researcher comes to code them to produce quantitative data, similar but non-identical answers may get lumped together into the same category.

As Marten Shipman (1997) says, when the researcher's categories are not the respondent's categories, 'pruning and bending' of the data is inevitable. The questionnaire imposes a straitjacket that distorts the respondents' meanings and undermines the validity of the data.

Analysis and Evaluation

In Schofield's (1965) research on the sexual behaviour of teenagers. a young girl was asked in a questionnaire, 'Are you a virgin?' She answered, 'No, not yet'. Identify the problems of questionnaire research that this suggests.

Topic summary

Questionnaires are lists of written questions, usually **closed-ended** and often posted. They can gather data on **large numbers** cheaply and quickly.

Positivists favour them because they are **reliable** and objective. However, **low response rates** can make findings **unrepresentative**.

Interpretivists claim they **lack validity**: they are inflexible, superficial snapshots and don't give a true account of respondents' meanings.

EXAMINING QUESTIONNAIRES

QuickCheck Questions

Check your answers at www.sociology.uk.net

1　What advantages are there to using closed-ended questions?
2　Why do critics argue that questionnaires lack flexibility?
3　Give three reasons why positivists prefer questionnaires.
4　Why are questionnaires seen as a detached and objective research method?

5　Suggest one reason why detachment might be a disadvantage in research.
6　Suggest reasons why questionnaires often have a low response rate.
7　In what ways might questionnaires impose the researcher's meanings on respondents?

Questions to try

Whether or not you're taking the AS exams during your A level course, trying the AS questions below is a very good way of testing your knowledge and understanding and practising your skills in preparation for your A level exams.

Item A　Questionnaires are widely used in sociological research. Positivist researchers in particular see mailed questionnaires as a very effective research tool because they are a reliable method that generates representative data. The standardised, pre-coded questions used in questionnaires generate the quantitative data that positivists require.

However, interpretivist sociologists argue that the data produced is of little value because it lacks validity.

AS questions
1　Outline two ways of improving the rate of response to questionnaires.　(4 marks)
2　Evaluate the strengths of using mailed questionnaires.　(16 marks)
A level question
3　Applying material from Item A and your knowledge, evaluate the claim that what questionnaires gain in reliability and representativeness, they lose in validity.　(20 marks)

The Examiner's Advice

Q2 Spend about 25 minutes on this. The question asks you to focus on mailed questionnaires so make sure part of your answer deals with the 'mailed' dimension and not just questionnaires in general. Discuss practical strengths such as that they are a quick, cheap way to gather a large amount of information from a wide geographical area, data is easy to quantify and process, and there is no need for trained interviewers. There are few ethical problems, because those receiving questionnaires can choose whether or not to complete and return them and there is no face-to-face interaction involved. Examine theoretical strengths such as reliability, representativeness, detachment and objectivity. Use concepts such as these and examples of issues that mailed questionnaires are particularly appropriate for the study of. Explain why positivists find mailed questionnaires attractive. Evaluate these strengths. Do this as you go through each strength rather than offer a list of limitations in a separate section at the end.

Q3 Spend about 30 minutes on this. Be clear about definitions of validity, reliability and representativeness. Use the debate between positivism and interpretivism as a context for your answer. Explain why positivists value reliability and representativeness, and why questionnaires are seen as producing reliable and representative data, e.g. research can be repeated using an identical questionnaire and mailed or emailed questionnaires can reach a geographically widespread research sample. Explain why interpretivists value validity, and why they feel questionnaires fail to deliver it. Evaluate the view, e.g. by considering why questionnaires might not be as reliable and representative as positivists claim. For example, low response rates may undermine representativeness. Use concepts and issues such as those mentioned above and quantitative and qualitative data, generalisation, values in research, hypothesis testing, sociology as a science, objectivity and detachment, superficiality etc. Use studies such as Hite, and Connor and Dewson, and develop points noted in Item A.

METHODS IN CONTEXT
using questionnaires to investigate education

Sociologists sometimes use questionnaires to study issues such as:

- Subject and university choice
- Bullying and the experience of schooling
- Achievement and school factors
- Parental attitudes to education.

> Before reading this section, re-visit Topic 2 to refresh your understanding of what is special about researching education.

Operationalisation of concepts

Operationalising concepts involves turning abstract ideas into a measurable form. This can be particularly difficult when creating a questionnaire for pupils. Because their grasp of abstract concepts is generally less than that of adults, it may be more difficult to turn sociological ideas such as 'deferred gratification' or 'cultural capital' into language that pupils will understand.

This may produce answers that are based on respondents' misunderstanding of what the questions mean. Alternatively, there is a danger that the sociologist may have to over-simplify the questions so much that they cease to have any sociological value.

Samples and sampling frames

Schools routinely keep lists of pupils, staff and parents. These can provide accurate sampling frames from which the sociologist can draw a representative sample. Schools also

Oxford University

▲ What problems might there be in using questionnaires to study students' reasons for their choice of university?

have ready-made opportunity samples of pupils and teachers, for example in the form of classes and teaching departments.

However, schools may not keep lists that reflect the researcher's interests. For example, the sociologist may wish to take a representative sample of pupils of a particular ethnic group, but the school may not keep lists of pupils sorted by ethnic origin, so there is no sampling frame available from which to draw the sample. Even where the relevant sampling frame does exist, schools may deny access to such confidential information.

Distributing questionnaires in schools is a fairly easy way to access a large number of potential respondents. However, the researcher will first need the school's permission to give them out.

Parents are harder than pupils or teachers to locate and contact, so using the school to distribute questionnaires is an effective way to overcome this difficulty. For example, the school can give out questionnaires for pupils to take home for their parents to complete.

Younger children in particular are more open to peer group pressure and it is difficult to prevent pupils who are completing questionnaires that have been distributed in class from discussing responses.

A questionnaire that does not involve the researcher being present when it is completed may help to overcome the problem of status differences between adult researcher and younger respondent. On the other hand, a questionnaire usually has the appearance of a formal document that pupils may find off-putting.

Access and response rate

Response rates for questionnaires are often low. Schools may be reluctant to allow sociologists to distribute questionnaires because of the disruption to lessons that it may cause, or because they object to the researcher's chosen topic. For example, some schools might object to questionnaires about under-age sexual activity.

However, when questionnaires are conducted in schools, response rates can often be higher than in other areas. This is because, once the head has given their consent and put their authority behind the research, teachers and pupils may be under pressure to cooperate.

Similarly, the head may authorise time to be taken out of lessons so that the questionnaires can be completed. The higher response rate may produce more representative data from which generalisations can be drawn.

Another reason why response rates might be higher is that pupils, teachers and parents are accustomed to completing questionnaires issued by the school, such as student satisfaction surveys. On the other hand, teachers are often too busy to complete a lengthy questionnaire and this may reduce the response rate.

Practical issues

Questionnaires are very useful for gathering large quantities of basic factual educational information quickly and cheaply. For example, Michael Rutter (1979) used questionnaires to collect large quantities of data from 12 inner London secondary schools.

From this, Rutter was able to correlate achievement, attendance and behaviour with variables such as school size, class size and number of staff. It would have been very difficult to do this with more labour-intensive methods such as interviewing or observation.

However, the data generated by questionnaires is often limited and superficial. In Rutter's study, the data provided correlations between variables such as class size and achievement, but not explanations for these correlations.

There are particular problems in using questionnaires to study children. Written questionnaires involve participants being able to read and understand the questions. Thus they are unsuitable for those who cannot read reasonably well, such as young children or those with certain learning difficulties.

> **Analysis and Evaluation**
>
> Suggest three problems you might have in designing a questionnaire to be completed by seven-year-old pupils on the subject of school rules.

Children generally have a shorter attention span than adults and so questionnaires need to be relatively brief if they are to stand a chance of being completed. This limits the amount of information that can be gathered.

Children's life experiences are narrower and their recall different from those of adults. This may mean that pupils, particularly those of primary school age, do not actually 'know the answers'. Consequently, questionnaires may be of little value.

Schools have very active informal communication channels. Word of the researcher's presence may spread rapidly on the 'grapevine'. If the questionnaire is delivered class by class, its purpose and questions may become known throughout the school long before all pupils or teachers have been given it. This may affect the responses given by later participants and so reduce the validity of the data.

Teachers are well-educated professionals who will almost certainly have had experience of completing questionnaires. They may well be able to analyse the pattern of questions and recognise the researcher's aims and intentions. They may then adjust their answers accordingly. This will result in invalid data.

Teachers are very busy professionals and may not cooperate fully if the questionnaire is a lengthy document that will take a long time to complete.

Anonymity and detachment

Questionnaires can be particularly useful when researching sensitive educational issues such as bullying, where their anonymity may overcome pupils' embarrassment or fear of retribution from bullies.

As a result, response rates may be higher and pupils may be more likely to reveal details of their experience of being bullied. This may produce more valid data than would a face-to-face structured interview, for example.

However, much depends on whether pupils are reassured that their anonymity will be safeguarded. Yet this reassurance may be difficult to achieve with such a detached method as a questionnaire, where there is little or no personal contact with the researcher.

Interpretivist sociologists emphasise the importance of developing rapport with research participants and so they reject questionnaires as a means of researching pupils. Because the lack of contact with respondents makes rapport difficult to establish, young people may be less likely to give full and honest responses.

Questionnaires are formal, official-looking documents and pupils may equate them with school and teacher authority – especially if they are completed in class, like a test. As a result, some pupils, particularly those in anti-school subcultures, may refuse to cooperate or to take the activity seriously. This will result in incomplete or invalid data.

Compared with face-to-face forms of research such as interviews, it is easy to make questionnaires anonymous. As a result, teachers may feel able to set aside concerns about their careers and so give more honest answers to sensitive questions about issues such as their attitudes to pupils.

> **Activity** **Research**
>
> What factors affect students' decisions about university?
>
> ...go to www.sociology.uk.net

EXAMINING QUESTIONNAIRES IN CONTEXT

Question to try

For both the AS and the A level exams, you must answer a Methods in Context question.

Item A

Investigating material deprivation in pupils' home backgrounds

Material deprivation is a widespread problem throughout the United Kingdom today. Some pupils experience material deprivation in their home background and this can have a negative effect on their educational achievement. For example, a lack of income with which to buy educational resources, or having to live in cramped conditions, can affect academic performance. Some parents may feel that they have failed if they cannot provide adequate income for their family.

Sociologists may use questionnaires to investigate material deprivation in pupils' home backgrounds. To use questionnaires effectively, sociologists need to identify and gain responses from parents, but accessing a suitable database of contacts may prove difficult. Parents may also not be willing to discuss such a sensitive issue as material deprivation. On the other hand, substantial quantitative data may be generated by using questionnaires, allowing sociologists to identify patterns and draw comparisons.

AS and A level question

1   Applying material from Item A and your knowledge of research methods, evaluate the strengths and limitations of questionnaires for the study of material deprivation in pupils' home backgrounds.   (20 marks)

The Examiner's Advice

Q1 Spend about 30 minutes on this question. It requires you to apply your knowledge of questionnaires to the study of the particular issue of material deprivation in pupils' home backgrounds. It is not enough simply to discuss the strengths and limitations of questionnaires in general. Use Item A to help you. For example, it suggests that one research characteristic of material deprivation in pupils' home backgrounds is that parents may feel that they have failed if they cannot provide adequate income for their family. As a result, they may not be entirely honest in their answers and may exaggerate their real level of income, or play down its effects on their children's education. With a self-completion questionnaire, the researcher cannot check the accuracy and validity of their responses. You should link other research characteristics of material deprivation in pupils' home backgrounds to the strengths and limitations of questionnaires. For example, there are some clear indicators of a family's material wealth – income, possessions, eligibility for free school meals, type of house etc – and these are fairly easy to operationalise in written questionnaires. Other research characteristics include the literacy capabilities of different groups of parents, the usefulness of the school in distributing questionnaires, concerns over the intentions behind the questionnaire etc. You should link these to particular strengths or limitations of the method.

An example

In your answer you should connect the strengths and limitations of questionnaires to the research characteristics of material deprivation and underachievement. Here's an example paragraph.

'Item A suggests that this is a society-wide issue. Written questionnaires therefore seem like a good method to use because they can be mailed out to a large, geographically dispersed sample. However, questionnaires often lack representativeness because only certain types of parent return them. For example, parents in materially deprived households may feel that acknowledging their poverty in writing reflects badly on themselves as parents and so they may not respond. However, using questionnaires to research material deprivation and achievement can bring a high response rate if poor parents think their children will benefit, and also because they are used to filling in forms from school.'

What would be the difficulties and the advantages of conducting group interviews with young children like these?

GETTING STARTED

1 Imagine you are being interviewed by a stranger about a personal topic you find difficult to speak about.

   a Make a note of some of the problems you might face when discussing this topic with a stranger. Would you be more comfortable with someone you know? Give your reasons.

   b Are there any ways of overcoming any of these problems?

2 Another way to investigate a difficult topic would be to use a questionnaire that you fill in without having to talk to anyone. Revisit Topic 4 on the advantages and disadvantages of questionnaires, and compare them with using a conversation as a means of obtaining data.

Learning objectives

After studying this Topic, you should:

- Understand the differences between structured and unstructured interviews.

- Be able to evaluate the strengths and limitations of the different types of interview.

- Be able to apply your understanding of interviews to the study of education.

INTERVIEWS

While social surveys can be conducted by means of written questionnaires, an alternative that is widely used by sociologists is to conduct interviews instead. These can be carried out either face-to-face or by telephone.

Although both written questionnaires and interviews gather data by asking people questions, the obvious difference is that interviews involve a social interaction between the interviewer and interviewee, whereas with written questionnaires the respondent usually answers the questions without the involvement of the researcher. For example, in a postal questionnaire, there will normally be no direct contact between the researcher and respondent – the research takes place at a distance.

Types of interview

Sociologists use different types of interview in their research. These range from completely structured to completely unstructured interviews. The difference between them lies in how free the interviewer is to vary the questions and the way they are asked:

- **Structured or formal interviews** are very similar to a questionnaire: the interviewer is given strict instructions on how to ask the questions. The interview is conducted in the same standardised way each time, asking each interviewee precisely the same questions, word for word, in the same order, tone of voice and so on.

- **Unstructured or informal interviews** (also called discovery interviews) are like a guided conversation. The interviewer has complete freedom to vary the questions, their wording, order and so on from one interview to the next, pursuing whatever line of questioning seems appropriate at the time, asking follow-up questions or probing more deeply.

- **Semi-structured interviews** lie in between these two extremes. Each interview has the same set of questions in common, but the interviewer can also probe for more information. For example, Aaron Cicourel and John Kitsuse (1963) always followed up their questions with 'How do you mean?' as a way of gaining more information. Additional questions can be asked where the interviewer thinks it relevant.

- **Group interviews** Most interviews are one-to-one, but some are group interviews, with up to a dozen or so people being interviewed together. Paul Willis (1977) used group interviews as part of his research into the 'lads' and schooling.

Focus groups are a form of group interview in which the researcher asks the group to discuss certain topics (such as how pupils feel about the school) and records their views. Group interviews have their own particular strengths and limitations, as Box 19 shows.

Box 19 — Group interviews

By comparison with one-to-one interviews, group interviews and focus group discussions have certain distinctive strengths and limitations.

Strengths

- Participants may feel more comfortable being with others and thus are more likely to open up.
- In a discussion, participants often throw ideas around the group, stimulating each other's thinking. This produces richer and more reflective data.
- They can be a useful way of generating initial ideas that can be followed up in later research.
- The researcher can combine questioning with the opportunity to observe group dynamics and norms.

Limitations

- One or two individuals may dominate the discussion, inhibiting others from contributing.
- Much depends on the researcher's ability to keep the group focused on the discussion topic.
- Peer group pressure to conform to group norms may lead to participants not saying what they really think.
- Data generated from group interaction is more complex and difficult to analyse.

Analysis and Evaluation

1 Which type of interview – structured or unstructured – do you think would:
   a be quicker to conduct
   b give you more insight?

2 Why might the results from two unstructured interviews on a given subject be harder to compare than the results from two structured interviews on that subject?

Structured interviews

Structured interviews are like questionnaires: both involve asking people a set of prepared questions. In both cases, the questions are usually closed-ended with pre-coded answers. The main difference is that in the interview, the questions are read out and the answers filled in by a trained interviewer rather than by the interviewee.

This basic similarity between structured interviews and questionnaires means that they share many of the same advantages and disadvantages. Where there are differences, these often come from the fact that structured interviews involve interaction between researcher and interviewee.

1 Practical issues

- Training interviewers is relatively straightforward and inexpensive, since all they are really required to do is follow a set of instructions. However, this is more costly than simply posting or emailing questionnaires to people.
- Surveys that use structured interviews can cover quite large numbers of people with relatively limited resources because they are quick and fairly cheap to administer (see Box 20). However, they still cannot match the potentially huge numbers reached by postal questionnaires.
- Structured interviews are suitable for gathering straightforward factual information such as a person's age or job (see Box 20).
- The results are easily quantified because they use closed-ended questions with coded answers. This makes them suitable for hypothesis testing.

2 Response rate

The large numbers who can be surveyed using structured interviews increase the chances of obtaining a representative sample of the population. Although the numbers that can be studied are lower than for questionnaires, structured interviews generally have a higher response rate. For example, of the 987 people Young and Willmott approached for their main sample, only 54 refused to be interviewed. This may be because people find it harder to turn down a face-to-face request, and some may welcome the opportunity to talk.

Response rates can be increased if the interviewer can make several call backs to pursue those who fail to respond initially. However, this increases the cost of the survey. High response rates help to produce a more representative result and therefore a better basis for making generalisations.

On the other hand, as with questionnaires, those with the time or willingness to be interviewed may be untypical (for example, they may be lonely or have time on their hands). If so, this will produce unrepresentative data and undermine the validity of any generalisations made from the findings.

Box 20	Using structured interviews

Young and Willmott (1962) used structured interviews in their research into the extended family in east London:

'The general sample being much larger – 933 people – we could not do the interviewing ourselves; these interviews were carried out by other interviewers we employed for the purpose. The interviews were formal and standardised, the questions precise and factual, with a limited range of alternative answers, on straightforward topics like people's age, job, religion, birthplace etc. The interviewers' task was to ring the appropriate code-number opposite the answer they received or, at a few points in the interview, to write in a fairly short and simple reply. Each interview took between about ten minutes and half an hour, depending on the number of relatives possessed by a particular informant.'

3 Reliability

If a method is reliable, another sociologist could repeat the research and get the same results. Structured interviews are seen as reliable because it is easy for the researcher to standardise and control them. They can ensure that each interview is conducted in precisely the same way, with the same questions, in the same order, with the same wording and tone of voice.

If each interviewer conducts every interview in exactly the same way, then any other researcher following the same interview procedures should get very similar results. The structured interview provides a 'recipe' for repeating the research: as in cookery, anyone who follows the recipe ought to get the same result. The fact that all interviewees are asked exactly the same questions also means that we can compare their answers easily to identify similarities and differences.

4 Validity

A valid method is one that provides a true, authentic picture of the topic being researched. Critics of structured interviews argue that, like questionnaires, they often produce a false picture of the subjects they are trying to study.

- Structured interviews usually use closed-ended questions that restrict interviewees to choosing from a limited number of pre-set answers. If none of these answers fits what the interviewee really wishes to say, the data obtained will be invalid.
- Structured interviews give interviewers very little freedom to explain questions or clarify misunderstandings. For example, they may be given one alternative form of words to use if the interviewee doesn't understand the question, but if this fails to do the trick the interviewer usually has to move on to the next question.

- People may lie or exaggerate. These responses will produce false data.

The interview is a social interaction and so there is always a risk that the interaction between interviewer and interviewee will influence the answers given. For example, gender and ethnic differences can affect the answers, as can the interviewee's desire to be seen in a favourable light (see page 130).

5 Inflexibility

Like self-completed questionnaires, structured interviews suffer from the inflexibility that comes from having to draw up the questions in advance. In doing so, the researcher has already decided what is important – yet this may not coincide with what the interviewee thinks is important.

As a result, the findings may lack validity because they do not reflect the interviewee's concerns and priorities. In particular, establishing the questions beforehand and then sticking to them rigidly will make it impossible to pursue any interesting leads that emerge in the course of the interviews, thereby losing valuable insights.

Also like questionnaires, structured interviews are merely snapshots taken at one moment in time, so they fail to capture the flowing, dynamic nature of social life – unlike participant observation, for example.

6 Feminist criticisms

Hilary Graham (1983) argues that survey methods such as questionnaires and structured interviews are patriarchal and give a distorted, invalid picture of women's experience. She argues that:

- The researcher, not the female interviewee, is in control of the interview and decides the line of questioning to be followed. This mirrors women's subordination in wider society.
- Survey methods treat women as isolated individuals rather than seeing them in the context of the power relationships that oppress them.
- Surveys impose the researcher's categories on women, making it difficult for them to express their experiences of oppression, thus concealing the unequal power relationships between the sexes.

These feminist criticisms are similar to those put forward by interpretivist sociologists, who argue that structured interviews fail to reveal how the interviewee sees their situation. Graham argues that sociologists need to use methods that allow the researcher to understand women's behaviour, attitudes and meanings. She therefore advocates the use of direct observation instead of structured interviews.

Other feminists favour unstructured interviews, which enable the researcher to build a more equal and collaborative relationship based on trust, empathy and support.

Unstructured interviews

Whereas a structured interview follows a standardised format, in an unstructured interview the interviewer has complete freedom to vary the interview. Supporters argue that this brings a number of important advantages.

Advantages of unstructured interviews

While structured interviews are criticised for their lack of validity, unstructured interviews are widely seen as a way of gathering valid data, enabling researchers to get a deeper understanding of the interviewee's world. There are several reasons for this, which we examine below.

1 Rapport and sensitivity

The informality of unstructured interviews allows the interviewer to develop a rapport (relationship of trust and understanding) with the interviewee. This is more likely to put the interviewee at their ease and encourage them to open up than a formal structured interview.

A good example of this is the work of William Labov (1973). When using a formal interview technique to study the language of black American children, Labov found that they appeared to be tongue-tied and 'linguistically deprived'. However, adopting a more relaxed, informal style – the interviewer sitting on the floor, the child allowed to have a friend present – brought a completely different response. The children opened up and spoke freely, showing that they were competent speakers.

Unstructured interviews are particularly useful when researching sensitive topics. For example, Dobash and Dobash used them to study domestic violence. The empathy and encouragement of the interviewer will help the interviewee to feel comfortable discussing difficult or personal subjects such as abuse.

2 The interviewee's view

Because there are no set questions, unstructured interviews allow the interviewee more opportunity to speak about those things they think are important. This contrasts with the structured interview, where the researcher decides in advance what questions are worth asking and limits interviewees to a fixed range of possible answers. By allowing them greater freedom to express their views, an unstructured interview is more likely to produce fresh insights and valid data. Similarly, the interviewer's probing can help formulate and develop interviewees' thoughts more clearly.

In their study of claimants' experiences of unemployment, Hartley Dean and Peter Taylor-Gooby (1992) used unstructured tape-recorded interviews, lasting up to 90 minutes, with 85 claimants. In their words:

'Questions were not put in any set order; the wording of questions was adapted to fit the circumstances of the respondent and/or the interview situation; questions which were evidently inappropriate were omitted altogether; additional questions or prompts were used at the interviewer's discretion to clarify or develop themes as they emerged.'

This approach gives interviewees the freedom to talk in their own terms about the issues that concern them.

> **Analysis and Evaluation**
> What disadvantages might there be in recording interviews?

3 Checking understanding

In structured interviews, there is a great danger that the interviewee misunderstands the question, or the interviewer misunderstands the answer.

A major advantage of unstructured interviews is that they make it much easier for interviewer and interviewee to check each other's meanings.

- If the interviewee doesn't understand a question, it can be explained.
- Similarly, if the interviewer is unsure what the interviewee's answer means, follow-up questions can be put to clarify matters.

4 Flexibility

Unstructured interviews are highly flexible. The interviewer is not restricted to a fixed set of questions in advance, but can explore whatever seems interesting or relevant. The researcher can formulate new ideas and hypotheses and then put them to the test as they arise during the course of the interview. There is no need to go away and draw up a new interview schedule, as there would be if using structured interviews.

5 Exploring unfamiliar topics

With structured interviews, researchers need to have some knowledge of the subject and preferably also a clear hypothesis before they start interviewing; otherwise, they will have little idea of what questions to ask.

However, where the subject is one that we don't yet know much about, unstructured interviews may be more useful, precisely because they are open-ended and exploratory. As with an ordinary conversation, we can start out knowing nothing and, by asking questions, learn as we go along. Some sociologists use unstructured interviews as a starting point to develop their initial ideas about a topic before going on to use more structured methods of investigation such as questionnaires.

Disadvantages of unstructured interviews

Despite their strengths, using unstructured interviews as a method of collecting data has a number of disadvantages.

1 Practical problems

Time and sample size Being in-depth explorations, unstructured interviews take a long time to conduct – often several hours each. This limits the number that can be carried out and means that the researcher will have a relatively small sample compared with the larger numbers who can be studied using structured interviews or questionnaires.

Training also needs to be more thorough than for someone conducting structured interviews. The interviewer needs to have a background in sociology so they can recognise when the interviewee has made a sociologically important point and so they can probe further with an appropriate line of questioning. All this adds to the cost of conducting unstructured interviews.

Interpersonal skills Interviewers also need good interpersonal skills so they can establish the rapport that is essential if interviewees are to answer fully and honestly.

2 Representativeness

The smaller numbers involved mean it is more likely that the sample interviewed will not be representative. This means that it will be harder to make valid generalisations based on the findings of the interviews.

3 Reliability

Unstructured interviews are not reliable because they are not standardised. Each interview is unique: interviewers are free to ask different questions in each case if they feel it is relevant to do so. This makes it virtually impossible for another researcher to replicate the interviews and check the findings or compare them with their own.

4 Quantification

Because unstructured interviews use mainly open-ended questions, the answers cannot be pre-coded. This makes it very difficult to count up and quantify the numbers of interviewees giving this or that answer. In turn, the lack of quantitative data makes unstructured interviews less useful for establishing cause-and-effect relationships and hypothesis testing that positivists prefer.

5 Validity

Unstructured interviews are generally seen as producing valid data. However, critics argue that the fact that they involve an interaction between interviewer and interviewee inevitably colours and distorts the information obtained.

As we have seen, structured interviews also face the same problem, even if not to the same extent. We examine the problems of interviews as interactions next.

Activity   Research

Comparing structured and unstructured interviews

...go to www.sociology.uk.net

See Box 12 on page 94 for more about positivism, interpretivism and research methods.

Box 21   Positivism, interpretivism and interviews

Positivists favour *structured* interviews because they achieve the main positivist goals of reliability, generalisability and representativeness:

- Standardised questions and answers produce reliable data because other researchers can replicate the interview.
- Pre-coded responses allow us to produce quantitative data, identify and measure behaviour patterns, and establish cause-and-effect relationships.
- Structured interviews are often large scale and thus more representative.

Interpretivists reject structured interviews because they impose the researcher's framework of ideas on interviewees.

Interpretivists favour *unstructured* interviews because they achieve the main interpretivist goal of validity:

- Absence of a pre-set structure means interviewees can discuss what is important to them.
- Open-ended questions allow interviewees to express themselves in their own words, thereby producing qualitative data that gives us an insight into their meanings.

Positivists reject unstructured interviews because each one is unique and cannot be replicated.

The interview as a social interaction

All interviews, whether structured or unstructured, involve a social interaction between interviewer and interviewee. The danger is that the interviewee may be responding not to the questions themselves but to the social situation in which they are asked.

Social interactions can threaten the validity of interviews in several ways.

1 Interviewer bias

The interviewer may ask 'leading' questions, where the wording 'tells' the interviewee how to answer. For example, the question, 'Wouldn't you agree that women should not go out to work when they have young children?' clearly implies that the interviewer expects the answer 'Yes'. (This is less of a danger in structured interviews, because the interview schedule restricts the interviewer to a particular set of questions and fixed wording.) Interviewers may also consciously or unconsciously influence the answer by their facial expression, body language or tone of voice.

Another source of interviewer bias is where the interviewer identifies too closely with the interviewees. For example, Ann Oakley (1982) admits that, as a mother herself, she found it difficult to remain detached and neutral when interviewing other women about maternity and childbirth.

2 Artificiality

Even the most relaxed of unstructured interviews is still an interview and not a normal conversation: both parties know it is an interview, in which one 'side' takes the initiative and asks the questions. Under these artificial conditions, it is sometimes doubtful whether truthful answers can be obtained.

3 Status and power inequalities

Inequalities between interviewer and interviewee may affect the interviewee's honesty or willingness to answer. In general, the bigger the status difference, the less valid the data. For example, Josephine Rich (1968) shows that when adults interview children, the child's need to please the interviewer will affect their answers.

Similarly, gender differences in power can shape the interview, while ethnic inequalities between interviewer and interviewee may make interviewing very difficult. This led John Howard Griffin (1962) to abandon interviewing in favour of using participant observation.

While all interviews risk distorting the data as a result of these factors, structured interviews may be less susceptible. This is because in a structured interview there are more controls over the nature of the interaction. For example, the interviewer has to follow a standard list of pre-set questions.

> **Application**
>
> 1 In what ways might gender differences between interviewer and interviewee affect the interview?
>
> 2 How might the social setting in which an interview takes place influence the interviewee's response?

4 Cultural differences

These may also undermine validity. For example, there may be misunderstandings as a result of different meanings being given to the same words.

The cultural gap may also mean that interviewers cannot tell when they are being lied to. For example, Margaret Mead's (1943) research on adolescents in Samoa in the western Pacific has been criticised on the grounds that Mead, who couldn't speak the language, was unable to spot that the girls she interviewed had deliberately misled her.

5 The social desirability effect

In social interaction, people often seek to win approval. This may be even truer in an interview, where interviewees may be on their best behaviour and give answers that present them in a favourable light.

They may also wish not to appear ignorant or uninteresting and so, instead of saying that they don't know or don't understand the question, they offer any answer at all rather than none.

6 Ethical issues

There are relatively few ethical problems with interviews. Nevertheless, because the interview is a social interaction, the interviewee may feel under some pressure to answer questions. Researchers should gain interviewees' informed consent, guarantee anonymity and make it clear that they have a right not to answer any of the questions that they do not wish to. Interviews on sensitive topics, or with vulnerable people, may also risk causing psychological harm.

Improving the validity of interviews

Some researchers use techniques to improve the chances of obtaining valid data. For example, to reduce the chance of interviewees making up answers or telling lies, Alfred Kinsey's (1953) interviews on sexual behaviour asked questions rapidly, giving interviewees little time to think, and used some questions to check the answers given to others. Follow-up interviews 18 months later were also used as a way of checking earlier answers.

Howard Becker (1971) developed another approach in his interviews with 60 Chicago schoolteachers. He used aggression, disbelief and 'playing dumb' as ways of extracting sensitive information from them that they might not otherwise have revealed, about how they classified pupils in terms of their social class and ethnic background. However, the success of such tactics requires the researcher to have special skills. For the same reason, this approach might also prove difficult to replicate.

Other researchers have overcome the problem of cultural differences by ensuring that interviewers and interviewees are ethnically and language-matched. For example, the interviews for James Nazroo's (1997) survey of the health of Britain's ethnic minorities were carried out in the language of the interviewee's choice.

All these techniques can help to improve the validity of answers.

Activity	Discussion
Age, ethnicity and interviewing	
	...go to www.sociology.uk.net

Topic summary

Structured interviews use closed-ended questions. They are quicker and cheaper than unstructured interviews, cover larger numbers and produce **reliable** and **representative** data, but **lack validity** and flexibility.

Unstructured interviews use open-ended questions, producing **valid** data by allowing interviewees to express themselves fully. However, they are **less representative**, and quantification is difficult.

All interviews are **social interactions** and face problems of **interviewer bias** and status or **cultural differences** between interviewer and interviewee.

EXAMINING INTERVIEWS

QuickCheck Questions

Check your answers at www.sociology.uk.net

1 Which of the following features do you associate with structured interviews and which with unstructured?

   a hard to analyse findings   b qualitative data

   c representative data   d formal

   e interviewer bias   f detachment

   g open-ended questions   h fixed questions

   i different from a questionnaire   j costly training

2 True or false? Structured interviews generally produce reliable data, whereas unstructured interviews produce valid data.

3 Suggest two benefits of using group interviews in sociological research.

4 What is meant by 'rapport' in relation to interviewing?

5 Identify two similarities between structured interviews and postal questionnaires.

6 Why might interviewer bias be more likely in an unstructured than a structured interview?

7 How might cultural differences between the interviewer and interviewee affect the interview?

8 Suggest two ways in which sociologists can improve the validity of interviews as a source of data.

Questions to try

Whether or not you're taking the AS exams during your A level course, trying the AS questions below is a very good way of testing your knowledge and understanding and practising your skills in preparation for your A level exams.

Item A Sociologists use different forms of interview in their research. Structured interviews, preferred by positivists, are similar to questionnaires with fixed questions and a standardised style of delivery. Unstructured and group interviews are more like guided conversations and are favoured by interpretivist and feminist researchers.

Whichever form of interview is used, they are face-to-face research encounters and this generates problems as well as benefits for the researcher.

AS questions

1 Outline two reasons why sociologists may choose to use group interviews. (4 marks)

2 Evaluate the difficulties that sociologists sometimes face in using structured interviews. (16 marks)

A level question

3 Applying material from Item A and your knowledge, evaluate the usefulness of different types of interviews in sociological research. (20 marks)

The Examiner's Advice

Q2 Spend about 25 minutes on this question. Focus on structured interviews and avoid drifting into unstructured interviews. Discuss practical problems such as that they take longer than questionnaires and the costs of training interviewers. Ethical problems may arise from the face-to-face interaction involved, such as interviewees feeling pressurised. Examine theoretical difficulties, most of which relate to validity. Closed-ended questions, limited opportunities to clarify questions, inability to explore new areas of interest, and the difficulties posed by the fact they are social interactions, all need examining. Use concepts such as validity, rapport, interviewer bias, status and power inequalities and social desirability. Explain why interpretivists and feminists see structured interviews as having difficulties. Evaluate these difficulties as you go through each one rather than in a separate section at the end. For example, evaluate the problem of using closed-ended questions by arguing that the benefit is that they generate easily quantifiable data.

Q3 Spend about 30 minutes on this. Be clear about the different types of interviews used by sociologists. Refer to structured, unstructured and group interviews. Relate the perceived strengths and limitations of different forms of interview to key concepts including validity, reliability and representativeness. Use the debate between positivism and interpretivism as a context for your answer. Explain why interpretivists and feminists see unstructured and group interviews as useful – for example in giving interviewees more control over the interview. Explain why positivists value structured interviews for their greater reliability and representativeness. Evaluate the strengths and limitations of each form of interview. Use concepts and issues such as quantitative and qualitative data, generalisation, sociology as a science, values in research, interviewer bias, artificiality, social desirability, verstehen, objectivity and subjectivity. Use studies such as Becker, Oakley, and Young and Wilmott, and develop points noted in Item A.

METHODS IN CONTEXT
using interviews to investigate education

Sociologists may use interviews to study issues such as:

- Pupil subcultures
- Pupils' experience of health and sex education
- Class, ethnicity and language
- Gender identity and the male gaze
- Class and parental choice of schools.

> Before reading this section, re-visit Topic 2 to refresh your understanding of what is special about researching education.

Practical issues

Young people's linguistic and intellectual skills are less developed than those of adults and this may pose practical problems for interviewers. Young interviewees may:

- Be less articulate or more reluctant to talk.
- Not understand long, complex questions or some abstract concepts.
- Have a more limited vocabulary and use words incorrectly or differently from adults, e.g. slang.
- Have a shorter attention span and poorer memory retrieval than adults.
- Read body language differently from adults.

These factors may lead to misunderstandings and incorrect or incomplete answers and thus undermine the validity of the data obtained. Such communication difficulties also mean that unstructured interviews may be more suitable than structured ones, since they allow the interviewer more scope to clear up misunderstandings by re-wording questions or explaining their meaning.

However, children may also have more difficulty in keeping to the point, especially in unstructured interviews. As Janet Powney and Mike Watts (1987) note, young children tend to be more literal minded and often pay attention to unexpected details in questions, and may use a different logic from adult interviewers. Training therefore needs to be more thorough for someone interviewing children, which adds to the costs of the research.

However, given that young people tend to have better verbal than literacy skills, interviews may be more successful than written questionnaires as a method of obtaining valid answers.

Another practical problem is that schools have very active informal communication channels. This means that the content of the interview – possibly an inaccurate version of it – may get around most pupils and teachers after only a few interviews have taken place. This may influence the responses given by later interviewees, thus reducing the validity of the data.

The location of the interview can also be problematic. If interviews are conducted on school premises, this may affect how comfortable the pupil or parent feels. The school and the classroom represent higher status and authority and some pupils and parents might find the location off-putting. Teachers too may be put off by the fear of colleagues or the head teacher overhearing, especially if the questions are of a sensitive nature.

> **Application**
>
> When interviewing parents, what effect might age, gender or ethnic differences between the interviewer and interviewee have on the response rate and on the validity of the answers given?

Unstructured interviews can often take an hour or more to conduct. Given the time constraints that most teachers work under, interviews with them would probably have to take place outside school hours. If the interviews are conducted during school time, there are likely to be interruptions and other distractions that are commonplace in a busy school environment.

Parents, too, often have busy work and parenting schedules and may only cooperate in lengthy interviews if they can see some benefit to their children's education.

For young children in particular, there is also the ethical issue that they may be unsettled by strange situations such as an interview, so researchers need to take particular care that the interview does not distress them.

Reliability and validity

Structured interviews produce reliable data because they are standardised: each interview is conducted in precisely the same way, with the same questions, in the same order, tone of voice and so on.

However, structured interviews may not produce valid data, since young people are unlikely to respond favourably to such a formal style – perhaps because it makes the interviewer appear too much like a teacher.

Instead of using this formal approach, therefore, Di Bentley (1987) began each interview by showing them a 'jokey' image of her fooling around with her daughter. During the interview, she maintained a relaxed atmosphere by nodding, smiling and making eye contact.

However, this is a very personal interviewing style that cannot easily be standardised. Thus, different interviewers would be likely to obtain very different results and this would reduce the reliability and comparability of their findings.

Access and response rate

Schools are hierarchical institutions and this can cause problems when seeking to interview teachers or pupils. As Powney and Watts note, the lower down the hierarchy the interviewee is, the more approvals that have to be obtained. Thus, to interview a teacher, a researcher might first have to obtain the permission of the head teacher, whereas to interview pupils may require parental consent as well.

Schools may also be reluctant to allow sociologists to conduct interviews during lesson time because of the disruption it causes, or because they object to the researcher's chosen topic. For example, some schools might object to interviews about drug use.

Similarly, there may be problems conducting interviews after school hours, whether on the school premises or in pupils' homes.

Parental permission may also be required to interview children. The likelihood of this being granted varies according to the subject of research. Field's (1987) study of pupils' experience of sex and health education in schools had a relatively high refusal rate of 29 per cent, mainly because of parents withholding consent.

On the other hand, if the researcher can obtain official support for the study, then the hierarchical nature of school may work in their favour. For example, heads can instruct teachers to release pupils from class for interviews and this may increase the response rate.

Analysis and Evaluation
1   What difficulties might you have in interviewing pupils (a) on school premises; (b) in their homes?
2   How might your research topic make a difference to where you might conduct the interview?

The interviewer as 'teacher in disguise'

Power and status inequalities can affect the outcome of interviews. If interviewees have less power than the interviewer, they may see it as being in their own interests to lie, exaggerate, conceal information or seek to please when answering questions. They may also be less self-confident and their responses less articulate. All this will reduce the validity of the data.

There are power and status inequalities between young people and adults. Interviewers are usually adults and children may see them as authority figures. This is even more likely in educational research, especially if the interviews are conducted on school premises. In this situation, Bell (1981) notes, pupils may see the interviewer as a 'teacher in disguise'.

This may affect the validity of the data in several ways. For example, pupils may seek to win the 'teacher's' approval by giving untrue but socially acceptable answers that show them in a favourable light, for example about how much time they spend on homework.

Similarly, pupils are accustomed to adults 'knowing better' and so may defer to them in interviews. For example, children are more likely than adults to change their original answer when the question is repeated because they think it must have been wrong.

There may be similar inequalities when interviewing certain parents. Working-class parents may perceive the interviewer as having a higher status than them and may feel that the questions are patronising or intrusive. By contrast, when interviewing middle-class teachers, power and status inequalities are likely to be less pronounced.

The interview is a social interaction. The inequalities between children and adults, pupils and teachers, may influence this interaction and thus distort the data obtained.

133

Improving the validity of interviews with pupils

As we have seen, interviews may not produce valid data. That is, they may not give a true picture of young people's attitudes and behaviour. However, researchers can adopt strategies to improve the validity of interviews with pupils and young people. For example, Sheila Greene and Diane Hogan (2005) argue that interviewers should:

- **Use open-ended** rather than closed-ended questions.
- **Not interrupt** children's answers.
- **Tolerate long pauses** to allow children to think about what they want to say.
- **Recognise that children are more suggestible** and so it is particularly important to avoid asking leading questions.
- **Avoid repeating questions**, since this makes children change their first answer because they think it was wrong.

Activity	Research
Researching sex education	
	...go to www.sociology.uk.net

In general, unstructured interviews may be more suitable for overcoming barriers of power and status inequality. Their informality can put young interviewees at their ease and establish rapport more easily. As Labov's research shows (page 127), this can encourage interviewees to open up and respond more fully, thus producing more valid data. This can be particularly useful when dealing with sensitive topics such as bullying.

Group interviews with pupils

An alternative to the conventional one-to-one interview is the group interview. This has both strengths and limitations as a method of studying education.

Pupils and young people are often strongly influenced by peer pressure and this may reduce the validity of the data gathered in a group interview, where individuals may conform to peer expectations rather than express what they truly think.

For example, the exchange in Box 22 reads like an authentic statement of the boys' shared values. Yet it is difficult to know whether the views expressed are genuinely shared or simply the product of the boys egging each other on to say similar things.

In addition, the free-flowing nature of group interviews makes it impossible to standardise the questions and this will reduce the reliability of the method and the comparability of findings.

On the other hand, Greene and Hogan argue that group interviews are particularly suitable for use with pupils. They create a safe peer environment and they reproduce the small group settings that young people are familiar with in classroom work. Peer support also reduces the power imbalance between adult interviewer and young interviewee found in one-to-one interviews.

Group interviews can also reveal the interactions between pupils. For example, Box 22 illustrates how the 'lads' reinforce each other's opposition to authority. However, peer pressure may influence individuals to give answers that conform to the group's values, rather than expressing their true opinions. For example, Spanksy begins to express a different view of teachers from the other lads, but then after a pause, conforms to the group's anti-teacher values.

Box 22	A group interview

In this extract from a group interview conducted by Paul Willis, four of the 'lads' are discussing teachers:

Joey   They're bigger than us, they stand for a bigger establishment than we do. Like, we're just little and they stand for bigger things, and you try to get your own back. It's, uh, resenting authority, I suppose.

Eddie   The teachers think they're high and mighty 'cos they're teachers, but they're nobody really, they're just ordinary people, ain't they?

Bill   Teachers think they're everybody. They are more, they're higher than us, but they think they're a lot higher and they're not.

Spanksy   Wish we could call them by their first names and that... [pause]... They think they're God.

Source: adapted from Willis (1976)

EXAMINING INTERVIEWS IN CONTEXT

Question to try

For both the AS and the A level exams, you must answer a Methods in Context question.

Item A

Investigating the extent of parental choice in education

Supporters of marketisation policies claim that an education market gives parents greater choice over which school their children can attend. Sociologists are interested in investigating just how much parental choice there actually is in this education market. Some parents are much more aware than others of how to 'work the system', even to the extent of manipulating the rules in their favour.

Sociologists may use structured interviews to investigate the extent of parental choice in education. However, although structured interviews are useful for gathering factual information, they are probably less effective when it comes to finding out parents' attitudes and feelings. Also, how far parents are likely to give honest answers to the questions put to them in a structured interview may depend upon whether they feel their role as a parent is being challenged by the questions asked.

AS and A level question

1   Applying material from Item A and your knowledge of research methods, evaluate the strengths and limitations of structured interviews for the study of the extent of parental choice in education.

(20 marks)

The Examiner's Advice

Q1 Spend about 30 minutes on this question. It requires you to apply your knowledge of structured interviews to the study of the particular issue of the extent of parental choice in education. It is not enough simply to discuss the strengths and limitations of structured interviews in general. Use Item A to help you. For example, it suggests that one research characteristic of the extent of parental choice in education is that some parents may be able to manipulate the system in some way. Consequently, they may not be prepared to divulge certain information in case this incriminates them, for example if they had used a relative's address to get their child into a particular school. The inability to use follow-up questions in a structured interview means the researcher cannot develop this line of enquiry. You should link other research characteristics of the extent of parental choice to the strengths and limitations of structured interviews. For example, there are some clear indicators of parental choice, e.g. whether parents got their child into their first choice school, whether they know about appeals procedures or have friends or relatives who are teachers. These are easily operationalised in interviews containing fixed questions. Other research characteristics include the difficulty of obtaining a representative sample of parents, operationalising some aspects of cultural capital, measuring the role of economic capital etc. You should link these to particular strengths or limitations of the method.

An example

In your answer you should connect the strengths and limitations of structured interviews to the research characteristics of parental choice. Here's an example paragraph.

'As Item A says, some parents are more aware of how to 'work the system' and one view is that these are likely to be middle-class parents. Structured interviews can be used to test this hypothesis by correlating answers to closed-ended questions about straightforward factual issues. For example, parents can be asked about their occupation in order to identify their class. This information can then be correlated with their answers to a question about whether they got their child into their first choice school. This will show if middle-class parents are more successful in exercising choice.'

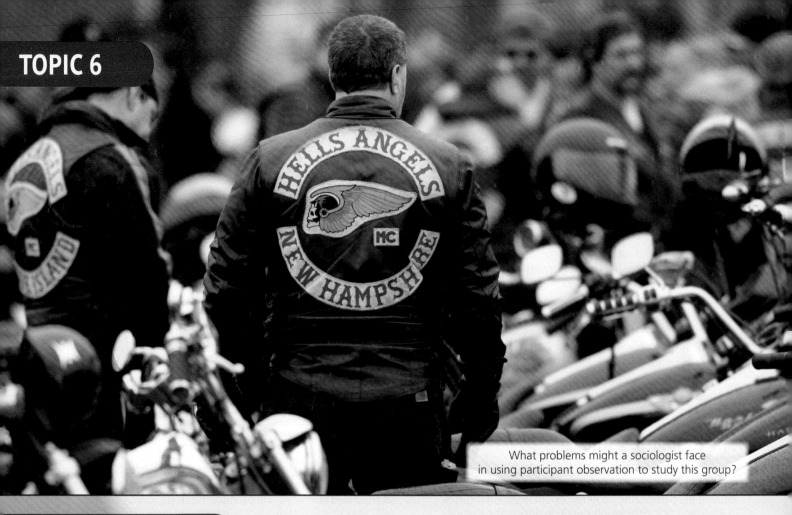

What problems might a sociologist face in using participant observation to study this group?

GETTING STARTED

Sociologists often want to study small groups or subcultures such as the bikers shown in the photograph above. One way to study such groups is by joining in with them.

1 Using the photograph, write a list of the personal characteristics you might need if you wanted to join in this group to study it.

2 Now carry out your own participant observation. The setting will be your own household. The activity you will observe is a mealtime. Your research aim is to describe the way the meal is organised. Make notes on what you observe, including who is present; when and where the meal takes place; how long it lasts; what is consumed and what tasks each of the people carry out.

3 In conducting your research, consider the following issues:

   a How might the fact that you probably know the group very well affect your research?

   b You are part of the group you are studying. What problems might this cause?

   c Will you tell the group that you are observing them or keep it secret? Give reasons for your choice.

   d How will you record your findings? Give reasons for your answer.

4 After completing the observation, summarise the advantages and disadvantages you found in using this method.

Learning objectives

After studying this Topic, you should:

- Know the different types of observational methods.
- Be able to explain the main stages in conducting a participant observation study.
- Be able to evaluate the strengths and limitations of overt and covert participant observation.
- Be able to apply your understanding of observational methods to the study of education.

PARTICIPANT OBSERVATION

As we have seen, one problem of using survey methods such as interviews or questionnaires to study people is that what they *say* they do and what they *actually* do may be two quite different things.

For example, in interviews, people may conceal information or lie about their real behaviour in order to please the interviewer, save face or create a better impression of themselves.

One way of overcoming this problem might be simply to see for ourselves what people really do by observing them in their normal everyday environment, rather than questioning them in an artificial interview situation.

By using observational methods rather than questioning people, we might hope to get a truer, more valid picture of social reality.

There are many techniques for observing people. In this Topic, we first look at the main types of observational method before focusing on the one that is used most often by sociologists – namely, participant observation.

Types of observation

There are several different types of observation. Firstly, we can distinguish between:

- **Non-participant observation** The researcher simply observes the group or event without taking part in it. For example, they may use a two-way mirror to observe children playing.
- **Participant observation** The researcher actually takes part in an event or the everyday life of the group while observing it.

Secondly, we can distinguish between:

- **Overt observation** The researcher makes their true identity and purpose known to those being studied. The sociologist is open about what they are doing.
- **Covert observation** The study is carried out 'under cover'. The researcher's real identity and purpose are kept concealed from the group being studied. The researcher takes on a false identity and role, usually posing as a genuine member of the group.

However, actual research does not always fit neatly into one or other of these categories. For example, William Whyte's (1955) study of 'Street Corner Society' was semi-overt (partly open). He revealed his real purpose to a key member of the group, Doc, but not to others.

In sociology, most observation is unstructured participant observation. However, positivist sociologists in particular do occasionally use structured observation, which is normally non-participant. Here, the researcher uses a structured observational schedule to categorise systematically what happens.

The schedule is a pre-determined list of the types of behaviour or situations the sociologist is interested in. Each time an instance of such behaviour occurs, the sociologist records it on the schedule, for example, how often boys and girls in a nursery play with particular toys. The researcher adds up the number of times each event occurs. This produces quantitative data, from which patterns and correlations can then be established. (See page 144 for an example of a structured observational schedule.)

Finally, observation may be used in conjunction with other methods. For example, when interviewing, the researcher may observe interviewees' body language to gauge whether or not they are telling the truth.

> **Analysis and Evaluation**
> 1 Why might a researcher choose to keep their real identity and purpose a secret from the group they are observing?
> 2 In what circumstances, if any, do you think it is acceptable for researchers to do this? Give your reasons.

Conducting a participant observation study

Sociologists face two main issues when conducting a participant observation study:

- **getting in, staying in and getting out** of the group being studied
- **whether to use overt or covert observation.**

Getting in

To do the study, we must first gain entry to the group. Some groups are easier to enter than others. For example, joining a football crowd is likely to be easier than joining a criminal gang.

making contact

Making the initial contact with the group may depend on personal skills, having the right connections, or even pure chance. Ned Polsky (1971), who was a good pool player himself, found his skill useful in gaining entry to the world of the poolroom hustler. James Patrick (1973) was able to join a Glasgow gang because he looked quite young and knew one of its members from having taught him in approved school (now called young offenders' institutions). Eileen Fairhurst (1977) found herself hospitalised by back trouble and used the opportunity to conduct a study on being a patient.

acceptance

To gain entry to a group, the researcher will have to win their trust and acceptance. It may help to make friends with a key individual, as Sarah Thornton (1995) did with Kate in her study of the clubbing and rave scene. Sometimes, though, the researcher's age, gender, class or ethnicity may prove an obstacle. Thornton found her age and nationality a barrier:

> 'I began my research when I was 23 and slowly aged out of the peer group I was studying. Also, as a Canadian investigating British clubs and raves, I was quite literally a stranger in a strange land.'

Thornton was met with suspicion at first. As Kate's brother put it, 'How do you know she won't sell this to the Daily Mirror?' However, such barriers can sometimes be overcome. A white researcher, Elliot Liebow (1967), succeeded in gaining acceptance by a black street-corner gang in Washington DC. Some researchers have gone to remarkable lengths to gain acceptance and pass as one of the group, but probably none more so than John Howard Griffin (1962).

Griffin was a white man who in 1959 used medication and sun lamp treatments to change his skin colour and pass as black. He then travelled around the Deep South of the USA, experiencing first hand the impact of white racism.

In the Deep South at that time, public amenities such as schools, cafes, hotels, transport and toilets were all racially segregated, and black people faced discrimination in housing, jobs and political and civil rights.

Activity | **Webquest**

Black Like Me

...go to www.sociology.uk.net

the observer's role

'Getting in' poses the question of what role the researcher should adopt. Ideally, it should:

- be one that does not disrupt the group's normal patterns
- offer a good vantage point from which to make observations.

Whyte succeeded in achieving both these aims by refusing all leadership roles, with the one exception of secretary of the community club, a position that allowed him to take ample notes under the guise of taking the minutes of meetings.

However, it is not always possible to take a role that is both unobtrusive and a good vantage point. Some roles may also involve taking sides in conflicts, with the result that the researcher may become estranged from one faction or the other, making observation more difficult.

> **Analysis and Evaluation**
>
> In what ways might the researcher's personal characteristics be an obstacle to gaining access to a group?

Staying in

Once accepted, the researcher needs to be able to stay in the group and complete the study. Here we can see a key problem for the participant observer: having to be both involved in the group so as to understand it fully, and yet at the same time detached from the group so as to remain objective and unbiased.

'going native'

One danger of staying in the group is that of becoming over-involved or 'going native'. By over-identifying with the group, the researcher becomes biased. When this happens, they have stopped being an objective observer and have simply become a member of the group.

For example, in his study of the Amsterdam police, Maurice Punch (1979) found that in striving to be accepted by the tightly-knit patrol group he was studying, he over-identified with them, even acting as a 'policeman' himself – chasing and holding suspects, searching houses, cars and people, and shouting at people who abused his police 'colleagues'.

At the other extreme, the researcher may preserve their detachment so as to avoid bias, but by remaining detached they risk not understanding the events they observe. Striking a balance between these two extremes is immensely difficult. As David Downes and Paul Rock (2011) put it:

> 'Participant-observers try to perform a most intricate feat. They are required to reach the probably unattainable state of one who is both insider and outsider, a person who sees a social world from within it in the manner of a member, yet who also stands apart and analyses it in the manner of a stranger.'

A further problem of staying in is that the more time the researcher spends with the group, the less strange its ways come to appear. After a while, the researcher may cease to notice things that would have struck them as unusual or noteworthy at an earlier stage of the research: the observer becomes less observant. As Whyte put it, 'I started as a non-participating observer and ended as a non-observing participator'.

Getting out

In practical terms, getting out of the group at the end of the study generally presents fewer problems than getting in or staying in. If the worst comes to the worst, the researcher can simply call a halt and leave. This was Patrick's experience of studying a Glasgow gang when, sickened by the violence, he abandoned the study abruptly. Others can leave more gracefully, particularly if their observation has been overt. Nevertheless, leaving a group with whom one has become close can be difficult.

Re-entering one's normal world can also be difficult. Whyte found that when he returned to Harvard University after his research, he was tongue-tied and unable to communicate with fellow academics. These problems can be made worse if the research is conducted on and off over a period of time, with multiple 'crossings' between the two worlds.

The researcher may also find that loyalty prevents them from fully disclosing everything they have learnt, for fear that this might harm members of the group. For example, in the case of criminal groups, exposure of their activities might lead to prosecution, or reprisals against the author. Clearly, such concealment of data will reduce the validity of the study.

Overt observation

Sociologists face the decision whether to use overt or covert observation. Many sociologists favour the use of overt observation, where the researcher reveals his or her true identity and purpose to the group and asks their permission to observe. This has several advantages:

- It avoids the ethical (moral) problem of obtaining information by deceit and, when studying deviant groups, that of being expected to join in their activities.
- It allows the observer to ask the kind of naïve but important questions that only an outsider could ask. For example, the researcher could ask a gang member, 'Why do you rob and steal?'
- The observer can take notes openly.
- It allows the researcher to use interview methods to check insights derived from observations.

However, overt observation has two major disadvantages:

- **A group may refuse the researcher permission** to observe them, or may prevent them from seeing everything. As two of the Amsterdam police officers that

Punch had done his research with later told him, 'When you were with us, we only let you see what we wanted you to see'.
- **It risks creating the Hawthorne Effect**, where those who know they are being observed begin to behave differently as a result. This undermines the validity of the data.

Covert observation

Because of these disadvantages, some sociologists choose to carry out covert observation. However, the use of covert observation raises several practical and ethical issues.

Practical issues

The main practical advantage of covert observation is that it reduces the risk of altering people's behaviour, and sometimes it is the only way to obtain valid information. This is particularly true where people are engaged in activities that they would rather keep secret. As Laud Humphreys (1970), who studied gay men's sexual encounters in public toilets, notes:

'There is only one way to watch highly discreditable behaviour and that is to pretend to be in the same boat with those engaging in it.'

If they knew they were being observed, they would change or conceal their behaviour and so the main advantage of observation – that it preserves the naturalness of people's behaviour – would be lost.

On the other hand, covert participant observation can pose practical problems.

Firstly, it requires the researcher to keep up an act, and may call for detailed knowledge of the group's way of life even before joining it. There is always a risk of one's cover being 'blown' by even a trivial mistake. Patrick was almost found out when he bought his suit with cash instead of credit and when he fastened the middle button of his jacket rather than the top one – things the gang would never have done. This is likely to bring the research to an abrupt end and may, in the case of some criminal groups, lead to physical harm. As Polsky advises, therefore:

'You damned well better not pretend to be "one of them" because they will test this claim out and you will either find yourself involved in illegal activities, or your cover will be blown.'

This was something Patrick also discovered when the gang handed him an axe to use in an expected fight.

Secondly, the sociologist cannot usually take notes openly and must rely on memory and the opportunity to write them in secret. Both Leon Festinger et al (1956), studying a religious sect that had predicted the imminent end of the world, and Jason Ditton (1977), studying theft among bread deliverymen, had to use toilets as a place for recording their observations. In Ditton's case, this eventually aroused suspicion.

Thirdly, the researcher cannot ask naïve but important questions, or combine observation with other methods, such as interviews.

Fourthly, although pretending to be an insider rather than an outsider reduces the risk of the Hawthorne Effect, the addition of a new member (the researcher) can still change the group's behaviour, thus reducing validity.

Ethical issues

Covert participant observation raises serious ethical (moral) issues for researchers. These often conflict with the practical advantage it brings of observing natural behaviour.

- It is immoral to deceive people, obtaining information by pretending to be their friend or 'in the same boat'. Researchers should obtain the informed consent of their subjects, and reveal the purpose of the study and the use to which its findings will be put. With covert observation, this cannot normally be done, at least until afterwards.
- Covert observers may have to lie about their reasons for leaving the group at the end of their research. Others, such as Patrick, simply abandon the group without explanation. Critics argue that this is unethical.
- They may have to participate in immoral or illegal activities as part of their 'cover' role.
- Similarly, as witnesses to such activities, they may have a moral or legal duty to intervene or to report them to the police.

Advantages of participant observation

According to its supporters, participant observation offers a range of advantages.

1 Validity

What people say they do when asked in a questionnaire, and what they actually do in real life, are not always the same thing. By contrast, by actually observing people we can obtain rich qualitative data that provides a picture of how they really live. Supporters of participant observation argue that this is the method's main strength, and most of its other advantages are linked to this.

2 Insight

The best way to truly understand what something is like is to experience it for ourselves. Sociologists call this personal or subjective understanding 'verstehen', a German word meaning 'empathy', or understanding that comes from putting yourself in another person's place.

Participant observation allows the researcher to gain empathy through personal experience. By actually living as a member of a group, we can gain insight into their way of life, their meanings and viewpoints, their values and problems. We can come to understand their 'life-world' as they themselves understand it. This closeness to people's lived reality means that participant observation can give uniquely valid, authentic data.

3 Flexibility

As we saw in Topics 4 and 5, research methods such as questionnaires and structured interviews involve

| Box 23 | Positivism, interpretivism and observation |

Interpretivists favour *unstructured participant* observation because it achieves their main goal of validity:
- Observation gives the researcher a true picture because it shows us what people do, rather than simply what they say they do.
- Participation in the group gives the researcher first hand insight into social actors' meanings and behaviour – especially if the observation is carried out covertly.

Positivists reject participant observation because its lack of structure means it cannot be replicated or results quantified.

Positivists favour *structured non-participant* observation because it achieves their main goals of reliability, generalisability and representativeness:
- Standardised behaviour categories produce reliable data because other researchers can replicate the observation.
- Pre-determined observational categories allow us to produce quantitative data, identify and measure behaviour patterns, and establish cause-and-effect relationships.
- Structured observation takes less time than unstructured observation, so a larger, more representative sample can be studied.

Interpretivists reject structured observation because it imposes the researcher's view of reality on those being observed, resulting in invalid data.

See Box 12 on page 94 for more about positivism, interpretivism and research methods.

beginning the research with a specific hypothesis and pre-set questions. Even before starting to collect the data, therefore, the researcher has already decided what questions are important. The obvious problem with this is that the questions the researcher thinks are important may not be the same as the ones the subjects think are important. This is especially true when starting to study a topic of which we have little or no previous knowledge.

By contrast, participant observation is a much more flexible method. Rather than starting with a fixed hypothesis, it allows the sociologist to enter the situation with a relatively open mind about what they will find. As new situations are encountered, new explanations can be formulated and the sociologist can change direction to follow them up there and then. In this way, any theories that the researcher produces are 'grounded' in real life.

This open-mindedness allows the researcher to discover things that other methods may miss. As Whyte noted, simply by observing, 'I learned answers to questions that I would not have had the sense to ask if I had been using interviews.' Similarly, Polsky offers some sound, if blunt, advice: 'initially, keep your eyes and ears open but keep your mouth shut'.

4 Practical advantages

Sometimes participant observation may be the only viable method for studying certain groups, particularly those engaged in activities that wider society sees as deviant or disreputable. Such groups are likely to be suspicious of outsiders who come asking questions. As Lewis Yablonsky (1973) points out, a teenage gang is likely to see researchers who come armed with questionnaires as the unwelcome representatives of authority.

By contrast, because participant observation enables the sociologist to build a rapport with the group and gain its trust, it has proved a successful method of studying delinquent gangs, football hooligans, thieves, drug users, religious sects and other 'outsider' groups.

Participant observation can also be used in other situations where questioning would be ineffective. This is shown in Aaron Cicourel's (1968) study of how police and probation officers categorise juveniles by making unconscious assumptions about whether they are criminal 'types'. Precisely because they are unaware of their assumptions, it would be pointless for the sociologist to ask them questions about these. For Cicourel, therefore, the only way to get at these assumptions is to observe the police directly in their work.

Disadvantages of participant observation

Despite the advantages offered by participant observation, it also faces a number of disadvantages.

1 Practical disadvantages

There are several practical disadvantages in using participant observation:

- It is very time-consuming. For example, Whyte's study took him four years to complete.
- The researcher needs to be trained so as to be able to recognise aspects of a situation that are sociologically significant and worth further attention.
- It can be personally stressful and demanding, especially if covert.
- It requires observational and interpersonal skills that not everyone possesses.
- Personal characteristics such as age, gender or ethnicity may restrict what kinds of groups can be studied. As Downes and Rock put it, 'not everyone would pass uneventfully into the world of punk rockers or Hell's Angels'.
- Many groups may not wish to be studied in this way, and some have the power to make access difficult. This is one reason why participant observation often focuses on relatively powerless groups who are less able to resist being studied, such as petty criminals.

Analysis and Evaluation

Why is covert participant observation more likely than overt to be stressful and demanding for the researcher?

2 Ethical problems

As we have seen, covert participant observation in particular raises serious ethical difficulties, including deceiving people in order to obtain information about them and participating in illegal or immoral activities in the course of sociological research.

3 Representativeness

Sociologists who use quantitative survey methods usually study large, carefully selected, representative samples that provide a sound basis for making generalisations. By contrast, in participant observation studies, the group studied is usually very small and the 'sample' is often selected haphazardly, for example by a chance encounter with someone who turns out to be a key informant.

This does not provide a sound basis for making generalisations. As Downes and Rock note, although participant observation may provide valid insights into the particular group being studied, it is doubtful how far these 'internally valid' insights are 'externally valid', that is, generalisable to the wider population.

4 Reliability

Reliability means that if another researcher repeats the method, they will obtain the same results. To achieve reliability, research procedures must be standardised so that other researchers can reproduce them. For example, in structured interviews all interviewers ask the same standard questions in the same way.

By contrast, in participant observation so much depends on the personal skills and characteristics of a lone researcher that it is unlikely any other investigator would be able to replicate the original study. For example, as Whyte recognised, his method was to some extent unique to him alone.

Also, because participant observation usually produces qualitative data, this can make comparisons with other studies difficult. As a result, it is unlikely to produce reliable data. Positivists, who see sociology as scientific, thus reject participant observation as an unsystematic method that cannot be replicated by other researchers.

5 Bias and lack of objectivity

Critics argue that participant observation studies lack objectivity.

- The risk of becoming too involved and 'going native' makes it difficult to remain objective and the sociologist may end up presenting a one-sided or biased view of the group.
- Sometimes, loyalty to the group or fear of reprisals leads the sociologist to conceal sensitive information. This denies those who read the published study a full and objective account of the research.
- Participant observation often attracts sociologists whose sympathies lie with the underdog. Since it is seen as an effective method for 'telling it like it is' from the actor's point of view, some of those who use it may be biased in favour of their subjects' viewpoint. For example, Willis was accused of presenting a romanticised account of the 'lads'.

6 Validity

According to its supporters, the great strength of participant observation lies in its validity. As a form of verstehen, allowing the sociologist to become an insider, it gives an authentic account of the actor's world.

Positivists reject this claim. They argue that the findings from such studies are merely the subjective and biased impressions of the observer. Rather than truly 'telling it like it is', participant observation simply tells it as the observer sees it.

Supporters of participant observation claim that it does not impose the sociologist's own categories and ideas on the facts, but positivists argue that in reality the researcher selects what facts they think are worth recording, and that these are likely to fit in with the researcher's pre-existing views and prejudices.

A further threat to validity comes from the Hawthorne Effect: the very presence of the observer may make the subjects act differently. This defeats the main aim of participant observation, to produce a 'naturalistic' account of human behaviour.

7 Lack of a concept of structure

Interactionists favour the use of participant observation. They see society as constructed through the small-scale, face-to-face interactions of its members and the meanings that individual actors give to their situation. In their view, participant observation is a useful tool for examining these micro-level interactions and meanings at first hand.

However, structural sociologists such as Marxists and functionalists see this as inadequate. They argue that because it focuses on the 'micro' level of actors' meanings, participant observation research tends to ignore the wider structural forces that shape our behaviour, such as class inequality or the norms and values into which we are socialised.

In the structuralist view, therefore, seeing things only through the actors' eyes will never give us the complete picture. For example, if the actors are unaware of the structural forces shaping their behaviour, then their own account of their lives, revealed through participant observation, will give us at best only a partial view.

Activity Research

The rules of the game

...go to www.sociology.uk.net

Topic summary

Participant observation (PO) involves joining in with a group to gain **insight**, and can be **overt** or **covert**. Research goes through three phases: getting in, staying in and getting out. Covert PO may produce more **valid** data, but is **ethically** questionable and faces practical problems of maintaining one's cover. **Interpretivists** claim that PO produces **valid** data, but **positivists** argue that it is **unreliable**, **unrepresentative** and lacks objectivity. They prefer **structured observation**, which is usually non-participant and collects quantitative data.

EXAMINING PARTICIPANT OBSERVATION

QuickCheck Questions

Check your answers at www.sociology.uk.net

1 Explain the difference between overt and covert observation.

2 What is a structured observation schedule?

3 Why should participant observers seek to avoid leadership roles within the group they are studying?

4 Suggest two reasons why it might be difficult for the observer to gain the trust of the group they wish to study.

5 Suggest reasons why participant observation can be described as a more flexible method than questionnaires.

6 Why do critics argue that participant observation studies lack objectivity?

7 Suggest two reasons why participant observation may produce valid data.

8 Why do some critics argue that participant observation does not produce valid data?

Questions to try

Whether or not you're taking the AS exams during your A level course, trying the AS questions below is a very good way of testing your knowledge and understanding and practising your skills in preparation for your A level exams.

AS questions

1 Outline two reasons why sociologists sometimes choose to use structured observation. (4 marks)

2 Evaluate the advantages that some sociologists see in using participant observation in their research. (16 marks)

A level question

3 Outline and explain two practical problems of covert observation. (10 marks)

The Examiner's Advice

Q2 Spend about 25 minutes on this question. It asks you to focus on participant observation, so avoid drifting into non-participant observation. Focus on evaluating the advantages that some sociologists see in participant observation. Discuss advantages such as rapport, sensitivity, insight, verstehen, flexibility, checking understanding, opening up new topic areas, accessing difficult to study social groups, greater validity. The question does not specify covert or overt, so make sure you draw out the advantages of each. In particular, explain how overt avoids the ethical problems of being covert while covert observation has the strength of avoiding the Hawthorne Effect. Use concepts such as those above and examples of studies such as Humphreys, Griffin and Whyte. Explain why interpretivists tend to see participant observation as having many advantages. Evaluate the advantages as you go through each one rather than listing limitations in a separate section at the end. For example, evaluate validity by arguing that the data may reflect the observer's own biases rather than the reality.

Q3 Spend about 15 minutes on this. Divide your time fairly equally between each problem. Don't write a separate introduction; just start on your first problem. Focus on practical problems. Possible problems include making contact with the group, gaining entry, finding and maintaining an appropriate cover role, leaving the group etc. You can refer to participant observation, non-participant observation, or both. Describe each problem in some detail. Do this by creating a chain of reasoning (see page 248). For example, in covert participant observation the researcher needs to adopt a role in the group. However, the role available to them may not give them access to all aspects of the group's life. This means the researcher will only gain an incomplete and possibly distorted view of the group. Use concepts and issues such as role, covert observation, 'going native', recording of findings, time, cost, and studies such as Patrick, Humphreys, Festinger or Ditton.

METHODS IN CONTEXT
using observation to investigate education

The main use of observational techniques in the study of education is to investigate classroom interaction and the behaviour, attitudes and values of teachers and pupils. Sociologists are interested in a range of possible classroom interaction issues. These include:

- Gender and classroom behaviour
- Teacher expectations and labelling
- Speech codes in the classroom
- Pupil subcultures
- Teacher and pupil racism
- The hidden curriculum.

> Before reading this section, re-visit Topic 2 to refresh your understanding of what is special about researching education.

Structured observation

There are several types of observation. At one extreme are highly structured methods using pre-categorised observational schedules. Positivists prefer these methods because they enable them to identify and make quantitative measurements of behaviour patterns. These methods are usually non-participant.

practical issues

One example of the structured observational schedules favoured by positivists is the Flanders system of interaction analysis categories (FIAC). This is used to measure pupil-pupil and pupil-teacher interaction quantitatively. The observer uses a standard chart to record interactions at three-second intervals, placing each observation in one of ten pre-defined behaviour categories. (See Box 24.)

Observations can thus easily be converted into quantitative data simply by counting the number of times each type of behaviour occurs. Thus, for example, Flanders (1970) found that in the typical American classroom, 68 per cent of the time is taken up by teacher talk, 20 per cent by pupil talk and 12 per cent lost in silence or confusion.

The relative simplicity of structured observational methods such as FIAC means that they are quicker, cheaper and require less training than less structured methods.

reliability

Structured observational techniques such as FIAC are likely to be easily replicated. This is because FIAC uses only ten categories of classroom interaction, which makes it relatively

Box 24	Flanders interaction analysis categories (FIAC)

Teacher Talk
1. Teacher accepts pupils' feelings.
2. Teacher praises or encourages pupils.
3. Teacher accepts or uses ideas of pupils.
4. Teacher asks questions.
5. Teacher lectures.
6. Teacher gives directions.
7. Teacher criticises pupils or justifies authority.

Pupil Talk
8. Pupils talk in response to teacher.
9. Pupils initiate talk.

Silence
10. Silence or confusion.

Source: Delamont (1976)

easy for other researchers to apply in a standardised way. It also generates quantitative data, which makes the findings easy to compare with those of other studies.

validity

Interpretivist sociologists criticise structured observation of classroom interaction for its lack of validity. For example, Sara Delamont argues that simply counting classroom behaviour and classifying it into a limited number of pre-defined categories ignores the meanings that pupils and teachers attach to it.

Unstructured observation

Interpretivists favour the use of less structured, more flexible, qualitative observational methods. These allow them to gain access to the meanings that teachers and pupils give to situations by immersing themselves in those situations. Unlike structured methods with their observation schedules, this approach does not make assumptions in advance about what the key research issues will be. Sociologists use these observational methods more often than structured ones.

Activity	Research

Classroom observation: structured or unstructured?

...go to www.sociology.uk.net

practical issues

Schools are complex places and more time-consuming to observe than many other settings. It took Lacey two months to familiarise himself with the school, while Eggleston (1976) needed over three months just to set up his cover role for his observations.

However, it may be easier to gain permission to observe lessons than to interview pupils and teachers. The head of the London school studied by Fuller decided not only that it would be good for the pupils to have a non-teaching adult around, but that permission from parents was not required for her to observe normal school behaviour – whereas it would have been if she had wanted to conduct interviews.

Personal characteristics such as age, gender and ethnicity affect the process of observation. At the time Wright (1992) was carrying out her research, there were few black teachers and she found that her African Caribbean ethnicity produced antagonistic reactions from some white teachers. On the other hand, she found that many black pupils held her in high esteem and would ask her for support.

Observation of interactions in school settings is limited by the restrictions of the school timetable, holidays, control over access, health and safety legislation and so on.

Schools are busy public places, so the observer may find it difficult to find the privacy needed to record observations. Hammersley found that noting down the staffroom conversations he overheard had to be done covertly and hurriedly, in one case on the back of his newspaper. More often, he jotted down notes after he had left the staffroom, trying to record the exact statements he had overheard. Hammersley acknowledges that he may well have made mistakes or relied on his own interpretation of the general sense of what was said.

ethical issues

The additional ethical issues relating to the observation of young people usually mean that a covert approach to studying pupils is not appropriate. Their greater vulnerability and limited ability to give informed consent means that observation normally has to be overt.

Delamont points out that every observer in a school sees and hears things that could get pupils into trouble. In some cases, this may even involve the law, such as when pupils steal from school.

What to do with this 'guilty knowledge' is both an ethical and a practical problem: ethically, it could be argued that the researcher is obliged to report the wrongdoing. However, doing so may breach the trust that pupils have placed in the researcher and may mean pupils will no longer confide in them or cooperate with their research.

Delamont also notes that, given the harm that can be done to pupils, teachers and schools, additional care should be taken to protect their identity. This is even more of an issue in a marketised education system where a good public image is important to the success of a school.

validity

For interpretivists, the main strength of observation, and especially participant observation, is its validity – it gives us an authentic understanding of the world-views of social actors. This understanding is particularly important when researching issues such as classroom interaction or labelling in schools.

However, the power difference between young people and adults is a major barrier to uncovering the real attitudes and behaviour of pupils. They may present a false image when being observed by an adult researcher, thus undermining the validity of the research.

Nevertheless, observation is more likely than most methods to overcome this problem, because it gives the researcher the opportunity to gain acceptance by pupils.

A further factor limiting validity is that teachers may be quite skilled at disguising their feelings and altering their behaviour when being observed – for example, by inspectors and school managers. This may mean that the sociologist's data from classroom observation lacks validity.

There is also the problem that the language of the pupil may be very different from that of the researcher. This makes it difficult for researchers to be certain that they understand pupils' meanings.

the Hawthorne Effect

It is very difficult to carry out covert observation of educational settings, especially classrooms. This is because there are few 'cover' roles the researcher can adopt and because he or she stands out as being much older than the pupils.

This means that most classroom observation has to be overt. However, this makes it very difficult to avoid the Hawthorne Effect, where the presence of the researcher influences the behaviour of those being observed.

For example, Ronald King (1984) tried to blend into the background in an infant school by initially spending short periods of time in the classroom to allow the children to become familiar with his presence. So as not to be seen as a teacher, he avoided eye contact and politely refused their requests for help. In an attempt to be unobtrusive, he even used the classroom's Wendy House as a 'hide'.

This example shows how difficult it is for an adult observer to reduce the effect of their presence on pupils' behaviour. As Ball (1993) asks, what did the children actually make of the tall man hiding in the Wendy House? In other words, the danger is that the children's awareness of King's presence may have changed their normal behaviour and so undermined the validity of his observations.

representativeness

The scale of the education system is vast. There are around 4,000 secondary and over 30,000 primary schools in England and Wales, as well as over 350 colleges. The average secondary school has around 70 classes taking place at any one time. The result is a huge amount of educational activity.

By contrast, most observational studies focus on a small number of pupils in just a single school. For example, Willis (1977) studied a core group of only twelve boys. The small scale of such studies results from the fact that it takes time to become familiar with the setting, gain the trust of teachers and pupils, and carry out the actual observations. The limited scale of the typical observational study, combined with the sheer size of the education system, mean that observing school interaction is unlikely to produce representative data.

Hammersley considered that the data he collected in the school staffroom was more open to sample bias than his classroom data. This was because, although he sought a wide range of contacts among the teachers, he found that many treated him with suspicion. As a result, he tended to associate largely with one group of teachers with whom he had more in common. This made his sample less representative.

reliability

Participant observation studies of education tend to lack reliability. This is because data recording is often unsystematic and hard to replicate. For example, as we saw earlier, Hammersley found that on one occasion he had to write his notes on the back of a newspaper because he was observing staffroom conversations covertly.

Secondly, the personal characteristics of different observers may evoke differing responses. For example, Wright found that as a black female, she was met with hostility by some white teachers, but was readily accepted by black pupils. A white male researcher may well have found the opposite.

Box 25	**Longitudinal studies**

Longitudinal studies follow the same sample or group over an extended period of time. Participant observation studies are generally longitudinal, though longitudinal studies often use other methods, such as questionnaires, interviews and documents. Examples of longitudinal studies of education include:

- Lacey's four-year participant observation study of Hightown grammar school.
- J.W.B. Douglas' study following 5,632 children all born in the first week in March 1946 through their schooling.
- The National Child Development Study (NCDS), a birth cohort study following the lives of all those born in Britain in the same week in 1958.
- Leon Feinstein (2003) used data from the NCDS and the British Cohort Study, which follows a group born in 1970, to study class differences in educational achievement.

Such studies have advantages and disadvantages:

- They trace developments over time, rather than just taking a one-off 'snapshot' of one moment.
- By making comparisons over time, they can identify causes. Douglas and Feinstein both used longitudinal studies to discover the causes of class differences in achievement.
- Sample attrition – people dropping out of the study. The NCDS lost a third of its original sample of 17,400 between 1958 and 1999. The drop-outs may not be typical of those who stay in, making the remaining sample less representative.
- The large amounts of data produced can be difficult to analyse – and by definition, results cannot be obtained quickly.
- Longitudinal studies can also be costly. Parker's (1998) five-year study of illegal drug use among 1,125 adolescents cost £380,000.

EXAMINING PARTICIPANT OBSERVATION IN CONTEXT

Question to try

For both the AS and the A level exams, you must answer a Methods in Context question.

Item A

Investigating the ways in which classroom interactions reinforce traditional gender identities

Some sociologists have pointed to the ease with which traditional gender identities can be reinforced in classroom interaction. Verbal abuse and other more subtle processes such as the 'male gaze' can have an impact on gender identity. Sociologists have found that some male teachers may even collude with male pupils in 'putting down' girls.

Sociologists may use non-participant observation to investigate the ways in which classroom interactions reinforce traditional gender identities. Observing classroom behaviour at first hand enables researchers to see what actually goes on rather than getting a verbal account after the event. There is also the potential for greater insight through direct experience of classroom interaction. However, it is very difficult for the observer to avoid being noticed and this can affect the behaviour both of teachers and of pupils.

AS and A level question

1   Applying material from Item A and your knowledge of research methods, evaluate the strengths and limitations of non-participant observation for the study of the ways in which classroom interactions reinforce traditional gender identities.

(20 marks)

The Examiner's Advice

Q1 Spend about 30 minutes on this question. It requires you to apply your knowledge of non-participant observation to the study of the particular issue of the ways in which classroom interactions reinforce traditional gender identities. It is not enough simply to discuss the strengths and limitations of non-participant observation in general. Use Item A to help you. For example, it suggests that one research characteristic of the ways in which classroom interactions may reinforce traditional gender identities is that some of the processes involved may be quite subtle such as the 'male gaze' – a way of looking at female pupils and teachers. Consequently, possibly the only way these may be identified is through careful observation of actual classroom interaction. You should link other research characteristics of the ways classroom interactions may reinforce gender identities to the strengths and limitations of non-participant observation. For example, reinforcing traditional gender identities may involve the rapid exchange of looks and words, something that cannot easily be captured after the event through interviews or questionnaires. Other research characteristics include the degree of difficulty of observing all the interactions in a busy classroom setting, the likelihood of this behaviour being hidden by teachers or pupils who are aware they are being observed, measuring the impact of any such behaviour on gender identities etc. You should link these to particular strengths or limitations of the method.

An example

In your answer you should connect the strengths and limitations of non-participant observation to the research characteristics of schooling and gender identities. Here's an example paragraph.

'Item A suggests that the gender of the researcher is likely to play a very important role when investigating this issue. The gender of the observer may alter the behaviour of both teachers and pupils. For example, the presence of a male sociologist in an all-girls' school may alter the normal dynamics of school life. In addition, teachers may disguise sexist attitudes in the observer's presence because they have a professional duty to treat all pupils equally. However, teachers may find it hard to sustain this 'front' when being observed over a prolonged period.'

Police statistics often underestimate the numbers on demonstrations.

GETTING STARTED

Official statistics are collected and published by the government. There are statistics relating to many areas of social life, for example unemployment, education, crime and health.

1 Why might governments collect these statistics?

2 Sociologists can sometimes use official statistics in their research. What advantages might there be in this for the sociologist?

3 Why might governments want to change the official definition that they use as the basis for collecting statistics on unemployment?

Learning objectives

After studying this Topic, you should:

- Know the different types of secondary data that sociologists use.
- Be able to evaluate the strengths and limitations of official statistics and documents.
- Be able to apply your understanding of documents and official statistics to the study of education.

Sociologists not only use data they have gathered themselves by primary methods such as observation or questionnaires. They also make use of information that other people have already created or gathered.

For example, governments collect statistics on the number of births, marriages and deaths, and private individuals often write letters and emails or keep diaries as a record of their experiences.

Sociologists often make use of information from such sources. Similarly, research findings previously made by one sociologist can be used later by another sociologist.

These are known as secondary sources, and the information from them is called secondary data. Secondary data is therefore data gathered or produced by other people for their own particular purposes, but which sociologists make use of in their research (Figure 3.2).

For example, we could use birth rate statistics to develop or test hypotheses about the family, or use diaries to gain a sense of what family life was like for people in the past.

There are two main sources of secondary data:

- Official statistics
- Documents.

In this Topic, we shall examine the strengths and limitations of these two sources of secondary data in sociological research.

Official statistics

Official statistics are quantitative data gathered by the government or other official bodies. Examples include statistics on births, deaths, marriages and divorces, exam results, school exclusions, crime, suicide, unemployment and health. The ten-yearly Census of the whole UK population is a major source of official statistics. Examples of many other official statistics can be found on the website of the Office for National Statistics.

The government collects official statistics to use in policy-making. For example, statistics on births help the government to plan the number of school places for the future. Similarly, Ofsted and the Department for Education use statistics on things such as exam results to monitor the effectiveness of schools and colleges.

There are two ways of collecting official statistics:

- **Registration** – for example, the law requires parents to register births.
- **Official surveys**, such as the Census or the General Household Survey.

In addition to official statistics produced by the government, organisations and groups such as trade unions, charities, businesses and churches also produce various kinds of statistics. For example, the educational pressure group, the National Grammar Schools Association, produces statistics on the comparative performance of grammar and non-selective schools.

Both the advantages and the disadvantages of official statistics stem largely from the fact that they are secondary data. That is, they are not collected by sociologists but by official agencies for their own particular purposes – which may not always be the same as those of the sociologist.

Analysis and Evaluation
Despite the legal requirement for every household to complete the Census form, in inner city areas there are often lower rates of completion than elsewhere. Suggest two reasons for this.

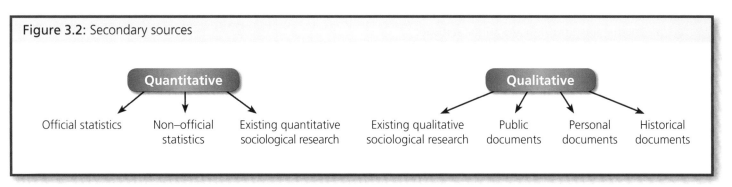

Figure 3.2: Secondary sources

Quantitative
- Official statistics
- Non–official statistics
- Existing quantitative sociological research

Qualitative
- Existing qualitative sociological research
- Public documents
- Personal documents
- Historical documents

1 Practical issues

Advantages Official statistics offer several practical advantages.

- They are a free source of huge amounts of data. Only the state can afford to conduct large-scale surveys costing millions of pounds, such as the Census covering every household in the UK. Likewise, only the government has the power to compel citizens to provide it with information, for example by requiring parents to register births. Sociologists can make use of this data, saving them time and money.
- Statistics allow comparisons between groups. For example, we can compare statistics on educational achievement, crime rates or life expectancy between classes, genders or ethnic groups.
- Because official statistics are collected at regular intervals, they show trends and patterns over time. This means sociologists can use them for 'before and after' studies to show cause-and-effect relationships. For example, we can compare divorce statistics before and after a change in the divorce law to measure what effect the new legislation has had.

Disadvantages Official statistics can have practical disadvantages.

- The government collects statistics for its own purpose and not for the benefit of sociologists, so there may be none available on the topic we are interested in. For example, Durkheim in his study of suicide found that there were no statistics specifically on the religion of suicide victims, presumably because the state had no use for the information. However, this was crucial to Durkheim's hypothesis about integration and suicide.
- The definitions that the state uses in collecting the data may be different from those that sociologists would use. For example, they may define 'poverty' or 'truancy' differently. In turn, this may lead to different views of how large the problem is.
- If definitions change over time, it may make comparisons difficult. For example, the official definition of unemployment changed over 30 times during the 1980s and early 1990s – so the unemployment statistics are not comparing like with like.

2 Representativeness

Because official statistics often cover very large numbers (sometimes even the entire population), and because care is taken with sampling procedures, they often provide a more representative sample than surveys conducted with the limited resources available to the sociologist. They may therefore provide a better basis for making generalisations and testing hypotheses.

However, some statistics are less representative than others. For example, statistics gathered by compulsory registration, such as birth and death statistics or the number of pupils in school, are likely to cover virtually all cases and therefore be highly representative.

By contrast, statistics produced from official surveys, such as the British Crime Survey or the General Household Survey, may be less representative because they are only based on a sample of the relevant population. Nonetheless, such official surveys are usually much bigger than most sociologists could carry out themselves. For example, the Crime Survey for England and Wales in 2014 had a sample size of 50,000 people.

3 Reliability

Official statistics are generally seen as a reliable source of data. They are compiled in a standardised way by trained staff, following set procedures. For example, government statisticians compile death rates for different social classes following a standard procedure that uses the occupation recorded on each person's death certificate to identify their class.

Official statistics are therefore reliable because, in principle, any person properly trained will allocate a given case to the same category.

However, official statistics are not always wholly reliable. For example, census coders may make errors or omit information when recording data from census forms, or members of the public may fill in the form incorrectly.

Box 26	Positivism, interpretivism and official statistics

Positivists favour official statistics as objective social facts that achieve the main positivist goals of reliability, generalisability and representativeness.

- They provide reliable data because their standardised categories and collection techniques can be easily replicated.
- Because they are collected at regular intervals, they show trends in behaviour over time.
- They provide quantitative data, allowing us to identify and measure behaviour patterns and establish cause-and-effect relationships.
- They are usually large scale and thus very representative.

Interpretivists reject official statistics, particularly 'soft' ones, such as crime statistics, as social constructs and not social facts. Official statistics fail to achieve the main interpretivist goal of validity.

See Box 12 on page 94 for more about positivism, interpretivism and research methods.

4 Validity: the 'dark figure'

A major problem with using official statistics is that of validity. Do they actually measure the thing that they claim to measure?

Hard and soft statistics Some 'hard' official statistics do succeed in doing this. For example, statistics on the number of births, deaths, marriages and divorces generally give a very accurate picture (although a small number of births and deaths do go unrecorded).

However, 'soft' statistics give a much less valid picture. For example, police statistics do not record all crimes. Similarly, educational statistics do not record all racist incidents occurring in schools.

Attempts have been made to compensate for the shortcomings of police statistics by using self-report or victim studies to give a more accurate picture of the amount of crime. For example, the Crime Survey for England and Wales asks people what crimes they have been victims of.

By comparing the results with the police statistics, we can see that the latter underestimate the 'real rate' of crime and from this we can make a more accurate estimate of the extent of crime. For example, the 2011 British Crime Survey found that only 38 per cent of crimes revealed by the survey were actually reported to the police, and the police did not record all of these.

Application

1 Suggest three types of crime that may not be reported to the police.
2 For each example, suggest why this may be so.
3 Suggest reasons why the police do not record all the crimes reported to them.

5 Official statistics: facts, constructs or ideology?

Whether we see official statistics as useful or not depends in part on which theoretical perspective we adopt.

positivism

Positivists such as Emile Durkheim (1897) see statistics as a valuable resource for sociologists. Positivists take for granted that official statistics are 'social facts'; that is, true and objective measures of the real rate of crime, suicide etc. They see sociology as a science and, just like natural scientists, they develop hypotheses to discover the causes of the behaviour patterns that the statistics reveal.

Positivists often use official statistics to test their hypotheses. For example, Durkheim put forward the hypothesis that suicide is caused by a lack of social integration. Using the

▲ A cannabis farm. Not all crimes get reported or recorded.

comparative method (see Topic 3), he argued that Protestant and Catholic religions differ in how well they integrate individuals into society. Using official suicide statistics, he was able to show that Protestants had a higher suicide rate than Catholics, and so was able to argue that this statistical evidence proved his hypothesis correct.

interpretivism

By contrast, interpretivists such as Maxwell Atkinson (1971) regard official statistics as lacking validity. They argue that statistics do not represent real things or 'social facts' that exist out there in the world. Instead, statistics are socially

---

Figure 3.3: Crime statistics – the official view

In the official view, statistics give a relatively accurate and true picture of society. The flow chart below indicates the official view of how crime statistics are created.

A crime is committed
↓
It is observed by witnesses or victims
↓
The crime is reported to the police
↓
Police record the crime
↓
Police investigate
↓
Police arrest the suspect
↓
The suspect is charged with the crime
↓
Suspect appears in court and, if found guilty, offender and crime are counted in the official crime statistics.

constructed – they merely represent the labels some people give to the behaviour of others.

In this view, suicide statistics do not represent the 'real rate' of suicides that have actually taken place, but merely the total number of decisions made by coroners to *label* some deaths as suicides. The statistics therefore tell us more about the way coroners label deaths than about the actual causes of these deaths.

Rather than taking statistics at face value, therefore, interpretivists argue that we should investigate how they are socially constructed. For example, Atkinson uses qualitative methods such as observing the proceedings of coroners' courts to discover how coroners reach their decisions to label some deaths as suicides, others as accidents and so on.

Marxism

Marxists such as John Irvine (1987) take a different view. Unlike interpretivists, they do not regard official statistics as merely the outcome of the labels applied by officials such as coroners. Instead they see official statistics as serving the interests of capitalism.

Marxists see capitalist society as made up of two social classes in conflict with each other, the capitalist ruling class

and the working class, whose labour the capitalists exploit for profit.

In this conflict, the state is not neutral, but serves the interests of the capitalist class. The statistics that the state produces are part of ruling-class ideology – that is, a part of the ideas and values that help to maintain the capitalist class in power.

Unemployment statistics are a good example of this process. The state has regularly changed the definition of unemployment over the years. This has almost always reduced the numbers officially defined as unemployed, thus disguising the true level of unemployment and its damaging effects on the working class.

Activity	Research

Comparing perspectives on official statistics

...go to www.sociology.uk.net

Similarly, Marxists argue that official police statistics systematically underestimate the number of people taking part in demonstrations against government policies. This gives the public the impression that there is less opposition to capitalism.

Documents

The term 'document' refers to any written text, such as personal diaries, government reports, medical records, novels, newspapers, letters, emails, blogs, web pages, parish registers, train timetables, shopping lists, bank statements – the list is almost endless. In fact, we can also take the term to include 'texts' such as paintings, drawings, photographs, maps and so on. We can also include sounds and images from film, television, radio and other media output.

We can distinguish between public and personal documents:

public documents

Public documents are produced by organisations such as government departments, schools, welfare agencies, businesses and charities. Some of this output may be available for researchers to use. It includes documents such as Ofsted reports of school inspections, minutes of council meetings, published company accounts and records of parliamentary debates.

Public documents also include the official reports of public enquiries such as the Black Report (1980) into inequalities in health, which became a major source of information for sociologists.

personal documents

Personal documents include items such as letters, diaries, photo albums and autobiographies. These are first-person accounts of social events and personal experiences, and they generally also include the writer's feelings and attitudes.

A famous early example of a study using personal documents is William Thomas and Florian Znaniecki's (1919) *The Polish Peasant in Europe and America*, a study of migration and social change. As interactionists, they were particularly interested in people's personal experiences of these events.

They used personal documents to reveal the meanings that individuals gave to their experience of migration. The documents included 764 letters bought after an advertisement in a Polish newspaper in Chicago and several autobiographies.

Thomas and Znaniecki also used public documents, such as newspaper articles and court and social work records. With these documents, they were able to explore the experiences of social change of some of the thousands of people who migrated from rural Poland to the USA in the early 20th century.

historical documents

A historical document is simply a personal or public document created in the past. If we want to study the past, historical documents are usually the only source of information (although in the case of the recent past, there may still be people alive who can be questioned).

The study of families and households illustrates some of the types of historical documents that have been used:

- Peter Laslett used parish records in his study of family structure in pre-industrial England.
- Michael Anderson used parliamentary reports on child labour, as well as statistical material from the 1851 Census, to study changes in family structure in 19th century Preston.
- Philippe Ariès used child-rearing manuals and paintings of children in his study of the rise of the modern notion of childhood.

Assessing documents

As John Scott (1990) argues, when it comes to assessing documentary sources, the general principles are the same as those for any other type of sociological evidence. He puts forward four criteria for evaluating documents: authenticity, credibility, representativeness and meaning.

1 authenticity

Is the document what it claims to be? Are there any missing pages, and if it is a copy, is it free from errors? Who actually wrote the document? For example, the so-called 'Hitler Diaries' were later proven to be fakes.

2 credibility

Is the document believable? Was the author sincere? Politicians may write diaries intended for publication that inflate their own importance. Thomas and Znaniecki's Polish immigrants may have lied in their letters home about how good life in the USA was, to justify their decision to emigrate.

▲ A 19th century portrait of a child – but how representative is it of children at the time?

Is the document accurate? For example, was the account of a riot written soon after the event, or years later? Stuart Stein (2003) notes that documents on the internet are often not checked for accuracy before publication.

3 representativeness

Is the evidence in the document typical? If we cannot answer this question, we cannot know whether it is safe to generalise from it:

- Not all documents survive: are the surviving documents typical of the ones that get destroyed or lost?
- Not all surviving documents are available for researchers to use. The 30-year rule prevents access to some official documents for 30 years and, if classified as

---

Box 27 **Positivism, interpretivism and documents**

Interpretivists tend to favour documents because they achieve the main interpretivist goal of validity:
- They are not usually written with research in mind and can thus be an authentic statement of their author's views.
- They provide qualitative data that gives us insight into the author's world-view and meanings.

Positivists tend to reject documents because they fail to achieve the main positivist goals of reliability, generalisability and representativeness:
- They are often unstandardised and unreliable; for example, every person's diary is unique. This also makes it difficult to draw generalisations from them.
- They are often unrepresentative; for example, only literate groups can write diaries and letters.
- In interpreting documents, researchers may impose their own meanings on them.

However, positivists do sometimes carry out content analysis on documents to produce quantitative data from them.

See Box 12 on page 94 for more about positivism, interpretivism and research methods.

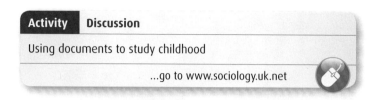

Activity Discussion

Using documents to study childhood

...go to www.sociology.uk.net

official secrets, they may not be available at all. Private documents such as diaries may never become available, or only after the death of the author.

- Certain groups may be unrepresented: the illiterate, and those with limited leisure time, are unlikely to keep diaries. The better educated classes are thus likely to be over-represented.

4 meaning

The researcher may need special skills to understand a document. It may have to be translated from a foreign language; words may change their meaning over time.

We also have to interpret what the document actually means to the writer and the intended audience. Different sociologists may interpret the same document differently. Thomas later admitted that the interpretations he and Znaniecki had offered in their book were not always based on the data from the documents.

Advantages of documents

Although documents need to be assessed carefully by the sociologist before they are used as sources of evidence, nevertheless they have several important advantages:

- Personal documents such as diaries and letters enable the researcher to get close to the social actor's reality, giving insight through their richly detailed qualitative data. Interpretivists favour them for this reason.
- Sometimes documents are the only source of information, for example in studying the past.
- By providing another source of data, documents offer an extra check on the results obtained by primary methods.
- They are a cheap source of data, because someone else has already gathered the information. For the same reason, using existing documents saves the sociologist time.

Content analysis

Content analysis is a method for dealing systematically with the contents of documents. It is best known for its use in analysing documents produced by the mass media, such as television news bulletins or advertisements.

Although such documents are usually qualitative, content analysis enables the sociologist to produce quantitative data from these sources.

Ros Gill (1988) describes how content analysis works as follows. Imagine we want to measure particular aspects of a media message; for example, how many female characters are portrayed as being in paid employment.

- First we decide what categories we are going to use, such as employee, full-time housewife etc.
- Next, we study the source (television broadcast, magazine article etc) and place the characters in it into the categories we have decided upon.
- We can then count up the number in each category, for example to compare how often women are portrayed as full-time housewives rather than employees.

We might then go on to compare the results of our content analysis with the official statistics for female employment to see if the media were presenting a false or stereotypical picture of women's roles.

Glenys Lobban (1974) used content analysis to analyse gender roles in children's reading schemes, while Gaye Tuchman (1978) used it to analyse television's portrayal of women. Lobban and Tuchman both found that females were portrayed in a range of roles that was both limited and stereotyped. For example, Lobban found that female characters were generally portrayed playing domestic roles.

Content analysis has several advantages:

- It is cheap.
- It is usually easy to find sources of material in the form of newspapers, television broadcasts and so on.
- Positivists see it as a useful source of objective, quantitative, scientific data.

However, interpretivist sociologists argue that simply counting up the number of times something appears in a document tells us nothing about its meaning.

Activity Research

How do newspapers report crime?

...go to www.sociology.uk.net

Topic summary

Secondary data include **official statistics** and **documents.**

Secondary sources save **time and money** and provide useful data, but they may not always be available.

Statistics may **lack validity**, measuring officials' decisions rather than real events.

Documents, such as diaries, letters and government reports, **may not be authentic or representative.** Some sociologists apply **content analysis** to documents.

EXAMINING SECONDARY SOURCES

QuickCheck Questions

Check your answers at www.sociology.uk.net

1 Why are official statistics and documents described as secondary data?
2 Explain the difference between registration and official surveys as ways of collecting official statistics.
3 What are the main uses of official statistics for sociologists?
4 Give one example of 'hard' statistics and one example of 'soft' statistics.
5 Suggest reasons why official crime statistics may not be a valid picture of the amount of crime.
6 Suggest two examples of personal documents.
7 What personal and public documents did Thomas and Znaniecki use in their study of Polish immigrants to America?
8 Name Scott's four criteria for evaluating documents.

Questions to try

Whether or not you're taking the AS exams during your A level course, trying the AS questions below is a very good way of testing your knowledge and understanding and practising your skills in preparation for your A level exams.

Item A   As well as their own primary data, sociologists use data that has been gathered by others. These secondary sources can be very useful. For example, the scale of data collected by governments in the form of official statistics is far beyond the resources of any sociologist. There are also some issues, such as suicide or historical events, which would be very difficult to investigate without having access to the personal or public documents left behind by those involved.

Positivist and interpretivist researchers tend to favour different forms of secondary data. Positivists prefer quantitative data, while interpretivists favour qualitative data.

AS questions

1 Outline two practical problems of using historical documents in sociological research.   (4 marks)
2 Evaluate the practical and theoretical issues involved in using statistics in studying society.   (16 marks)

A level

3 Applying material from Item A and your knowledge, evaluate the usefulness of different kinds of secondary data in sociological research.   (20 marks)

The Examiner's Advice

Q2 Spend about 25 minutes on this question. Discuss practical issues such as that governments may not collect statistics on some areas of sociological interest, their definitions may change over time and differ from those of the sociologist. Examine theoretical issues, especially the issue of validity. Differentiate here between 'hard' and 'soft' statistics. The former are usually straightforward headcounts (e.g. births) and so very accurate. 'Soft' statistics often have an unrecorded 'dark figure'. Use examples (e.g. unemployment and crime figures) to illustrate the social construction of statistics. Although usually seen as representative and reliable, statistics may also contain errors in the recording of data. Explain why interpretivists and Marxists tend to reject official statistics as a source of data. Evaluate these problems as you go through each one rather than offering a list of strengths in a separate section at the end. For example, point out that recording errors in some types of official statistics e.g. the Census, are relatively minor.

Q3 Spend about 30 minutes on this. Be clear about the different kinds of secondary data including public documents, personal documents and official statistics. Use the debate between positivism and interpretivism as a context for your answer. Explain why interpretivists see personal documents as useful in producing valid data. Explain why positivists value statistics for their reliability and representativeness. Evaluate the view, e.g. by considering why statistics might not be as reliable or representative as positivists claim. Compare the usefulness of secondary data with that of primary data (e.g. in terms of cost and time). Use concepts and issues such as quantitative and qualitative data, validity, reliability, representativeness, sociology as a science, social construction of statistics, objectivity and subjectivity. Use studies such as Durkheim, Atkinson, official crime surveys, the Census, Thomas and Znaniecki, Scott and Gill, and develop points noted in Item A.

METHODS IN CONTEXT
using secondary sources to investigate education

Sociologists use secondary sources to study a variety of educational issues. The main secondary sources that they use are official statistics and a variety of documents, both personal and public. We shall examine the usefulness of each of these in turn.

Before reading this section, re-visit Topic 2 to refresh your understanding of what is special about researching education.

Using official statistics to investigate education

Education is one of the key services provided by the state and as such is closely monitored. As a result, schools, colleges, local authorities and the Department for Education collect a wide range of official statistics on education. These cover many issues that sociologists are interested in, including:

- Ethnicity, class, gender and educational achievement
- School attendance, truancy and inclusion
- League tables, marketisation and school performance
- Gender and subject choice
- Education, work and training.

practical issues

Much of this data is published and thus available to the sociologist, saving them both time and money. For example, the government collects statistics on over 30,000 primary and 4,000 secondary schools. In practice, it would be too costly and time-consuming for a sociologist to gather information on so many schools themselves.

Educational statistics allow sociologists to make comparisons between the achievements of different social groups based on ethnicity, gender and social class.

Also, because educational statistics are collected at regular and frequent intervals, sociologists can make comparisons over time. For example, annually gathered exam statistics enable the sociologist to see trends in results.

Governments gather statistics to monitor the effectiveness of their educational policies, such as those dealing with the curriculum, subject choice, raising standards and reducing inequality of achievement. Such issues are also of great relevance to sociologists, so the statistics produced by government may be very useful to researchers.

However, governments collect statistics for their own policy purposes and these may not be the same as those of sociologists. For example, sociologists are very interested in the relationship between language, social class and achievement, but there are no official statistics available on this.

Even where the state collects educational statistics of sociological interest, the definitions of key concepts may differ from those that sociologists use. For example, official definitions of pupils' social class are based on parental occupation, whereas Marxist sociologists define class in terms of property ownership.

Also, the state may not collect statistics on pupils' social class as such, but only on pupils who are entitled to free school meals.

Because of the stigma and peer group bullying sometimes associated with receiving free school meals, some pupils don't claim them even when entitled to do so. Furthermore, because official statistics are secondary data, they cannot tell the sociologist about the interaction processes in school that may lead to this under-claiming.

Also, although free school meals are used as an indicator of low class position, not all those entitled to them are working-class (for example some lower middle-class pupils from large families may qualify for them). Nor are all working-class children entitled to free school meals - only those from relatively poor backgrounds will qualify.

representativeness

Some official statistics on education are highly representative. For example, all state schools have to complete a school census three times a year. This collects information on pupils' attendance, ethnicity and gender, the numbers receiving free school meals and so on. Because these statistics cover virtually every pupil in the country, they are highly representative.

reliability

Positivists favour official statistics because their reliability means that they can be used to test and re-test hypotheses and thus discover cause-and-effect relationships. For example, statistics on exam results showing social class differences in educational achievement may correlate with statistics on parental income. From this, positivists may be able to conclude that poverty causes under-achievement.

Although it is possible for errors to creep into the production of official statistics on education, they are generally very reliable.

This is because the government imposes standard definitions and categories for their collection, which all schools must use. This enables the process to be replicated from year to year, allowing direct comparisons to be made, for example of school performance over time.

However, governments may change the definitions and categories. For example, when the Conservatives first introduced league tables of school performance in 1988, a school's position was based purely on its exam results. This generally meant that schools with middle-class pupils were placed higher than those with working-class intakes.

However, in 2006, the Labour government introduced a new measure of school performance called Contextual Value Added (CVA). This took into account not just exam results, but also the level of deprivation pupils suffer.

In many cases, CVA 'turns the tables' and results in schools with disadvantaged pupils being placed higher than those with middle-class intakes. Changing the definitions on which educational statistics are based makes it difficult for sociologists to draw comparisons over time.

validity

Interpretivists question the validity of educational statistics. They argue that such statistics are socially constructed. For example, they see truancy statistics as the outcome of a series of definitions and decisions made by a variety of social actors, such as parents, teachers and pupils.

Schools may manipulate their attendance figures by re-defining poor attenders as being on study leave or additional work experience. They may be tempted to do so because, in an education market, there is pressure on schools to present themselves in the best possible light in order to maintain their funding and parental support. However, this deliberate distorting of attendance figures undermines the validity of educational statistics.

Activity | **Research**

Does absence cause underachievement?

...go to www.sociology.uk.net

Using documents to investigate education

Schools, colleges, local authorities and the Department for Education generate a wide range of public documents. Also, because pupils produce large amounts of paper-based work, there is the opportunity for the researcher to use personal educational documents. But these are not the only documents that sociologists can use, as Box 28 shows.

Documents cover many educational issues that sociologists are interested in, including:

▲ A wide variety of documents about education is available to the researcher.

- Ethnic, class and gender differences in achievement
- The curriculum
- Gender stereotyping in school books
- Racist incidents in schools
- Special educational needs.

practical issues

Public documents on education are often easily accessible. Partly because of government policies emphasising parental choice, schools make a large amount of information available to the public, which researchers may then use.

For example, David Gillborn (1995), in his study of racism and schooling, was able to access a wide range of school documents, including school policy statements, local authority guidelines on anti-racism and the minutes of staff meetings and working parties.

These documents gave Gillborn the 'official' picture of what was happening in terms of racism and anti-racism in the schools he studied. Gillborn then compared this with the data he collected from interviews and observation.

Similarly, Gewirtz et al (1995), in their study of marketisation and education, found that school brochures and prospectuses were a useful free source of information about how schools presented themselves in the education 'marketplace'.

Personal documents can be more difficult to access. Valerie Hey (1997) made use of the notes girls passed to each other in class to understand their friendship patterns. However, the notes were not always easy to obtain, as the girls were experts at hiding them from teachers.

Some educational documents are confidential, such as teachers' personnel files and pupils' disciplinary records; so sociologists may be unable to gain access to them.

Box 28	Examples of documents in education	
Public documents	**Personal documents**	
School websites	Pupils' written work	
Government guidance to schools and colleges	School reports on pupils	
School prospectuses	Pupils and teachers' diaries	
Government enquiries	Pupils and teachers' autobiographies	
Novels and films about school life	Graffiti on school buildings, desks etc	
School textbooks	Notes passed between pupils in class	
Recordings of playground songs and games	Letters from parents, e.g. explaining absences	
Media reports about education	Text messages between pupils	
Ofsted inspection reports		

Analysis and Evaluation

Why might (a) school prospectuses and (b) Ofsted inspection reports not give a valid picture of school life?

ethical issues

There are few ethical concerns with using public documents produced by schools. Having been placed in the public domain by the organisation that produced them, permission for their use is not required.

However, there are more ethical problems with personal documents. For example, Hey collected in the notes that girls had passed to each other in class. In some cases, the girls offered her the notes freely, but in others Hey collected them from desks at the end of the lesson and, in one case, a teacher took them from the wastepaper bin and offered them to her. Thus in some cases, informed consent for their use had not been obtained.

representativeness

Some official documents are legally required of all schools and colleges, such as records of racist incidents. This makes it more likely that we can form a representative picture of racism in schools across the whole country. However, of course, not all racist incidents may be documented.

Personal documents are often less representative. For example, Hey collected about 70 notes, but the unsystematic way in which she came by them makes it likely that her sample was unrepresentative.

reliability

Many public documents, for example attendance registers, are produced in a systematic format. This enables researchers to make direct comparisons of the absence rates of pupils in different schools.

However, deliberate falsifications or accidental mistakes made when filling in registers reduce their reliability because teachers are not applying the measure of attendance consistently.

Some educational documents can also be used in ways that other researchers can replicate. Lobban examined 179 stories from six school reading schemes looking for gender stereotyping. She analysed the content of each story using the same set of categories, counting the number of times images fell into each category. Future researchers can easily apply systematic content analysis of this kind to create comparative data from educational documents.

validity

Documents can provide important insights into the meanings held by teachers and pupils and can therefore be high in validity. For example, Hey initially examined girls' friendships in schools through observation and interviews. Eventually, however, she realised that she was ignoring a useful source of insight into girls' feelings and actions – the notes they passed to each other in class.

Although teachers considered these notes to be 'bits of silliness', Hey found that they offered valuable insights into the nature of girls' friendships. This is because they were spontaneous expressions of the girls' feelings and attitudes.

However, all documents are open to different interpretations. For example, we cannot be sure that Hey's interpretation of the meaning of the notes was the same as that of the girls. Also, because the girls sometimes handed Hey the notes after the class, it is possible that they were written with her in mind and may not have been spontaneous.

EXAMINING OFFICIAL STATISTICS IN CONTEXT

Question to try

For both the AS and the A level exams, you must answer a Methods in Context question.

Item A

Investigating social class differences in achievement

Many sociologists have examined the relationship between social class and achievement and have found that there is a clear pattern of middle-class pupils outperforming working-class pupils. However, sociologists also want to understand the reasons for this pattern.

Sociologists may use official statistics to investigate social class differences in achievement. These allow researchers to see trends and patterns over time which can help to reveal cause-and-effect relationships. Official statistics can be highly representative because they are often collected across a wide range of institutions. However, it is very difficult for the researcher to be sure that official statistics have not been manipulated in some way by the organisations responsible for their collection.

AS and A level question

1   Applying material from Item A and your knowledge of research methods, evaluate the strengths and limitations of official statistics for the study of social class differences in achievement.   (20 marks)

The Examiner's Advice

Q1 Spend about 30 minutes on this question. It requires you to apply your knowledge of official statistics to the study of the particular issue of class differences in achievement. It is not enough simply to discuss the strengths and limitations of official statistics in general. Use Item A to help you. For example, it suggests that one research characteristic of class differences in achievement is that although there is a clear pattern of class inequality, sociologists also want to know the reasons behind this. Official statistics are very useful for identifying the pattern but give few indications as to the reasons for the pattern. Schools collect lots of data about achievement over time but little else that could be used to correlate with it. You should link other research characteristics of class differences in achievement to the strengths and limitations of official statistics. For example, achievement can be measured at various stages and schools collect statistics at several points in a pupil's educational career. This gives trends over time. Other research characteristics include the need to cover a wide range of schools, the possible influence of many different school and non-school factors on achievement, the self-esteem of pupils in relation to their achievement etc. You should link these to particular strengths or limitations of the method.

An Example

In your answer you should connect the strengths and limitations of official statistics to the research characteristics of class differences in achievement. Here's an example paragraph.

'Item A suggests that organisations such as schools may try to manipulate official statistics. For example, there is a great pressure on them to present their results as positively as possible within the education market. However, they have little room to manipulate examination results because all pupils take the same range of exams, and because pupils are easily categorised into those who are eligible for free school meals (FSM) and those who are not, which some researchers use as a way of operationalising the concept of class. Statistics that correlate FSM and exam results are publicly available. However, FSM in not a very valid measure of class. For example, many working-class pupils may not be eligible for FSM because their parental income is just above the threshold.'

CHAPTER 3

EXAMINING RESEARCH METHODS

Item A   When deciding which research methods to use, sociologists are influenced by a range of factors. Although the researcher's theoretical standpoint leads them to favour either quantitative or qualitative methods, practical factors are arguably more important. Issues such as cost, time, access and the views of whoever is funding the research are impossible to ignore when selecting a method.

AS questions

1   Outline two practical factors affecting sociologists' choice of research topic.   (4 marks)
2   Evaluate the reasons why some sociologists use unstructured interviews.   (16 marks)

A level questions

3   Outline and explain two ethical problems of covert research.   (10 marks)
4   Applying material from Item A and your knowledge, evaluate the claim that practical factors are more important
    than theoretical factors in determining the sociologist's choice of method.   (20 marks)

The examiner's advice for AS question 2 is on page 256. For A level question 4, see the answer below along with the examiner's comments and mark.

Answer by Viola

A level question 4: Applying material from Item A and your knowledge, evaluate the claim that practical factors are more important than theoretical factors in determining the sociologist's choice of method.

Many factors affect a sociologist's choice of research method. Not only are they influenced by practical considerations and their theoretical standpoint but ethical factors also have an influence. When deciding, much depends on the topic and group being studied.

Good to introduce ethical issues early but last point needs developing.

Positivist researchers much prefer to use quantitative data. They see the social world as an objective fact (like the natural world) and want to establish cause-and-effect relationships between social factors, for example, between gender and educational achievement. To do this, they need quantitative data that is easily analysed for trends, patterns and correlations. For example, Durkheim used official statistics to examine the links between suicide and religious beliefs. Interpretivists, on the other hand, want to use methods that produce qualitative data, such as participant observation (PO), because they focus on the meanings social actors hold.

Good knowledge of theoretical perspectives, but could link them to a wider range of methods and sources than just statistics and PO.

In many cases, practical issues prevent researchers from choosing the method they would prefer. Time and money are important considerations. A longitudinal study will be very expensive, requiring funding over many years, and there may not be a suitable funding body to do this. Alternatively, a short PO study such as that carried out over a few weekends by Patrick, is not really limited by cost.

Some good use of examples of practical issues involving particular methods.

Other practical factors include the research opportunity and gaining access to a group. Sometimes an opportunity to do research occurs out of the blue, as with Patrick. This often leads to using PO as there is no time to carefully prepare a questionnaire, set up a sample etc to use in another method.

Good links made between practical issues and a particular method.

At the end of the day, however, it may be ethics that really determines the choice of method. Researchers cannot just act however they wish. They have to take into consideration ethical concerns like getting informed consent, maintaining privacy and confidentiality, and the effect research can have on people. In some cases, these will outweigh theoretical and practical factors.

Reference to ethics needs linking to practical or theoretical issues, e.g. the conflict between validity and ethics when using covert methods.

In the real world of research, funding is crucial and whoever is funding the study will have a major say in what is studied and how it is studied. Research funded by the government is usually focused on gathering quantitative data as they want to see patterns in order to make policy decisions. So an interpretivist might have to tailor their personal preference for qualitative methods in order to get the funding.

Good explanation of influence of government funding body's preferences.

Theoretical perspective is what many researchers would prefer to base their choice of method on – this is a positive element in the choice. However, practical factors act as limits on what can be done, so arguably they are the most important consideration.

Good evaluative point here – positive factor versus limiting factor.

Which of the factors that affect choice of method is most important will also depend on the research subject. In some cases, like studying sensitive or secretive groups, simply whether or not a particular method is practical will be the determining factor.

Another evaluative point though not developed fully. The answer would benefit from an overall conclusion.

You should spend about 30 minutes on this. Viola's answer has a good range of material, referring to theoretical and practical factors and introducing ethical concerns too. Although the question does not mention ethical issues, it would be legitimate (though not required) to conclude that ethical factors are more important than either practical or theoretical ones. However, although ethical factors get some mention in the answer, their influence is stated rather than developed.

There is some focus in the answer on the theoretical versus practical issue that the question points to, e.g. at the start of paragraph 3 and the end of paragraphs 4 and 6. The last two paragraphs also attempt a clear answer to the question although the final paragraph is not developed fully.

The answer could be improved by referring to more studies and their methods in order to show how the different factors influenced the choice of method.

161

EXAMINING METHODS IN CONTEXT

Item A
Investigating pupils with learning difficulties

Some pupils experience learning difficulties, especially in relation to literacy. As a result, they often do badly in school and may be embarrassed by this, and this can lead to low self-esteem. In some cases, pupils with learning difficulties become members of anti-school subcultures.

Sociologists may use written questionnaires to investigate this issue. Respondents can fill questionnaires in quickly and easily by simply selecting one answer from a fixed set of answers. Written questionnaires can also be distributed fairly easily. However, one limitation of written questionnaires is that usually there is no direct contact between researcher and respondents.

Applying material from Item A and your knowledge of research methods, evaluate the strengths and limitations of written questionnaires for the study of pupils with learning difficulties.

(20 marks)

Answer by Brendan

Positivist researchers favour this method because it produces data that is easily quantifiable, reliable and representative. Positivists look for links between factors and these are more easily seen through numerical data. However, interpretivists reject their use, arguing that the data created lacks validity. Written questionnaires are also cheaper and quicker to carry out on a large scale, so they have many practical advantages.

> Theory is an excellent way to start – but he needs to link it to the research issue of learning difficulties.

As Item A says, written questionnaires are quickly and easily filled in as respondents only have to select an answer from a list created by the researcher. This might well help when studying pupils with learning difficulties as this is much easier than asking them to write or speak at length – something their learning difficulties might stop them from doing.

> Excellent – uses Item and then develops the point, linking a characteristic of the pupils to a strength of questionnaires.

Written questionnaires are also very useful for researching sensitive issues like this. They can be anonymous so there is no need for pupils (or teachers) to hold back with their answers out of fear of being identified. There would be no 'comeback' on them. However, interpretivists argue that this means no rapport and trust is built, making it harder to get to people's real meanings.

> Needs to explain why it's a sensitive issue for pupils (or teachers), so as to link it to anonymity. A missed opportunity.

Schools are often reluctant to let researchers in. Heads and other 'gatekeepers' may feel the school's reputation is at stake if the research finds that they have a lot of pupils with learning difficulties.

> Good point about access and school's reputation but needs linking specifically to questionnaires.

On the other hand, once a head admits the researcher, there are some big advantages. The head can allow the sociologist to distribute the questionnaires, for example in tutor time, and they can impose a deadline on their completion. This gets over one of the big problems with questionnaires – their low rate of return.

> Good link between two features of questionnaires and researching in schools – but still needs linking to the study of learning difficulties.

There are few ethical issues with written questionnaires as it is up to the respondent whether or not they fill them in and return them. There's not the same pressure as with face-to-face research. However, if they are distributed by the school, the pupil – or parent – may feel pressurised into completing them.

Pupils with learning difficulties may not have enough reading and writing skills to understand the written questionnaire. They may also be too embarrassed about their own weaknesses to fill it in. This is especially true with written questionnaires, because there is no-one to help them.'

> Accurate, but not linked to studying the specific issue or even education in general – so just a general point.

> Excellent – clearly links a characteristic of the specific issue (literacy) to two features of the method (written and no help available).

Spend about 30 minutes on this question. The key skill to show here is Application: you must apply your knowledge of the method to the particular issue in the question. Don't just talk about written questionnaires in general.

Brendan's answer has good coverage of strengths and limitations of written questionnaires, including practical (time, cost, access), ethical (limited ethical constraints) and theoretical issues (positivism vs interpretivism).

In paragraphs 2 and 7, Brendan does extremely well – he links a strength or limitation of the method to a characteristic of the particular issue of pupils with learning difficulties. This is what examiners are looking for and these two paragraphs earn a lot of marks because they show good Application skills.

Elsewhere, he gives a strength or limitation of written questionnaires in general (e.g. paragraph 6) but needs to link it to the issue. Likewise, he makes a good point about issues to do with studying schools in general (e.g. paragraph 5) but needs to link it to studying learning difficulties in particular.

Listing the method's strengths and limitations and then attempting to link them to the particular issue can be a very effective approach, as Brendan's mark shows. However, doing it the other way round can also be effective. First take a characteristic of the research issue and then link it to a strength or limitation of the method. Look at Brendan's last paragraph in which he does this.

 17/20

CHAPTER 4

Families and Households

Brighton, 2014. One of the UK's first gay weddings.

What is a family? What is a household?

A household is a person living alone or a group of people living together (e.g. sharing meals, bills, housework etc). This group may or may not be related to one another.

Defining the family is harder. One definition is that it involves monogamous marriage between a man and a woman, plus their child(ren), all sharing the same residence. This *nuclear* family is often held up as the ideal. However, this definition rules out groups that many would see as families, such as unmarried cohabiting couples.

At the other extreme is the idea that any set of arrangements that those involved see as a family, *is* a family. This has the advantage of not requiring us to make judgements about other people's lifestyles: if you define your own personal set-up as a family, sociologists have no right to disagree.

However, some would see this approach as too broad, since literally any group can count as a family – so it may include households that some would not see as 'proper' families.

Key questions about the family

In this chapter, we shall be examining some of the different aspects of family life that sociologists are interested in. These include:

- Are husbands and wives today equal?
- How far have the position of children and our attitudes towards childhood changed?
- Changes in the size of families, birth and death rates, and in the population as a whole.
- Changes in marriage, cohabitation, divorce and parenthood, and the increasing diversity of family types today.
- The impact on families of government policies and laws.

The AQA Specification

The specification is the syllabus produced by the exam board, telling you what you have to study. The AQA specification for Families and Households requires you to examine the following:

- The relationship of the family to the social structure and social change, with particular reference to the economy and to state policies.
- Changing patterns of marriage, cohabitation, separation, divorce and childbearing and the life-course, including the sociology of personal life, and the diversity of contemporary family and household structures.
- Gender roles, domestic labour and power relationships within the family in contemporary society.
- The nature of childhood, and changes in the status of children in the family and society.
- Demographic trends in the UK since 1900: birth rates, death rates, family size, life expectancy, ageing population, and migration and globalisation.

For more about the specification, visit www.aqa.org.uk

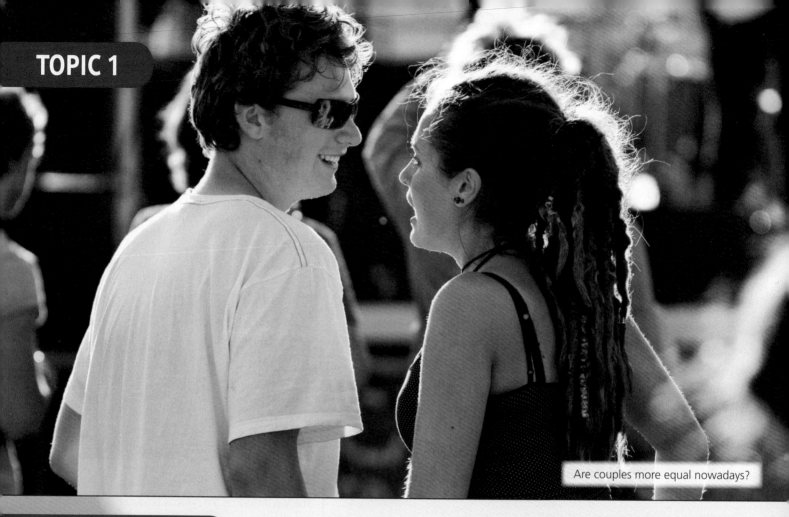

TOPIC 1

Are couples more equal nowadays?

GETTING STARTED

Note down who was responsible for each of the following tasks in your family when you were young: (A) always mother; (B) mainly mother; (C) shared equally by both parents; (D) mainly father; (E) always father; (F) other person (state who).

1 Doing the laundry
2 Making small repairs in the house
3 Caring for sick family members
4 Shopping for groceries
5 Doing the household cleaning

6 Preparing the meals
7 Taking you to the park
8 Reading to you at bedtime
9 Supervising your bath
10 Taking you to and picking you up from school

Now collate everyone's answers so that you have results for the whole class.

a As a class, identify any patterns you can see. For example, are certain tasks always done by the same person?

b What reasons can you think of for the patterns?

c Do you think these patterns show a fair division of labour?

Learning objectives

After studying this Topic, you should:

- Know about gender roles in the domestic division of labour.

- Know about power relationships between couples, including decision-making, control of resources and domestic violence.

- Be able to analyse how far these roles and relationships have changed over time.

- Be able to evaluate different sociological views on couples' roles and relationships.

COUPLES

In the 19th century, the Victorian family was very patriarchal – that is, the man was in every sense the head of the household. For example, on marrying, a woman's property became her husband's. Similarly, grounds for divorce were very unequal – a man could gain a divorce on the grounds of his wife's adultery, but a woman had to prove her husband's cruelty or another 'matrimonial offence' in addition to adultery.

This Topic is about married and cohabiting couples. It looks at equality and inequality in families and households.

Sociologists are interested in how far couples have a more equal relationship today. Some of the key questions they ask about couples are:

- Do men and women share housework and childcare equally?
- Do men and women have an equal say in family decisions and do they get equal shares of the household's income?
- Why does domestic violence occur and who commits it?

The domestic division of labour

The domestic division of labour refers to the roles that men and women play in relation to housework, childcare and paid work. Sociologists are interested in whether men and women share domestic tasks equally.

Parsons: instrumental and expressive roles

In the traditional nuclear family, the roles of husbands and wives are segregated – separate and distinct from one another. In Talcott Parsons' (1955) functionalist model of the family, for example, there is a clear division of labour between spouses:

- **The husband has an instrumental role**, geared towards achieving success at work so that he can provide for the family financially. He is the breadwinner.
- **The wife has an expressive role**, geared towards primary socialisation of the children and meeting the family's emotional needs. She is the homemaker, a full-time housewife rather than a wage earner.

Parsons argues that this division of labour is based on biological differences, with women 'naturally' suited to the nurturing role and men to that of provider. He claims that this division of labour is beneficial to both men and women, to their children and to wider society. Some conservative thinkers and politicians, known as the New Right, also hold this view.

However, other sociologists have criticised Parsons:

- Michael Young and Peter Willmott (1962) argue that men are now taking a greater share of domestic tasks and more wives are becoming wage earners.
- Feminist sociologists reject Parsons' view that the division of labour is natural. In addition, they argue that it only benefits men.

Joint and segregated conjugal roles

Elizabeth Bott (1957) distinguishes between two types of conjugal roles; that is, roles within marriage:

- **Segregated conjugal roles**, where the couple have separate roles: a male breadwinner and a female homemaker/carer, as in Parsons' instrumental and expressive roles. Their leisure activities also tend to be separate.
- **Joint conjugal roles**, where the couple share tasks such as housework and childcare and spend their leisure time together.

Young and Willmott identified a pattern of segregated conjugal roles in their study of traditional working-class extended families in Bethnal Green, east London, in the 1950s. Men were the breadwinners. They played little part in home life and spent their leisure time with workmates in pubs and working men's clubs. Women were full-time housewives with sole responsibility for housework and childcare, helped by their female relatives. The limited leisure women had was also spent with female kin.

The symmetrical family

Young and Willmott (1973) take a 'march of progress' view of the history of the family. They see family life as gradually improving for all its members, becoming more equal and democratic. They argue that there has been a long-term trend away from segregated conjugal roles and towards joint conjugal roles and the 'symmetrical family'.

By the symmetrical family they mean one in which the roles of husbands and wives, although not identical, are now much more similar:

- Women now go out to work, although this may be part-time rather than full-time.

- Men now help with housework and childcare.
- Couples now spend their leisure time together instead of separately with workmates or female relatives.

In their study of families in London, Young and Willmott found that the symmetrical family was more common among younger couples, those who are geographically and socially isolated, and the more affluent (better off). Young and Wilmott see the rise of the symmetrical nuclear family as the result of major social changes that have taken place during the past century:

- **Changes in women's position,** including married women going out to work
- **Geographical mobility** – more couples living away from the communities in which they grew up
- **New technology** and labour-saving devices
- **Higher standards of living.**

Many of these factors are inter-linked. For example, married women bringing a second wage into the home raises the family's standard of living. This means the couple can afford more labour-saving devices. This makes housework easier and encourages men to do more.

> **Application**
> Explain how geographical mobility might help to give rise to symmetrical families.

A feminist view of housework

Feminist sociologists reject this 'march of progress' view. They argue that little has changed: men and women remain unequal within the family and women still do most of the housework. They see this inequality as stemming from the fact that the family and society are male-dominated or patriarchal. Women occupy a subordinate and dependent role within the family and in wider society.

The feminist Ann Oakley (1974) criticises Young and Willmott's view that the family is now symmetrical. She argues that their claims are exaggerated. Although Young and Willmott found that most of the husbands they interviewed 'helped' their wives at least once a week,

this could include simply taking the children for a walk or making breakfast on one occasion. For Oakley, this is hardly convincing evidence of symmetry.

In her own research on housewives, Oakley found some evidence of husbands helping in the home but no evidence of a trend towards symmetry. Only 15% of husbands had a high level of participation in housework, and only 25% had a high level of participation in childcare.

Husbands were more likely to share in childcare than in housework, but only its more pleasurable aspects. Most couples defined the father's role as one of 'taking an interest'. A good father was one who would play with the children in the evenings and 'take them off her hands' on Sunday morning. However, this could mean that mothers lost the rewards of childcare, such as playing with the children, and were simply left with more time for housework.

Later research supports Oakley's findings. Mary Boulton (1983) found that fewer than 20% of husbands had a major role in childcare. She argues that Young and Willmott exaggerate men's contribution by looking at the tasks involved in childcare rather than the responsibilities. A father might help with specific tasks, but it was almost always the mother who was responsible for the child's security and well-being.

Similarly, research in the 1990s by Alan Warde and Kevin Hetherington (1993) found that sex-typing of domestic tasks remained strong. For example, wives were 30 times more likely to be the last person to have done the washing, while husbands were four times more likely to be the last person to wash the car.

In general, Warde and Hetherington found that men would only carry out routine 'female' tasks when their partners were not around to do them. Nevertheless, they did find evidence of a slight change of attitude among younger men. They no longer assumed that women should do the housework, and were more likely to think they were doing less than their fair share.

> **Analysis and Evaluation**
> What problems might there be in trying to research how much housework people do?

Are couples becoming more equal?

The impact of paid work

Most of the women in Oakley's study in the 1970s were full-time housewives, but today many more wives go out to

work, either full-time or part-time. This trend towards both partners working raises two questions:

- Is it leading to a more equal division of domestic tasks, with a 'new man' taking responsibility and doing an equal share of the housework and childcare? This is a march of progress view.

- Or does it simply mean that women now have to carry a 'dual burden' of paid work as well as domestic work? This is a feminist view.

The march of progress view

Like Young and Willmott's symmetrical family described earlier, some recent sociologists take an optimistic view. They argue that women going out to work is leading to a more equal division of labour at home. In this march of progress view, men are becoming more involved in housework and childcare just as women are becoming more involved in paid work outside the home.

For example, Jonathan Gershuny (1994) argues that women working full-time is leading to a more equal division of labour in the home. Using time studies, he found that these women did less domestic work than other women.

Similarly, Oriel Sullivan's (2000) analysis of nationally representative data collected in 1975, 1987 and 1997 (see Table 4A) found a trend towards women doing a smaller share of the domestic work and men doing more. Her analysis also showed an increase in the number of couples with an equal division of labour and that men were participating more in traditional 'women's' tasks.

These trends reflect changes in attitudes to the traditional division of labour. For example, the British Social Attitudes survey (2013) found a fall in the number of people who think it is the man's job to earn money and the woman's job to look after home and family. In 1984, 45% of men and 41% of women agreed with this view, but by 2012 only 13% of men and 12% of women agreed.

Table 4A	Women's percentage share of domestic work, by employment status of partners, Great Britain		
	1975	1987	1997
Husband full-time, wife full-time	68	62	60
Husband full time, wife part-time	80	70	69
Husband full time, wife not employed	82	73	73
All	77	67	63

Source: adapted from Sullivan (2000)

The feminist view

In the view of feminist sociologists, women going into paid work has not led to greater equality in the division of domestic labour. There is still little sign of the 'new man' who does an equal share of housework and childcare, while women now carry a dual burden, as the following evidence from the British Social Attitudes survey shows.

Table 4B	Household tasks undertaken by men and women in heterosexual couples, 1994-2012		
Individual always/usually undertaking task	1994 %	2002 %	2012 %
Cares for sick family members			
Always/usually the man	1	3	5
Both equally	45	44	38
Always/usually the woman	48	48	36
Does the laundry			
Always/usually the man	1	6	6
Both equally	18	15	20
Always/usually the woman	79	78	70
Does the household cleaning			
Always/usually the man	n/a	5	8
Both equally	n/a	29	29
Always/usually the woman	n/a	59	56
Prepares the meals			
Always/usually the man	n/a	11	16
Both equally	n/a	29	27
Always/usually the woman	n/a	58	55
Makes small repairs around the house			
Always/usually the man	75	71	75
Both equally	18	17	10
Always/usually the woman	5	7	7

n/a = not asked. The percentages do not add up to 100% because we have not shown the very few responses that said they couldn't choose or the task is done by someone else.

Source: adapted from British Social Attitudes (2013)

How much do men do? The survey found that in 2012 men on average did eight hours of housework a week, whereas women did 13 hours. Similarly, men spent 10 hours on care for family members, whereas women spent 23 hours. Overall, therefore, women did twice as much as men. 60% of women felt this division of labour was unjust because they were doing more than their fair share.

Who does what? The survey also found that couples continue to divide household tasks along traditional gender lines (see Table 4B). For example, women were much more likely to do the laundry, care for sick family members, shop for groceries, do the cleaning and prepare the meals, while men were more likely to do small repairs around the house. These patterns were much the same as they had been in 1994.

One thing that such surveys do not measure is the qualitative differences in the tasks men and women perform. For example, Graham Allan (1985) argues that women's tasks, such as washing and cleaning, are less intrinsically satisfying.

Taking responsibility for children

Another problem with such surveys is that they often focus only on easily quantifiable aspects such as who performs which tasks or how much time they spend doing them.

While useful, this tells us nothing about who takes responsibility for ensuring that the tasks are done. As we saw earlier, Boulton (1983) points out that although fathers may help by performing specific childcare tasks, it is usually the mother who takes responsibility for the child's security and well-being.

Boulton's view is supported by a number of studies:

- **Ferri and Smith** (1996) found that fathers took responsibility for childcare in fewer than 4% of families.
- **Dex and Ward** (2007) found that, although fathers had quite high levels of involvement with their three-year-olds (for example, 78% played with their children), when it came to caring for a sick child, only 1% of fathers took the main responsibility.
- **Braun, Vincent and Ball** (2011) found that in only three families out of 70 studied was the father the main carer. Most were 'background fathers'; helping with childcare was more about their relationship with their partner than their responsibility towards their children. Most fathers held a 'provider ideology' that their role was as breadwinners, while the mothers saw themselves as the primary carers. This was underpinned by ideas about 'intensive mothering' in the media telling women how to be good mothers.

These findings are in some ways very similar to those of Oakley four decades earlier.

emotion work and the triple shift

Another aspect of taking responsibility for other family members is what Arlie Russell Hochschild (2013) calls 'emotion work'. Feminists have noted that women are often required to perform emotion work, where they are responsible for managing the emotions and feelings of family members, such as handling jealousies and squabbles between siblings, ensuring everyone is kept happy and so on, while at the same time exercising control over their own emotions. Jean Duncombe and Dennis Marsden (1995) argue that women have to perform a 'triple shift' of housework, paid work and emotion work.

Taking responsibility for 'quality time'

Another responsibility is that of coordinating, scheduling and managing the family's 'quality time' together – a responsibility that usually falls to mothers, according to Dale Southerton (2011).

This has become more difficult in today's late modern society with recent social changes such as the emergence

▲ Literally, 'ready to eat'. Does the availability of fast food reduce the burden of housework for women?

of the 24/7 society and flexible working patterns. These changes have led to people's time being more fragmented and 'de-routinised'. As Southerton argues:

> 'Achieving quality time is becoming more and more difficult as working mothers find themselves increasingly juggling the demands of work and career, personal leisure time and family, while at the same time managing and coordinating their own and their families' social activities.'

Being 'pushed for time' in this way does not show up in the quantitative measures that time studies such as Gershuny's use.

Southerton also notes that, although some studies now show that men and women have more or less equal amounts of leisure time, they have different experiences of it. For example, men are more likely to experience consolidated 'blocks' of uninterrupted leisure time, whereas women's leisure is often punctuated by child care. Women are also more likely to multi-task than men. This indicates that women are carrying a dual burden in which they face an increased volume of activities to be managed.

summary

The evidence we have considered above suggests there may have been some movement towards an equal division of labour, but perhaps not very much. There is conflicting evidence on how much time men and women spend on domestic tasks – some findings, such as Gershuny's, suggesting a move towards greater equality, whereas other evidence (for example, from the British Social Attitudes survey) indicates continuing inequality. When it comes to responsibility for housework and especially for childcare, however, equality appears to be some way off.

Explaining the gender division of labour

Rosemary Crompton and Claire Lyonette (2008) identify two different explanations for the unequal division of labour.

The cultural or ideological explanation of inequality
In this view, the division of labour is determined by patriarchal norms and values that shape the gender roles in our culture. Women perform more domestic labour simply because that is what society expects them to do and has socialised them to do.

The material or economic explanation of inequality
In this view, the fact that women generally earn less than men means it is economically rational for women to do more of the housework and childcare while men spend more of their time earning money.

What evidence is there for these explanations and therefore what is the likelihood of the division of labour becoming more equal in the future?

Evidence for the cultural explanation

From this perspective, equality will be achieved only when norms about gender roles change. This would involve changes in men and women's attitudes, values and expectations, role models and socialisation. There is some evidence for this explanation:

- **Gershuny** (1994) found that couples whose parents had a more equal relationship are more likely to share housework equally themselves. This suggests parental role models are important. He argues that social values are gradually adapting to the fact that women are now

working full-time, establishing a new norm that men should do more domestic work.

- **Man Yee Kan** (2001) found that younger men do more domestic work. Similarly, according to the Future Foundation (2000), most men claimed to do more housework than their father and most women claimed to do less than their mother. This suggests a generational shift in behaviour is occurring.
- **The British Social Attitudes survey** (2013) found that less than 10% of under-35s agreed with a traditional division of labour, as against 30% of the over-65s. This indicates a long-term change in norms, values and attitudes, reflecting changes in the gender role socialisation of younger age groups in favour of more equal relationships.
- **Gillian Dunne** (1999) found that lesbian couples had more symmetrical relationships because of the absence of traditional heterosexual 'gender scripts', that is, norms that set out the different gender roles men and women are expected to play (see Box 29).

Evidence for the material explanation

From this perspective, if women join the labour force and earn as much as their partners, we should expect to see men and women doing more equal amounts of domestic work. There is some evidence for this explanation:

- **Kan** found that for every £10,000 a year more a woman earns, she does two hours less housework per week.
- **Sara Arber and Jay Ginn** (1995) found that better-paid, middle-class women were more able to buy in commercially produced products and services, such as labour-saving devices, ready meals, domestic help and childcare, rather than having to spend time carrying out labour-intensive domestic tasks themselves.
- **Xavier Ramos** (2003) found that where the woman is the full-time breadwinner and the man is unemployed, he does as much domestic labour as she does.
- **Sullivan** shows that working full-time rather than part-time makes the biggest difference in terms of how much domestic work each partner does (see Table 4A).

Box 29	Same-sex couples and gender scripts

Dunne's study of 37 lesbian couples with dependent children found that they were more likely than heterosexual women to:

- Describe their relationship as equal, share housework and childcare equally, and view childcare positively.
- Give equal importance to both partners' careers.

Dunne argues that this is because heterosexuals are under pressure to conform to deeply ingrained masculine or feminine 'gender scripts' by performing different kinds of domestic tasks that confirm their gender identities. By contrast, in lesbian relationships household tasks are not linked to particular gender scripts. This allows lesbian couples to create a more equal relationship.

This supports the radical feminist view that relationships between men and women are inevitably patriarchal and that women can only achieve equality in a same-sex relationship.

Similarly, Jeffrey Weeks (1999) and Carol Smart (2007) argue that same-sex relationships offer greater possibilities of equality because the division of labour is open to negotiation and agreement, and not based on patriarchal tradition.

However, Dunne also found that where one partner did much more paid work than the other, the time that each partner spent on domestic work was likely to be unequal. This suggests that paid work still affects the division of labour even in same-sex relationships.

Sullivan suggests that this may be because working full-time brings women's earnings much closer to those of their partners.

However, women continue to earn less than men: in seven out of eight households, men earn more. This is partly because women, especially those with young children, are more likely to work part-time. Rosemary Crompton (1997) thus concludes that there is no immediate prospect of a more equal division of labour if this depends on economic equality between the sexes.

Conclusion

- There is some evidence that a woman being in paid work leads to more equality in the division of labour, especially if she is in full-time work.
- Many feminists argue that, in reality, the extent of this is limited: women still continue to shoulder a dual or triple burden. And even if men are doing more in the home, domestic tasks themselves remain gendered. Furthermore, it is women who are expected to take responsibility for housework and childcare.
- Feminists argue that the root of the problem is patriarchy. Patriarchal norms and values shape society's expectations about the domestic roles that men and women ought to perform. Patriarchy also ensures that women earn less at work and so have less bargaining power in the home. Until patriarchy is successfully challenged in the home and in the workplace, therefore, the domestic division of labour is likely to remain unequal.

Activity   Research

Are couples becoming more equal?

...go to www.sociology.uk.net

Resources and decision-making in households

As we have seen, there is inequality in who does what in the home. There is also inequality in who gets what – in how the family's resources are shared out between men and women. This is linked to who controls the family's income and who has the power to make decisions about how it is spent.

Michelle Barrett and Mary McIntosh (1991) note that:

- Men gain far more from women's domestic work than they give back in financial support.
- The financial support that husbands give to their wives is often unpredictable and comes with 'strings' attached.
- Men usually make the decisions about spending on important items.

Research shows that family members do not share resources such as money and food equally. For example, Elaine Kempson (1994) found that among low income families, women denied their own needs, seldom going out, and eating smaller portions of food or skipping meals altogether in order to make ends meet.

In many households, a woman has no entitlement to a share of household resources in her own right. As a result, she is likely to see anything she spends on herself as money that ought to be spent on essentials for the children. Even in households with apparently adequate incomes, resources may be shared unequally, leaving women in poverty.

Money management

The feminist sociologists Jan Pahl and Carolyn Vogler (1993) identify two main types of control over family income:

- **The allowance system,** where men give their wives an allowance out of which they have to budget to meet the family's needs, with the man retaining any surplus income for himself.
- **Pooling,** where both partners have access to income and joint responsibility for expenditure; for example, a joint bank account.

Pooling is on the increase and is now the most common money management system.

Decision-making

It is often assumed that pooling indicates more equality in decision-making and control over resources, and it is more common among couples where both partners work full-time.

However, where the pooled income is controlled by the husband, this tends to give men more power in major financial decisions (although not as much as in an allowance system). Pahl and Vogler (2007) found that even where there was pooling, the men usually made the major financial decisions.

Similarly, Irene Hardill's (1997) study of 30 dual-career professional couples found that the important decisions were usually taken either by the man alone or jointly and that his career normally took priority when deciding whether to move house for a new job. This supports Janet Finch's (1983) observation that women's lives tend to be structured around their husbands' careers.

Similarly, Stephen Edgell's (1980) study of professional couples found that:

- **Very important decisions,** such as those involving finance, a change of job or moving house, were either taken by the husband alone or taken jointly but with the husband having the final say.
- **Important decisions,** such as those about children's education or where to go on holiday, were usually taken jointly, and seldom by the wife alone.
- **Less important decisions,** such as the choice of home decor, children's clothes or food purchases, were usually made by the wife.

Edgell argues that the reason men are likely to take the decisions is that they earn more. Women usually earn less than their husbands and, being dependent on them economically, have less say in decision-making.

However, there is some evidence of a limited move towards greater equality in financial decision-making. Laurie and Gershuny (2000) found that by 1995, 70% of couples said they had an equal say in decisions. Significantly, though, they found that women who were high earning, well qualified professionals were more likely to have an equal say.

Cultural versus material explanations

Gershuny and Laurie's findings provide support for the economic or material explanation of gender inequality described earlier by Crompton and Lyonette (see page 171).

However, feminists argue that inequalities in decision-making are not simply the result of inequalities in earnings. They argue that in patriarchal society, the cultural definition of men as decision-makers is deeply ingrained in both men and women and instilled through gender role socialisation. Until this definition is challenged, decision-making is likely to remain unequal. This view reflects the cultural explanation of gender inequality described by Crompton and Lyonette.

The meaning of money

As Pahl notes, just pooling money doesn't necessarily mean there is equality. We also need to know who controls the pooled money and whether each partner contributes equally (despite any differences in their incomes). For example, if a man earns twice as much as his wife, but both put the same amount into the joint account, does this count as equality?

Nor does each partner keeping their money separately always mean inequality. For example, Vogler et al found that cohabiting couples were less likely to pool their money – perhaps from a desire to maintain their independence. Yet evidence suggests that cohabiting couples are more likely than married couples to share domestic tasks equally.

These ideas point to the fact that we need to understand the meaning of money for couples. As Charlott Nyman (2003) notes, money has no automatic, fixed or natural meaning and different couples can define it in different ways. These meanings can reflect the nature of the relationship.

Application

Why do you think pooling of resources is less likely to be found among older couples?

A 'personal life' perspective on money

The personal life perspective focuses on the meanings couples give to who controls the money.

From this perspective, the meanings that money may have in relationships cannot be taken for granted. For example, while we might assume that one partner controlling the money is a sign of inequality in the relationship, for some couples it may not have this meaning.

For example, there is evidence that same-sex couples often give a different meaning to the control of money in the relationship. Carol Smart (2007) found that some gay men and lesbians attached no importance to who controlled the money and were perfectly happy to leave this to their partners. They did not see the control of money as meaning either equality or inequality in the relationship.

Similarly, Weeks et al (2001) found that that the typical pattern was pooling some money for household spending, together with separate accounts for personal spending. This money management system thus reflects a value of 'co-independence' – where there is sharing, but where each partner retains control over some money and maintains a sense of independence. This is like the pattern among cohabiting couples found by Vogler et al.

Smart found that there is greater freedom for same-sex couples to do what suits them as a couple. She suggests that this may be because they do not enter relationships with the same 'historical, gendered, heterosexual baggage of cultural meanings around money' that see money as a source of power. (For more about the personal life perspective, see page 194.)

Hence supporters of the personal life perspective argue that it is essential always to start from the personal meanings of the actors involved in the situation. This echoes Weeks' and Smart's point about the division of labour in same-sex couples (see Box 29).

Activity | **Discussion**

Resources and sharing of decisions

...go to www.sociology.uk.net

Domestic violence

The Home Office (2013) defines domestic violence and abuse as:

'Any incident or pattern of incidents of controlling, coercive or threatening behaviour, violence or abuse between those aged 16 or over who are or have been intimate partners or family members regardless of gender or sexuality.'

This can include psychological, physical, sexual, financial and emotional violence or abuse.

A common view of domestic violence is that it is the behaviour of a few disturbed or 'sick' individuals, and that its causes are psychological rather than social. However, sociologists have challenged this view:

- **Domestic violence is far too widespread** to be simply the work of a few disturbed individuals. According to the Women's Aid Federation (2014), domestic violence accounts for between a sixth and a quarter of all recorded violent crime.
  The Crime Survey for England and Wales (2013) found that two million people reported having been victims of domestic abuse during the previous year.

- **Domestic violence does not occur randomly** but follows particular social patterns and these patterns have social causes. The most striking of these patterns is that it is mainly violence by men against women.
  For example, Kathryn Coleman et al (2007) found that women were more likely than men to have experienced 'intimate violence' across all four types of abuse – partner abuse, family abuse, sexual assault and stalking.
  According to Coleman and Osborne (2010), two women a week – or one third of all female homicide victims – are killed by a partner or former partner.

This pattern is confirmed by Russell and Rebecca Dobash's (1979: 2007) research in Scotland, based on police and court records and interviews with women in women's refuges. They cite examples of wives being slapped, pushed about, beaten, raped or killed by their husbands.

Dobash and Dobash found that violent incidents could be set off by what a husband saw as a challenge to his authority, such as his wife asking why he was late home for a meal. They argue that marriage legitimates violence against women by conferring power and authority on husbands and dependency on wives.

While most victims are women, however, the Crime Survey for England and Wales (2013) found a relatively narrow gender gap: 7.3% of women (1.2 million) compared with 5% of men (800,000) reported having experienced domestic abuse in the previous year. However, other studies report a wider gap.

But just knowing how many victims there are tells us nothing about the frequency, severity or effects of the abuse they suffer – and here there is a very significant gender gap:

- **Sylvia Walby and Jonathan Allen** (2004) found that women were much more likely to be victims of multiple incidents of abuse and of sexual violence.

- **Donna Ansara and Michelle Hindin** (2011) found that women suffered more severe violence and control, with more serious psychological effects. They also found that women were much more likely than men to be fearful of their partners.

- **Aliyah Dar** (2013) points out that it can also be difficult to count separate domestic violence incidents, because abuse may be continuous (for example, living under constant threat), or may occur so often that the victim cannot reliably count the instances.

Official statistics

Official statistics on domestic violence understate the true extent of the problem for two main reasons.

Firstly, victims may be unwilling to report it to the police. Stephanie Yearnshire (1997) found that on average a woman suffers 35 assaults before making a report. Domestic violence is the violent crime least likely to be reported.

Dar argues that victims of domestic violence are less likely than victims of other forms of violence to report the offence because they believe that it is not a matter for the police or that it is too trivial, or from fear of reprisals.

Secondly, police and prosecutors may be reluctant to record, investigate or prosecute those cases that are reported to them. According to David Cheal (1991), this reluctance is due to the fact that police and other state agencies are not prepared to become involved in the family. They make three assumptions about family life:

- that the family is a private sphere, so access to it by state agencies should be limited
- that the family is a good thing and so agencies tend to neglect the 'darker side' of family life
- that individuals are free agents, so it is assumed that if a woman is experiencing abuse she is free to leave. However, this is not true. Male violence is often coupled with male economic power: abused women are often financially dependent on their husbands and unable to leave.

Lack of action by police and prosecutors means that cases successfully prosecuted are merely the tip of a much larger iceberg of abuse. For example, during 2006-11, conviction rates stood at a mere 6.5% of incidents reported to the police.

Explanations of domestic violence

We saw earlier that Crompton and Lyonette identify two types of explanation of gender inequality in the division of labour – one that emphasises cultural factors such as ideas and values, and one that emphasises material factors such as gender inequalities in earnings.

Similarly, we can identify two types of explanation of domestic violence:

- **The radical feminist explanation** This emphasises the role of patriarchal ideas, cultural values and institutions.
- **The materialist explanation** This emphasises economic factors such as lack of resources.

The radical feminist explanation

Radical feminists interpret findings such as those of Dobash and Dobash as evidence of patriarchy. For example, Kate Millett (1970) and Shulamith Firestone (1970) argue that all societies have been founded on patriarchy. They see the key division in society as that between men and women. Men are the enemy: they are the oppressors and exploiters of women.

Radical feminists see the family and marriage as the key institutions in patriarchal society and the main source of women's oppression. Within the family, men dominate women through domestic violence or the threat of it.

For radical feminists, widespread domestic violence is an inevitable feature of patriarchal society and serves to preserve the power that all men have over all women.

In their view, this helps to explain why most domestic violence is committed by men. Radical feminists give a sociological, rather than a psychological, explanation by linking patterns of domestic violence to dominant social norms about marriage.

Furthermore, in their view, male domination of state institutions helps to explain the reluctance of the police and courts to deal effectively with cases of domestic violence. (For more about the radical feminist perspective, see Topic 3.)

evaluation

However, Faith Robertson Elliot (1996) rejects the radical feminist claim that all men benefit from violence against women. Not all men are aggressive and most are opposed to domestic violence. Radical feminists ignore this.

Radical feminists also fail to explain female violence, including child abuse by women and violence against male

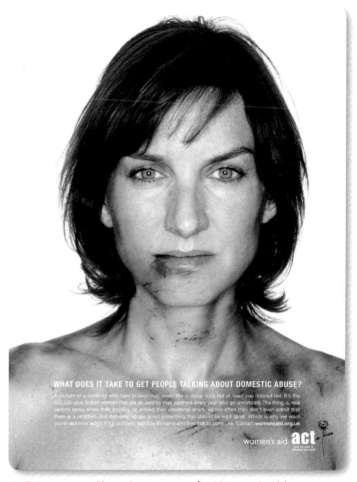

▲ TV presenter Fiona Bruce poses for Women's Aid campaign poster.

partners and within lesbian relationships. For example, the Crime Survey for England and Wales (2013) found that 18% of men (2.9 million) have experienced domestic violence since the age of 16.

Radical feminists use the concept of patriarchy to explain why most victims of domestic violence are women, but they wrongly assume that all women are equally at risk of patriarchal violence. They explain why it is women and not men who are victims, but they fail to explain which women are most likely to be victims.

For example, evidence from the Office for National Statistics (2014) suggests that women from some social groups face a greater risk of domestic violence. These include:

- young women
- those in the lowest social classes and those living in the most deprived areas
- those on low incomes or in financial difficulties
- those living in shared and rented accommodation
- those with high levels of alcohol consumption or using illegal drugs
- those with a long term illness or disability.

Some of these groups overlap. For example, statistics show that children from lower social classes appear at higher risk of abuse and violence.

Furthermore, men who suffer domestic violence are also likely to belong to these groups.

The materialist explanation

The materialist explanation of domestic violence focuses on economic and material factors such as inequalities in income and housing to explain why some groups are more at risk than others. For example, Richard Wilkinson and Kate Pickett (2010) see domestic violence as the result of stress on family members caused by social inequality.

> **Application**
> Suggest two reasons why poorer families are more likely to end up in the child abuse statistics than better-off families.

Inequality means that some families have fewer resources than others. Those on low incomes or living in overcrowded accommodation are likely to experience higher levels of stress. This reduces their chances of maintaining stable, caring relationships and increases the risk of conflict and violence. For example:

- worries about money, jobs and housing may spill over into domestic conflict as tempers become frayed
- lack of money and time restricts people's social circle and reduces social support for those under stress.

The findings of Wilkinson and Pickett show that not all people are equally in danger of suffering domestic violence: those with less power, status, wealth or income are often at greatest risk.

evaluation

Wilkinson and Pickett's approach is useful in showing how social inequality produces stress and triggers conflict and violence in families. As those in lower social classes face greater hardship and thus stress, this helps to explain the class differences in the statistics on domestic violence.

However, unlike the radical feminist approach, Wilkinson and Pickett do not explain why women rather than men are the main victims.

Marxist feminists also see inequality causing domestic violence. For example, Fran Ansley (1972) describes wives as 'takers of shit'. She argues that domestic violence is the product of capitalism: male workers are exploited at work and they take out their frustration on their wives.

This helps to explain why domestic violence is male violence against females. However, it fails to explain why not all male workers commit acts of violence against their partners and it doesn't account for cases of female domestic violence. (See Topic 3 for more about Marxist feminism.)

> **Activity**   Media
> Why don't domestic violence victims leave?
> ...go to www.sociology.uk.net

Topic summary

Sociologists disagree as to whether couples are becoming more equal. **Functionalists** argue for the necessity of **segregated conjugal roles** based on biological differences between the sexes.

However, '**march of progress**' sociologists argue that the family is becoming more **symmetrical**, with joint conjugal roles.

Feminists disagree, arguing that men's contribution remains minimal and women now shoulder a **dual burden** of paid and unpaid work, or even perform a **triple shift** that also includes emotion work.

Couples remain unequal in terms of **decision making** and **control of resources**. Men earn more and are more likely to take the major decisions, even where incomes are pooled. **The personal life perspective** argues that we need to understand the different meanings money can have within a relationship.

Radical feminists argue that **domestic violence** is an extreme form of **patriarchal power** over women. However, though most victims are female, not all women are equally at risk.

EXAMINING COUPLES

QuickCheck Questions

1 Distinguish between instrumental and expressive roles.
2 State two features of the symmetrical family.
3 'Patriarchal norms shape gender roles in couples.' Is this a cultural or a material explanation?
4 What reason does Edgell give for why men have more power to influence family decision-making?

5 Why according to Smart is control of money less of an issue in some same-sex couples?
6 Suggest two reasons why domestic violence is not simply the behaviour of a few psychologically disturbed individuals.
7 Identify two other groups apart from women who are at risk of domestic violence.

Questions to try

Whether or not you are taking the AS exams during your A level course, answering the AS questions below is a very good way of testing your knowledge and understanding and practising your skills in preparation for your A level exams.

Item A   March of progress sociologists argue that the family is becoming more equal. Increasingly today, both partners are likely to have jobs outside the home and they both carry out household chores and provide childcare. However, feminist sociologists reject this claim. They argue that the family is still patriarchal and that women today carry a dual burden.

Item B   Domestic violence accounts for up to a quarter of all recorded violent crime. Victims are more likely to be female and offenders male: domestic violence is linked to gender roles in patriarchal society. However, not all women are equally likely to suffer domestic violence. Victims – both female and male – are more likely to belong to disadvantaged social groups and live under difficult circumstances.

AS questions

1 Define the term 'dual burden'. (2 marks)
2 Using one example, explain why the 'pooling' system of managing household finances may not always show equality between spouses. (2 marks)
3 Outline three characteristics of the symmetrical family. (6 marks)

AS and A level question

4 Applying material from Item A and your knowledge, evaluate the view that the division of labour in couples is now equal. (20 marks)

A level question

5 Applying material from Item B, analyse two reasons for patterns of domestic violence. (10 marks)

The Examiner's Advice

Q4 Spend about 30 minutes on this. Focus on the division of labour, not on domestic violence or resources. Cover a range of issues, including both housework and childcare, and who is responsible for organising it, not just who does it, whether tasks themselves are gendered, the division of labour in same-sex couples etc. Develop points from Item A, e.g. on the dual burden, patriarchy and the impact of women's paid work. Use these and other key concepts and issues such as emotion work and triple shift, 'quality time', background fathers, gender scripts etc. Use evidence from studies such as Gershuny, Sullivan, Kan, Boulton, Braun et al, British Social Attitudes surveys, Dex and Ward, Crompton and Lyonette, Southerton and Dunne. Evaluate how useful different views are in explaining the evidence, especially march of progress and feminist views, and material and cultural explanations.

Q5 Spend about 15 minutes on this question. Divide your time fairly equally between the two reasons. You don't need a separate introduction; just start on your first reason. To answer this question, it's essential that you take two points from the Item and show through a chain of reasoning (see page 248) how each reason explains a pattern. (It is a very good idea to quote from the Item when doing so.) You could use patriarchy, social disadvantage or living conditions. For example, in patriarchal society, men exercise power over women. This means domestic violence is used to ensure women fulfil subordinate roles. Use concepts and issues such as radical feminism, the materialist explanation, stress, class inequality, alcohol abuse etc, and studies such as Dobash and Dobash, Firestone, Wilkinson and Pickett, Dar, Cheal, Ansley and Robertson Elliot. Include some brief evaluation.

Child soldiers

GETTING STARTED

In pairs, complete the following:

1 What stereotypes of childhood does the picture challenge?
2 List five words that you would associate with childhood in the UK.
3 Find out the age at which you are permitted to do the following in the UK:

a serve in the army   e drive a car
b smoke   f leave education
c get married   g vote in an election
d have sexual intercourse   h drink alcohol at home.

4 Compare your answers to questions 1 to 3 with the rest of the class.
5 Why do you think sociologists argue that childhood is not a fixed biological stage?

Learning objectives

After studying this Topic, you should:

- Understand why sociologists see childhood as a social construction.
- Know the reasons for the emergence of the modern notion of childhood.
- Be able to analyse and evaluate different views of the position of children today.
- Be able to analyse and evaluate different views of the future of childhood.

Sociologists are interested in how the status of different family members has changed over time. For example, as we saw in Topic 1, there have been debates about whether couples have become more equal today than in the past.

In this Topic, we look at changes in childhood and the position of children in the family and society, as well as the factors responsible for these changes.

We examine three major issues:

- How childhood is socially constructed; that is, how it is created and defined by society.
- Is the position of children better today than it was in the past?
- What is the future of childhood likely to be?

Childhood as a social construct

Sociologists see childhood as socially constructed; in other words, as something created and defined by society. They argue that what people mean by childhood, and the position that children occupy in society, is not fixed but differs between different times, places and cultures. We can see this by comparing the western idea of childhood today with childhood in the past and in other societies.

The modern western notion of childhood

It is generally accepted in our society today that childhood is a special time of life and that children are fundamentally different from adults. They are regarded as physically and psychologically immature and not yet competent to run their own lives. There is a belief that children's lack of skills, knowledge and experience means that they need a lengthy, protected period of nurturing and socialisation before they are ready for adult society and its responsibilities.

As Jane Pilcher (1995) notes, the most important feature of the modern idea of childhood is separateness. Childhood is seen as a clear and distinct life stage, and children in our society occupy a separate status from adults.

This is emphasised in several ways, for instance through laws regulating what children are allowed, required or forbidden to do. Their difference from adults is also emphasised through differences in dress, especially for younger children, and through products and services specially for children, such as toys, food, books, entertainments, play areas and so on.

Related to the separateness of children's status is the idea of childhood as a 'golden age' of happiness and innocence. However, this innocence means that children are seen as vulnerable and in need of protection from the dangers of the adult world and so they must be kept 'quarantined' and separated from it. As a result, children's lives are lived largely in the sphere of the family and education, where adults provide for them and protect them from the outside world. Similarly, unlike adults, they lead lives of leisure and play and are largely excluded from paid work.

However, this view of childhood as a separate age-status is not found in all societies. It is not universal. As Stephen Wagg (1992) puts it:

'Childhood is socially constructed. It is, in other words, what members of particular societies, at particular times and in particular places, say it is. There is no single universal childhood, experienced by all. So, childhood isn't "natural" and should be distinguished from mere biological immaturity.'

This means that, while all humans go through the same stages of physical development, different cultures construct or define this process differently.

In western cultures today, children are defined as vulnerable and unable to fend for themselves. However, other cultures do not necessarily see such a great difference between children and adults. We can see this by looking at examples both from other cultures today and from European societies of the past.

Application
1. Explain what is meant by the phrase 'childhood is a social construct'.
2. Suggest two ways in which children in our society occupy a separate status from adults.

Cross-cultural differences in childhood

A good way to illustrate the social construction of childhood is to take a comparative approach – that is, to look at how children are seen and treated in other times and places than our own. The anthropologist Ruth Benedict (1934) argues that children in simpler, non-industrial societies are generally treated differently from their modern western counterparts in three ways:

- **They take responsibility at an early age.** For example, Samantha Punch's (2001) study of childhood in rural

Bolivia found that, once children are about five years old, they are expected to take work responsibilities in the home and in the community. Tasks are taken on without question or hesitation.

Similarly, Lowell Holmes' (1974) study of a Samoan village found that 'too young' was never given as a reason for not permitting a child to undertake a particular task: 'Whether it be the handling of dangerous tools or the carrying of extremely heavy loads, if a child thinks he can handle the activity, parents do not object'.

- **Less value is placed on children showing obedience to adult authority.** For example, Raymond Firth (1970) found that among the Tikopia of the western Pacific, doing as you are told by a grown-up is regarded as a concession to be granted by the child, not a right to be expected by the adult.
- **Children's sexual behaviour is often viewed differently.** For example, among the Trobriand Islanders of the south-west Pacific, Bronislaw Malinowski (1957) found that adults took an attitude of 'tolerance and amused interest' towards children's sexual explorations and activities.

Benedict argues that in many non-industrial cultures, there is much less of a dividing line between the behaviour expected of children and that expected of adults. Such evidence illustrates the key idea that childhood is not a fixed thing found universally in the same form in all human societies, but is socially constructed and so differs from culture to culture.

The globalisation of western childhood

Some sociologists argue that western notions of childhood are being globalised. International humanitarian and welfare agencies have exported and imposed on the rest of the world, western norms of what childhood should be – a separate life stage, based in the nuclear family and school, in which children are innocent, dependent and vulnerable, and have no economic role.

For example, campaigns against child labour, or concerns about 'street children' in developing countries, reflect western views about how childhood 'ought' to be – whereas in fact, such activity by children may be the norm for the culture and an important preparation for adult life. In this view, western-style 'childhood' is spreading throughout the world. However, arguably such campaigns have little impact on the position of children in developing countries.

Historical differences in childhood

The position of children differs over time as well as between societies. Many sociologists and historians argue that childhood as we understand it today is a relatively recent 'invention'.

The historian Philippe Ariès (1960) argues that in the Middle Ages (from about the 10th to the 13th centuries), 'the idea of childhood did not exist'. Children were not seen as having a different 'nature' or needs from adults – at least, not once they had passed the stage of physical dependency during infancy.

In the Middle Ages, childhood as a separate age-stage was short. Soon after being weaned, the child entered wider society on much the same terms as an adult, beginning work from an early age, often in the household of another family. Children were in effect 'mini-adults' with the same rights, duties and skills as adults. For example, the law often made no distinction between children and adults, and children often faced the same severe punishments as those meted out to adults.

As evidence of his view, Ariès uses works of art from the period. In these, children appear without 'any of the characteristics of childhood: they have simply been depicted on a smaller scale'. The paintings show children and adults dressed in the same clothing and working and playing together.

Parental attitudes towards children in the Middle Ages were also very different from those today. Edward Shorter (1975) argues that high death rates encouraged indifference and neglect, especially towards infants. For example, it was not uncommon for parents to give a newborn baby the name of a recently dead sibling, to refer to the baby as 'it', or to forget how many children they had had.

▲ Adults and children are barely distinguishable from each other in Bruegel the Younger's famous 16th century painting.

The modern cult of childhood

According to Ariès, however, elements of the modern notion of childhood gradually began to emerge from the 13th century onwards:

- Schools (which previously adults had also attended) came to specialise purely in the education of the young. This reflected the influence of the church, which increasingly saw children as fragile 'creatures of God' in need of discipline and protection from worldly evils.
- There was a growing distinction between children's and adults' clothing. By the 17th century, an upper-class boy would be dressed in 'an outfit reserved for his own age group, which set him apart from adults'.
- By the 18th century, handbooks on childrearing were widely available – a sign of the growing child-centredness of family life, at least among the middle classes.

According to Ariès, these developments culminate in the modern 'cult of childhood'. He argues that we have moved from a world that did not see childhood as in any way special, to a world that is obsessed with childhood. He describes the 20th century as 'the century of the child'.

Some sociologists have criticised Ariès for arguing that childhood did not exist in the past. Linda Pollock (1983) argues that it is more correct to say that in the Middle Ages, society simply had a different notion of childhood from today's.

However, Ariès' work is valuable because it shows that childhood is socially constructed: he demonstrates how ideas about children and their social status have varied over time.

Analysis and Evaluation

What problems might there be in using evidence such as paintings and diaries, as Ariès does, to understand childhood or family life in the past?

Reasons for changes in the position of children

There are many reasons for the changes in the position of children. These include the following changes during the 19th and 20th centuries:

- **Laws restricting child labour and excluding children from paid work.** From being economic assets who could earn a wage, children became an economic liability, financially dependent on their parents.
- **The introduction of compulsory schooling** in 1880 had a similar effect, especially for the children of the poor (middle- and upper-class children were already receiving education). The raising of the school-leaving age has extended this period of dependency.
- **Child protection and welfare legislation,** such as the 1889 Prevention of Cruelty to Children Act. Exactly a century later, the 1989 Children Act made the welfare of the child the fundamental principle underpinning the work of agencies such as social services.
- **The growth of the idea of children's rights** For example, the Children Act defines parents as having 'responsibilities' rather than 'rights' in relation to children, while the United Nations Convention on the Rights of the Child (1989) lays down basic rights such as entitlement to healthcare and education, protection from abuse and the right to participate in decisions that affect them, such as custody cases.
- **Declining family size and lower infant mortality rates** have encouraged parents to make a greater financial and emotional investment in the fewer children that they now have.
- **Children's development became the subject of medical knowledge.** Jacques Donzelot (1977) observes how theories of child development that began to appear from the 19th century stressed that children need supervision and protection.
- **Laws and policies that apply specifically to children,** such as minimum ages for a wide range of activities, from sex to smoking, have reinforced the idea that children are different from adults and so different rules must be applied to their behaviour.

Industrialisation Most sociologists agree that the process of industrialisation – the shift from agriculture to factory production as the basis of the economy – underlies many of the above changes. For example, modern industry needs an educated workforce and this requires compulsory schooling of the young.

Similarly, the higher standards of living and better welfare provision that industry makes possible lead to lower infant mortality rates. Industrialisation is thus a key factor in bringing about the modern idea of childhood and the changed status of children.

The future of childhood

So far, we have looked at how childhood has changed and developed from pre-industrial to modern society. But if childhood is socially constructed, we can expect it to continue to change in the future as society itself changes, for example from modern to postmodern society.

The disappearance of childhood

One influential view of the future of childhood is put forward by Neil Postman (1994). Postman argues that childhood is 'disappearing at a dazzling speed'. He points to the trend towards giving children the same rights as adults, the disappearance of children's traditional unsupervised games, the growing similarity of adults' and children's clothing, and even to cases of children committing 'adult' crimes such as murder.

In Postman's view, the cause first of the emergence of childhood, and now its disappearance, lies in the rise and fall of print culture and its replacement by television culture.

During the Middle Ages, most people were illiterate, and speech was the only skill needed for participation in the adult world. Children were able to enter adult society from an early age. Childhood was not associated with innocence, nor the adult world with mystery. There was no division between the world of the adult and that of the child.

the information hierarchy

Postman argues that childhood emerged as a separate status along with mass literacy, from the 19th century on. This is because the printed word creates an information hierarchy: a sharp division between adults, who can read, and children, who cannot.

This gave adults the power to keep knowledge about sex, money, violence, illness, death and other 'adult' matters a secret from children. These things became mysteries to them, and childhood came to be associated with innocence and ignorance.

However, television blurs the distinction between childhood and adulthood by destroying the information hierarchy. Unlike the printed word, TV does not require special skills to access it, and it makes information available to adults and children alike. The boundary between adult and child is broken down, adult authority diminishes, and the ignorance and innocence of childhood is replaced by knowledge and cynicism.

The counterpart of the disappearance of childhood is the disappearance of adulthood, where adults' and children's tastes and styles become indistinguishable.

> **Application**
>
> Suggest three ways in which children's and adults' leisure, dress and food are now similar.

evaluation

Unlike Postman, Iona Opie (1993) argues that childhood is not disappearing. Based on a lifetime of research into children's unsupervised games, rhymes and songs, conducted with her husband Peter Opie, she argues that there is strong evidence of the continued existence of a separate children's culture over many years.

Postman's study is valuable in showing how different types of communication technology, such as print and television, can influence the way in which childhood is constructed. However, he over-emphasises a single cause – television – at the expense of other factors that have influenced the development of childhood.

Childhood in postmodernity

Unlike Postman, Christopher Jenks (2005) does not believe childhood is disappearing, but he does believe it is changing.

Jenks agrees with Ariès that childhood was a creation of modern society. For Jenks, modern society (especially the 20th century) was concerned with 'futurity' and childhood was seen as a preparation for the individual to become a productive adult in the future. To achieve this, the vulnerable, undeveloped child needed to be nurtured, protected and controlled, especially by the 'child-centred' family and by the education system, which imposed discipline and conformity on children.

Now, however, Jenks argues, childhood is once again undergoing change as society moves from modernity to postmodernity. In modern society, adults' relationships were more stable, but in postmodern society, the pace of change speeds up and relationships become more unstable. For example, divorce becomes much more common.

This generates feelings of insecurity. In this context, relationships with their children become more important as a source of adults' identity and stability. While your marriage may end in divorce, you are still the parent of your child.

In postmodern society, relationships with their children thus become adults' last refuge from the constant uncertainty and upheaval of life. As a result, adults become even more fearful for their children's security and even more preoccupied with protecting them from perceived dangers such as child abuse.

This further strengthens the prevailing view of children as vulnerable and in need of protection that we have already seen in the modern notion of childhood, resulting in even greater surveillance and regulation of children's lives.

For this reason, Jenks does not agree with Postman that we are seeing the disappearance of childhood. Childhood continues to be a separate status, and the legal and other restrictions placed on what children can do continues to mark them off from adults.

evaluation

Evidence both for and against Jenks is limited. There is some evidence that parents see their relationship with their children as more important than that with their partners, and that parents are very concerned about the risks they believe their children face. However, the evidence comes from small, unrepresentative studies.

Jenks is guilty of over-generalising. Despite the greater diversity of family and childhood patterns found today (such as lone-parent families, stepfamilies etc), he makes rather sweeping statements that imply that all children are in the same position.

Activity Media

The accordion family

...go to www.sociology.uk.net

Has the position of children improved?

As we have seen, childhood is socially constructed and varies between times, places and cultures. There are important differences between childhood in western societies today as compared with both present-day developing countries and European societies in the past. For example, in the Middle Ages, child labour was a basic fact of life for almost all children, while schooling was available only to the wealthy.

The march of progress view

These differences raise the question of whether the changes in the status of childhood that we looked at earlier represent an improvement. The march of progress view argues that, over the past few centuries, the position of children in western societies has been steadily improving and today is better than it has ever been. This view paints a dark picture of the past. As Lloyd De Mause (1974) puts it:

> 'The history of childhood is a nightmare from which we have only recently begun to awaken. The further back in history one goes, the lower the level of childcare, and the more likely children are to be killed, abandoned, beaten, terrorised and sexually abused.'

Writers such as Ariès and Shorter hold a march of progress view. They argue that today's children are more valued, better cared for, protected and educated, enjoy better health and have more rights than those of previous generations.

For example, children today are protected from harm and exploitation by laws against child abuse and child labour, while an array of professionals and specialists caters for their educational, psychological and medical needs. The government spends huge sums on their education.

Better healthcare and higher standards of living also mean that babies have a much better chance of survival now than a century ago. In 1900, the infant mortality rate was 154 per 1,000 live births; today, it is 4 per 1,000.

the child-centred family

Higher living standards and smaller family sizes (down from 5.7 births per woman in the 1860s to 1.83 in 2014) also mean that parents can afford to provide for children's needs properly. According to one estimate, by the time a child reaches their 21st birthday, they will have cost their parents over £227,000.

March of progress sociologists argue that the family has become child-centred. Children are no longer to be 'seen and not heard', as they were in Victorian times. Instead they are now the focal point of the family, consulted on many decisions as never before. Parents invest a great deal in their children emotionally as well as financially, and often have high aspirations for them to have a better life and greater opportunities than they themselves have had.

Furthermore, it is not just the family that is now child-centred; so is society as a whole. For example, much media output and many leisure activities are designed specifically for children.

Activity Webquest

The cost of child-centredness

...go to www.sociology.uk.net

toxic childhood

As against the view that the position of children now is better than it has ever been, some writers suggest that children in the UK today are experiencing what Sue Palmer (2007; 2010) calls 'toxic childhood'. She argues that rapid technological and cultural changes in the past 25 years have damaged children's physical, emotional and intellectual development. These changes range from junk food, computer games, and intensive marketing to children, to the long hours worked by parents and the growing emphasis on testing in education.

Concerns have also been expressed about young people's health and behaviour. For example, UK youth have above average rates in international league tables for obesity, self-harm, drug and alcohol abuse, violence, early sexual experience and teenage pregnancies. A UNICEF survey in 2013 ranked the UK 16th out of 29 for children's well being.

The conflict view

The march of progress view is that the position of children has improved dramatically in a relatively short period of time. However, conflict sociologists such as Marxists and feminists dispute this. They argue that society is based on a conflict between different social groups such as social classes or genders. In this conflict, some groups have more power, status or wealth than others. Conflict sociologists see the relationship between groups as one of domination and subordination, in which the dominant group act as oppressors.

Conflict sociologists argue that the march of progress view of modern childhood is based on a false and idealised image that ignores important inequalities. They criticise the march of progress view on two grounds:

- There are inequalities *among children* in terms of the opportunities and risks they face: many today remain unprotected and badly cared for.
- The inequalities *between children and adults* are greater than ever: children today experience greater control, oppression and dependency, not greater care and protection.

Inequalities among children

Not all children share the same status or experiences. For example, children of different *nationalities* are likely to experience different childhoods and different life chances. 90% of the world's low birth-weight babies are born in developing countries.

There are also *gender* differences between children. For example, according to Mayer Hillman (1993), boys are more likely to be allowed to cross or cycle on roads, use buses, and go out after dark unaccompanied. Jens Bonke (1999) found that girls do more domestic labour – especially in lone-parent families, where they do five times more housework than boys.

Table 4C	Children who were the subject of a child protection plan at 31 March 2013: England	
Type of abuse		**numbers**
Neglect		17,930
Physical abuse		4,670
Sexual abuse		2,030
Emotional abuse		13,640
Multiple abuse		4,870

Source: DFE (2013)

Analysis and Evaluation

1 What difficulties might there be in defining emotional abuse?

2 Suggest reasons why these statistics might not be an accurate measure of the true extent of child abuse.

Similarly, there are *ethnic* differences: Julia Brannen's (1994) study of 15-16 year olds found that Asian parents were more likely than other parents to be strict towards their daughters. Similarly, Ghazala Bhatti (1999) found that ideas of *izzat* (family honour) could be a restriction, particularly on the behaviour of girls.

There are also important *class* inequalities between children:

- Poor mothers are more likely to have low birth-weight babies, which in turn is linked to delayed physical and intellectual development.
- Children of unskilled manual workers are over three times more likely to suffer from hyperactivity and four times more likely to experience conduct disorders than the children of professionals.
- Children born into poor families are also more likely to die in infancy or childhood, to suffer longstanding illness, to be shorter in height, to fall behind at school, and to be placed on the child protection register.

Thus we cannot speak of 'children' in general as if they were all equal – social class, gender and ethnic differences affect their life chances.

Inequalities between children and adults

There are also major inequalities of power between children and adults. March of progress writers argue that adults use this power for the benefit and protection of children, for example by passing laws against child labour.

However, critics such as Shulamith Firestone (1979) and John Holt (1974) argue that many of the things that march of progress writers see as care and protection are in fact just new forms of oppression and control. For example, Firestone argues that 'protection' from paid work is not a benefit to children but a form of inequality. It is a way of forcibly segregating children, making them more dependent, powerless and subject to adult control than previously.

These critics see the need to free children from adult control, and so their view is described as 'child liberationism'. Adult control takes a number of forms.

neglect and abuse

Adult control over children can take the extreme form of physical neglect or physical, sexual or emotional abuse. In 2013, 43,000 children were subject to child protection plans because they were deemed to be at risk of significant harm – most often from their own parents (see Table 4C). The charity ChildLine receives over 20,000 calls a year from children saying that they have been sexually or physically abused. Such figures indicate a 'dark side' to family life of which children are the victims.

controls over children's space

Children's movements in industrial societies such as Britain are highly regulated. For example, shops may display

▲ Constant supervision?

signs such as 'no schoolchildren'. Children are told to play in some areas and forbidden to play in others. There is increasingly close surveillance over children in public spaces such as shopping centres, especially at times when they should be in school.

Similarly, fears about road safety and 'stranger danger' have led to more and more children being driven to school rather than travelling independently. For example, in 1971, 86% of primary school children were allowed to travel home from school alone. By 2010, this had fallen to 25%. According to Hugh Cunningham (2007), the 'home habitat' of 8 year olds (the area in which they are able to travel alone) has shrunk to one-ninth of the size it was 25 years earlier.

This control and surveillance contrasts with the independence of many children in developing countries today. For example, Cindi Katz (2004) describes how rural Sudanese children roam freely both within the village and for several kilometres outside it.

controls over children's time

Adults in modern society control children's daily routines, including the times when they get up, eat, go to school, come home, go out, play, watch television and sleep. Adults also control the speed at which children 'grow up'. It is they who define whether a child is too old or too young for this or that activity, responsibility or behaviour. This contrasts with Holmes' finding that among Samoans, 'too young' is never given as a reason for not letting a child undertake a particular task.

controls over children's bodies

Adults exercise enormous control over children's bodies, including how they sit, walk and run, what they wear (sun hats, make-up, glasses), their hairstyles and whether or not they can have their ears pierced. It is taken for granted that children's bodies may be touched (in certain ways by certain adults): they are washed, fed and dressed, have their heads patted and hands held, are picked up, cuddled and kissed, and they may be disciplined by smacking.

At the same time, adults restrict the ways in which children may touch their own bodies. For example, a child may be told not to pick their nose, suck their thumb or play with their genitals. This contrasts with the sexual freedoms enjoyed by children in some non-industrial cultures such as the Trobriand Islands.

control over children's access to resources

In industrial societies, children have only limited opportunities to earn money, and so they remain dependent economically on adults:

- Labour laws and compulsory schooling exclude them from all but the most marginal, low-paid, part-time employment.
- Although the state pays child benefit, this goes to the parent not the child.
- Pocket money given by parents may depend on 'good behaviour' and there may be restrictions on what it can be spent on.

All this contrasts with the economic role of children in developing societies today and in European societies in the past. For example, Katz found that Sudanese children were already engaged in productive work from the age of three or four.

Age patriarchy

Diana Gittins (1998) uses the term 'age patriarchy' to describe inequalities between adults and children. Just as feminists use the concept of patriarchy to describe male domination and female dependency, Gittins argues that there is also an age patriarchy of adult domination and child dependency. In fact, patriarchy means literally 'rule by the father' and as Gittins points out, the term 'family' referred originally to the power of the male head over all other members of the household, including children and servants as well as women.

Today this power may still assert itself in the form of violence against both children and women. For example, according to Cathy Humphreys and Ravi Thiara (2002), a quarter of the 200 women in their study left their abusing partner because they feared for their children's lives. (See Topic 1 for more about domestic violence.) Such findings support Gittins' view that patriarchy oppresses children as well as women.

Evidence that children may experience childhood as oppressive comes from the strategies that they use to resist the status of child and the restrictions that go with it. Jennifer Hockey and Allison James (1993) describe one strategy as 'acting up' – acting like adults by doing things that children are not supposed to do, such as swearing, smoking, drinking alcohol, joy riding and under-age sexual activity. Similarly, children may exaggerate their age ('I'm nearly 9').

'Acting down' – behaving in ways expected of younger children – is also a popular strategy for resisting adult control (e.g. by reverting to 'baby talk' or insisting on being carried). Hockey and James conclude that modern childhood is a status from which most children want to escape.

However, critics of the child liberationist view argue that some adult control over children's lives is justified on the grounds that children cannot make rational decisions and so are unable to safeguard their interests themselves.

Critics also argue that, although children remain under adult supervision, they are not as powerless as the child liberationists claim. For example, as we saw earlier, the 1989 Children Act and the United Nations Convention on the Rights of the Child establish the principle that children have legal rights to be protected and consulted.

Activity	Discussion

Has the position of children improved?

...go to www.sociology.uk.net

The 'new sociology of childhood'

The views we have examined so far see childhood as socially constructed; that is, shaped by social processes such as industrialisation, laws and government policies, and institutions such as the family and education system.

While this helps us to understand how childhood changes over time, there is a danger of seeing children as merely passive objects who have no part in making their own childhoods. It risks seeing children from what Berry Mayall (2004) calls an 'adultist' viewpoint. That is, it may see children as mere 'socialisation projects' for adults to mould, shape and develop, of no interest in themselves, but only for what they will become in the future.

A different view is taken by the 'new sociology of childhood'. This approach doesn't see children as simply 'adults in the making'. Instead, it sees children as active agents who play a major part in creating their own childhoods.

the child's point of view

For this reason, as Carol Smart (2011) says, the new approach aims to include the views and experiences of children themselves while they are living through childhood. As Mayall says, we need to focus on 'the present tense of childhood' to study ordinary everyday life from the child's perspective.

For example, Jennifer Mason and Becky Tipper (2008) show how children actively create their own definitions of who is 'family' – which may include people who are not 'proper' aunts or grandfathers etc, but who they regard as 'close'.

Similarly, Smart et al's (2001) study of divorce found that, far from being passive victims, children were actively involved in trying to make the situation better for everyone.

Studies like these use research methods such as informal, unstructured interviews, which empower children to express their own views and allow researchers to see the world from the child's point of view.

This enables sociologists to explore the diverse, multiple childhoods that exist even within a single society. For example, as Smart notes, there are 'disabled childhoods, Chinese childhoods, girls' childhoods, the childhoods of adopted children, poor childhoods and so on'.

Because it allows children to express their point of view, the new sociology of childhood also draws attention to the fact that children often lack power in relation to adults. As such, it is an approach favoured by child liberationists who campaign in favour of children's rights and priorities.

Topic summary

Childhood is a **social construction** and varies between times, places and groups. Most sociologists see our idea of childhood as a fairly recent one, the result of **industrialisation** and other social changes. Modern society constructs childhood as a time of **vulnerability, innocence and segregation** from the adult world. Some argue that we are witnessing the **disappearance of childhood** as the media erode the boundary between childhood and adulthood. In **postmodernity**, adult surveillance and control increase.

'March of progress' sociologists believe we live in an increasingly **child-centred society**. They state that children have never had it so good. Critics argue that this ignores the continued existence of child poverty, abuse and exploitation.

Child liberationists argue that children in modern western society are victims of **age patriarchy** and are subject to adult control. **The new sociology of childhood** argues that we must take the perspective of the child.

EXAMINING CHILDHOOD

QuickCheck Questions

1 Suggest three ways in which childhood in non-industrial cultures often differs from childhood in the west.
2 Give two examples of parental neglect or indifference towards children in the Middle Ages.
3 Why does Jenks think parents have become more fearful for their children's security?
4 Why are children less of an economic asset to their parents today than they were in the past?
5 Give one example of class differences between children.
6 What is age patriarchy?
7 Give one disadvantage of seeing childhood from an 'adultist' viewpoint.

Questions to try

Whether or not you are taking the AS exams during your A level course, answering the AS questions below is a very good way of testing your knowledge and understanding and practising your skills in preparation for your A level exams.

Item A According to some sociologists, children in today's supposedly child-centred society lead lives that are segregated and controlled, but childhood was not always like this. Ariès describes a medieval world where there was little distinction between children and adults in either work or leisure. According to this view, industrial society brought major changes. Children's lives became increasingly confined and regulated by adults. Not all sociologists share this view. Some argue that the distinction between childhood and adulthood is again becoming blurred.

Item B A popular view is that childhood is a fixed, universal, biological stage of physical and psychological immaturity that is common to all human beings. Everyone will pass through it on the way to biological maturity and adulthood. However, evidence shows that what counts as childhood, what experiences children undergo and what roles they play, are far from universal.

AS questions
1 Define the term 'child-centred society'.   (2 marks)
2 Using one example, explain how the difference between adulthood and childhood may be becoming less clear.   (2 marks)
3 Outline three ways in which adults control children's time, space or bodies.   (6 marks)

AS and A level question
4 Applying material from Item A and your knowledge, evaluate sociological explanations of changes in the status of childhood.   (20 marks)

A level question
5 Applying material from Item B, analyse two arguments against the view that childhood is a fixed, universal stage.   (10 marks)

The Examiner's Advice

Q4 Spend about 30 minutes on this. Explain the concept of social construction and apply historical examples of how childhood varies. Develop points from Item A, e.g. on children in medieval society and the emergence of the modern notion of childhood as segregated, innocent etc. Discuss industrialisation, child protection legislation, schooling, literacy etc. Consider whether childhood is now changing again, e.g. the blurring of the distinction between children and adults. Use these and other key concepts and issues such as age patriarchy, the role of the media, toxic childhood etc. Use evidence from studies such as Ariès, Shorter, Postman, De Mause, Gittins, Hockey and James, Mayall, Palmer etc. Evaluate by considering debates between march of progress and child liberationist views on the status of children today, whether childhood is disappearing etc.

Q5 Spend about 15 minutes on this. Divide your time fairly equally between the two arguments. You don't need a separate introduction; just start on your first argument. To answer this question, it's essential that you take two points from the Item and show through a chain of reasoning (see page 248) how each demonstrates that childhood is not a fixed, universal stage. (It is a very good idea to quote from the Item when doing so.) You could use changes over time, cross-cultural differences, or differences within the same society. For example, compulsory education changed children's status by removing them from the workforce. This meant they became economically dependent on adults. Use concepts such as social construction, industrialisation, legislation, work, literacy, the media etc. Include some brief evaluation, e.g. that all societies distinguish between children and adults.

Family spending performs an important function for the economy.

GETTING STARTED

Different sociologists have different views of the role of the family. These views often focus on whether or not they see the family as beneficial for its members and for wider society.

In pairs, using what you learned from Topics 1 and 2 as well as your own ideas, make a list of:

1 All the positive points you can think of about families.
   For each point, suggest how it benefits (a) society and (b) the individual members of the family.

2 All the negative points you can think of about families.
   For each point, suggest what negative effects the family may have on (a) the individual members of the family and (b) society.

Learning objectives

When you have studied this Topic, you should:

- Understand the functionalist, Marxist, feminist and personal life perspectives on the family.

- Be able to analyse the similarities and differences between these perspectives.

- Be able to evaluate the usefulness of these perspectives on the family.

So far in this chapter, we have looked at some of the key members of the family – husbands and wives, parents and children – and at how far their roles and relationships may have changed. We now turn our attention to how the family fits into wider society.

This Topic deals with theories about the role or purpose of the family – what it does for its members and for society. We look at the answers sociologists have given to the question, 'What are the functions of the family?'

Sociologists have studied the family from a number of different perspectives or viewpoints and reached different conclusions as to its role or functions. In this Topic, we shall examine the following sociological theories of the family:

- **Functionalism** – a consensus perspective
- **Marxism** – a class conflict perspective
- **Feminism** – a gender conflict perspective
- **The personal life perspective.**

The functionalist perspective on the family

Functionalists believe that society is based on a value consensus – a set of shared norms and values – into which society socialises its members. This enables them to cooperate harmoniously to meet society's needs and achieve shared goals.

Functionalists regard society as a system made up of different parts or sub-systems that depend on each other, such as the family, the education system and the economy. Functionalists often compare society to a biological organism like the human body.

For example, just as organs such as the heart or lungs perform functions vital to the well being of the body as a whole, so the family meets some of society's essential needs, such as the need to socialise children.

Functionalists see the family as a particularly important sub-system – a basic building block of society. For example, George Peter Murdock (1949) argues that the family performs four essential functions to meet the needs of society and its members:

- **Stable satisfaction of the sex drive** with the same partner, preventing the social disruption caused by a sexual 'free-for-all'.
- **Reproduction of the next generation**, without which society could not continue.
- **Socialisation of the young** into society's shared norms and values.
- **Meeting its members' economic needs**, such as food and shelter.

Application

What similarities and differences can you see between society and a biological organism such as the human body?

Criticisms of Murdock

Murdock accepts that other institutions could perform these functions. However, he argues that the sheer practicality of the nuclear family as a way of meeting these four needs explains why it is universal – found in all human societies without exception.

However, while few sociologists would doubt that most of these are important functions, some argue that they could be performed equally well by other institutions, or by non-nuclear family structures.

Others have criticised Murdock's approach. Marxists and feminists reject his 'rose-tinted' harmonious consensus view that the family meets the needs of both wider society and all the different members of the family. They argue that functionalism neglects conflict and exploitation:

- **Feminists** see the family as serving the needs of men and oppressing women.
- **Marxists** argue that it meets the needs of capitalism, not those of family members or society as a whole.

Activity	Webquest

Alternatives to the nuclear family

...go to www.sociology.uk.net

Parsons' 'functional fit' theory

Apart from the functions identified by Murdock, the family may meet other needs too. For example, it may perform welfare, military, political or religious functions. In the view of Talcott Parsons (1955), the functions that the family performs will depend on the kind of society in which it is found.

Furthermore, the functions that the family has to perform will affect its 'shape' or structure. Parsons distinguishes between two kinds of family structure:

- **The nuclear family** of just parents and their dependent children.
- **The extended family** of three generations living under one roof.

Parsons argues that the particular structure and functions of a given type of family will 'fit' the needs of the society in which it is found.

According to Parsons, there are two basic types of society – modern industrial society and traditional pre-industrial society. He argues that the nuclear family fits the needs of industrial society and is the dominant family type in that society, while the extended family fits the needs of pre-industrial society.

In Parsons' view, when Britain began to industrialise, from the late 18th century onwards, the extended family began to give way to the nuclear. This was because the emerging industrial society had different needs from pre-industrial society, and the family had to adapt to meet these needs. Parsons sees industrial society as having two essential needs:

1 A geographically mobile workforce

In traditional pre-industrial society, people often spent their whole lives living in the same village, working on the same farm. By contrast, in modern society, industries constantly spring up and decline in different parts of the country, even different parts of the world, and this requires people to move to where the jobs are.

Parsons argues that it is easier for the compact two-generation nuclear family to move, than for the three-generation extended family. The nuclear family is better fitted to the need that modern industry has for a geographically mobile workforce.

2 A socially mobile workforce

Modern industrial society is based on constantly evolving science and technology and so it requires a skilled, technically competent workforce. It is therefore essential that talented people are able to win promotion and take on the most important jobs, even if they come from very humble backgrounds.

In modern society, an individual's status is achieved by their own efforts and ability, not ascribed (fixed at birth) by their social and family background, and this makes social mobility possible. For example, the son of a labourer can become a doctor or lawyer through ability and hard work.

For this reason, Parsons argues, the nuclear family is better equipped to meet the needs of industrial society. In the extended family, adult sons live at home in their father's house – where the father has a higher ascribed status as head of the household.

However, at work, the son may have a higher achieved status (a more important job) than his father. This would

Box 30	The evidence against Parsons

Other sociologists and historians have produced evidence that contradicts Parsons' claims of a 'functional fit' between the extended family and pre-industrial society, and between the nuclear family and industrial society. We can summarise these criticisms in terms of the following three questions:

1 Was the extended family dominant in pre-industrial society?

According to Young and Willmott (1973), the pre-industrial family was nuclear, not extended as Parsons claims, with parents and children working together, for example in cottage industries such as weaving. Similarly, Peter Laslett's (1972) study of English households from 1564 to 1821 found that they were almost always nuclear. A combination of late childbearing and short life expectancy meant that grandparents were unlikely to be alive for very long after the birth of their first grandchild.

2 Did the family become nuclear in early industrial society?

According to Parsons, industrialisation brought the nuclear family. However, Young and Willmott argue that the hardship of the early industrial period gave rise to the 'mum-centred' working-class extended family, based on ties between mothers and their married daughters, who relied on each other for financial, practical and emotional support.

The idea that individuals break off or maintain family ties because of the costs or benefits involved is called exchange theory.

Michael Anderson's (1980) study of mid-19th century Preston uses exchange theory to explain the popularity of the working-class extended family. He shows how the harsh conditions of the time – poverty, sickness, early death and the absence of a welfare state – meant that the benefits of maintaining extended family ties greatly outweighed the costs. These benefits included using older kin for childcare while parents worked, and taking in orphaned relatives to produce extra income and help towards the rent.

3 Is the extended family no longer important in modern society?

There is partial support for Parsons' claim that the nuclear family has become the dominant family type today. Young and Willmott argue that, from about 1900, the nuclear family emerged as a result of social changes that made the extended family less important as a source of support. These changes included higher living standards, married women working, the welfare state and better housing.

However, the extended family has not disappeared. Studies show that it continues to exist because it performs important functions, for example providing financial help, childcare and emotional support (see Topic 5).

inevitably give rise to tensions and conflict if they both lived under the same roof.

The solution therefore is for adult sons to leave home when they marry and form their own nuclear family. The nuclear family therefore encourages social mobility as well as geographical mobility.

The result is the mobile nuclear family, which is 'structurally isolated' from its extended kin (relatives). Though it may keep in touch with them, it has no binding obligations towards them – unlike the pre-industrial extended family, where relatives had an overriding duty to help one another, for example at harvest or in times of hardship or crisis.

Loss of functions

The pre-industrial family was a multi-functional unit. For example, it was both a unit of production in which family members worked together, for example on the family farm, and a unit of consumption, feeding and clothing its members. It was a more self-sufficient unit than the modern nuclear family, providing for its members' health and welfare and meeting most individual and social needs.

However, according to Parsons, when society industrialises, the family not only changes its structure from extended to nuclear, it also loses many of its functions.

For example, the family ceases to be a unit of production: work moves into the factories and the family becomes a unit of consumption only. It also loses most of its other functions to other institutions, such as schools and the health service.

In Parsons' view, as a result of this loss of functions, the modern nuclear family comes to specialise in performing just two essential or 'irreducible' functions:

▲ Helping out at harvest time on the family farm

- **The primary socialisation of children** to equip them with basic skills and society's values, to enable them to cooperate with others and begin to integrate them into society.
- **The stabilisation of adult personalities:** the family is a place where adults can relax and release tensions, enabling them to return to the workplace refreshed and ready to meet its demands. This is functional for the efficiency of the economy.

The Marxist perspective on the family

While functionalists see society as based on value consensus (agreement), Marxist sociologists see capitalist society as based on an unequal conflict between two social classes:

- **the capitalist class,** who own the means of production
- **the working class,** whose labour the capitalists exploit for profit.

Marxists see all society's institutions, such as the education system, the media, religion and the state, along with the family, as helping to maintain class inequality and capitalism.

Thus, for Marxists, the functions of the family are performed purely for the benefit of the capitalist system. This view

contrasts sharply with the functionalist view that the family benefits both society as a whole and all the individual members of the family.

Marxists have identified several functions that they see the family as fulfilling for capitalism:

1 Inheritance of property

Marxists argue that the key factor determining the shape of all social institutions, including the family, is the mode of production – that is, who owns and controls society's productive forces (such as tools, machinery, raw materials, land and labour). In modern society, it is the capitalist class that owns and controls these means of production. As the mode of production evolves, so too does the family.

Marx called the earliest, classless society, 'primitive communism'. In this society, there was no private property. Instead, all members of society owned the means of production communally.

At this stage of social development, there was no family as such. Instead, there existed what Friedrich Engels called the 'promiscuous horde' or tribe, in which there were no restrictions on sexual relationships.

private property

However, as the forces of production developed, society's wealth began to increase. Along with increased wealth came the development of private property, as a class of men emerged who were able to secure control of the means of production. This change eventually brought about the patriarchal monogamous nuclear family.

In Engels' view, monogamy became essential because of the inheritance of private property – men had to be certain of the paternity of their children in order to ensure that their legitimate heirs inherited from them.

In Engels' view, the rise of the monogamous nuclear family represented a "world historical defeat of the female sex". This was because it brought the woman's sexuality under male control and turned her into "a mere instrument for the production of children".

Marxists argue that only with the overthrow of capitalism and private ownership of the means of production will women achieve liberation from patriarchal control. A classless society will be established in which the means of production are owned collectively, not privately. There will no longer be a need for the patriarchal family, since there will be no need to have a means of transmitting private property down the generations.

2 Ideological functions

Marxists argue that the family today also performs key ideological functions for capitalism. By 'ideology', Marxists mean a set of ideas or beliefs that justify inequality and maintain the capitalist system by persuading people to accept it as fair, natural or unchangeable.

One way in which the family does this is by socialising children into the idea that hierarchy and inequality are inevitable. Parental (especially paternal) power over children accustoms them to the idea that there always has to be someone in charge (usually a man) and this prepares them

for a working life in which they will accept orders from their capitalist employers.

According to Eli Zaretsky (1976), the family also performs an ideological function by offering an apparent 'haven' from the harsh and exploitative world of capitalism outside, in which workers can 'be themselves' and have a private life. However, Zaretsky argues that this is largely an illusion – the family cannot meet its members' needs. For example, it is based on the domestic servitude of women.

> **Application**
> What other social institutions in addition to the family socialise children into the idea that hierarchy and inequality are inevitable?

3 A unit of consumption

Capitalism exploits the labour of the workers, making a profit by selling the products of their labour for more than it pays them to produce these commodities. The family therefore plays a major role in generating profits for capitalists, since it is an important market for the sale of consumer goods:

- Advertisers urge families to 'keep up with the Joneses' by consuming all the latest products.
- The media target children, who use 'pester power' to persuade parents to spend more.
- Children who lack the latest clothes or 'must have' gadgets are mocked and stigmatised by their peers.

Thus, Marxists see the family as performing several functions that maintain capitalist society: the inheritance of private property, socialisation into acceptance of inequality, and a source of profits. In the Marxist view, while these may benefit capitalism, they do not benefit the members of the family.

Criticisms of the Marxist perspective

- Marxists tend to assume that the nuclear family is dominant in capitalist society. This ignores the wide variety of family structures found in society today.
- Feminists argue that the Marxist emphasis on class and capitalism underestimates the importance of gender inequalities within the family. In the feminist view, these are more fundamental than class inequalities and the family primarily serves the interests of men, not capitalism.
- Functionalists argue that Marxists ignore the very real benefits that the family provides for its members.

Which of the following statements about the family are likely to be put forward by (a) a functionalist (b) a Marxist (c) both?

1   It fulfils the needs of its individual members.
2   It is important in socialising children.
3   Its structure is determined by economic factors.
4   It provides consumers to buy goods.

5   It provides a 'safety valve' away from work.
6   It fulfils its functions for society.
7   It is universal and necessary everywhere.
8   It has an important reproductive role.
9   It keeps women under patriarchal control.
10 It performs its functions for capitalism.

Feminist perspectives on the family

Like Marxists, feminists take a critical view of the family. They argue that it oppresses women – as we saw in Topic 1, they have focused on issues such as the unequal division of domestic labour and domestic violence against women. They do not regard gender inequality as natural or inevitable, but as something created by society.

However, feminism is a broad term covering several types. Each type approaches the family in a different way and offers different solutions to the problem of gender inequality. We shall examine four main types of feminism.

1   Liberal feminism

Liberal feminists are concerned with campaigning against sex discrimination and for equal rights and opportunities for women (e.g. equal pay and an end to discrimination in employment).

- They argue that women's oppression is being gradually overcome through changing people's attitudes and through changes in the law such as the Sex Discrimination Act (1975), which outlaws discrimination in employment.
- They believe we are moving towards greater equality, but that full equality will depend on further reforms and changes in the attitudes and socialisation patterns of both sexes.

In terms of the family, they hold a view similar to that of 'march of progress' theorists such as Young and Willmott (see Topic 1). Although liberal feminists do not believe full gender equality has yet been achieved in the family, they argue that there has been gradual progress.

For example, some studies suggest that men are doing more domestic labour, while the way parents now socialise their sons and daughters is more equal than in the past and they now have similar aspirations for them.

However, other feminists criticise liberal feminists for failing to challenge the underlying causes of women's oppression and for believing that changes in the law or in people's attitudes will be enough to bring equality. Marxist and radical feminists believe instead that far-reaching changes to deep-rooted social structures are needed.

2   Marxist feminism

Marxist feminists argue that the main cause of women's oppression in the family is not men, but capitalism. Women's oppression performs several functions for capitalism:

▲ Marxist feminists see women as a reserve army of labour.

- **Women reproduce the labour force** through their unpaid domestic labour, by socialising the next generation of workers and maintaining and servicing the current one.
- **Women absorb anger** that would otherwise be directed at capitalism. Fran Ansley (1972) describes wives as 'takers of shit' who soak up the frustration their husbands feel because of the alienation and exploitation they suffer at work. For Marxists, this explains male domestic violence against women.
- **Women are a reserve army of cheap labour** that can be taken on when extra workers are needed. When no longer needed, employers can 'let them go' to return to their primary role as unpaid domestic labour.

Marxist feminists see the oppression of women in the family as linked to the exploitation of the working class. They argue that the family must be abolished at the same time as a socialist revolution replaces capitalism with a classless society.

3 Radical feminism

Radical feminists argue that all societies have been founded on patriarchy – rule by men. For radical feminists, the key division in society is between men and women:

- **Men are the enemy:** they are the source of women's oppression and exploitation.
- **The family and marriage are the key institutions** in patriarchal society. Men benefit from women's unpaid domestic labour and from their sexual services, and they dominate women through domestic and sexual violence or the threat of it.

For radical feminists, the patriarchal system needs to be overturned. In particular, the family, which they see as the root of women's oppression, must be abolished. They argue that the only way to achieve this is through *separatism* – women must organise themselves to live independently of men.

Many radical feminists argue for 'political lesbianism' – the idea that heterosexual relationships are inevitably oppressive because they involve 'sleeping with the enemy'. Similarly, Germaine Greer (2000) argues for the creation of all-

female or 'matrilocal' households as an alternative to the heterosexual family.

However, for liberal feminists such as Jenny Somerville (2000), radical feminists fail to recognise that women's position has improved considerably – with better access to divorce, better job opportunities, control over their own fertility, and the ability to choose whether to marry or cohabit.

Somerville also argues that heterosexual attraction makes it unlikely that separatism would work.

However, Somerville does recognise that women have yet to achieve full equality. She argues that there is a need for 'family friendly' policies, such as more flexible working, to promote greater equality between partners.

4 Difference feminism

The feminist approaches we have considered so far all tend to assume that most women live in conventional nuclear families and that they share a similar experience of family life.

However, difference feminists argue that we cannot generalise about women's experiences. They argue that lesbian and heterosexual women, white and black women, middle-class and working-class women, have very different experiences of the family from one another.

For example, by regarding the family purely negatively, white feminists neglect black women's experience of racial oppression. Instead, black feminists view the black family positively as a source of support and resistance against racism.

However, other feminists argue that difference feminism neglects the fact that all women share many of the same experiences. For example, they all face a risk of domestic violence and sexual assault, low pay and so on.

> **Analysis and Evaluation**
> Which of the four feminist perspectives do you find most convincing? Give reasons for your answer.

The personal life perspective on families

As we have seen, there are major differences between functionalist, Marxist and feminist theories of the family. However, the personal life perspective argues that they all suffer from two weaknesses:

1 **They tend to assume that the traditional nuclear family is the dominant family type.** This ignores the

increased diversity of families today. Compared with 50 years ago, many more people now live in other families, such as lone-parent families, stepfamilies and so on. We examine family diversity in Topic 5.

2 **They are all structural theories.** That is, they assume that families and their members are simply passive puppets

Beyond ties of blood and marriage

As well as taking a bottom up approach to relationships, the personal life perspective also takes a wider view of relationships than just traditional 'family' relationships based on blood or marriage ties

For example, a woman who may not feel close to her own sister and may be unwilling to help her in a crisis, may at the same time be willing to care for someone to whom she is not related, such as the elderly woman who cohabited with her late father. Without knowing what meaning each of these relationships has for her, we would not be able to understand how she might act.

By focusing on people's meanings, the personal life perspective draws our attention to a range of other personal or intimate relationships that are important to people even though they may not be conventionally defined as 'family'. These include all kinds of relationships that individuals see as significant and that give them a sense of identity, belonging or relatedness, such as:

- **Relationships with friends** who may be 'like a sister or brother' to you.
- **Fictive kin:** close friends who are treated as relatives, for example your mum's best friend who you call 'auntie'.
- **Gay and lesbian 'chosen families'** made up of a supportive network of close friends, ex-partners and others, who are not related by blood or marriage.
- **Relationships with dead relatives** who live on in people's memories and continue to shape their identities and affect their actions.
- **Even relationships with pets** For example, Becky Tipper (2011) found in her study of children's views of family relationships, that children frequently saw their pets as 'part of the family'.

These and similar relationships raise questions about what counts as family from the point of view of the individuals involved. For example, Petra Nordqvist and Carol Smart's (2014) research on donor-conceived children explores "what counts as family when your child shares a genetic link with a 'relative stranger' but not with your partner?"

Analysis and Evaluation

How legitimate is it to count pets, friends and dead relatives as part of your family? Give reasons for your answer.

Donor-conceived children

In their research, Nordqvist and Smart found that the issue of blood and genes raised a range of feelings. Some parents emphasised the importance of social relationships over genetic ones in forming family bonds.

▲ Pets: part of the family?

manipulated by the structure of society to perform certain functions – for example, to provide the economy with a mobile labour force, or to serve the needs of capitalism or of men.

Sociologists influenced by interactionist and postmodernist perspectives reject the structural view. They argue that structural theories ignore the fact that we have some *choice* in creating our family relationships.

They argue that to understand the family today, we must focus on the meanings its members give to their relationships and situations, rather than on the family's supposed 'functions'.

The sociology of personal life

The sociology of personal life is a new perspective on families. It is strongly influenced by interactionist ideas and argues that to understand families, we must start from the point of view of the individuals concerned and the meanings they give to their relationships. This contrasts with the other perspectives we have looked at in this Topic:

- Functionalism, Marxism and feminism all take a 'top down', structural approach.
- By contrast, the personal life perspective shares the 'bottom up' approach of interactionism. It emphasises the meanings that individual family members hold and how these shape their actions and relationships.

For example, Erin, the mother of an egg donor-conceived child, defined being a mum in terms of the time and effort she put into raising her daughter: "that's what makes a mother and not the cell that starts it off".

However, difficult feelings could flare up for a non-genetic parent if somebody remarked that the child looked like them. Differences in appearance also led parents to wonder about the donor's identity, about possible 'donor siblings' and whether these counted as family for their child.

Where couples knew their donor, they had to resolve other questions about who counted as family. Do the donor's parents count as grandparents of a donor-conceived child? Is the donor-conceived child a (half) sibling to the donor's other children?

For lesbian couples, there were additional problems. These included concerns about equality between the genetic and non-genetic mothers and that the donor might be treated as the 'real' second parent.

Activity | **Media**

Donor-conceived children

...go to www.sociology.uk.net

Evaluation of the personal life perspective

Nordqvist and Smart's study illustrates the value of the personal life perspective as compared with top down, structural approaches. It helps us to understand how people themselves construct and define their relationships as 'family', rather than imposing traditional sociological definitions of the family (based on blood or genes, for example) from the outside.

However, the personal life perspective can be accused of taking too broad a view. Critics argue that, by including a wide range of different kinds of personal relationships, we ignore what is special about relationships that are based on blood or marriage.

The personal life perspective rejects the top down view taken by other perspectives, such as functionalism.

Nevertheless, it does see intimate relationships as performing the important function of providing us with a sense of belonging and relatedness.

However, unlike functionalism, the personal life perspective recognises that relatedness is not always positive. For example, people may be trapped in violent, abusive relationships or simply in ones where they suffer everyday unhappiness, hurt or lack of respect.

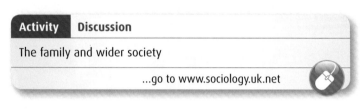

Activity | **Discussion**

The family and wider society

...go to www.sociology.uk.net

Topic summary

Functionalists take a **consensus** view of the family. They see it as a **universal** institution that performs essential functions for society as a whole and for all its members.

Parsons sees a **functional fit** between the nuclear family and modern society's need for a **mobile labour force**.

Marxists see the family as serving the economic and ideological needs of **capitalism**, such as the transmission of private property from one generation of capitalists to the next.

Feminists see the family as perpetuating **patriarchy**. **Liberal, radical and Marxist feminists** differ over the cause of women's subordination and the solution to it.

Functionalist, Marxist and feminist theories have all been criticised for neglecting family **diversity** and individuals' capacity to **choose** their family arrangements.

The **personal life perspective** argues that we must focus on the meanings people give to relationships and on how they define what counts as family.

EXAMINING THEORIES OF THE FAMILY

QuickCheck Questions

Check your answers at www.sociology.uk.net

1 List the four functions of the family that Murdock identifies.
2 How does the family perform an ideological function, according to Marxists?
3 Give two criticisms of the Marxist view of the family.

4 Explain the difference between Marxist feminism and radical feminism.
5 What is meant by a 'bottom up' approach to the family?
6 Give three examples of relationships that some people regard as 'family' but are not based on blood or marriage.

Questions to try

Whether or not you are taking the AS exams during your A level course, answering the AS questions below is a very good way of testing your knowledge and understanding and practising your skills in preparation for your A level exams.

Item A   Despite their disagreements, functionalist, Marxist and feminist approaches to the family share certain similarities. They are all structural approaches: they see the family as a structure that performs certain functions — although they disagree about what these functions are and who benefits from them. Similarly, they all assume that by 'the family' we mean the conventional nuclear family.

Other sociologists reject this structural approach. For example, the personal life perspective takes a bottom-up view that focuses on people's meanings and how they themselves define what counts as 'family'.

Item B   Capitalist society is based on a wealthy capitalist class exploiting the labour of a propertyless working class in order to extract a profit. However, to obtain their profit, capitalists must sell what has been produced and this requires people who are willing to buy it. For capitalism to continue, the proletariat must be persuaded to accept their exploitation. Capitalists also need to retain control of their wealth in order to maintain their privileged position.

AS questions

1 Define the term 'patriarchy'.   (2 marks)
2 Using one example, explain how liberal feminists see gender inequality in the family being overcome.   (2 marks)
3 Outline three functions that functionalists see the family as performing.   (6 marks)

AS and A level question

4 Applying material from Item A and your knowledge, evaluate the usefulness of structural approaches to our understanding of families and households.   (20 marks)

A level question

5 Applying material from Item B, analyse two functions that the family may perform for capitalism.   (10 marks)

The Examiner's Advice

Q4 Spend about 30 minutes on this. You could start by developing points from Item A, e.g. on the similarities and differences between different structural perspectives, in terms of what functions they see the family performing and who benefits. Use concepts such as economic and ideological functions, primary socialisation, stabilisation of adult personalities, reserve army of labour, reproduction of the labour force or patriarchy etc. Use evidence from studies such as Murdock, Parsons, Engels, Ansley, Greer, Tipper, Nordqvist and Smart etc. Evaluate structural approaches by considering debates between functionalists, Marxists and feminists mentioned above, but you should also deal with criticisms from the personal life perspective. Make use of evidence on how people define 'family', e.g. donor-conceived children, fictive kin, chosen families, pets as family etc.

Q5 Spend about 15 minutes on this. Divide your time fairly equally between the two functions. You don't need a separate introduction. It's essential that you take two points from the Item and show through a chain of reasoning (see page 248) how each relates to a function for capitalism. (It is a very good idea to quote from the Item when doing so.) You could use functions such as ideological indoctrination, providing a consumer market, or inheritance of wealth. For example, the family is based on parental authority. This means children are socialised into the idea that there must always be someone in charge, thus making them willing to accept their employers' orders. Use concepts such as commodities, unit of consumption, pester power, advertising, primitive communism, paternity, the family as haven etc, and studies such as Ansley, Engels or Zaretsky. Include some brief evaluation.

TOPIC 4

A Victorian-style funeral – but death rates today are far lower than in the 19th century.

GETTING STARTED

Study Figure 4.2 on page 200 and then answer these questions:

1 When did the number of births per year in the UK first start to fall?

2 Identify the three periods during which the number of births showed steep rises. Can you suggest any reasons for a rise during these periods?

3 When did the UK experience periods with low numbers of births? Can you suggest any reasons for this?

4 Why do you think that numbers of births and deaths were so similar around 1941?

5 Why do you think the number of deaths is projected to rise in the coming decades?

6 Summarise in two sentences what has happened to births and deaths in the UK since 1901.

Learning objectives

After studying this Topic, you should:

- Know the main population trends in the UK since 1900.

- Understand and be able to evaluate the reasons for population changes, including birth and death rates, family size, life expectancy, the ageing population and migration and globalisation.

- Understand and be able to evaluate the consequences of these changes.

DEMOGRAPHY

Family and population are closely linked. For example, new members of the population are mostly born into and raised by families, while the kind of care they receive from their family affects their chances of survival. Similarly, as the study by Anderson shows (Box 30, page 190), when people migrate from country to country or from region to region, they often rely on kin to facilitate their move.

The study of populations and their characteristics is called demography. These characteristics include:

- **Size:** is the population large or small, growing or declining?
- **Age structure:** is the average age of the population rising or falling?

As Figure 4.1 shows, the factors that most directly affect the size of a country's population are:

- **Births:** how many babies are born.
- **Deaths:** how many people die.
- **Immigration:** how many people enter the country from elsewhere.
- **Emigration:** how many people leave the country to live elsewhere.

In this Topic, we examine some of the main features of the UK population, and how and why it has changed. Britain in 1801 had a population of 10.5 million. By 1901, this stood at 37 million. The current population of the UK is approximately 65 million and one projection is that it will rise to 71 million by 2031.

Until the 1980s, UK population growth was largely the product of **natural change** – that is, the result of there being more births than deaths. However, since the 1980s, most of the growth has come from **net migration** – that is, more immigration than emigration.

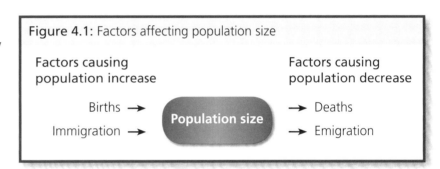

Figure 4.1: Factors affecting population size

Factors causing population increase		Factors causing population decrease
Births →	**Population size**	→ Deaths
Immigration →		→ Emigration

Births

The number of births obviously affects population size. Sociologists use the concept of **birth rate** to measure births. The birth rate is defined as the number of live births per thousand of the population per year.

As Figure 4.2 shows, there has been a long-term decline in the number of births since 1900. In that year, England and Wales had a birth rate of 28.7, but by 2014 it had fallen to an estimated 12.2.

However, as Figure 4.2 shows, there have been fluctuations in births, with three 'baby booms' in the 20th century. The first two came after the two world wars (1914-18 and 1939-45), as returning servicemen and their partners started families that they had postponed during the war years.

There was a third baby boom in the 1960s, after which the birth rate fell sharply during the 1970s. The rate rose during the 1980s, before falling again after the early 1990s, with some increase since 2001.

The total fertility rate

The factors determining the birth rate are, firstly, the proportion of women who are of childbearing age (usually taken to be aged 15-44) and, secondly, how fertile they are – that is, how many children they have. The total fertility

rate (TFR) is the average number of children women will have during their fertile years.

The UK's TFR has risen in recent years, but it is still much lower than in the past. From an all-time low of 1.63 children per woman in 2001, it rose to 1.83 by 2014. However, this is still far lower than the peak of 2.95 children per woman reached in 1964 during the 1960s baby boom.

These changes in fertility and birth rates reflect the fact that:

- More women are remaining childless than in the past.
- Women are postponing having children: the average age for giving birth is now 30, and fertility rates for women in their 30s and 40s are on the increase. Older women may be less fertile and have fewer fertile years remaining, and so they produce fewer children.

Reasons for the decline in the birth rate

Sociologists have identified a number of reasons for the long-term decline in the birth rate since 1900. These reasons involve a range of social, economic, cultural, legal, political and technological factors.

1 Changes in women's position

There were major changes in the position of women during the 20th century. These include:

- Legal equality with men, including the right to vote.
- Increased educational opportunities – girls now do better at school than boys.
- More women in paid employment, plus laws outlawing unequal pay and sex discrimination.
- Changes in attitudes to family life and women's role.
- Easier access to divorce.
- Access to abortion and reliable contraception, giving women more control over their fertility.

According to Sarah Harper (2012), the education of women is the most important reason for the long-term fall in birth and fertility rates. It has led to a change in mind-set among women, resulting in fewer children. Not only are educated women more likely to use family planning, they now see other possibilities in life apart from the traditional role of housewife and mother. Many are choosing to delay childbearing, or not to have children at all, in order to pursue a career. For example, in 2012, one in five women aged 45 was childless – double the number of 25 years earlier.

Harper also notes that, once a pattern of low fertility lasts for more than one generation, cultural norms about family size change. Smaller families become the norm and large ones come to be seen as deviant or less acceptable.

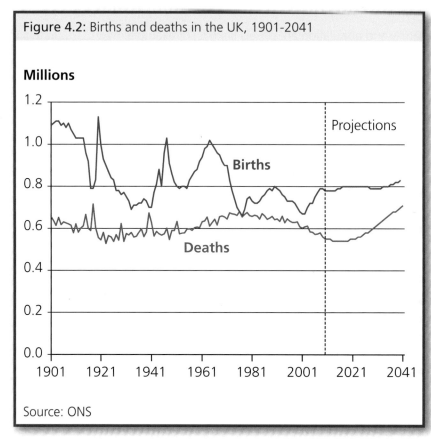

Figure 4.2: Births and deaths in the UK, 1901-2041

Source: ONS

Analysis and Evaluation

Apart from education, which of the factors listed above do you think is the most important reason for the fall in birth and fertility rates. Explain your answer.

2 Decline in the infant mortality rate

The infant mortality rate (IMR) measures the number of infants who die before their first birthday, per thousand babies born alive, per year.

Harper argues that a fall in the IMR leads to a fall in the birth rate. This is because, if many infants die, parents have more children to replace those they have lost, thereby increasing the birth rate. By contrast, if infants survive, parents will have fewer of them.

In 1900, the IMR for the UK was 154. In other words, over 15% of babies died within their first year. These figures are higher than those of less developed countries today. For example, in 2014, the world's highest estimated IMR was that of Afghanistan, at 117.

During the first half of the 20th century, the UK's IMR began to fall. This was due to several reasons:

- Improved housing and better sanitation, such as flush toilets and clean drinking water, reduced infectious disease. Infants are much more susceptible to infection because of their less developed immune system.
- Better nutrition, including that of mothers.
- Better knowledge of hygiene, child health and welfare, often spread via women's magazines.
- A fall in the number of married women working may have improved their health and that of their babies.
- Improved services for mothers and children, such as antenatal and postnatal clinics.

Before the mid-20th century, it is doubtful whether specifically medical factors had much effect on the IMR – although indirectly, the medical profession had a significant impact through its campaigns to improve public health measures.

However, from about the 1950s, medical factors began to play a greater role. For example, mass immunisation against childhood diseases such as whooping cough, diphtheria and later measles, the use of antibiotics to fight infection and improved midwifery and obstetric techniques, all contributed to a continuing fall in the IMR.

As a result of all the above developments, by 1950 the UK's IMR had fallen to 30 and by 2012 it stood at 4 – barely one fortieth of its 1900 figure.

However, while many sociologists claim that the falling IMR led to a fall in birth rates, Brass and Kabir (1978) argue that the trend to smaller families began not in rural areas, where the IMR first began to fall, but in urban areas, where the IMR remained higher for longer.

3 Children are now an economic liability

Until the late 19th century, children were economic assets to their parents because they could be sent out to work from an early age to earn an income. However, since the late 19th century children have gradually become an economic liability. (See Topic 2, page 181.)

- **Laws** banning child labour, introducing compulsory schooling and raising the school leaving age mean that children remain economically dependent on their parents for longer and longer.
- **Changing norms** about what children have a right to expect from their parents in material terms mean that the cost of bringing up children has risen.

As a result of these financial pressures, parents now feel less able or willing than in the past to have a large family.

4 Child centredness

As we saw in Topic 2, the increasing child centredness both of the family and of society as a whole means that childhood is now socially constructed as a uniquely important period in the individual's life. In terms of family size, this has encouraged a shift from 'quantity' to 'quality' – parents now have fewer children and lavish more attention and resources on these few.

Future trends in birth rates

As a result of the above factors, birth rates, fertility rates and family sizes have fallen over the last century. However, as we saw earlier, there has been a slight increase in births since 2001.

One reason for this is the increase in immigration because, on average, mothers from outside the UK have a higher fertility rate than those born in the UK. Babies born to mothers from outside the UK accounted for 25% of all births in 2011. However, as Figure 4.2 shows, the projection for the period up to 2041 expects the annual number of births to be fairly constant, at around 800,000 per year.

Effects of changes in fertility

Changes in the number of babies born affect several aspects of society. These include the family, the dependency ratio, and public services and policies.

The family

Smaller families mean that women are more likely to be free to go out to work, thus creating the dual earner couple typical of many professional families. However, family size is only one factor here. For example, better off couples may be able to have larger families and still afford childcare that allows them both to work full-time.

> **Application**
> What other effects might the decline in the number of babies being born have on families and their members?

The dependency ratio

The dependency ratio is the relationship between the size of the working or productive part of the population and the size of the non-working or dependent part of the population.

The earnings, savings and taxes of the working population must support the dependent population. Children make up a large part of the dependent population, so a fall in the number of children reduces the 'burden of dependency' on the working population.

However, in the longer term, fewer babies being born will mean fewer young adults and a smaller working population and so the burden of dependency may begin to increase again.

Vanishing children Falling fertility rates mean fewer children. As a result, childhood may become a lonelier experience as fewer children will have siblings, and more childless adults may mean fewer voices speaking up in support of children's interests. Conversely, fewer children could mean they will come to be more valued.

Public services and policies

A lower birth rate has consequences for public services. For example, fewer schools and maternity and child health services may be needed. It also affects the cost of maternity and paternity leave and the types of housing that need to be built. However, we should remember that many of these are political decisions. For example, instead of reducing the number of schools, the government could decide to have smaller class sizes.

An ageing population One effect of women having fewer babies is that the average age of the population is rising: there are more old people relative to young people. This ageing of the population has a number of important effects, which we deal with later in this Topic.

Deaths

The death rate is the number of deaths per thousand of the population per year. In 1900, the death rate stood at 19, whereas by 2012 it had more than halved, to 8.9.

The death rate had already begun falling from about 1870 and continued to do so until 1930. It rose slightly during the 1930s and 1940s – the period of the great economic depression, followed by World War II – but since the 1950s it has declined slightly.

Reasons for the decline in the death rate

There are several reasons why the death rate declined during the 20th century.

According to Tranter (1996), over three-quarters of the decline in the death rate from about 1850 to 1970 was due to a fall in the number of deaths from infectious diseases such as diphtheria, measles, smallpox, typhoid and above all tuberculosis (TB). Deaths from infectious disease were commonest in the young and most of the decline in the death rate occurred among infants, children and young adults.

By the 1950s, so-called 'diseases of affluence' (wealth) such as heart disease and cancers had replaced infectious diseases as the main cause of death. These degenerative diseases affect the middle aged and old more than the young.

There are several possible reasons for the decline in deaths from infection. It is possible that the population began to develop some natural resistance or that some diseases became less virulent (powerful).

However, social factors probably had a much greater impact on infectious diseases. These include the following:

Improved nutrition

Thomas McKeown (1972) argues that improved nutrition accounted for up to half the reduction in death rates, and was particularly important in reducing the number of deaths from TB. Better nutrition increased resistance to infection and increased the survival chances of those who did become infected.

However, McKeown does not explain why females, who receive a smaller share of the family food supply, lived longer than males. Similarly, he fails to explain why deaths from some infectious diseases, such as measles and infant diarrhoea, actually rose at a time of improving nutrition.

Medical improvements

Before the 1950s, despite some important innovations, medical improvements played almost no part in the reduction of deaths from infectious disease.

However, after the 1950s, improved medical knowledge, techniques and organisation did help to reduce death rates. Advances included the introduction of antibiotics, immunisation, blood transfusion, improved maternity services, as well as the setting up of the National Health Service in 1948. More recently, improved medication, by-pass surgery and other developments have reduced deaths from heart disease by one-third.

Smoking and diet

According to Harper, the greatest fall in death rates in recent decades has come not from medical improvements, but simply from a reduction in the number of people smoking. However, in the 21st century, obesity has replaced smoking as the new lifestyle epidemic. For example, in 2012, one quarter of all UK adults were obese.

Yet, although obesity has increased dramatically, deaths from obesity have been kept low as a result of drug therapies. Harper suggests that we may be moving to an 'American' health culture where lifestyles are unhealthy but where a long lifespan is achieved by use of costly medication.

Public health measures

In the 20th century, more effective central and local government with the necessary power to pass and enforce laws led to a range of improvements in public health and the quality of the environment.

These included improvements in housing (producing drier, better ventilated, less overcrowded accommodation), purer drinking water, laws to combat the adulteration of food and drink, the pasteurisation of milk, and improved sewage disposal methods. Similarly, the Clean Air Acts reduced air pollution, such as the smog that led to 4,000 deaths in five days in 1952.

Other social changes

Other social changes also played a part in reducing the death rate during the 20th century. These included:

- The decline of dangerous manual occupations such as mining
- Smaller families reduced the rate of transmission of infection

- Greater public knowledge of the causes of illness
- Lifestyle changes, especially the reduction in the number of men who smoke.
- Higher incomes, allowing for a healthier lifestyle.

Life expectancy

Life expectancy refers to how long on average a person born in a given year can expect to live. As death rates have fallen, so life expectancy has increased. For example:

- Males born in England in 1900 could expect on average to live until they were 50 (57 for females).
- Males born in England in 2013 can expect to live for 90.7 years (94 for females).

Over the past two centuries, life expectancy has increased by about two years per decade.

One reason for lower average life expectancy in 1900 was the fact that so many infants and children did not survive beyond the early years of life. To put the improvement in life expectancy into perspective, we can note that a newborn baby today has a better chance of reaching its *65th* birthday than a baby born in 1900 had of reaching its *first* birthday.

If the trend to greater longevity (long lifespan) continues, Harper predicts that we will soon achieve 'radical longevity', with many more centenarians (people aged over 100). Currently there are about 10,000 in the UK; by 2100 there are projected to be one million.

Class, gender and regional differences

Despite the overall reduction in the death rate and the increase in life expectancy over the last 100 years, there are still important class, gender and regional differences. For example, women generally live longer than men – although the gap has narrowed due to changes in employment and in lifestyle (such as more women smoking).

Similarly, those living in the North and Scotland have a lower life expectancy than those in the South, while working-class men in unskilled or routine jobs are nearly three times as likely to die before they are 65 compared with men in managerial or professional jobs.

According to Walker (2011), those living in the poorest areas of England die on average seven years earlier than those in the richest areas, while the average difference in disability-free life expectancy is 17 years.

Suggest three reasons why manual workers have higher death rates than professionals.

The ageing population

The average age of the UK population is rising. In 1971, it was 34.1 years. By 2013, it stood at 40.3. By 2037, it is projected to reach 42.8. There are fewer young people and more old people. The number aged 65 or over equalled the number of under-15s for the first time ever in 2014.

Another way of illustrating the changing age-profile of the population is by means of 'age pyramids' such as the ones in Figure 4.3. These show how older age groups are growing as a proportion of the population, while younger groups are shrinking. In fact, as Donald Hirsch (2005) notes, the traditional age 'pyramid' is disappearing and being replaced by more or less equal-sized 'blocks' representing the different age groups. For example, by 2041 there will be as many 78 year olds as five year olds.

This ageing of the population is caused by three factors:

- **Increasing life expectancy** – people are living longer into old age
- **Declining infant mortality,** so that nowadays hardly anyone dies early in life
- **Declining fertility** – fewer young people are being born in relation to the number of older people in the population.

Effects of an ageing population

We have already examined the reasons for changes in life expectancy, infant mortality and fertility that are causing an ageing population. We shall now focus on the effects or consequences of an ageing population.

Public services

Older people consume a larger proportion of services such as health and social care than other age groups. This is particularly true of the 'old old' (usually defined as 75 or over) as against the 'young old' (65-74). However, we should beware of over-generalising, since many people remain in relatively good health well into old age.

In addition to increased expenditure on health care, an ageing population may also mean changes to policies and provision of housing, transport or other services.

One-person pensioner households

The number of pensioners living alone has increased and one-person pensioner households now account for about

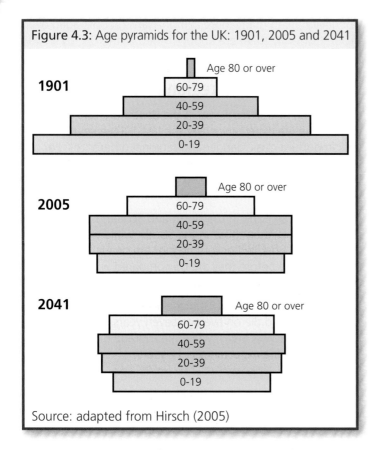

Figure 4.3: Age pyramids for the UK: 1901, 2005 and 2041

1901

Age 80 or over
60-79
40-59
20-39
0-19

2005

Age 80 or over
60-79
40-59
20-39
0-19

2041

Age 80 or over
60-79
40-59
20-39
0-19

Source: adapted from Hirsch (2005)

12.5% or one in eight of all households. Most of these are female, both because women generally live longer than men, and because they are usually younger than their husbands.

Among the over-75s, there are twice as many women as men. This has been described as the 'feminisation of later life'.

The dependency ratio

Like the non-working young, the non-working old are an economically dependent group who need to be provided for by those of working age, for example through taxation to pay for pensions and health care.

As the number of retired people rises, this increases the dependency ratio and the burden on the working population. In 2015, there were 3.2 people of working age for every one pensioner. This ratio is predicted to fall to 2.8 to one by 2033.

However, it would be wrong to assume that 'old' necessarily equals 'economically dependent'. For example, the age at which people can draw their pension is rising – from 2020 both men and women will have to wait until they are 66 to access the state pension, rising to 67 from 2026.

Also, while an increase in the number of old people raises the dependency ratio, in an ageing population this is offset by a declining number of dependent children.

Ageism, modernity and postmodernity

One consequence of the ageing population in modern society is the growth of ageism – the negative stereotyping and unequal treatment of people on the basis of their age. Ageism towards older people shows itself in many ways, such as discrimination in employment and unequal treatment in health care. Similarly, much of the discourse (way of speaking and thinking) about old age and ageing has been constructed as a 'problem' – for example in terms of the cost of pensions or health care for the old.

Modern society and old age

Many sociologists argue that ageism is the result of 'structured dependency'. The old are largely excluded from paid work, leaving them economically dependent on their families or the state. In modern society, our identity and status are largely determined by our role in production. Those excluded from production by compulsory retirement have a dependent status and a stigmatised identity.

Similarly, from a Marxist perspective, Phillipson (1982) argues that the old are of no use to capitalism because they are no longer productive. As a result, the state is unwilling to support them adequately and so the family, especially female relatives, often has to take responsibility for their care.

In modern society, life is structured into a fixed series of stages, such as childhood, youth and so on. Age becomes important in role allocation, creating fixed life stages and age-related identities, such as worker or pensioner. The old are thus excluded from a role in the labour force and made dependent and powerless.

Postmodern society and old age

Postmodernist sociologists argue that in today's postmodern society, the fixed, orderly stages of the life course have broken down. For example, trends such as children dressing in adult styles, later marriage and early retirement all begin to blur the boundaries between the life stages. This gives individuals a greater choice of lifestyle, whatever their age.

Unlike in modern society, consumption, not production, becomes the key to our identities. We can now define ourselves by what we consume. As Hunt (2005) argues, this means we can choose a lifestyle and identity regardless of age: our age no longer determines who we are or how we live.

As a result, the old become a market for a vast range of 'body maintenance' or 'rejuvenation' goods and services through which they can create their identities. These include cosmetic surgery, exercise equipment, gym memberships and anti-ageing products.

These trends begin to break down the ageist stereotypes found in modern society. Two other features of postmodern society also undermine old age as a stigmatised life stage:

The centrality of the media Media images now portray positive aspects of the lifestyles of the elderly.

The emphasis on surface features The body becomes a surface on which we can write identities. Anti-ageing products enable the old to write different identities for themselves.

> **Activity** | **Research**
>
> Media portrayals of older people
>
> ...go to www.sociology.uk.net

Inequality among the old

However, while the orderly stages of the life course may have broken down somewhat, Pilcher (1995) argues that inequalities such as class and gender remain important. Many of these are related to the individual's previous occupational position.

Class The middle class have better occupational pensions and greater savings from higher salaries. Poorer old people have a shorter life expectancy and suffer more infirmity (making it more difficult to maintain a youthful self-identity).

Gender Women's lower earnings and career breaks as carers mean lower pensions. They are also subject to sexist as well as ageist stereotyping, for example being described as 'old hags'.

Postmodernists understate the importance of such inequalities. These are related to the structure of wider society and they play a major part in shaping the experience of old age, often restricting the freedom of the elderly to choose an identity through their consumption. Older people also face discrimination that limits their choices: Age Concern (2004) found more people (29%) reported suffering age discrimination than any other form.

> **Analysis and Evaluation**
>
> How far can the points made above about old people also be applied to children and young people?

Policy implications

Donald Hirsch (2005) argues that a number of important social policies will need to change to tackle the new problems posed by an ageing population. The main problem will be how to finance a longer period of old age. This can be done by paying more from our savings and taxes while we are working, or by working for longer, or both.

Similarly, housing policy may need to change to encourage older people to 'trade down' into smaller accommodation. This would release wealth to improve their standard of living and free up housing for younger people.

As Hirsch recognises, these policy changes also require a cultural change in our attitudes towards old age. His view illustrates the notion that old age is a social construct – not a fixed, purely biological fact, but something shaped and defined by society. For example, in an ageing society, our idea of how old is old enough to retire may change.

Migration

In addition to natural change (births and deaths), the other factor affecting the size and age of the population is migration. Migration refers to the movement of people from place to place. It can be internal, within a society, or international.

- **Immigration** refers to movement into a society.
- **Emigration** refers to movement out.
- **Net migration** is the difference between the numbers of immigrants and the numbers of emigrants, and is expressed as a net increase or a net decrease due to migration.

In the UK, for most of the 20th century until the 1980s, there were fewer immigrants than emigrants.

Immigration

From 1900 until the Second World War (1939-45), the largest immigrant group were the Irish, mainly for economic reasons, followed by Eastern and Central European Jews, who were often refugees fleeing persecution, and people of British descent from Canada and the USA. Very few immigrants were non-white.

By contrast, during the 1950s, black immigrants from the Caribbean began to arrive in the UK, followed during the 1960s and 1970s by South Asian immigrants from India, Pakistan, Bangladesh and Sri Lanka, and by East African Asians from Kenya and Uganda.

One consequence is a more ethnically diverse society. By 2011, ethnic minority groups accounted for 14% of the population. One result has been a greater diversity of family patterns. (See Topic 5.)

However, as previously, more people left the UK than entered and most immigrants were white.

Despite this, however, a series of immigration and nationality acts from 1962 to 1990 placed severe restrictions on non-white immigration. By the 1980s, non-whites accounted for little more than a quarter of all immigrants, while the mainly white countries of the European Union became the main source of settlers in the UK.

Emigration

From as early as the mid-16th century until the 1980s, the UK was almost always a net exporter of people: more emigrated to live elsewhere than came to settle in the UK. Since 1900, emigrants have gone to the USA, Canada, Australia, New Zealand and South Africa.

The main reasons for emigration have been economic:

- 'push' factors such as economic recession and unemployment at home
- 'pull' factors such as higher wages or better opportunities abroad.

These economic reasons for migration contrast with those of some other groups, who have been driven to migrate by religious, political or racial persecution.

The impact of migration on UK population structure

Recent years have seen an increase in both immigration and emigration. These trends affect the size of the UK population, its age structure and the dependency ratio.

Population size The UK population is currently growing, partly as a result of immigration:

- Net migration is high (for example, 260,000 in 2014), with more immigrants (583,000) than emigrants (323,000). 47% of the immigrants were non-EU citizens, 38% were EU citizens (mainly from Eastern Europe) and 14% were British citizens returning to the UK.
- There is also a natural increase, with births exceeding deaths. However, births to UK born mothers remain low. Births to non-UK born mothers are higher (see Table 4D) and account for about 25% of all births, but even with

these, births remain below the replacement level of 2.1 per woman (the number needed to keep population size stable). If not for net migration, therefore, the UK's population would be shrinking.

Table 4D	Total fertility rate (births per woman), 2001 and 2011	
	2001	**2011**
All women	1.63	1.93
UK born women	1.56	1.84
Non-UK born women	2.21	2.21

Sources: 2011 Census; Migration Observatory (2014)

Age structure Immigration lowers the average age of the population both directly and indirectly:

- **Directly** Immigrants are generally younger. For example, in 2011, the average age of UK passport holders was 41, whereas that of non-UK passport holders living in Britain was 31.
- **Indirectly** Being younger, immigrants are more fertile and thus produce more babies.

The dependency ratio Immigration has three effects:

- Immigrants are more likely to be of working age and this helps to lower the dependency ratio. In addition, many older migrants return to their country of origin to retire.
- However, because they are younger, immigrants have more children, thereby increasing the ratio. Over time, however, these children will join the labour force and help to lower the ratio once again.
- Finally, the longer a group is settled in the country, the closer their fertility rate comes to the national average, reducing their overall impact on the dependency ratio.

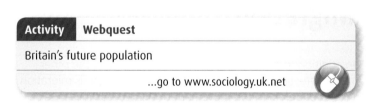

Activity	Webquest

Britain's future population

...go to www.sociology.uk.net

Globalisation and migration

'Globalisation' is the idea that barriers between societies are disappearing and people are becoming increasingly interconnected across national boundaries.

Globalisation is the result of many processes, including the growth of communication systems and global media,

the creation of global markets, the fall of communism in Eastern Europe and the expansion of the European Union.

Many see globalisation as producing rapid social changes. One such change is increased international migration – the movement of people across borders. We can identify several trends in global migration.

Acceleration

There has been a speeding up of the rate of migration. For example, according to the United Nations (2013), between 2000 and 2013 international migration increased by 33%, to reach 232 million or 3.2% of the world's population. In the same year, 862,000 people either entered or left the UK.

Differentiation

There are many types of migrant. These include permanent settlers, temporary workers, spouses, and forced migrants such as refugees and asylum seekers. Some may have legal entitlement while others enter without permission. Globalisation is increasing the diversity of types of migrant. For example, students are now a major group of migrants; in the UK in 2014, there were more Chinese-born (26%) than UK-born (23%) postgraduate students.

Before the 1990s, immigration to the UK came from a fairly narrow range of former British colonies. Most of these migrants had the right to settle and become citizens. They formed a small number of stable, geographically concentrated and homogenous ethnic communities.

Super-diversity However, since the 1990s globalisation has led to what Steven Vertovec (2007) calls 'super-diversity'. Migrants now come from a much wider range of countries. Even within a single ethnic group, individuals differ in terms of their legal status; for example, as citizens or spouses. A given ethnic group may also be divided by culture or religion and be widely dispersed throughout the UK.

There are also class differences among migrants. For example, Robin Cohen (2006) distinguishes three types of migrant:

- **Citizens** with full citizenship rights (e.g. voting rights and access to benefits). Since the 1970s, the UK state has made it harder for immigrants to acquire these rights.
- **Denizens** are privileged foreign nationals welcomed by the state, e.g. billionaire 'oligarchs' or highly paid employees of multinational companies.
- **Helots** (literally, slaves) are the most exploited group. States and employers regard them as 'disposable units of labour power', a reserve army of labour. They are found in unskilled, poorly paid work and include illegally trafficked workers, and those legally tied to particular employers, such as domestic servants.

The feminisation of migration

In the past, most migrants were men. Today, however, almost half of all global migrants are female. This has been called the globalisation of the gender division of labour, where female migrants find that they are fitted into patriarchal stereotypes about women's roles as carers or providers of sexual services.

Barbara Ehrenreich and Arlie Hochschild (2003) observe that care work, domestic work and sex work in western countries like the UK and USA is increasingly done by women from poor countries. This is a result of several trends:

1 The expansion of service occupations (which traditionally employ women) in western countries has led to an increasing demand for female labour.

2 Western women have joined the labour force and are less willing or able to perform domestic labour.

3 Western men remain unwilling to perform domestic labour.

4 The failure of the state to provide adequate childcare.

The resulting gap has been partly filled by women from poor countries. For example, Isabel Shutes (2011) reports that 40% of adult care nurses in the UK are migrants. Most of these are female.

There is also a global transfer of women's emotional labour. For example, migrant nannies provide care and affection for their employers' children at the expense of their own children left behind in their home country.

Migrant women also enter western countries as 'mail order' brides. This often reflects gendered and racialised stereotypes, for example of oriental women as subservient. Women migrants also enter the UK as illegally trafficked sex workers, often kept in conditions amounting to slavery.

Migrant identities

We all have multiple sources of identity: family, friends, neighbourhood, ethnicity, religion, nationality and so on all give us a sense of belonging and of who we are. For migrants and their descendants, their country of origin may provide an additional or alternative source of identity.

For example, migrants may develop hybrid identities made up of two or more different sources. John Eade (1994) found that second generation Bangladeshi Muslims in Britain created hierarchical identities: they saw themselves as Muslim first, then Bengali, then British. Those with hybrid identities may find that others challenge their identity claims ('you're not really one of us') or accuse them of not 'fitting in'.

Transnational identities

According to Thomas Hylland Eriksen (2007), globalisation has created more diverse migration patterns, with back-and-forth movements of people through networks rather than permanent settlement in another country.

As a result, migrants are less likely to see themselves as belonging completely to one culture or country. Instead, they may develop transnational 'neither/nor' identities and loyalties. Modern technology also makes it possible to sustain global ties without having to travel.

The globalised economy means that migrants may have more links to other migrants around the world than to either their country of origin or of settlement.

For example, Eriksen describes Chinese migrants in Rome who found Mandarin (the main language of China) more useful for everyday life than Italian – simply because Mandarin was important for their global connections with Chinese in other countries around the world. Migrants in a globalised world are thus less likely to desire assimilation into the host culture.

The politicisation of migration

With increased global flows of migrants, migration has become an important political issue. States now have policies that seek to control immigration, absorb migrants into society and deal with increased ethnic and cultural diversity. More recently, immigration policies have also become linked to national security and anti-terrorism policies.

Assimilationism was the first state policy approach to immigration. It aimed to encourage immigrants to adopt the language, values and customs of the host culture to make them 'like us'.

However, assimilationist policies face the problem that transnational migrants with hybrid identities may not be willing to abandon their culture or to see themselves as belonging to just one nation-state.

Multiculturalism accepts that migrants may wish to retain a separate cultural identity. However, in practice, this acceptance may be limited to more superficial aspects of cultural diversity. For example, Eriksen distinguishes between 'shallow diversity' and 'deep diversity':

- **Shallow diversity**, such as regarding chicken tikka masala as Britain's national dish, is acceptable to the state.
- **Deep diversity**, such as arranged marriages or the veiling of women, is not acceptable to the state.

Similarly, critics argue that multicultural education policies celebrate shallow diversity – superficial cultural differences, such as 'samosas, saris and steel bands' – while failing to address deeper problems facing children from migrant backgrounds, such as racism.

From the 1960s there was a move towards multiculturalism but since the '9/11' Islamist terror attack in 2001, many politicians have swung back towards demanding that migrants assimilate culturally. For example, in France, veiling of the face in public was made illegal in 2010.

However, Castles (2000) argues that assimilationist policies are counter-productive because they mark out minority groups as culturally backward or 'Other'. This can lead to minorities responding by emphasising their difference, as in the case of Islamic fundamentalism. This increases the hosts' suspicion of them as an 'enemy within' and may promote anti-terrorism policies that target them. This breeds further marginalisation, defeating the goal of assimilation.

A divided working class Assimilationist ideas may also encourage workers to blame migrants for social problems such as unemployment, resulting in racist scapegoating. According to Castles and Kosack (1973), this benefits capitalism by creating a racially divided working class and preventing united action in defence of their interests.

Activity	Webquest

The 'Life in the UK' test

...go to www.sociology.uk.net

Topic summary

Population size is influenced by **natural change** (births and deaths) and **net migration** (immigration and emigration).

Since 1900, the **birth rate** has **declined**, producing smaller family sizes. Reasons include **lower infant mortality** and changes in the **position of women and children**.

The **death rate declined** and **life expectancy increased**, largely due to **social changes**. Effects of an **ageing population** include greater costs of health care and **pensions, ageism,** and an increase in the **dependency ratio**. In **modernity,** exclusion from work makes old age a dependent status, but in **postmodernity,** age no longer determines identity.

Migration affects age structure and fertility rates. Reasons for migration can involve **push** and **pull** factors. **Globalisation** has increased migration. There is more **diversity** in types of migration, and **transitional identities** are more common. Migration has become politicised, but **assimilationist** policies may be self-defeating.

EXAMINING DEMOGRAPHY

QuickCheck Questions

Check your answers at www.sociology.uk.net

1 Identify two factors that have led to a decline in the death rate since 1900.
2 Suggest two reasons for the decline in the birth rate since 1900, apart from changes in women's position.
3 Suggest two reasons for class differences in infant mortality.
4 How might population trends in the UK be related to the increase in the proportion of married women working?

5 What is meant by 'ageism'?
6 What is meant by the 'dependency ratio'?
7 What is meant by a 'hybrid identity'?
8 What is meant by the 'structured dependency of the old'?
9 What is the difference between citizens, denizens and helots?
10 Explain the difference between assimilationism and multiculturalism.

Questions to try

Whether or not you are taking the AS exams during your A level course, answering the AS questions below is a very good way of testing your knowledge and understanding and practising your skills in preparation for your A level exams.

Item A   In modern society, people's lives were made up of fixed age-stages, with the final stage defined by compulsory retirement and, for many, poverty. The old also faced prejudice and discrimination.

By contrast, some sociologists argue that the position of the old in today's postmodern society is changing for the better. In postmodern society, individuals can choose a lifestyle and identity that does not depend on their age. This has freed the old from their previous disadvantaged status in society.

However, critics argue that many old people remain disadvantaged in today's society.

AS questions
1 Define the term 'birth rate'.   (2 marks)
2 Using one example, explain how migration may affect the age structure of the population.   (2 marks)
3 Outline three factors that may affect the dependency ratio, apart from migration.   (6 marks)

AS and A level questions
4 Outline and explain two reasons for changes in the size of families and households in the last 50 years or so.   (10 marks)
5 Applying material from Item A and your knowledge, evaluate the view that the position of the old in today's society is changing for the better.   (20 marks)

The Examiner's Advice

Q4 Spend about 15 minutes on this question. Divide your time fairly equally between the two reasons. You don't need a separate introduction; just start on your first reason. Possible reasons include increased divorce, the changing position of women, consumerism, child centredness and increased life expectancy. Describe each reason in some detail. Explain how each has resulted in a change in family and/or household size in the last 50 years or so. Do this by creating a chain of reasoning (see page 248). For example, increased child centredness means parents invest more, economically and emotionally, in their children. This means they are less willing or able to have many children, resulting in smaller families and households. Use concepts and issues such as singletons, lone-parent families, geographical mobility, the rising cost of children, the ageing population, later marriage, decline of the three-generation household, the impact of feminist ideas and the welfare state.

Q5 Spend about 30 minutes on this question. You could start by making a case for the view in the question. Use Item A to begin an explanation of the difference between modern and postmodern society and how postmodernists see this affecting the old. Use concepts and issues such as ageism, structured dependency, stigmatised age-related identities (in modernity); and consumption choices, blurred boundaries, role of the media and emphasis on surface features (in postmodernity). You can evaluate the view by making a case against it. Consider issues such as structural inequalities (e.g. class and gender inequalities in terms of poverty and access to pensions); whether the old can in fact choose youthful identities; the existence of ageist stereotyping and abuse. Also consider public services for the old, the dependency ratio, and the pensions 'time bomb' to evaluate the view in the question. Use evidence from studies such as Phillipson, Hunt, Pilcher and Hirsch.

Are women's demands driving changes in the family?

GETTING STARTED

In pairs, complete the following:

1 Look at the list of changing family and household patterns at the top of the next page. Identify all of the different family or household types that are mentioned in the list.

2 Choose three or four of these types. For each type, note whether it is becoming more common or less common in the UK today.

3 Suggest reasons for each of these trends, e.g. why are there more lone-parent families today?

4 Share your answers with the rest of the class. Are there any common factors in your reasons?

Learning objectives

After studying this Topic, you should:

- Know the main changes in partnerships, including marriage, divorce, cohabitation and civil partnerships, as well as one-person and extended family households.

- Know the main changes in childbearing and childrearing, including births outside marriage, lone-parent families and stepfamilies.

- Understand how these changes have contributed to greater family diversity.

- Be able to analyse and evaluate the explanations for these changes in families and households.

CHANGING FAMILY PATTERNS

In the past 40 or 50 years there have been some major changes in family and household patterns. For example:

- The number of traditional nuclear family households – a married couple with their dependent children – has fallen.
- Divorce rates have increased.
- There are fewer first marriages, but more re-marriages.
- People are marrying later in life.
- More couples are cohabiting.
- Same-sex relationships can be legally recognised through civil partnerships or marriages.

- Women are having fewer children and having them later.
- There are more births outside marriage.
- There are more lone-parent families.
- More people live alone.
- There are more stepfamilies, and more couples without children.

In this Topic, we examine the changes in patterns of family life in Britain and the reasons for them. These changes include marriage, cohabitation and divorce. Such changes are contributing to greater family diversity, and we examine how sociologists have interpreted them.

Divorce

We look first at divorce because divorce is a major cause of changing family patterns and greater family diversity. For example, most re-marriages involve a divorcee, and divorce creates both lone-parent families and one-person households.

Changing patterns of divorce

Since the 1960s, there has been a great increase in the number of divorces in the United Kingdom, as Figure 4.4 shows. The number of divorces doubled between 1961 and 1969, and doubled again by 1972. The upward trend continued, peaking in 1993 at 165,000.

Since then, numbers have fallen somewhat, but still stood at 118,000 in 2012 – about six times higher than in 1961. This rate means that about 40% of all marriages will end in divorce.

One reason for the fall in the number of divorces since the 1990s is that fewer people are marrying in the first place and are choosing to cohabit instead.

About 65% of petitions (applications) for divorce now come from women. This is in sharp contrast to the situation in the past. For example, in 1946, only 37% of petitions came from women – barely half today's

figure. The commonest reason for a woman to be granted a divorce is the unreasonable behaviour of her husband.

Some couples are more likely than others to divorce. Couples whose marriages are at greatest risk include those who marry young, have a child before they marry or cohabit before marriage, and those where one or both partners have been married before.

Figure 4.4: Marriages and divorces: England and Wales, 1932-2012

Source: ONS

Application

Study Figure 4.4 and answer the following questions:

1 Approximately how many divorces were there in 1972?

2 Approximately how many marriages were there in 2012?

3 Suggest three reasons why the total number of marriages has been declining.

Box 31	A brief history of divorce law

Before 1857, divorce was virtually non-existent and only obtainable by a special and costly Act of Parliament.

1857 Men could divorce unfaithful wives, but women also had to prove husbands' cruelty or another matrimonial offence in addition to adultery. Divorce still very costly.

1921 3,000 divorces.

1923 Grounds for divorce equalised for men and women.

1937 Grounds widened to include desertion and cruelty.

1949 Legal aid available, making divorce more affordable.

1961 27,000 divorces – nine times higher than in 1921.

1969 Divorce Law Reform Act passed (came into effect in 1971). The idea of a matrimonial offence or 'guilty party' was abolished. This made 'irretrievable breakdown' of marriage the sole ground for divorce, established by proving unreasonable behaviour, adultery, desertion, or separation either with or without consent. Divorce available after two years' agreed separation, or five years if only one spouse wants divorce.

1984 The minimum period after marriage before a divorce petition could be filed was reduced from three years to one.

1996 Family Law Act encourages couples to seek mediation but allows divorce by agreement after a 'period of reflection'.

2004 Civil Partnership Act allows for legal dissolution of a civil partnership on the same grounds as for a marriage – irretrievable breakdown.

2007 Appeal Court ruling: in divorce settlements, the principle of equality applies, so the starting point is a 50-50 split of all assets, including salaries and pension rights.

2014 Same-sex marriages became law. Same grounds for divorce apply to both same-sex and opposite-sex couples.

Explanations for the increase in divorce

Sociologists have identified the following explanations for the increase in divorce.

1 Changes in the law

Divorce was very difficult to obtain in 19th-century Britain, especially for women. Gradually, changes in the law have made divorce easier. There have been three kinds of change in the law:

- **Equalising the grounds** (the legal reasons) for divorce between the sexes
- **Widening the grounds** for divorce
- **Making divorce cheaper.**

When the grounds were equalised for men and women in 1923, this was followed by a sharp rise in the number of divorce petitions from women. Similarly, the widening of the grounds in 1971 to 'irretrievable breakdown' made divorce easier to obtain and produced a doubling of the divorce rate almost overnight. The introduction of legal aid for divorce cases in 1949 lowered the cost of divorcing. Divorce rates have risen with each change in the law. (See Box 31.)

Although divorce is the legal termination of a marriage, couples can and do find other solutions to the problem of an unhappy marriage. These include:

- **Desertion**, where one partner leaves the other but the couple remain legally married
- **Legal separation**, where a court separates the financial and legal affairs of the couple but where they remain married and are not free to re-marry
- **'Empty shell' marriage**, where the couple continue to live under the same roof but remain married in name only.

However, as divorce has become easier to obtain, these solutions have become less popular.

Yet although changes in the law have given people the freedom to divorce more easily, this does not in itself explain why more people should choose to take advantage of this freedom. To fully explain the rise in divorce rates we must therefore look at other changes too. These include changes in public attitudes towards divorce.

2 Declining stigma and changing attitudes

Stigma refers to the negative label, social disapproval or shame attached to a person, action or relationship. In the past, divorce and divorcees have been stigmatised. For example, churches tended to condemn divorce and often refused to conduct marriage services involving divorcees. Juliet Mitchell and Jack Goody (1997) note that an important change since the 1960s has been the rapid decline in the stigma attached to divorce.

As stigma declines and divorce becomes more socially acceptable, couples become more willing to resort to divorce as a means of solving their marital problems.

In turn, the fact that divorce is now more common begins to 'normalise' it and reduces the stigma attached to it. Rather than being seen as shameful, today it is more likely to be regarded simply as a misfortune.

3 Secularisation

Secularisation refers to the decline in the influence of religion in society. Many sociologists argue that religious institutions and ideas are losing their influence and society is becoming more secular. For example, church attendance rates continue to decline.

As a result of secularisation, the traditional opposition of the churches to divorce carries less weight in society and people are less likely to be influenced by religious teachings when making decisions about personal matters such as whether or not to file for divorce.

At the same time, many churches have also begun to soften their views on divorce and divorcees, perhaps because they fear losing credibility with large sections of the public and with their own members.

4 Rising expectations of marriage

Functionalist sociologists such as Ronald Fletcher (1966) argue that the higher expectations people place on marriage today are a major cause of rising divorce rates. Higher expectations make couples less willing to tolerate an unhappy marriage.

This is linked to the ideology of romantic love – an idea that has become dominant over the last couple of centuries. This is the belief that marriage should be based solely on love, and that for each individual there is a Mr or Miss Right out there.

It follows that if love dies, there is no longer any justification for remaining married and every reason to divorce so as to be able to renew the search for one's true soulmate.

In the past, by contrast, individuals often had little choice in who they married, and at a time when the family was also a unit of production, marriages were often contracted largely for economic reasons or out of duty to one's family.

Under these circumstances, individuals were unlikely to have the high expectations about marriage as a romantic union of two souls that many couples have today. Entering marriage with lower expectations, they were therefore less likely to be dissatisfied by the absence of romance and intimacy.

Today, on the other hand, marriage is increasingly viewed not as a binding contract, but as a relationship in which individuals seek personal fulfilment, and this encourages couples to divorce if they do not find it. As Graham Allan and Graham Crow (2001) put it:

> 'Love, personal commitment and intrinsic satisfaction are now seen as the cornerstones of marriage. The absence of these feelings is itself justification for ending the relationship.'

However, despite today's high divorce rates, functionalists such as Fletcher take an optimistic view. They point to the continuing popularity of marriage. Most adults marry, and the high rate of re-marriage after divorce shows that although divorcees may have become dissatisfied with a particular partner, they have not rejected marriage as an institution.

However, feminist critics argue that this is too rosy a view. They argue that the oppression of women within the

▲ Reduced legal costs have made divorce widely available.

family is the main cause of marital conflict and divorce, but functionalists ignore this. Although functionalists offer an explanation of rising divorce rates, they fail to explain why it is mainly women rather than men who seek divorce.

We should also note that, although most adults do marry, marriage rates have fallen significantly in the past 50 years, as Figure 4.4 shows.

5 Women's increased financial independence

One reason for women's increased willingness to seek divorce is that improvements in their economic position have made them less financially dependent on their husband and therefore freer to end an unsatisfactory marriage.

- Women today are much more likely to be in paid work. The proportion of women working rose from 53% in 1971 to 67% in 2013.
- Although women generally still earn less than men, equal pay and anti-discrimination laws have helped to narrow the pay gap.
- Girls' greater success in education now helps them achieve better-paid jobs than previous generations.
- The availability of welfare benefits means that women no longer have to remain financially dependent on their husbands.

These developments mean that women are more likely to be able to support themselves in the event of divorce.

Allan and Crow put forward a similar view. They argue that "marriage is less embedded within the economic system" now. There are fewer family firms and the family is no longer a unit of production, so spouses are not so dependent on each other economically.

In particular, women now have their own separate source of income from paid work. Not having to rely on their husband financially, women therefore do not have to tolerate conflict or the absence of love, and in such circumstances they are more willing to seek divorce.

6   Feminist explanations

Feminists argue that married women today bear a dual burden: they are required to take on paid work in addition to performing domestic labour (housework and childcare). In the view of feminists, this has created a new source of conflict between husbands and wives, and this is leading to a higher divorce rate than in the past.

While there may have been big improvements in women's position in the public sphere of employment, education, politics and so on, feminists argue that in the private sphere of family and personal relationships, change has been limited and slow. They argue that marriage remains patriarchal, with men benefiting from their wives' 'triple shift' of paid work, domestic work and emotion work (see page 170).

Similarly, Arlie Hochschild (1997) argues that for many women, the home compares unfavourably with work. At work, women feel valued. At home, men's continuing resistance to doing housework is a source of frustration and makes marriage less stable. In addition, the fact that both partners now go out to work leaves less time and energy for the emotion work needed to address the problems that arise. Both these factors may contribute to a higher divorce rate.

According to Wendy Sigle-Rushton (ESRC, 2007), mothers who have a dual burden of paid work and domestic work are more likely to divorce than non-working mothers in marriages with a traditional division of labour. But where the husband of a working wife is actively involved in housework, the divorce rate is the same as for couples with a traditional division of labour.

However, Cooke and Gash (2010) found no evidence that working women are more likely to divorce. They argue that this is because working has now become the accepted norm for married women.

Radical feminists such as Jessie Bernard (1976) observe that many women feel a growing dissatisfaction with patriarchal marriage. She sees the rising divorce rate, and the fact that most petitions come from women, as evidence of their

growing acceptance of feminist ideas: women are becoming conscious of patriarchal oppression and more confident about rejecting it.

7   Modernity and individualisation

Sociologists such as Ulrich Beck (1992) and Anthony Giddens (1992) argue that in modern society, traditional norms, such as the duty to remain with the same partner for life, lose their hold over individuals.

As a result, each individual becomes free to pursue his or her own self-interest. This view has become known as the individualisation thesis.

Relationships thus become more fragile, because individuals become unwilling to remain with a partner if the relationship fails to deliver personal fulfilment. Instead, they seek what Giddens calls the 'pure relationship' – one that exists solely to satisfy each partner's needs and not out of a sense of duty, tradition or for the sake of the children. This results in higher divorce rates.

At the same time, the rising divorce rate 'normalises' divorce and further strengthens the belief that marriage exists solely to provide personal fulfilment.

Modern society also encourages individualism in other ways. For example, women as well as men are now expected to work and are encouraged to pursue their own individual career ambitions. This can cause conflicts of interest between spouses and contribute to marital breakdown.

Some sociologists also argue that modernity encourages people to adopt a neoliberal, consumerist identity based on the idea of freedom to follow one's own self-interest. This pursuit of self-interest is likely to pull spouses apart.

The meaning of a high divorce rate

Sociologists disagree about the effects of today's high divorce rate on society and on individual family members.

The New Right see a high divorce rate as undesirable because it undermines marriage and the traditional nuclear family, which they regard as vital to social stability.

In their view, a high divorce rate creates a growing underclass of welfare-dependent female lone parents who are a burden on the state and it leaves boys without the adult male role model they need. They believe it also results in poorer health and educational outcomes for children.

Feminists see a high divorce rate as desirable because it shows that women are breaking free from the oppression of the patriarchal nuclear family.

Postmodernists and the individualisation thesis see a high divorce rate as showing that individuals now have the freedom to choose to end a relationship when it no longer meets their needs. They see it as a major cause of greater family diversity.

Functionalists argue that a high divorce rate is not necessarily a threat to marriage as a social institution. It is simply the result of people's higher expectations of marriage today. The high rate of re-marriage shows people's continuing commitment to the idea of marriage.

Interactionists aim to understand what divorce means to the individual. David Morgan (1996) argues that we cannot generalise about the meaning of divorce, because every individual's interpretation of it is different.

Mitchell and Goody provide a good example of this. One of their interviewees described the day her father left as the best day of her life, whereas another said that she had never recovered from her father deserting the family.

The personal life perspective accepts that divorce can cause problems, such as financial difficulties (especially for women) and lack of daily contact between children and non-resident parents.

However, writers from this perspective, such as Carol Smart (2011), argue that divorce has become 'normalised' and that family life can adapt to it without disintegrating. Rather than seeing divorce as a major social problem, we should see it as just 'one transition amongst others in the life course'.

Activity	Media

The impact of divorce on children

...go to www.sociology.uk.net

Partnerships

Marriage

There have been a number of important changes in the pattern of marriage in recent years:

- Fewer people are marrying: marriage rates are at their lowest since the 1920s. In 2012, there were 175,000 first marriages for both partners – less than half the number for 1970.
- However, there are more re-marriages (marriages where one or both partners have been married before). In 2012, one third of all marriages were re-marriages for one or both partners. For many people, this is leading to 'serial monogamy': a pattern of marriage – divorce – re-marriage.
- People are marrying later: the average age of first marriage rose by seven years between 1971 and 2012, when it stood at 32 years for men and 30 for women.
- Couples are less likely to marry in church. In 1981, 60% of weddings were conducted with religious ceremonies, but by 2012 this had fallen to 30%.

Reasons for changing patterns of marriage

First marriages Many of the reasons for a fall in the number of first marriages are similar to the reasons for the increase in divorce examined earlier. They include the following:

- Changing attitudes to marriage There is less pressure to marry and more freedom for individuals to choose the type of relationship they want. There is now a widespread belief that the quality of a couple's relationship is more important than its legal status. The norm that everyone ought to get married has greatly weakened.

▲ Marriage rates are at their lowest since the 1920s.

- **Secularisation** The churches are in favour of marriage, but as their influence declines people feel freer to choose not to marry. For example, according to the 2001 Census, only 3% of young people with no religion were married, as against up to 17% of those with a religion.

- **Declining stigma attached to alternatives to marriage** Cohabitation, remaining single, and having children outside marriage are all now widely regarded as acceptable, so that pregnancy no longer automatically leads to a 'shotgun wedding'. In 1989, 70% believed that couples who want children should get married but by 2012 only 42% thought so.

- **Changes in the position of women** With better educational and career prospects, many women are now less economically dependent on men. This gives them greater freedom not to marry. The feminist view that marriage is an oppressive patriarchal institution may also dissuade some women from marrying.

- **Fear of divorce** With the rising divorce rate, some may be put off marrying because they see the increased likelihood of marriage ending in divorce.

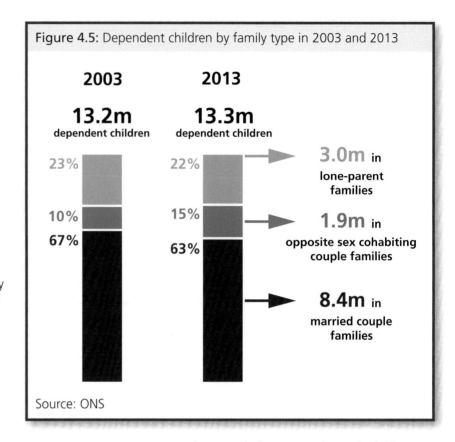

Figure 4.5: Dependent children by family type in 2003 and 2013

Source: ONS

Reasons for other changes in patterns of marriage include the following:

Remarriages The main reason for the increase in re-marriages is the rise in the number of divorces. The two have grown together so that the rising number of divorcees provides a supply of people available to re-marry.

Age on marrying The age at which couples marry is rising because young people are postponing marriage in order to spend longer in full-time education, and perhaps to establish themselves in a career first. Another reason is that more couples are now cohabiting for a period before they marry.

Church weddings Couples nowadays are less likely to marry in church for two main reasons:

- Secularisation: fewer people see the relevance of religious ceremony.
- Many churches refuse to marry divorcees (who make up a growing proportion of those marrying) and divorcees may in any case have less desire to marry in church.

Cohabitation

Cohabitation involves an unmarried couple in a sexual relationship living together. While the number of marriages has been falling, the number of couples cohabiting continues to increase:

- As Figure 4.5 shows, cohabiting couples with children are a fast-growing family type.
- There are 2.9 million cohabiting heterosexual couples in Britain. About one in eight adults are now cohabiting – double the number in 1996.
- There are an estimated 69,000 same-sex cohabiting couples.
- About a fifth of all those cohabiting are 'serial cohabitants' who have had one or more previous cohabitations.

Reasons for the increase in cohabitation

- Increased cohabitation rates are a result of the decline in stigma attached to sex outside marriage. In 1989, only 44% of people agreed that 'premarital sex is not wrong at all', but 65% took this view by 2012.
- The young are more likely to accept cohabitation.
- Increased career opportunities for women may mean they have less need for the financial security of marriage and are freer to opt for cohabitation.
- Secularisation: young people with no religion are more likely to cohabit than those with a religion.

Analysis and Evaluation

What view would you expect (a) the New Right and (b) feminists to take of cohabitation? Give your reasons.

The relationship between cohabitation and marriage

Although cohabitation is increasing as marriage decreases, the relationship between the two is not clear-cut. For some couples, cohabitation is just a step on the way to getting married, whereas for others it is a permanent alternative to marriage.

Robert Chester argues that for most people, cohabitation is part of the process of getting married. For example, according to Ernestina Coast (2006), 75% of cohabiting couples say that they expect to marry each other.

a trial marriage?

Many see cohabitation as a trial marriage and intend to marry if it goes well. Most cohabiting couples decide to marry if they have children. In some cases, cohabitation is a temporary phase before marriage because one or both partners are awaiting a divorce.

On the other hand, some couples see cohabitation as a permanent alternative to marriage. André Bejin (1985) argues that cohabitation among some young people represents a conscious attempt to create a more personally negotiated and equal relationship than conventional patriarchal marriage. For example, Shelton and John (1993) found that women who cohabit do less housework than their married counterparts.

Clearly, then, cohabitation does not mean the same thing to every couple. The term covers a diverse range of partnerships and the relationship between marriage and cohabitation is a complex and variable one.

Activity | **Discussion**

Cohabitation is becoming 'marriage by another name'

...go to www.sociology.uk.net

Same-sex relationships

Stonewall (2012), the campaign for lesbian, gay and bisexual rights, estimates that about 5 to 7% of the adult population today have same-sex relationships. It is impossible to judge whether this represents an increase because in the past, stigma and illegality meant that such relationships were more likely to be hidden.

There is evidence of increased social acceptance of same-sex relationships in recent years. Male homosexual acts were decriminalised in 1967 for consenting adults over 21. More recently the age of consent has been equalised with heterosexuals. Opinion polls show more tolerance of homosexuality.

Social policy now treats all couples more equally. For example, since 2002, cohabiting couples have had the same right to adopt as married couples. In 2004, the Civil Partnership Act gave same-sex couples similar legal rights to married couples in respect of pensions, inheritance, tenancies and property. Since 2014, same-sex couples have been able to marry.

chosen families

Jeffrey Weeks (1999) argues that increased social acceptance may explain a trend towards same-sex cohabitation and stable relationships that resemble those found among heterosexuals. Weeks sees gays as creating families based on the idea of 'friendship as kinship', where friendships become a type of kinship network. He describes these as 'chosen families' and argues that they offer the same security and stability as heterosexual families.

Similarly, Kath Weston (1992) describes same-sex cohabitation as 'quasi-marriage' and notes that many gay couples are now deciding to cohabit as stable partners. She contrasts this with the gay lifestyle of the 1970s, which largely rejected monogamy and family life in favour of casual relationships.

Others sociologists have noted the effect on same-sex relationships of a legal framework such as civil partnerships and marriage. For example, Allan and Crow argue that, because of the absence of such a framework until recently, same-sex partners have had to negotiate their commitment and responsibilities more than married couples. This may have made same-sex relationships both more flexible and less stable than heterosexual relationships.

Similarly, Anna Einasdottir (2011) notes that, while many gays and lesbians welcome the opportunity to have their partnerships legally recognised, others fear that it may limit the flexibility and negotiability of relationships. Rather than adopt what they see as heterosexual relationship norms, they wish their relationships to be different.

One-person households

Fewer people today are living in couples:

- There has been a big rise in the number of people living alone. In 2013, almost three in ten households (7.7 million people) contained only one person – nearly three times the figure for 1961. (See Figure 4.6.)
- 40% of all one-person households are over 65. Pensioner one-person households have doubled since 1961, while those of non-pensioners tripled. Men under 65 were the group most likely to live alone.
- By 2033, over 30% of the adult population will be single (unpartnered and never-married).

Reasons for the changes

The increase in separation and divorce has created more one-person households, especially among men under 65. This is because, following divorce, any children are more likely to live with their mother; their father is more likely to leave the family home.

The decline in the numbers marrying, and the trend towards marrying later, also mean more people are remaining single. The proportion of adults who are single has risen by half since 1971. Many of these are living alone. It is possible that a growing number are opting for 'creative singlehood' – the deliberate choice to live alone.

However, while many of these choose to remain single and live alone, some are alone because there are too few partners available in their age group. These are mainly older widows.

'Living apart together'

It is often assumed that those not living with a partner do not have one, whether from choice or not. However, research by Simon Duncan and Miranda Phillips for the British Social Attitudes survey (2013) found that about one in 10 adults are 'living apart together' or 'LATs' – that is, in a significant relationship, but not married or cohabiting. This is about half of all the people officially classified as single. It has been suggested that this may reflect a trend towards less formalised relationships and 'families of choice'.

However, Duncan and Phillips found that both choice and constraint play a part in whether couples live together. For example, some said they could not afford to. However, a minority actively chose to live apart, for example because

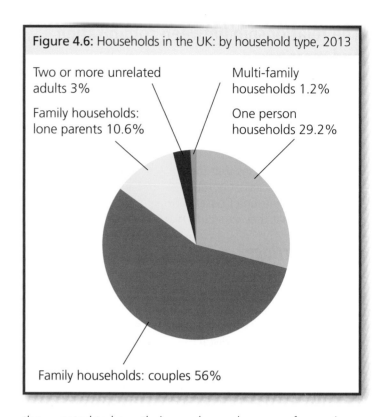

Figure 4.6: Households in the UK: by household type, 2013

Two or more unrelated adults 3%

Multi-family households 1.2%

Family households: lone parents 10.6%

One person households 29.2%

Family households: couples 56%

they wanted to keep their own home, because of a previous troubled relationship or because it was 'too early' to cohabit.

Public attitudes towards LATs are favourable. A majority believe that 'a couple do not need to live together to have a strong relationship', while 20% see LATs as their 'ideal relationship' (more than the number who prefer cohabitation).

Duncan and Phillips conclude that, while being a LAT is no longer seen as abnormal, it probably does not amount to a rejection of more traditional relationships.

Parents and children

Childbearing

- Nearly half (47%) of all children are now born outside marriage: over twice as many as in 1986 (see Figure 4.7). However, nearly all these births are jointly registered by both parents. In most cases, the parents are cohabiting.
- Women are having children later: between 1971 and 2012, their average age at the birth of their first child rose by four years to 28.1 years.
- Women are having fewer children than in the 20th century, though the number increased slightly in the early 21st century. The average number of children per woman fell from a peak of 2.95 in 1964 to a record low of 1.63 in 2001, rising somewhat to a peak of 1.94 in 2010.

- More women are remaining childless: it is predicted that a quarter of those born in 1973 will be childless when they reach the age of 45.

Reasons for the changes

- Reasons for the increase in births outside marriage include a decline in stigma and increase in cohabitation. For example, only 28% of 25-34 year olds now think marriage should come before parenthood.
- The later age at which women are having children, smaller family sizes and the fact that more women are remaining childless, all reflect the fact that women now have more options than just motherhood. Many are seeking to establish themselves in a career before starting a family, or instead of having children at all.

Lone-parent families

Lone-parent families now make up 22% of all families with children. One child in four lives in a lone-parent family.

- Over 90% of these families are headed by lone mothers.
- Until the early 1990s, divorced women were the biggest group of lone mothers. From the early 1990s, single (never married) women became the biggest group of lone mothers.
- A child living with a lone parent is twice as likely to be in poverty as a child living with two parents.

Reasons for the patterns

The number of lone-parent families has risen due to the increase in divorce and separation and more recently, due to the increase in the number of never-married women having children.

This is linked to the decline in stigma attached to births outside marriage. In the past, the death of one parent was a common cause of lone-parent families, but this is no longer very significant.

Lone-parent families tend to be female-headed for several reasons. These include:

- the widespread belief that women are by nature suited to an 'expressive' or nurturing role
- the fact that divorce courts usually give custody of children to mothers
- the fact that men may be less willing than women to give up work to care for children.

Single by choice Many lone-parent families are female-headed because the mothers are single by choice. They may not wish to cohabit or marry, or they may wish to limit the father's involvement with the child. Jean Renvoize (1985) found that professional women were able to support their child without the father's involvement.

Equally, as Ellis Cashmore (1985) found, some working-class mothers with less earning power chose to live on welfare benefits without a partner, often because they had experienced abuse. Feminist ideas, and greater opportunities for women, may also have encouraged an increase in the number of never-married lone mothers.

Lone parenthood, the welfare state and poverty

The New Right thinker Charles Murray (1984) sees the growth of lone-parent families as resulting from an over-generous welfare state providing benefits for unmarried mothers and their children.

Murray argues that this has created a 'perverse incentive'; that is, it rewards irresponsible behaviour, such as having children without being able to provide for them. The welfare state creates a 'dependency culture' in which people assume that the state will support them and their children.

For Murray, the solution is to abolish welfare benefits. This would reduce the dependency culture that encourages births outside marriage.

However, critics of New Right views argue that welfare benefits are far from generous and lone-parent families are much more likely to be in poverty. Reasons for this include:

- Lack of affordable childcare prevents lone parents from working: 60% of them are unemployed. This is twice as high as among mothers with partners.
- Inadequate welfare benefits.
- Most lone parents are women, who generally earn less than men.
- Failure of fathers to pay maintenance, especially if they have formed a second family that they have to support.

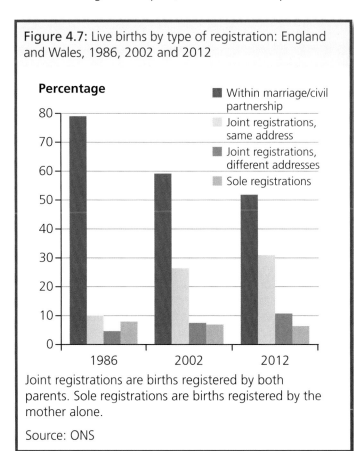

Figure 4.7: Live births by type of registration: England and Wales, 1986, 2002 and 2012

Legend:
- Within marriage/civil partnership
- Joint registrations, same address
- Joint registrations, different addresses
- Sole registrations

Joint registrations are births registered by both parents. Sole registrations are births registered by the mother alone.

Source: ONS

▲ There were 222,000 fewer births in 2013 than in 1960.

Stepfamilies

- Stepfamilies (often called reconstituted families) account for over 10% of all families with dependent children in Britain.
- In 85% of stepfamilies, at least one child is from the woman's previous relationship, while in 11% there is at least one child from the man's previous relationship. In 4% of stepfamilies there are children from both partners' previous relationships.
- Elsa Ferri and Kate Smith (1998) found that stepfamilies are very similar to first families in all major respects, and that the involvement of stepparents in childcare and childrearing is a positive one. However, they found that stepfamilies are at greater risk of poverty.
- According to Graham Allan and Graham Crow (2001), stepfamilies may face particular problems of divided loyalties and issues such as contact with the non-resident parent can cause tensions.
- Jane Ribbens McCarthy et al (2003) conclude that there is diversity among these families and so we should speak of 'stepfamilies' plural rather than 'the stepfamily'. Some have few tensions, while for those that do, the tensions are not so different from those in 'intact' families.

Reasons for the patterns

- Stepfamilies are formed when lone parents form new partnerships. Thus the factors causing an increase in the number of lone parents, such as divorce and separation, are also responsible for the creation of stepfamilies.
- More children in stepfamilies are from the woman's previous relationship than the man's because, when marriages and cohabitations break up, children are more likely to remain with their mother.
- Stepparents are at greater risk of poverty because there are often more children and because the stepfather may also have to support children from a previous relationship.
- Some of the tensions faced by stepfamilies may be the result of a lack of clear social norms about how individuals should behave in such families.

Ethnic differences in family patterns

Immigration into Britain since the 1950s has helped to create greater ethnic diversity. Analysis of the 2011 Census shows that 86% of the UK population were White. Of the 14% belonging to an ethnic minority, the main groups were Asian and Asian British (7.5%) Black and Black British (3.3%) and Mixed (2.2%). Greater ethnic diversity has contributed to changing family patterns in the UK.

Black families

Black Caribbean and Black African people have a higher proportion of lone-parent households. In 2012, just over half of families with dependent children headed by a black person were lone-parent families (see Table 4E). This compared with only one in nine Asian families and just under a quarter for the population as a whole.

The high rate of female-headed, lone-parent black families has sometimes been seen as evidence of family disorganisation that can be traced back to slavery or, more recently, to high rates of unemployment among black males.

Table 4E	Families with dependent children: by child's ethnicity, UK 2012		
Percentages	Married couples*	Cohabiting couples	Lone parents
White	61	16	23
Mixed	53	12	36
Asian and Asian British	88	1	11
Black and Black British	43	6	51
Other ethnic group	71	6	23
All families	62	14	24

*includes civil partnership couples
Source: ONS; LFS

Under slavery, when couples were sold separately, children stayed with the mother. It is argued that this established a pattern of family life that persists today. It is also argued that male unemployment and poverty have meant that black men are less able to provide for their family, resulting in higher rates of desertion or marital breakdown.

However, Heidi Safia Mirza (1997) argues that the higher rate of lone-parent families among blacks is not the result of disorganisation, but rather reflects the high value that black women place on independence. Tracey Reynolds (2010) argues that the statistics are misleading, in that many apparently 'lone' parents are in fact in stable, supportive but non-cohabiting relationships.

Asian families

Bangladeshi, Pakistani and Indian households tend to be larger than those of other ethnic groups, at 4.4, 4.3 and 3 persons per household respectively, compared with 2.4 for both Black Caribbean and White British households.

Such households sometimes contain three generations, but most are in fact nuclear rather than extended. Larger household sizes are partly a result of the younger age profile of British Asians, since a higher proportion are in the childbearing age groups compared with the population as a whole.

Larger Asian households also to some extent reflect the value placed on the extended family in Asian cultures. However, practical considerations, such as the need for assistance when migrating to Britain, are also important. For example, Roger Ballard (1982) found that extended family ties provided an important source of support among Asian migrants during the 1950s and 1960s.

In this early period of migration, houses were often shared by extended families. Later, although most Asian households were now nuclear, relatives often lived nearby. There was frequent visiting, and kinship networks continued to be a source of support. Today, Sikhs, Muslims and Hindus are still more likely than other ethnic or religious groups to live in extended family units.

The extended family today

The existence of the extended family among minority ethnic groups raises the question of how widespread or important this kind of family is in the UK today. As we saw in Topic 3, according to functionalists such as Parsons, the extended family is the dominant family type in pre-industrial society, but in modern industrial society it is replaced by the nuclear family.

For example, as Nickie Charles' (2008) study of Swansea found, the classic three-generation family all living together under one roof is now "all but extinct". The only significant exceptions she found were among the city's Bangladeshi community.

However, while the extended family may have declined, it has not entirely disappeared. Instead, as Peter Willmott (1988) argues, it continues to exist as a 'dispersed extended family', where relatives are geographically separated but maintain frequent contact through visits and phone calls.

Similarly, Mary Chamberlain's (1999) study of Caribbean families in Britain found that, despite being geographically dispersed, they continue to provide support. She describes them as 'multiple nuclear families' with close and frequent contact between siblings, uncles, aunts and cousins, who often make a big contribution to childrearing.

As Chamberlain suggests, the extended family survives because it performs important functions

for its members. For example, Colin Bell's (1968) earlier research in Swansea found that both working-class and middle-class families had emotional bonds with kin and relied on them for support:

- Among the middle class, there was more financial help from father to son.

▲ Three generations celebrate a wedding, Bethnal Green, 1952. Is the extended family now 'all but extinct'?

• Working-class families had more frequent contact (they lived closer) and there was more domestic help from mothers to daughters.

The 'beanpole' family

Bell's findings suggest the importance of the so-called 'beanpole' family. The beanpole family is a particular type of extended family, which Julia Brannen (2003) describes as 'long and thin':

• **It is extended vertically** (up and down) through three or more generations: grandparents, parents and children.
• **But it is not extended horizontally** (sideways): it doesn't involve aunts, uncles, cousins etc.

For example, Charles found the same high level of contact between mothers and adult daughters that Bell had found in the 1960s. However, in the case of brothers and sisters, there had been a sharp decline in both support and contact. This suggests a 'beanpole' structure.

Beanpole families may partly be the result of two demographic changes:

• **Increased life expectancy** means more surviving grandparents and great-grandparents.
• **Smaller family sizes** mean people have fewer siblings and thus fewer horizontal ties.

Obligations to relatives

Yet despite the rise of the beanpole family, many people still feel a sense of obligation to help their wider extended kin. For example, Janet Finch and Jennifer Mason (1993) found that over 90% of people had given or received financial help, and about half had cared for a sick relative.

However, there is some variability in what can be expected of different relatives. For example, Finch and Mason found that more is expected of females than males. Similarly, Cheal (2002) argues that, when it comes to help with household tasks:

> 'A systematic set of rules exists for deciding who has the greatest obligation to assist. Help should be given: first, by a spouse; second, by a daughter; third, by a daughter-in-law; fourth, by a son; fifth, by other relatives; and sixth, by non-relatives.'

Cheal notes that where personal care for an elderly woman is needed, a daughter or daughter-in-law is preferred if the husband is not available. Sons are rarely chosen as caregivers for an elderly woman. On the other hand, daughters are rarely chosen as appropriate people to provide money.

But while daughters are more likely than sons to take responsibility for the care of elderly relatives, not all the daughters in a family necessarily play an equal part. As Mason (2011) found, much depends on the history of the relationship, the particular obligations women feel towards their relatives, and what other responsibilities they have that would give them 'legitimate excuses' not to be involved.

> **Application**
> What 'legitimate excuses' might people give for not offering help to relatives who are in need?

Similarly, Finch and Mason found that the principle of reciprocity or balance is also important – people felt that help received should be returned to avoid any feelings of indebtedness.

Overall, evidence suggests that the extended family continues to play an important role for many people today, providing both practical and emotional support when called upon. However, this is very different from Parsons' classic extended family, whose members lived and worked together, and who were bound by strong mutual obligations. Nevertheless, some sense of obligation does remain, at least to some kin and as a last resort in times of crisis.

Activity | **Research**

Patterns of obligation

...go to www.sociology.uk.net

Topic summary

Recent decades have seen some major changes in family patterns. **Changes in partnerships** include fewer first marriages, more divorces, re-marriages and cohabitations. **Changing patterns of parenting** include more births outside marriage, lone parents and stepfamilies. There are more **one-person** households and **same-sex** families. There are also **ethnic differences** in household composition. The **extended family** survives mainly in dispersed form.

Reasons for these changes include greater **individualism, secularisation, reduced stigma** and **changes in attitudes,** changes in **the law** (e.g. regarding divorce and homosexuality) and in the **position of women.**

EXAMINING CHANGING FAMILY PATTERNS

QuickCheck Questions

Check your answers at www.sociology.uk.net

1 Approximately what percentage of marriages end in divorce?
2 Why might the 'pure relationship' lead to more divorce?
3 What proportion of marriages are re-marriages?
4 Give one reason for the increase in the number of one-person households.

5 Identify two changes in childbearing patterns in recent years.
6 Identify three changes in family patterns where decline in stigma may be partly responsible for the changes.
7 Suggest two reasons why lone-parent families tend to be poorer than couple families.

Questions to try

Whether or not you are taking the AS exams during your A level course, answering the AS questions below is a very good way of testing your knowledge and understanding and practising your skills in preparation for your A level exams.

Item A   There has been a significant increase in the number of divorces since 1970. One important factor behind the increase has been the changes in the law relating to divorce. However, legal changes alone may not be enough to explain the trend and sociologists have suggested a number of possible causes of a higher divorce rate. One of these is a decline in the influence of traditional norms about marriage that used to stigmatise divorce.

Item B   The different cultural traditions, migration patterns and economic circumstances of different minority ethnic groups are reflected in the ethnic differences in family and household patterns seen in the United Kingdom today. These include differences in the proportions of people from different ethnic groups who live in single person, nuclear family, lone-parent and extended family households.

AS questions

1 Define the term 'beanpole' family.   (2 marks)
2 Using one example, explain how changes in the position of women have led to changes in patterns of marriage.   (2 marks)
3 Outline three reasons why lone-parent families are generally headed by the mother.   (6 marks)

AS and A level question

4 Applying material from Item A and your knowledge, evaluate sociological contributions to our understanding of the trends in divorce in the United Kingdom since 1970.   (20 marks)

A level question

5 Applying material from Item B, analyse two reasons for ethnic differences in family and household patterns.   (10 marks)

The Examiner's Advice

Q4 Spend about 30 minutes on this. Start by outlining the main trends in divorce since 1970. You need to consider a range of explanations of the trend. Use Item A to examine changes in the law (e.g. widening grounds) and link the decline in traditional norms to other factors, such as secularisation, changing attitudes etc. Examine other explanations, including rising expectations of marriage, the individualisation thesis, changes in women's position, feminist views etc. Link these explanations to different perspectives where possible. Use concepts such as the pure relationship, individualisation, financial independence, dual burden and the ideology of romantic love. Use evidence from studies such as Allan and Crow, Fletcher, Bernard, Giddens, Hochschild, Sigle-Rushton and Smart. Evaluate by debating how different perspectives interpret divorce.

Q5 Spend about 15 minutes on this. Divide your time fairly equally between each reason. You don't need a separate introduction; just start on your first reason. To answer this question, it's essential that you take two points from the Item and show through a chain of reasoning (see page 248) how each results in particular ethnic differences in family or household patterns. (It is a very good idea to quote from the Item when doing so.) You could use cultural traditions, patterns of migration and settlement, and the economic position of migrant groups. For example, African-Caribbean cultural traditions, possibly originating from slavery, stress the importance of women's economic independence. This means female headed families are common. Use concepts such as living apart together, matrifocal families, economic and cultural factors, racism, and studies such as Reynolds, Mirza, Charles, Chamberlain and Ballard. Include some brief evaluation.

TOPIC 6

A traditional nuclear family?

GETTING STARTED

For the Getting Started activity in the previous topic, you may have made a list of different family and household types. If so, return to it now. If not, quickly skim Topic 5 and write down as many family and household types as you can spot there. Don't include nuclear and extended families.

1 From your list, identify three or four of these types and from your knowledge of them briefly summarise some of the reasons why they are on the increase.

2 Can you see any common factors in these reasons (such as the changing position of women)?

3 Do you think the trend towards more people living in non-nuclear family and household types is good or bad? Give your reasons. (You might want to think about whether it is good or bad for society as a whole, for the individual, for men, women, children, the old etc.)

Learning objectives

After studying this Topic, you should:

- Be able to describe a range of different sociological views of family diversity.
- Understand the difference between modernist and postmodernist approaches to family diversity.
- Be able to analyse and evaluate sociological explanations of family diversity.

The changing family patterns that we examined in Topic 5 are bringing about increased family diversity in the UK today. For example, there are now fewer households containing a nuclear family and more lone-parent families and one-person households than there were in the 1970s. More couples, both straight and gay, now cohabit, many more children are born outside marriage than previously, and many more marriages end in divorce.

In this Topic, we turn our attention to the ways in which sociologists have classified the different types of family diversity and how they have tried to understand the causes and meaning of increased diversity today.

For example, does family diversity mean the breakdown of the family – or a new era of choice and personal fulfilment? Will individuals and society benefit from increased diversity, or is the decline of the traditional family likely to damage us?

Modernism and the nuclear family

Perspectives such as functionalism and the New Right have been described as 'modernist'. That is, they see modern society as having a fairly fixed, clear-cut and predictable structure. They see one 'best' family type – the nuclear family – as slotting into this structure and helping to maintain it by performing certain essential functions.

Functionalism

Thus, according to Talcott Parsons, there is a 'functional fit' between the nuclear family and modern society. As we saw in Topic 3, Parsons sees the nuclear family as uniquely suited to meeting the needs of modern society for a geographically and socially mobile workforce, and as performing two 'irreducible functions' – the primary socialisation of children and the stabilisation of adult personalities. These contribute to the overall stability and effectiveness of society.

In the functionalist view, therefore, because of the family's ability to perform these essential functions, we can generalise about the type of family that we will find in modern society - namely, a nuclear family with a division of labour between husband and wife.

Hence, other family types can be considered as dysfunctional, abnormal or even deviant, since they are less able to perform the functions required of the family.

Analysis and Evaluation

Why do functionalists believe that the nuclear family enables the workforce in modern society to be geographically and socially mobile?

The New Right

The New Right have a conservative and anti-feminist perspective on the family. They are firmly opposed to family diversity.

Like functionalists, the New Right hold the view that there is only one correct or normal family type. This is the traditional

or conventional patriarchal nuclear family consisting of a married couple and their dependent children, with a clear-cut division of labour between the breadwinner-husband and homemaker-wife.

▲ Are lone-parent families dysfunctional?

This is the same as the functionalist distinction between the instrumental and expressive roles performed by husband and wife respectively (see Topic 1).

The New Right see this family as 'natural' and based on fundamental biological differences between men and women. In their view, this family is the cornerstone of society; a place of refuge, contentment and harmony.

The New Right oppose most of the changes in family patterns that we examined in Topic 5, such as cohabitation, gay marriage and lone parenthood. They argue that the decline of the traditional nuclear family and the growth of family diversity are the cause of many social problems.

In particular, the New Right are concerned about the growth of lone-parent families, which they see as resulting from the breakdown of couple relationships. They see lone-parent families as harmful to children. They argue that:

- Lone mothers cannot discipline their children properly.
- Lone-parent families leave boys without an adult male role model, resulting in educational failure, delinquency and social instability.
- Such families are also likely to be poorer and thus a burden on the welfare state and taxpayers.

Cohabitation versus marriage

The New Right claim that the main cause of lone-parent families is the collapse of relationships between cohabiting couples. For example, Harry Benson (2006) analysed data on the parents of over 15,000 babies. He found that, over the first three years of the baby's life, the rate of family breakdown was much higher among cohabiting couples: 20%, compared with only 6% among married couples. In the New Right view, only marriage can provide a stable environment in which to bring up children.

Benson (2010; 2011) argues that couples are more stable when they are married. For example, the rate of divorce among married couples is lower than the rate of breakups among cohabiting couples.

In Benson's view, marriage is more stable because it requires a deliberate commitment to each other, whereas cohabitation allows partners to avoid commitment and responsibility.

New Right thinkers and Conservative politicians have used such evidence and arguments to support the view that both the family and society at large are 'broken'.

- They argue that only a return to 'traditional values', including the value of marriage, can prevent social disintegration and damage to children.
- They regard laws and policies such as easy access to divorce, gay marriage and widespread availability of welfare benefits as undermining the conventional family.

Benson therefore argues that government needs to encourage couples to marry by means of policies that support marriage. (For more on the New Right view of government policy and the family, see Topic 7.)

Activity	Media
The conventional nuclear family	
	...go to www.sociology.uk.net

Criticisms of the New Right

The New Right view has been criticised:

- The feminist Ann Oakley (1997) argues that the New Right wrongly assume that husbands and wives' roles are fixed by biology. Instead, cross-cultural studies show great variation in the roles men and women perform within the family. Oakley believes that the New Right view of the family is a negative reaction against the feminist campaign for women's equality.
- Feminists also argue that the conventional nuclear family favoured by the New Right is based on the patriarchal oppression of women and is a fundamental cause of gender inequality. In their view, it prevents women working, keeps them financially dependent on men, and denies them an equal say in decision-making.
- Critics of the New Right argue that there is no evidence that children in lone-parent families are more likely to be delinquent than those brought up in a two-parent family of the same social class.
- The New Right view that marriage equals commitment, while cohabitation does not, has been challenged. As we saw in Topic 5, it depends on the meaning of the relationship to those involved. Some people see cohabitation as a temporary phase, while others see it as a permanent alternative to marriage.
- The rate of cohabitation is higher among poorer social groups. Therefore, as Carol Smart (2011) points out, it may be poverty that causes the breakdown of relationships, rather than the decision not to marry.

Chester: the neo-conventional family

Robert Chester (1985) recognises that there has been some increased family diversity in recent years. However, unlike the New Right, he does not regard this as very significant, nor does he see it in a negative light. Chester argues that the only important change is a move from the dominance of the traditional or conventional nuclear family, to what he describes as the 'neo-conventional family'.

By the conventional family, Chester means the type of nuclear family described by the New Right and Parsons, with its division of labour between a male breadwinner and a female homemaker.

By contrast, Chester defines the neo-conventional family as a dual-earner family in which both spouses go out to work and not just the husband. This is similar to the symmetrical family described by Young and Willmott (see Topic 1).

Apart from this, Chester does not see any other evidence of major change. He argues that most people are not choosing to live in alternatives to the nuclear family (such as lone-parent families) on a long-term basis, and the nuclear family remains the ideal to which most people aspire.

Although many people are not part of a nuclear family at any one time, Chester argues that this is largely due to the life cycle. Many of the people who are currently living in a one-person household, such as elderly widows, divorced men or young people who have not yet married, were either part of a nuclear family in the past or will be in the future.

Statistics on household composition are thus misleading because they are merely a snapshot of a single moment in time. They don't show us the fact that most people will spend a major part of their lives in a nuclear family.

As evidence of his view that little has changed, Chester identifies a number of patterns:

- Most people live in a household headed by a married couple.
- Most adults marry and have children. Most children are reared by their two natural parents.
- Most marriages continue until death. Divorce has increased, but most divorcees remarry.
- Cohabitation has increased, but for most couples it is a temporary phase before marrying or re-marrying. Most couples get married if they have children.
- Although births outside marriage have increased, most are jointly registered, indicating that the parents are committed to bringing up children as a couple.

For Chester, then, the extent and importance of family diversity has been exaggerated. Like the functionalists, Chester sees the nuclear family as dominant.

The only important difference between Chester's view and that of the functionalists is that Chester sees a change from a conventional to a neo-conventional nuclear family where both spouses play an 'instrumental' or breadwinner role.

The Rapoports: five types of family diversity

Unlike Chester, Rhona and Robert Rapoport (1982) argue that diversity is of central importance in understanding family life today. They believe that we have moved away from the traditional nuclear family as the dominant family type, to a range of different types. Families in Britain have adapted to a pluralistic society – that is, one in which cultures and lifestyles are more diverse. In their view, family diversity reflects greater freedom of choice and the widespread acceptance of different cultures and ways of life in today's society.

Unlike the New Right, the Rapoports see diversity as a positive response to people's different needs and wishes, and not as abnormal or a deviation from the assumed norm of a 'proper' nuclear family.

They identify five different types of family diversity in Britain today:

Organisational diversity This refers to differences in the ways family roles are organised. For example, some couples have joint conjugal roles and two wage-earners, while others have segregated conjugal roles and one wage-earner.

Cultural diversity Different cultural, religious and ethnic groups have different family structures. For example, there is a higher proportion of female-headed lone-parent families among African-Caribbean households and a higher proportion of extended families among Asian households.

Social class diversity Differences in family structure are partly the result of income differences between households of different social classes. Likewise, there are class differences in child-rearing practices.

▲ There is a higher proportion of extended families among Asian communities than among other ethnic groups.

Life-stage diversity Family structures differ according to the stage reached in the life cycle – for example, young newlyweds, couples with dependent children, retired couples whose children have grown up and left home, and widows who are living alone.

Generational diversity Older and younger generations have different attitudes and experiences that reflect the historical periods in which they have lived. For example, they may have different views about the morality of divorce or cohabitation.

Postmodernism and family diversity

As we have seen, modernist perspectives such as functionalism emphasise the dominance of one family type in modern society, namely the nuclear family. Modernist approaches take a structural or 'top down' view. That is, they see the family as a structure that shapes the behaviour of its members so that they perform the functions society requires.

In this view, individuals have no real choice about the pattern of family life. In terms of family patterns, our behaviour is orderly, structured and predictable: most people marry, go on to have children and so on. At most, there may be some limited variety in family life, such as the five types of diversity identified by the Rapoports.

By contrast, postmodernists such as David Cheal (1993) go much further than the Rapoports. Postmodernists start from the view that we no longer live in 'modern' society with its predictable, orderly structures such as the nuclear family. In their view, society has entered a new, chaotic, postmodern stage.

In postmodern society, there is no longer one single, dominant, stable family structure such as the nuclear family. Instead, family structures have become fragmented into many different types and individuals now have much more choice in their lifestyles, personal relationships and family arrangements (see Box 32).

Some writers argue that this greater diversity and choice brings with it both advantages and disadvantages:

- It gives individuals greater freedom to plot their own life course – to choose the kind of family and personal relationships that meet their needs.
- But greater freedom of choice in relationships means a greater risk of instability, since these relationships are more likely to break up.

Stacey: postmodern families

Judith Stacey (1998) argues that greater freedom and choice has benefited women. It has enabled them to free themselves from patriarchal oppression and to shape their family arrangements to meet their needs.

Stacey used life history interviews to construct a series of case studies of postmodern families in Silicon Valley, California. She found that women rather than men have been the main agents of changes in the family.

For example, many of the women she interviewed had rejected the traditional housewife-mother role. They had worked, returned to education as adults, improved their job prospects, divorced and re-married. These women had often created new types of family that better suited their needs.

One of these new family structures Stacey calls the 'divorce-extended family', whose members are connected by divorce rather than marriage. The key members are usually female and may include former in-laws, such as mother- and daughter-in-law, or a man's ex-wife and his new partner.

For example, Stacey describes in one of her case studies how Pam Gamma created a divorce-extended family. Pam married young, then divorced and cohabited for several years before re-marrying. Her second husband had also been married before.

By the time the children of Pam's first marriage were in their twenties, she had formed a divorce-extended family with Shirley, the woman cohabiting with her first husband. They helped each other financially and domestically, for example by exchanging lodgers in response to the changing needs of their households.

Such cases illustrate the idea that postmodern families are diverse and that their shape depends on the active choices people make about how to live their lives — for example, whether to get divorced, cohabit, come out as gay etc.

Thus, as David Morgan (1996; 2011) argues, it is pointless trying to make large-scale generalisations about 'the family' as if it were a single thing, as functionalists do. Rather, a family is simply whatever arrangements those involved choose to *call* their family. In this view, sociologists should focus their attention on how people create their own diverse family lives and practices. One way of exploring this is by means of life course analysis, as Box 33 explains.

The individualisation thesis

While not accepting everything postmodernism says about the nature of society today, sociologists such as Anthony Giddens and Ulrich Beck have been influenced by postmodernist ideas about today's society and have applied some of these to understanding family life.

In particular, Giddens and Beck explore the effects of increasing individual choice upon families and relationships. Their views have therefore become known as the individualisation thesis.

The individualisation thesis argues that traditional social structures such as class, gender and family have lost much of their influence over us. According to the thesis, in the past, people's lives were defined by fixed roles that largely prevented them from choosing their own life course. For example, everyone was expected to marry and to take up their appropriate gender role. By contrast, individuals in today's society have fewer such certainties or fixed roles to follow.

According to the individualisation thesis, therefore, we have become freed or 'disembedded' from traditional roles and structures, leaving us with more freedom to choose how we lead our lives. As Beck (1992) puts it, the 'standard biography' or life course that people followed in the past

▲ Flat hunting. Does having your own place mean you are an adult?

has been replaced by the 'do-it-yourself biography' that individuals today must construct for themselves.

For Giddens and Beck, this change has huge implications for family relationships and family diversity, which we shall now examine.

Box 33	Life course analysis

Life course analysis is a method of research developed by Tamara Hareven (1978). Using in-depth, unstructured interviews, it explores the meanings that individual family members give to the relationships they have and the choices they make at various turning points in their lives, such as the decision to have a baby or come out as gay.

Similarly, Clare Holdsworth and David Morgan (2005) examine what it means for young people to leave home and become independent or 'adult' and how parents, friends and others influence their decisions.

In the view of its supporters, life course analysis has two major strengths:

1 It focuses on what family members themselves consider important, rather than what sociologists may regard as important. It looks at families and households from the viewpoint of the people involved and the meanings they give to their lives, relationships and choices.

2 It is particularly suitable for studying families in today's postmodern or 'late modern' society, where there is more choice about personal relationships and more family diversity. Family structures are increasingly just the result of the choices made by their members.

Giddens: choice and equality

Anthony Giddens (1992) argues that in recent decades the family and marriage have been transformed by greater choice and a more equal relationship between men and women. This transformation has occurred because:

- Contraception has allowed sex and intimacy rather than reproduction to become the main reason for the relationship's existence.
- Women have gained independence as a result of feminism and because of greater opportunities in education and work.

As a result, the basis of marriage and the family has changed. Giddens argues that in the past, traditional family relationships were held together by external forces such as the laws governing the marriage contract and by powerful norms against divorce and sex outside marriage.

By contrast, today couples are free to define their relationship themselves, rather than simply acting out roles that have been defined in advance by law or tradition. For example, a couple nowadays don't have to marry to have children and divorce is readily accessible so they don't have to stay together 'til death do us part'.

The pure relationship

According to Giddens, what holds relationships together today is no longer law, religion, social norms or traditional institutions. Instead, intimate relationships nowadays are based on individual choice and equality.

Giddens describes this kind of relationship as the 'pure relationship'. He sees the pure relationship as typical of today's late modern society, in which relationships are no longer bound by traditional norms.

The key feature of the pure relationship is that it exists solely to satisfy each partner's needs. As a result, the relationship is likely to survive only so long as both partners think it is in their own interest to do so. Couples stay together because of love, happiness or sexual attraction, rather than because of tradition, a sense of duty or for the sake of the children.

Individuals are thus free to choose to enter and to leave relationships as they see fit. Relationships become part of the process of the individual's self-discovery or self-identity: trying different relationships becomes a way of establishing 'who we are'.

However, Giddens notes that with more choice, personal relationships inevitably become less stable. The pure relationship is a kind of 'rolling contract' that can be ended more or less at will by either partner, rather than a permanent commitment. This in turn produces greater family diversity by creating more lone-parent families, one person households, stepfamilies and so on.

Same-sex couples as pioneers

Giddens sees same-sex relationships as leading the way towards new family types and creating more democratic and equal relationships.

In Giddens' view, this is because same-sex relationships are not influenced by tradition to the extent that heterosexual relationships are (indeed they have generally been stigmatised and even criminalised). As a result, same-sex couples have been able to develop relationships based on choice rather than on traditional roles, since these were largely absent.

This has enabled those in same-sex relationships to negotiate personal relationships and to actively create family structures that serve their own needs, rather than having to conform to pre-existing norms in the way that heterosexual couples have traditionally had to do.

For example, Weston (1992) found that same-sex couples created supportive 'families of choice' from among friends, former lovers and biological kin, while Weeks (2000) found that friendship networks functioned as kinship networks for gay men and lesbians.

▲ Christians protesting outside Parliament against the Marriage Bill that allows gay couples to marry.

Beck: the negotiated family

Another version of the individualisation thesis is put forward by Ulrich Beck (1992). Beck argues that we now live in a 'risk society' where tradition has less influence and people have more choice. As a result, we are more aware of risks. This is because making choices involves calculating the risks and rewards of the different options open to us.

This contrasts with an earlier time when people's roles were more fixed by tradition and rigid social norms dictated how they should behave.

For example, in the past, people were expected to marry for life and, once married, men were expected to play the role of breadwinner and disciplinarian and to make the important financial decisions, while women took responsibility for the housework, childcare and care of the sick and elderly.

Although this traditional patriarchal family was unequal and oppressive, it did provide a stable and predictable basis for family life by defining each member's role and responsibilities. However, the patriarchal family has been undermined by two trends:

- **Greater gender equality**, which has challenged male domination in all spheres of life. Women now expect equality both at work and in marriage.
- **Greater individualism**, where people's actions are influenced more by calculations of their own self-interest than by a sense of obligation to others.

These trends have led to a new type of family replacing the patriarchal family. Ulrich Beck and Elisabeth Beck-Gernsheim (1995) call this the 'negotiated family'. Negotiated families do not conform to the traditional family norm, but vary according to the wishes and expectations of their members, who decide what is best for themselves by negotiation. They enter the relationship on an equal basis.

Application

Suggest three reasons why there is now greater gender equality in the family and society.

However, although the negotiated family is more equal than the patriarchal family, it is less stable. This is because individuals are free to leave if their needs are not met. As a result, this instability leads to greater family diversity by creating more lone-parent families, one person households, re-marriages and so on.

the zombie family

Although in today's uncertain risk society people turn to the family in the hope of finding security, in reality family relationships are themselves now subject to greater risk and uncertainty than ever before.

For this reason, Beck describes the family as a 'zombie category': it appears to be alive, but in reality it is dead. People want it to be a haven of security in an insecure world, but today's family cannot provide this because of its own instability.

The personal life perspective

Sociologists who take a personal life perspective, such as Carol Smart (2007) and Vanessa May (2013), agree that there is now more family diversity but they disagree with Beck and Giddens' explanation of it. They make several criticisms of the individualisation thesis.

criticisms of the individualisation thesis

Firstly, the individualisation thesis exaggerates how much choice people have about family relationships today. As Shelley Budgeon (2011) notes, this reflects the neoliberal ideology that individuals today have complete freedom of choice. In reality, however, traditional norms that limit people's relationship choices have not weakened as much as the thesis claims.

Secondly, the thesis wrongly sees people as disembedded, 'free-floating', independent individuals. It ignores the fact that that our decisions and choices about personal relationships are made within a social context.

Thirdly, the individualisation thesis ignores the importance of structural factors such as social class inequalities and patriarchal gender norms in limiting and shaping our relationship choices.

As May notes, this is because Giddens' and Beck's view of the individual is simply 'an idealised version of a white, middle-class man'. They ignore the fact that not everyone has the same ability as this privileged group to exercise choice about relationships.

The connectedness thesis

Reflecting these criticisms, sociologists from the personal life perspective propose an alternative to the individualisation thesis. Smart calls this the 'connectedness thesis'.

Instead of seeing us as disembedded, isolated individuals with limitless choice about personal relationships, Smart argues that we are fundamentally social beings whose choices are always made 'within a web of connectedness'.

According to the connectedness thesis, we live within networks of existing relationships and interwoven personal histories, and these strongly influence our range of options and choices in relationships.

For example, Finch and Mason's (1993) study of extended families found that, although individuals can to some extent negotiate the relationships they want, they are also embedded within family connections and obligations that restrict their freedom of choice. (For more on Finch and Mason, see page 222.)

Such findings challenge the notion of the pure relationship. Families usually include more than just the couples that Giddens focuses on, and even couple relationships are not always 'pure' relationships that we can walk away from at will.

For example, parents who separate remain linked by their children, often against their wishes. As Smart says, 'where lives have become interwoven and embedded, it becomes impossible for relationships to simply end'. Smart therefore emphasises the importance of always putting individuals in the context of their past and the web of relationships that shape their choices and family patterns.

class and gender

The connectedness thesis also emphasises the role of the class and gender structures in which we are embedded. These structures limit our choices about the kinds of relationships, identities and families we can create for ourselves. For example:

- After a divorce, gender norms generally dictate that women should have custody of the children, which may limit their opportunity to form new relationships. By contrast, men are freer to start new relationships and second families.
- Men are generally better paid than women and this gives them greater freedom and choice in relationships.
- The relative powerlessness of women and children as compared with men means that many lack freedom to choose and so remain trapped in abusive relationships.

> **Application**
> In what ways might an individual's age or ethnicity limit their choices about the kinds of family and personal relationships they can create?

The power of structures

As we saw earlier, Beck and Giddens argue that there has been a disappearance or weakening of the structures of class, gender and family that traditionally controlled our lives and limited our choices.

However, as May argues, these structures are not disappearing, they are simply being re-shaped. For example, while women in the past 150 years have gained important

rights in relation to voting, divorce, education and employment, this does not mean that they now 'have it all'.

For example, while women can now pursue traditionally 'masculine' goals such as careers, they are still expected to be heterosexual. As Anna Einasdottir (2011) argues, while lesbianism is now tolerated, heteronormativity (norms favouring heterosexuality) means that many lesbians feel forced to remain 'in the closet' and this limits their choices about their relationships and lifestyles.

Thus, the personal life perspective does not see increased diversity simply as a result of greater freedom of choice, as Beck and Giddens do. Instead, it emphasises the importance of social structures in shaping the freedoms many people now have to create more diverse types of families.

Thus, although there is a trend towards greater diversity and choice, the personal life perspective emphasises the continuing importance of structural factors such as patriarchy and class inequality in restricting people's choices and shaping their family lives.

Activity | **Discussion**

Is the nuclear family best?

...go to www.sociology.uk.net

Topic summary

Modernists such as **functionalists** and the **New Right** see only the nuclear family as normal and other family types as deviant. **Chester** sees only one major change – **the neo-conventional family** – whereas the **Rapoports** identify five types of diversity.

Sociologists influenced by **postmodernism** believe that in today's postmodern society, individuals have more **choice** in their relationships and family practices.

The individualisation thesis argues that traditional structures have lost influence, leading to more **choice** and diversity but also more **risk and instability.** Individuals now seek the **pure relationship,** based solely on satisfying their own needs.

The connectedness thesis argues that people are not simply isolated individuals and that wider **structures still limit choice** and diversity.

EXAMINING FAMILY DIVERSITY

QuickCheck Questions

Check your answers at www.sociology.uk.net

1 Why do the New Right see cohabitation as a problem?
2 State two criticisms of the New Right view of the family.
3 What is the difference between the conventional and the neo-conventional family?
4 What is the divorce-extended family?

5 What is the individualisation thesis?
6 Name two features of postmodernity that make family life more diverse.
7 Why does Giddens see same-sex relationships as more likely to be equal?

Questions to try

Whether or not you are taking the AS exams during your A level course, answering the AS questions below is a very good way of testing your knowledge and understanding and practising your skills in preparation for your A level exams.

Item A Recent decades have seen a move to a more diverse range of family arrangements. While some sociologists see this as harmful for society, others welcome it because they see it as bringing greater individual choice about relationships.

However, some sociologists argue that the extent of change should not be exaggerated: most people live in something resembling a conventional nuclear family, and many individuals still find their choices limited. For example, while being gay or lesbian is less stigmatised than in the past, it is not always easy for people to 'come out'.

Item B According to the individualisation thesis, greater individual choice has transformed family and intimate relationships. Unlike in the past, when individuals' lives were governed by tradition, today both men and women are free to make their own choices about relationships, sexuality and so on, following their own self-interest. Class, gender and family structures no longer limit our choices.

AS questions

1 Define the term 'the pure relationship'.   (2 marks)
2 Using one example, explain how greater gender equality may lead to family instability.   (2 marks)
3 Outline three types of diversity in family structures.   (6 marks)

AS and A level question

4 Applying material from Item A and your knowledge, evaluate sociological contributions to our understanding of family diversity.   (20 marks)

A level question

5 Applying material from Item B, analyse two criticisms of the individualisation thesis.   (10 marks)

The Examiner's Advice

Q4 Spend about 30 minutes on this. Start by outlining some of the main types of diversity, e.g. cohabitation, same-sex couples, lone parents etc. Consider a range of explanations, e.g. the New Right, postmodernism, feminism, Chester, the individualisation thesis and connectedness thesis. Link the material in Item A to some of these. Item A gives you a way to organise your answer, into two debates: whether diversity is good or bad (paragraph one) and how much increased diversity is there in fact (paragraph two). This will enable you to develop evaluation by contrasting different explanations. Use concepts and issues such as patriarchy, the neo-conventional family, the zombie family, increased gender equality, the pure relationship, individualisation, disembedding, families of choice etc. Use evidence from studies such as Parsons, Benson, Chester, Rapoport and Rapoport, Beck, Giddens, Cheal, Stacey, Weeks and Smart.

Q5 Spend about 15 minutes on this. Divide your time fairly equally between the two criticisms. You don't need a separate introduction. Take two points from the Item and show through a chain of reasoning (see page 248) the nature of the criticism. (It is a very good idea to quote from the Item when doing so.) You could criticise the idea that individuals' lives in the past were always governed by fixed roles, that women are as free as men to choose, or that structures no longer limit our choices. For example, divorce usually results in children remaining with their mother. This means her chances of forming a new relationship may be more limited. Use concepts such as patriarchy, the pure relationship, neoliberalism, disembeddedness, connectedness, heteronormativity and class inequality, and studies such as Beck, Giddens, Weeks, Sharp, May, Budgeon and Einasdottir.

一对夫妇只生一个孩子

Poster promoting China's one-child policy.

GETTING STARTED

Despite often being considered a private sphere, the family is also subject to external influence from government in the form of laws and social policies. These laws and policies may depend on which political party is in power and they may change over time.

In pairs, using what you have learned from the other topics in this chapter and your knowledge:

1 Make a list of government policies and laws that can affect family life. These could be policies and laws that are directly aimed at the family, such as child benefit, or they could be policies about other areas such as education that have an effect on the family, for example, compulsory schooling.

2 For each policy or law you have identified, outline how the policy affects family life. This may be an effect on different individual family members or on the family as a whole.

Learning objectives

After studying this Topic, you should:

● Know some of the ways in which social policies may affect families.

● Understand the different sociological perspectives on families and social policy.

● Be able to analyse these perspectives and evaluate their usefulness in explaining the relationship between families and social policy.

FAMILIES AND SOCIAL POLICY

Social policy refers to the plans and actions of state agencies, such as health and social services, the welfare benefits system, schools and other public bodies.

Policies are usually based on laws introduced by government that provide the framework within which these agencies operate. For example, laws lay down who is entitled to each specific welfare benefit.

Most social policies affect families in some way or other. Some are aimed directly at families, such as laws governing marriage and divorce, abortion and contraception, child protection, adoption and so on.

Other policies, although not necessarily aimed directly at families, still have an effect on them. For example:

- The policy of compulsory education enables parents to go out to work while schools provide a free 'childminding' service.
- The policy of 'care in the community' often means that it is family members rather than hospitals or nursing homes who have to care for the sick or elderly.
- Taxation policies affect how much money is taken from families and how much is made available to pay for the services provided for families.

A comparative view of family policy

The actions and policies of governments can sometimes have profound effects on families and their members.

Cross-cultural examples from different societies and historical periods can show us some of the more extreme ways in which the state's policies can affect family life. This can help us to see the relationship between families and social policies in a new light. A good example of this is China's one-child policy.

China's one-child policy In China, the government's population control policy has aimed to discourage couples from having more than one child.

The policy is supervised by workplace family planning committees; women must seek their permission to try to become pregnant, and there is often both a waiting list and a quota for each factory.

Couples who comply with the policy get extra benefits, such as free child healthcare and higher tax allowances. An only child will also get priority in education and housing later in life.

Couples who break their agreement to have only one child must repay the allowances and pay a fine. Women face pressure to undergo sterilisation after their first child.

Communist Romania At the other extreme, the former communist government of Romania in the 1980s introduced a series of policies to try to drive up the birth rate, which had been falling as living standards declined.

It restricted contraception and abortion, set up infertility treatment centres, made divorce more difficult, lowered the legal age of marriage to 15, and made unmarried adults and childless couples pay an extra 5% income tax.

Nazi family policy In Nazi Germany in the 1930s, the state pursued a twofold policy. On the one hand, it encouraged the healthy and supposedly 'racially pure' to breed a 'master race' (for example, by restricting access to abortion and contraception).

Official policy sought to keep women out of the workforce and confine them to 'children, kitchen and church', the better to perform their biological role.

On the other hand, the state compulsorily sterilised 375,000 disabled people that it deemed unfit to breed on grounds of 'physical malformation, mental retardation, epilepsy, imbecility, deafness or blindness'. Many of these people were later murdered in Nazi concentration camps.

Democratic societies By contrast with these extreme examples, some people argue that in democratic societies such as Britain, the family is a private sphere of life in which the government does not intervene, except perhaps when things 'go wrong', for example in cases of child abuse.

However, sociologists argue that in fact, even in democratic societies, the state's social policies play a very important role in shaping family life. In this Topic we shall examine a range of ways in which this occurs.

Activity	Media

China's one-child policy

...go to www.sociology.uk.net

Perspectives on families and social policy

Although sociologists agree that social policy can have important effects on family life, they hold different views about what kinds of effects it has and whether these are desirable. We shall examine a range of different sociological views or perspectives on the impact of social policy on families.

Functionalism

Functionalists see society as built on harmony and consensus (shared values), and free from major conflicts. They see the state as acting in the interests of society as a whole and its social policies as being for the good of all. Functionalists see policies as helping families to perform their functions more effectively and make life better for their members.

For example, Ronald Fletcher (1966) argues that the introduction of health, education and housing policies in the years since the industrial revolution has gradually led to the development of a welfare state that supports the family in performing its functions more effectively.

For instance, the existence of the National Health Service means that with the help of doctors, nurses, hospitals and medicines, the family today is better able to take care of its members when they are sick.

Application

1 Identify two functions that families perform for their members apart from healthcare.
2 Suggest ways in which welfare policies may help families to carry out each of these two functions more effectively.

However, the functionalist view has been criticised on two main counts:

- **It assumes that all members of the family benefit equally** from social policies, whereas feminists for example argue that policies often benefit men at the expense of women.
- **It assumes that there is a 'march of progress'**, with social policies steadily making family life better and better. However, Marxists for example argue that policies can also turn the clock back and reverse progress previously made, for example by cutting welfare benefits to poor families.

Donzelot: policing the family

Jacques Donzelot (1977) offers a very different perspective on the relationship between the family and state policies from that of the functionalists. Rather than a consensus view of policy as benefiting the family, Donzelot has a conflict view of society and he sees policy as a form of state power and control over families.

Donzelot uses Michel Foucault's (1976) concept of surveillance (observing and monitoring). Foucault sees power not just as something held by the government or state, but as diffused (spread) throughout society and found within all relationships.

In particular, Foucault sees professionals such as doctors and social workers as exercising power over their clients by using their expert knowledge to turn them into 'cases' to be dealt with.

Donzelot applies these ideas to the family. He is interested in how professionals carry out surveillance of families. He argues that social workers, health visitors and doctors use their knowledge to control and change families. Donzelot calls this 'the policing of families'.

Surveillance is not targeted equally on all social classes. Poor families are more likely to be seen as 'problem' families and as the cause of crime and anti-social behaviour. These are the families that professionals target for 'improvement'.

For example, as Rachel Condry (2007) notes, the state may seek to control and regulate family life by imposing compulsory Parenting Orders through the courts. Parents of young offenders, truants or badly behaved children may be forced to attend parenting classes to learn the 'correct' way to bring up their children.

Donzelot rejects the functionalists' march of progress view that social policy and the professionals who carry it out have created a better, freer or more humane society. Instead, he sees social policy as a form of state control of the family.

By focusing on the micro level of how the 'caring professions' act as agents of social control through their surveillance of families, Donzelot shows the importance of professional knowledge as a form of power and control.

However, Marxists and feminists criticise Donzelot for failing to identify clearly who benefits from such policies of surveillance. Marxists argue that social policies generally operate in the interests of the capitalist class, while feminists argue that men are the main beneficiaries.

The New Right

The New Right are strongly in favour of the conventional or 'traditional' nuclear family based on a married, heterosexual couple, with a division of labour between a male provider and a female homemaker. They see this family type as naturally self-reliant and capable of caring and providing for its members, especially the successful socialisation of children.

In their view, the changes that have led to greater family diversity, such as increases in divorce, cohabitation, same-sex partnerships and lone parenthood, are threatening the conventional family and producing social problems such as crime and welfare dependency.

For the New Right, state policies have encouraged these changes and helped to undermine the nuclear family. For example, Brenda Almond (2006) argues that:

- Laws making divorce easier undermine the idea of marriage as a lifelong commitment between a man and a woman.
- The introduction of civil partnerships (and since 2014 marriage) for gay and lesbian couples sends out the message that the state no longer sees heterosexual marriage as superior to other domestic set-ups.
- Tax laws discriminate against conventional families with a sole (usually male) breadwinner. They cannot transfer the non-working partner's (usually the wife's) tax allowances to the working partner, so they tend to pay more tax than dual-earner couples, each of whom has a tax allowance.

Similarly, the New Right point out that increased rights for unmarried cohabitants, such as adoption rights and succession to council house tenancies and pension rights when a partner dies, begin to make cohabitation and marriage more similar. This sends out the signal that the state does not see marriage as special or better.

Lone parents, welfare policy and the dependency culture

New Right commentators such as Charles Murray (1984; 1990) are particularly critical of welfare policy. In their view, providing 'generous' welfare benefits, such as council housing for unmarried teenage mothers and cash payments to support lone-parent families, undermines the conventional nuclear family and encourages deviant and dysfunctional family types that harm society.

Murray argues that these welfare benefits offer 'perverse incentives' – that is, they reward irresponsible or anti-social behaviour. For example:

- If fathers see that the state will maintain their children, some of them will abandon their responsibilities towards their families.
- Providing council housing for unmarried teenage mothers encourages young girls to become pregnant.
- The growth of lone-parent families, encouraged by generous benefits, means more boys grow up without a male role model and authority figure. This lack of paternal authority is responsible for a rising crime rate among young males.

Thus for the New Right, social policy has a major impact on family roles and relationships. Current policies are encouraging a dependency culture, where individuals come to depend on the state to support them and their children rather than being self-reliant. This threatens two essential functions that the family fulfils for society:

- the successful socialisation of the young
- the maintenance of the work ethic among men.

the New Right's solution

The New Right's solution to these problems is simple. They argue that the policy must be changed, with cuts in welfare spending and tighter restrictions on who is eligible for benefits.

In their view, this would have several advantages. For example, cutting welfare benefits would mean that taxes could also be reduced, and both these changes would give fathers more incentive to work and to provide for their families.

Similarly, denying council housing to unmarried teenage mothers would remove a major incentive to become pregnant when very young.

The New Right also advocate policies to support the traditional nuclear family, such as taxes that favour married rather than cohabiting couples, and making absent fathers financially responsible for their children.

Whereas functionalists take the view that state welfare policies can benefit the family and make it better able to meet its members' needs, the New Right disagree.

In their view, the less the state 'interferes' in families, the better family life will be. Greater self-reliance, and not reliance on the state, is what will enable the family to meet its members' needs most effectively.

Evaluation of the New Right view

The New Right view of policy has been criticised on several counts:

- Feminists argue that it is an attempt to justify a return to the traditional patriarchal nuclear family that subordinated women to men and confined them to a domestic role.
- It wrongly assumes that the patriarchal nuclear family is 'natural' rather than socially constructed.
- Pam Abbott and Claire Wallace (1992) argue that cutting benefits would simply drive many poor families into even greater poverty and make them even less self-reliant.
- The New Right ignore the many policies that support and maintain the conventional nuclear family rather than undermine it. (See the section on feminism below.)

Analysis and Evaluation

What is meant by the idea that the patriarchal nuclear family is socially constructed rather than natural?

The New Right's influence on policies

The New Right is a conservative view of the family that first developed in the 1970s. Therefore we might expect it to have had a strong influence on the Conservative Party's policies towards the family. However, Conservative policies since the 1970s show a more mixed picture.

We can also see some similarities between New Right ideas and New Labour policies.

Conservative governments 1979-97

Reflecting a New Right view, Mrs Thatcher's Conservative government banned the promotion of homosexuality by local authorities. This included a ban on teaching that homosexuality was an acceptable family relationship.

The Conservatives also defined divorce as a social problem – a view held by the New Right – and emphasised the continued responsibility of parents for their children after divorce. They set up the Child Support Agency to enforce maintenance payments by absent parents (usually fathers).

On the other hand, the Conservatives introduced measures opposed by the New Right, such as making divorce easier and giving 'illegitimate' children (those born outside marriage) the same rights as those born to married parents.

New Labour governments 1997-2010

We can see some similarities between New Right views and those of New Labour. Like the New Right, New Labour took the view that the family is the bedrock of society and saw a family headed by a married, heterosexual couple as the best environment for bringing up children.

Also like the New Right, New Labour emphasised the need for parents to take responsibility for their children, for example by introducing Parenting Orders for parents of truants and young offenders.

However, as Elizabeth Silva and Carol Smart (1999) note, New Labour rejected the New Right view that the family should have just one (male) earner and recognised that women too now go out to work.

Thus New Labour policies favoured the kind of dual-earner neo-conventional family described by Robert Chester (see Topic 6). These policies included:

- Longer maternity leave, three months' unpaid leave for both parents and the right to seek time off work for family reasons. These policies made it easier for both parents to work.
- Working Families Tax Credit, enabling parents to claim some tax relief on childcare costs.
- The New Deal, helping lone parents to return to work.

These policies reflect a further difference with the New Right, who oppose state intervention. New Labour argued instead that certain kinds of state intervention can improve life for families.

For example, their welfare, taxation and minimum wage policies were partly aimed at lifting children out of poverty by re-distributing income to the poor through higher benefits, whereas the New Right disapprove of re-distributing income through taxes and benefits.

A final area of difference with the New Right was in New Labour's support for alternatives to the conventional heterosexual nuclear family. This included policies such as:

- civil partnerships for same-sex couples
- giving unmarried couples the same rights to adopt as married couples
- outlawing discrimination on grounds of sexuality.

Conservative-led governments from 2010

The Conservatives have long been divided between what Richard Hayton (2010) calls:

- **Modernisers** who recognise that families are now more diverse and are willing to reflect this in their policies
- **Traditionalists** who favour a New Right view and reject diversity as morally wrong.

This division means that the Conservative Party has found it difficult to maintain a consistent policy line on the family. For example, the Conservative-led Coalition government introduced gay marriage – a policy opposed by New Right traditionalists. The influence of traditionalists was also weakened by the fact that the Conservatives had to share power in a coalition with the Liberal Democrats.

Critics argue that the Conservative government's financial austerity policies reflected the New Right's desire to cut public spending. However, the government failed to introduce policies that specifically promote the New Right ideal of a conventional heterosexual nuclear family. For example, Browne (2012) found that two-parent families with children fared particularly badly as a result of the government's tax and benefits policies.

Feminism

Feminists take a conflict view. They see society as patriarchal (male-dominated), benefiting men at women's expense. They argue that all social institutions, including the state and its policies, help to maintain women's subordinate position and the unequal gender division of labour in the family.

Policy as self-fulfilling prophecy

Policies are often based on assumptions about what the 'normal' family is like. Feminists such as Hilary Land (1978) argue that many social policies assume that the ideal family is the patriarchal nuclear family with a male provider and female homemaker plus their dependent children.

This norm of what the family should be like affects the kind of policies governing family life. In turn, the effect of the policies is often to reinforce that particular type of family at the expense of other types, creating a self-fulfilling prophecy.

For example, if the state assumes that 'normal' families are based on marriage and offers tax incentives to married couples that are not available to cohabiting couples, this policy may encourage marriage and discourage cohabitation.

In effect, the policy makes it more difficult for people to live in other family types than the one that policymakers assume they live in.

Policies supporting the patriarchal family

Feminists identify numerous examples of policies that help to maintain the conventional patriarchal nuclear family and reinforce women's economic dependence. These include the following.

Tax and benefits policies may assume that husbands are the main wage-earners and that wives are their financial dependants.

This can make it impossible for wives to claim social security benefits in their own right, since it is expected that their husbands will provide. This then reinforces women's dependence on their husbands.

Childcare While the government pays for some childcare for pre-school children, this is not enough to permit parents to work full-time unless they can meet the additional costs themselves. Likewise, policies governing school timetables and holidays make it hard for parents (usually the mothers) to work full-time unless they can afford extra childcare.

This means that women are restricted from working and placed in a position of economic dependence on their partners.

Care for the sick and elderly Government policies often assume that the family will provide this care. In general, this means it is middle-aged women who are expected to do the caring. In turn, this often prevents them from working full-time, increasing their economic dependence on their partners.

Furthermore, as Diana Leonard (1978) argues, even where policies appear to support women, they may still reinforce the patriarchal family and act as a form of social control over women.

For example, although maternity leave policies benefit women, they also reinforce patriarchy in the family. Maternity leave entitlement is much more generous than that for paternity leave and this encourages the assumption that the care of infants is the responsibility of mothers rather than fathers. Maternity benefits are also low, thereby increasing mothers' economic dependence on their partners.

▲ In some countries, grandparents are often the only providers of childcare where both parents work.

Similarly, child benefit is normally paid to the mother. Although this gives her a source of income that does not depend on the father, it also assumes that the child's welfare is primarily her responsibility.

Examples such as these show the importance of social policies in the social construction of family roles and relationships. By making it easier for women to take responsibility for the care of infants or by assuming that men are the main economic providers, social policies help to create and maintain the patriarchal roles and relationships that they assume to be the norm.

evaluation of the feminist view

Not all policies are directed at maintaining patriarchy. For example, equal pay and sex discrimination laws, the right of lesbians to marry, benefits for lone parents, refuges for women escaping domestic violence and equal rights to divorce could all be said to challenge the patriarchal family. Similarly, rape within marriage was made a criminal offence in 1991. These policies can all be said to improve the position of women in the family and wider society.

Activity	Webquest

Improving family policy

...go to www.sociology.uk.net

Gender regimes

As we have seen, feminists argue that social policy reinforces the patriarchal family. By examining policy from a comparative perspective across different societies, we can see whether this is inevitable, or whether different policies can encourage more equal family relationships.

For example, a country's policies on taxation, childcare, welfare services and equal opportunities will all affect whether women can work full-time, or whether they have to forgo paid work to care for children or elderly relatives.

Eileen Drew (1995) uses the concept of 'gender regimes' to describe how social policies in different countries can either encourage or discourage gender equality in the family and at work.

She identifies two types of gender regime following different types of family policies:

- **familistic gender regimes**, where policies are based on a traditional gender division between male breadwinner and female housewife and carer.

  In Greece, for example, there is little state welfare or publicly funded childcare. Women have to rely heavily on support from their extended kin and there is a traditional division of labour.

- **individualistic gender regimes**, where policies are based on the belief that husbands and wives should be treated the same. Wives are not assumed to be financially dependent on their husbands, so each partner has a separate entitlement to state benefits.

  In Sweden, for example, policies treat husbands and wives as equally responsible both for breadwinning and domestic tasks. Equal opportunities policies, state provision of childcare, parental leave and good quality welfare services mean that women are less dependent on their husbands and have more opportunities to work.

Application

In what ways might individualistic gender regimes undermine the patriarchal family?

State versus market

Drew argues that most European Union countries are now moving towards more individualistic gender regimes. This is likely to bring a move away from the traditional patriarchal family and towards greater gender equality in family roles and relationships.

However, policies such as publicly funded childcare do not come cheap, and they involve major conflicts about who should benefit from social policies and who should pay for them. It would therefore be naïve to assume that there is an inevitable 'march of progress' towards gender equality.

For example, feminists argue that since the global recession began in 2008, cutbacks in government spending throughout Europe have led to pressure on women to take more responsibility for caring for family members as the state retreats from providing welfare.

During this period, there has also been a trend towards neo-liberal welfare policies, in which individuals and families are encouraged to use the market rather than the state to meet their needs, for example through private pension provision and private care of the old.

Nevertheless, the differences between European countries show that social policies can play an important role in promoting or preventing gender equality in the family.

Activity   **Discussion**

The impact of policy on family life

...go to www.sociology.uk.net

Topic summary

Examples from China and elsewhere show how government policies may affect family life.

Functionalists see social policies as supporting the family in performing its functions for the benefit of all its members.

Donzelot argues that state professionals exercise control and **surveillance**, intervening to regulate family life.

Social policies may work to undermine or support different kinds of family. The **New Right** argue that over-generous **welfare benefits** to unmarried mothers encourage a **dependency culture**.

Feminists disagree, arguing that government policies **legitimate** the heterosexual **patriarchal nuclear family** and make other family types seem less valid.

Countries with **individualistic gender regimes** follow policies promoting women's equality. **Familistic** regimes perpetuate women's patriarchal dependence.

EXAMINING FAMILIES AND SOCIAL POLICY

QuickCheck Questions

Check your answers at www.sociology.uk.net

1 Give one example of how the state may control family life.
2 What is meant by 'perverse incentives' in relation to social policies?
3 Give two examples of New Right policies introduced by governments.
4 Name two New Labour policies that did not reflect a New Right view of the family.

5 Why do feminists argue that family policies may create a self-fulfilling prophecy?
6 Why do feminists favour an individualistic rather than a familistic gender regime?
7 What is meant by neoliberal welfare policies?

Questions to try

Whether or not you are taking the AS exams during your A level course, answering the AS questions below is a very good way of testing your knowledge and understanding and practising your skills in preparation for your A level exams.

Item A   According to feminist sociologists, the main function of laws and policies on families and households is to support the conventional heterosexual nuclear family and reproduce patriarchy. For example, policies concerning the care of children or the old often make the assumption that these are women's responsibility. Even policies seemingly designed to benefit women, such as paying child benefit to the mother, may have the effect of reinforcing their gender role.

By contrast, New Right thinkers argue that many policies offer 'perverse incentives' that actually undermine rather than support the conventional family.

AS questions

1 Define the term 'gender regime' in relation to social policies on the family. (2 marks)
2 Using one example, explain how functionalists see the role of social policies. (2 marks)
3 Outline three social policies or laws that may affect household or family size. (6 marks)

AS and A level questions

4 Outline and explain two social policies or laws that have affected the position of children in the family. (10 marks)
5 Applying material from Item A and your knowledge, evaluate the view that the main function of laws and policies on families and households is to reproduce patriarchy. (20 marks)

The Examiner's Advice

Q4 Spend about 15 minutes on this question. Divide your time fairly equally between the two policies or laws. You don't need a separate introduction; just start on your first policy. Possible policies include China's one child policy, child benefit, child protection, compulsory schooling, age restrictions (for sex, marriage, working etc). Describe each policy in some detail. Explain how each has affected the position of children in the family – avoid simply describing how it affects their position in society generally. Do this by creating a chain of reasoning (see page 248). For example, child labour legislation effectively keeps children out of the labour market. This means they have little or no independent source of income and this reinforces parental power and children remain economically dependent, unlike in pre-industrial society. Use concepts and issues such as social construction of childhood, cross-cultural and historical comparisons, age patriarchy, and industrialisation. You may find it useful to re-visit Topic 2 for this question.

Q5 Spend about 30 minutes on this question. You could use Item A as your starting point to consider New Right and feminist perspectives. Use key concepts from the item, e.g. patriarchy, gender role and perverse incentives. Add other concepts such as structured dependency, self-fulfilling prophecy, dependency culture, the underclass, gender regimes etc into your account of these perspectives. You should refer to a range of policies, including those that seem to support the conventional nuclear family and those that may undermine it. These could include policies on childcare, care of the sick and elderly, housing, taxes and benefits, maternity and paternity leave, gay marriage, outlawing of rape within marriage etc. You can evaluate the view by creating a debate between the New Right and feminism. You could also apply cross-cultural examples and policies in other areas (e.g. equal pay) that may affect gender roles or relationships in the family. You can also evaluate by suggesting other views of the main function of policy, e.g. from Donzelot or Fletcher.

CHAPTER 4

EXAMINING FAMILIES AND HOUSEHOLDS

AS questions

Item A   There have been important changes in the position of men and women in couple roles and relationships in the last 50 years or so. For example, it is now the norm for married women to take paid work, although often this is part-time rather than full-time. There are also signs of a 'new man' who is more involved in housework and childcare. However, feminists argue that such changes have done little to change the family from a patriarchal institution based on male power and female subordination.

1   Define the term 'dependency ratio'. (2 marks)
2   Using one example, explain how social policies may encourage family diversity. (2 marks)
3   Outline three reasons for the increase in the divorce rate in the last 50 years or so. (6 marks)
4   Outline and explain two functions that functionalist sociologists see the family as performing. (10 marks)
5   Applying material from Item A and your knowledge, evaluate the view that the family today remains a patriarchal institution. (20 marks)

A level questions

Item A   There have been significant changes in family patterns in the last few decades. These include changes in attitudes towards many aspects of family life. At the same time, there have been changes in wider society affecting men and women, for example in the labour market, education and laws relating to the family. Some sociologists argue that relationships have become more unstable as a result of all these changes.

Item B   In the view of Marxist sociologists, all of society's institutions contribute to maintaining the capitalist system. These institutions include the family, which Marxists see as performing important functions for capitalism. For example, its role in socialising the young helps to ensure that capitalism is provided with the next generation of docile workers.

However, critics argue that the Marxist view of the family ignores issues such as family diversity as well as inequalities within the family.

1   Outline and explain two ways in which laws and policies may affect roles and/or relationships in the family. (10 marks)
2   Applying material from Item A, analyse two reasons for changing patterns of marriage in recent decades. (10 marks)
3   Applying material from Item B and your knowledge, evaluate the usefulness of the work of Marxist sociologists for the study of families and households today. (20 marks)

The examiner's advice for AS questions 4 and 5, and for A level questions 1 and 2, is on page 257.

For A level question 3, see the answer on the next page along with the examiner's comments and mark.

Answer by Anna

A level question 3: Applying material from Item B and your knowledge, evaluate the usefulness of the work of Marxist sociologists for the study of families and households today.

Marxists have made an important contribution to the way we understand family life. They recognise that the family has been romanticised by functionalists as meeting all its members' needs. Instead, as Item B says, Marxists see it as an institution that upholds the capitalist system by performing vital functions. Their basic idea is that the family benefits capitalism rather than its own members.

> A good opening that applies Item B to explain the key idea in the Marxist view. Plus brief evaluation of functionalism.

Marxists argue that it does so in three major ways. Firstly it socialises the next generation of passive, docile workers, as Item B says. From an early age, we are taught to obey the authority of our parents, so it becomes ingrained in us that there is always someone above us and that unequal power is natural. This serves capitalism well because it accustoms us to obeying orders from our employers so they can exploit us. However, this could be criticised because not all children (or workers) are obedient.

> Good knowledge of the first Marxist contribution, making use of Item, plus brief evaluation.

The second contribution of Marxism is to see how important the family is for passing on property. The difference between the working class and capitalists is that the capitalists are property owners, so the family is a way of passing property down the generations to keep it within the ruling class. This means men must know who their heirs are in order to hand on their wealth to them and this is what the monogamous family provides. However, this assumes men can know for sure that they are the fathers of their wives' children, which before DNA testing was impossible.

> Again, relevant knowledge and some limited evaluation.

A last contribution is that workers spend most of their wages on providing for their families. Selling food and other consumer goods to families provides a big market for capitalists in which to make profit. A lot of advertising is targeted on 'family' spending, e.g. on family leisure activities, nice comfortable 'family homes' etc. Some advertising targets children, who then use pester power to get parents to spend their money. However, this seems to contradict the Marxist idea of well socialised children dutifully obeying their parents.

> A further function for capitalism, plus good evaluation point about children to indicate a contradiction in the Marxist view.

But Marxists don't offer a complete picture of family life. It seems very negative and deterministic. Would people stay in families if it only served the needs of capitalism and not their own needs? Functionalists would argue that it not only meets society's needs, but also the needs of mothers, fathers and children. Also, as Item B says, Marxism ignores family diversity and assumes everyone still lives in a heterosexual nuclear family, which seems old fashioned. Feminists have also criticised Marxism for ignoring gender inequalities (Item B), although Marxist feminists have tried to combine the two approaches. Overall, therefore, Marxism makes a useful contribution to understanding family life, but an incomplete one.

> A lot of good evaluative points here that could do with separating out and discussing fully. Could say more, especially about Marxist feminists.

> You should spend about 30 minutes on this. Anna's answer shows a well organised knowledge of the Marxist view of the family and its functions for capitalism, which she analyses successfully, and she makes brief but explicit evaluation points as she goes along. However, her answer would benefit from a few more Marxist concepts, such as exploitation, oppression etc.
>
> A strength of her answer is that it keeps a good focus on Marxism rather than giving equal weight to all the different perspectives on the family. However, she goes a little too far in this direction: her final paragraph is interesting because it raises several very important issues (determinism, diversity, gender inequality), any one of which would have benefited from a paragraph to itself. For example, a discussion of Marxist feminism would have been very useful and would have allowed for some analysis of the similarities and differences between Marxism and feminism. Equally, she could have developed a contrast with functionalism or other approaches.

17/20

CHAPTER 5

Preparing for the Exams

GETTING STARTED

Here are some things to help you prepare for your exams.

1. Make a list of the Topics in Chapters 2, 3 and 4. This will give you a framework for your revision.

2. Organise your class notes, activities and homework assignments for each Topic. Use the subheadings in each Topic as a guide to how you can organise your notes etc. You might want to work with a partner or in a small group and share your work or fill in any gaps you may have together.

3. In preparing to tackle the exams, make a list of the main issues covered in each Topic and the debates about them, e.g. the issue of the domestic division of labour and the debate about whether men are now doing a more equal share of it. Using these issues and debates, go to your notes and textbook to find the material you need in order to understand them.

4. From your notes and textbook, make a list of the key concepts needed for each Topic. Link these to the debates and issues.

5. To familiarise yourself with some possible exam questions for each Topic, look at the questions at the end of each Topic and each chapter, and at the practice papers in this chapter.

For further revision help and advice, see our revision guide, 'Succeed at A level Sociology – Book One', at www.sociology.uk.net

This chapter focuses on the examinations. It deals with:

- The knowledge and skills you have to show in your AS and A level exams
- The format of the exam papers
- The different types of question and how to tackle them.

The assessment objectives

In the AS and A level sociology exams, your answers are assessed in terms of three aims or 'assessment objectives', or AOs for short. These are:

AO1 Knowledge and Understanding

AO2 the skill of Application

AO3 the skills of Analysis and Evaluation.

Roughly 45% of the marks are for AO1 and the remaining 55% or so are for AO2 and AO3, so it's very important that you show evidence of all of the assessment objectives in your answers. Let's take a closer look at the kind of knowledge, understanding and skills you need to demonstrate in your answers.

Knowledge and Understanding

You need to know about and understand some of the main theories, research methods and concepts (ideas) that sociologists use in their work.

You also need to be familiar with some of the studies they have carried out and what these studies have found.

Application

The skill of Application includes:

- Linking ideas, concepts, theories, studies and methods to each other and to the question.
- Showing how the material you have selected is relevant to the question. In questions on methods in context, connecting the strengths and limitations of a method to the characteristics of a particular research issue.
- Using material from an Item when the question tells you to, linking it to your own knowledge and to the question.
- Using relevant examples. These could be from studies, news and current events, personal experience, other topics you have studied in sociology etc.
- Linking ideas from one area in sociology to material in another area.

Analysis

The skill of Analysis includes:

- Breaking down an argument or explanation into the ideas that make it up and showing how they fit together.
- Comparing and contrasting ideas to show their similarities and differences.
- Organising your essays with a well focused introduction and a clear, logical chain of reasoning from paragraph to paragraph, leading to an appropriate conclusion.

Evaluation

Evaluation is about weighing things up, giving informed opinions or making balanced judgments about something. The 'something' could be different evidence, ideas, views, theories or methods.

The skill of Evaluation includes:

- Looking at the arguments and evidence for and against a particular view.
- Examining a theory's assumptions or linking it to a particular perspective.

- Putting forward alternative views or perspectives to create a debate.
- Discussing the strengths (or advantages) and limitations (or disadvantages) of a research method.

In practice, the different assessment objectives are often interlinked. For example, in order to apply the right information (AO2), you first need to know and understand some sociology (AO1).

The assessment objectives are the same for both AS and A level. However, the AS and A level exams each have their own distinctive features, which we will now examine. We start with the AS exams and then go on to look at the A level exams.

Preparing for the AS exams

For AS level Sociology, you will take two written exam papers.

Each paper is one hour 30 minutes long and is worth 60 marks – so that's one and a half minutes per mark.

Each paper is worth half the overall marks for your AS level.

AS Paper 1

There are six questions and you must answer all of them:

- The first five questions are on Education, worth a total of 40 marks.
- The sixth question is on Methods in Context (Education), worth 20 marks.

Questions 01, 02 and 03 are short questions on Education worth a total of 10 marks.

Question 04 is a longer question on Education worth 10 marks.

Question 05 is a 20-mark essay question on Education. It is accompanied by Item A, which contains stimulus material for you to apply in your answer.

Question 06 is the Methods in Context question. It is accompanied by Item B, which contains stimulus material for you to apply in your answer.

Before reading on, turn to page 252 and take a look at the practice paper for AS Paper 1. Focus on the overall structure of the paper rather than trying to figure out the answers to the questions, and check the paper against the points above.

AS Paper 2

There are two sections to this paper: Section A and Section B.

Section A is on Research Methods and is worth 20 marks.

Section B is divided into four optional topics: B1 Culture and Identity, B2 Families and Households, B3 Health, and B4 Work, Poverty and Welfare. Each option is worth 40 marks.

Now look at the practice paper for AS Paper 2 on page 253. Focus again on its overall structure and check it against the points above. You will see that in Section B we have only included the questions on Families and Households, since that is the topic you will choose if you have been using this book.

You should also note that in the real exam paper, the subsection on Families and Households is the second subsection in Section B (after Culture and Identity), not the first. Don't make the mistake of diving in and starting to answer questions in the wrong subsection!

Section A has two compulsory research methods questions:

- One short question worth 4 marks.
- One essay question worth 16 marks.

Your chosen optional topic in Section B (Families and Households) has five compulsory questions:

- Three short questions worth a total of 10 marks.
- One longer question worth 10 marks.
- One essay question worth 20 marks. This is accompanied by an Item containing stimulus material for you to apply in your answer.

Further details of the different types of question in the AS papers are given below, along with advice on how to tackle them.

How long to spend on each question

Now that you've got an idea of the overall structure of the AS papers, you need to be aware of how much time to spend on each question. Luckily, there's a simple rule you can apply to give you an idea of how much time to invest in each answer, which is this:

Take the number of marks the question is worth and multiply it by one and a half. This will give you the number of minutes you should spend on it.

For example, if the question is worth 10 marks, you should spend about 15 minutes answering it. If it's worth 20 marks, spend about 30 minutes on it.

However, in practice, you might be able to answer the short questions (ones worth less than 10 marks) a bit more quickly. This will give you a few extra minutes for the 10 and 20 mark questions, where you need to do a little more thinking, planning and studying the stimulus Item.

Answering the short questions

The short questions carry two, four or six marks. Across the two AS papers they are worth 20% of the total marks. It's by no means impossible to get all of these marks and if you do, this could get you halfway to a pass even before you tackle the longer questions. But it's very important not to spend too much time writing long answers to them – you're not expected or required to do so. And as well as wasting time, long answers are often less clear and may end up scoring lower marks.

Two-mark questions

These occur on both papers. There are two kinds of two-mark questions. The first kind asks you to define a term or concept. For example:

Define the term 'meritocracy'.

points to remember

- To get both the marks, you must give a clear definition or explanation of the term. Simply giving an example might get you one mark, but it's not enough for both marks.
- Avoid repeating the word or phrase that you're being asked about in your definition – e.g. simply writing, 'Meritocracy is a system of rewards based on merit' doesn't show the examiner that you really know the meaning of the term. Put it in different words to make it clear.
- Your definition should be a whole sentence, though it doesn't need to be a long one.

The second kind of two-mark question takes the following form: Using one example, briefly explain… For example:

Using one example, briefly explain how pupils' cultural background may affect their level of educational achievement.

points to remember

- Give an example of the idea or concept in the question (e.g. the concept of cultural background) and explain how it affects or leads to the outcome stated in the question (e.g. educational achievement). For instance,

you could say, 'Middle-class parents value education highly, so they make great efforts to enable their children to succeed, e.g. by helping with homework'.

- If you only give an example of the term or concept without an explanation, you may get one mark but not both.
- Your answer should not be more than one or two sentences long.

Four-mark and six-mark questions

These questions ask you to outline two things (for 4 marks) or three things (for 6 marks). These could be things such as factors, features, reasons, causes, effects, functions, ways, problems, advantages, disadvantages, criticisms or other issues. For example:

Outline two advantages of using group interviews in sociological research.

Outline three ways in which the ethnocentric curriculum may operate in schools.

There is a six-mark 'Outline' question on both Education (Paper 1) and Families and Households (Paper 2). There is a four-mark 'Outline' question on Research Methods (Paper 2).

points to remember

- Your answers should be quite short: for each advantage, way, reason etc that you are asked to provide, one or two sentences will be enough. For example, you could write, 'The ethnocentric curriculum operates through only teaching European languages and not offering languages spoken by pupils from minority ethnic backgrounds, such as Urdu or Bengali.'
- Start each point on a separate line.
- If you're not sure whether all your points are right but you can think of an extra one, you can put this one down too. But remember, the more points you give, the more time you use up.

Answering the longer questions

On the AS papers, there are four types of longer question:

- **10-mark questions** on Education and on Families and Households. These require you to 'Outline and explain two' factors, features, reasons, causes, effects, functions, ways, problems, advantages, disadvantages, criticisms or other issues.
- **16-mark questions** on Research Methods. These require you to evaluate a method or related issue (such as ethical, practical or theoretical issues in choice of research method).
- **20-mark questions** on Education and Families and Households.
- **20-mark questions** on Methods in Context (Education).

We shall now look at what each of these involves.

The 10-mark 'Outline and explain' questions

These require you to outline and explain two factors, features, reasons, causes, effects, functions, ways, problems, advantages, disadvantages, criticisms or other issues in Education and in Families and Households. For example:

*Outline and explain **two** forms of pupil response to teacher racism and negative labelling.*

*Outline and explain **two** reasons for increases in family diversity.*

The instruction to explain rather than just outline (as in the short questions) means you need to show your knowledge and understanding by going into each reason, factor etc, in some detail. You should do this by creating a chain of reasoning to link your ideas into a clear explanation. See Box 35 for more about chains of reasoning.

The 16- and 20-mark questions

These are essay questions that require you to evaluate something.

The 16-mark questions ask you to evaluate a research method or related issue. For example:

Evaluate the limitations of using participant observation when conducting sociological research.

For these questions, you need to show knowledge and understanding of the different research methods, including the factors that affect sociologists' choice of methods and topics. You need to show the AO2 skill of Application by using your knowledge in ways relevant to the question, as well as the AO3 skills of Analysis and Evaluation, for example through a discussion of the strengths and limitations of different methods. Look back at page 245 to remind yourself of ways in which you can show AO2 and AO3 skills in your answers.

The 20-mark questions on Education and on Families and Households also ask you to evaluate something, such as an explanation or a view. For example:

Applying material from Item A and your knowledge, evaluate the view that social class differences in educational achievement are the result of factors outside schools.

In these questions, as well as showing knowledge and understanding of relevant sociological theories, concepts and studies, you need to show the AO2 skill of Application and the AO3 skills of Analysis and Evaluation. Again, look back at page 245 to remind yourself of how you can show these skills. You will also find it very useful to study Box 36 *Using the Items*, because these questions require you to apply material from the Item.

See also 'Points to remember for essay questions' below for further advice on answering 16- and 20-mark questions.

The 20-mark Methods in Context questions

Both AS and A level exams have a Methods in Context question. In both cases the context of the questions is a particular issue in Education. Both questions are accompanied by an Item containing stimulus material for you to apply in your answer. Both AS and A level questions always have the same format as the following example:

Applying material from Item B and your knowledge, evaluate the strengths and limitations of using questionnaires to investigate parental attitudes to education.

The questions always ask you about *one* research method and how it applies to *one* particular issue in education.

The research method could be any one of those named in the specification: questionnaires, interviews, participant and non-participant observation, experiments, documents

Box 35	The chain of reasoning

A chain of reasoning is a series of steps in an explanation, where each idea is like a link that connects to the one before it, leading eventually to a reasoned conclusion. For example, in a question on gender differences in subject choice, you could take the idea that science is in the male gender domain, link it to how this idea is projected (through textbooks, role models etc), then link this to its effect in putting girls off science.

Often, you can add further links, so your conclusion itself becomes part of a longer chain of reasoning and a more developed conclusion.

Building chains of reasoning is important in both AS and A level, because it shows the examiner you can put together sociological arguments to reach conclusions. This means chains of reasoning are essential to every question where you have to write more than a sentence or two. That is, any question worth 10 marks or more.

When you answer these questions, write in full sentences organised into paragraphs. A basic chain of reasoning could be put in a single paragraph, while a more extended chain could run for two or more paragraphs, depending on the point you are developing and the time you have available to answer the question.

Your ideas for chains of reasoning will come from your own knowledge, but in questions with an Item, always study the Item for possible points to include in your chains of reasoning. At A level, there is also a special case where you *must* use points from the Item. These are the questions that begin 'Applying material from the Item, analyse two...' For these, your chains of reasoning must draw directly from the Item. As you have to analyse two things, you need to create a separate chain for each. Each one should therefore incorporate a point from the Item. This point doesn't need to start your chain, but it must appear somewhere within it.

and official statistics. This includes any variants of these methods, such as structured, unstructured and group interviews, overt and covert observation, and postal questionnaires.

The particular issue could be any topic in education that sociologists might be interested in studying, such as labelling in schools or parental attitudes to education, for example.

What you need to know

To answer Methods in Context questions, you need to know two main sorts of things.

The methods You need to know all the research methods that you will find in Chapter 3. For each method, make sure you know its key features, along with all its practical, ethical and theoretical strengths and limitations.

The research characteristics of the main groups and areas of education that sociologists study: pupils, teachers, classrooms, schools and parents. By research characteristics, we mean the main features that a sociologist would have to take into account when choosing a method of studying them. For example, teachers are busy professionals who may not have time for long unstructured interviews; some pupils may not have the literacy skills needed to fill in a questionnaire and so on. For a full account of research characteristics, see Chapter 3, Topic 2 *Education: the research context.*

You should also study the *Investigating* boxes found in every Topic in Chapter 2, because these contain many examples of the research characteristics of particular issues in education, such as racism in schools, gender and subject choice, teachers' expectations of pupils, and anti-school subcultures.

What you need to do

Although you need to know about research characteristics and about the different research methods, answering Methods in Context questions successfully is not just about knowledge.

Above all, you must **apply** your knowledge of research methods to the study of the educational issue that the question asks you about. You will find it useful to study the examples of Methods in Context questions and examiner's advice at the end of Chapter 3, Topics 2 to 7, as well as the practice questions on pages 252 and 254.

In applying your knowledge of the method, be as specific as you can to the issue in the question. For example, in the question above about using questionnaires to study parental attitudes to education, you might say that this is a problematic method because parents are often too busy to fill in questionnaires. This shows some application, because the fact that parents are often busy is one of their obvious

Box 36	Using the Items

For both AS and A level, many questions require you to apply material from the Item. Items are an important source of help, so read them through carefully at least twice, and keep checking back to the question. Highlight any words that seem important. Think how you can connect your own knowledge to points in the Item, such as:

- Criticisms of a view in the Item, or alternative views to those in the Item.
- Examples from studies, statistics, facts etc that support or contradict ideas in the Item.
- Any relevant concepts that link to points in the Item.
- Explanations or definitions of key ideas in the Item.

You will be rewarded for applying material from the Item – so draw the examiner's attention to the fact that you have done so by using a phrase like, 'as Item A says'. You can quote from the Item or put it in your own words, but you must always build on it by linking it to the question and your own knowledge. Don't just copy it out or paraphrase it.

Below is an example of how you might use an Item for a 20- or 30-mark question. We have highlighted key words you could use in answering the question and suggested how you could link them to other material and the question. Always look for ways to link the Item to what you know and to the question.

Item A

According to some sociologists, children in today's supposedly child-centred society lead lives that are segregated and controlled,

but childhood was not always like this. Ariès describes a medieval world where there was little distinction between children and adults in either work or leisure. According to this view, industrial society brought major changes. Children's lives became increasingly confined and regulated by adults.

Not all sociologists share this view. Some argue that the distinction between childhood and adulthood is again becoming blurred.

Essay Applying material from Item A and your knowledge, evaluate sociological explanations of changes in the status of childhood. (20 marks)

Here are some ways you could use the Item to stimulate your thinking and make links to other material and the question:

- What does child-centred society mean? Why and how are we child-centred?
- Explain why Ariès argues that the medieval world made little distinction between children and adults.
- In what ways might industrial society have changed children's position? Link to the 'march of progress' view.
- Give examples of how children are confined and regulated. E.g. how do adults control children's time, space and bodies? Link to age patriarchy and the child liberationist view and discuss these.
- Not all... share this view... blurred. Examine contrasting views, e.g. Postman's claim that childhood is disappearing.

research characteristics. But your application of the method would be more specific to the issue in the question (parental attitudes) if you said for example that some parents have little interest in their children's education and so they see no point in completing the questionnaire.

You should try to draw conclusions about the usefulness of the method for studying the particular educational issue in the question. Do so as you go along, rather than leaving it until the end of your answer.

You should make good use of the material in the Item. This will give you clues both on some of the method's strengths and limitations, and on some of the research characteristics of the issue.

Preparing for the A level exams

As you are only halfway through the A level course, we would not expect you to have reached the same standard that you will have achieved by the end of your second year. For example, by the end of your course, you will know a lot more sociology from having studied other topics such as Beliefs in Society and Crime and Deviance, and you will find this gives you a broader and deeper understanding of the topics you have *already* studied in your first year.

Likewise, in your second year you will study Theory and Methods, which will give you new insights into what you have already learned from studying Research Methods in your first year. This means that, when you come to answer questions about research methods at A level, your answers will be strengthened by your new knowledge of sociological theory.

The practice papers

As you will see on pages 252–5, this chapter includes the following papers designed to give you practice:

- Papers covering the whole of the AS level course.
- Papers covering those parts of the A level course that you have already completed in your first year of study.

The companion to this book, 'AQA A level Sociology Book Two' covers the remaining A level topics of Beliefs in Society, Crime and Deviance, and Theory and Methods.

Use the AS papers for A level practice

Whether or not you are taking the AS exams midway through your A level course, it's still a good idea to attempt the AS level practice papers (and also the AS questions at the end of the different topics and chapters throughout this book) for several reasons:

- Most of the AS question types are the same as at A level, so you can use them to practise answering the kind of questions you will find at A level.
- The material you will need to answer questions on Education, Methods in Context and Families and Households is the same for both AS and A level. You will also need all the material you studied for Research Methods (an AS topic) to help you answer A level Theory and Methods questions.

- The AS level standard is the level we would expect you to have reached by the end of the first year of your A level course. This means that the AS practice papers are at the right level for you at this stage and are a good way of assessing your progress halfway through your A level course.

The A level exam papers

For A level, you will take three written exam papers.

Each paper is two hours long and is worth 80 marks – so that's one and a half minutes per mark, the same as for AS.

Each paper is worth one-third of the total marks for your A level.

A level Paper 1

There are six questions and you must answer all of them. Questions 01 to 04 are on Education, worth a total of 50 marks.

Questions 01 and 02 are short questions worth a total of 10 marks (four plus six).

Question 03 is worth 10 marks. This question type only appears at A level, not at AS. It comes with an Item containing material for you to apply in your answer. The question begins: 'Applying material from Item A, analyse two'. This could be two reasons, effects, factors, changes etc. Here is an example:

> *Applying material from Item A, analyse **two** factors outside schools that contribute to working-class underachievement.*

For these questions, you must find two points in the Item and use them in your answer by building them into chains of reasoning. (See Box 35.)

Question 04 is a 30-mark essay question on Education. It is accompanied by Item B, which contains material for you to apply in your answer. Here is an example:

*Applying material from **Item B** and your knowledge, evaluate the view that although Marxist and functionalist approaches focus on similar issues, they reach very different conclusions about the role of education.*

Although this question takes the same form as the 20-mark essays at AS (see above), it is worth more marks so you should spend longer on it. Your answer should show more breadth and depth of knowledge and you should develop your evaluation points more fully.

Question 05 is a Methods in Context (Education) question worth 20 marks. It is accompanied by Item C, which contains stimulus material for you to apply. This takes exactly the same form as the AS Methods in Context question. See above for details of how to tackle Methods in Context questions at both AS and A level.

Question 06 is on Theory and Methods and is worth 10 marks. This takes the same form as the 10-mark questions at AS. Here is an example:

*Outline and explain **two** reasons why some sociologists choose to use official statistics in their research.*

The instruction to explain means you need to show your knowledge and understanding by going into each reason, factor, effect etc, in some detail. Do this by creating a chain of reasoning to link your ideas into a clear explanation. (See Box 35.)

A level Paper 2

This paper has two sections: A and B. Each section has four optional topics in it and you must choose one from each section. Each option is worth 40 marks.

Section A options are A1 Culture and Identity, A2 Families and Households, A3 Health, and A4 Work, Poverty and Welfare. (These are the same as the options on AS level Paper 2.)

Section B options are B1 Beliefs in Society, B2 Global Development, B3 The Media, and B4 Stratification and Differentiation.

If you have used this book in your first year course, you will have studied Families and Households as your Section A option. (In your second year, you will study Beliefs in Society as your Section B option. You will find a mock exam covering that topic in Book Two.)

The Families and Households option has three compulsory questions:

A 10-mark question asking you to 'Outline and explain two' things. This is just like the 10-mark AS questions described above. Here is an example:

*Outline and explain **two** causes of increased diversity of family structures in the last 50 years.*

A 10-mark question like Question 03 on Paper 1 (see above). This question is accompanied by an Item. Here is an example:

*Applying material from Item A, analyse **two** changes in the status of childhood since the 19th century.*

For these questions, you must find two points in the Item and use them in your answer by building them into chains of reasoning. (See Box 35.)

A 20-mark essay question accompanied by an Item containing stimulus material for you to apply in your answer. Here is an example:

*Applying material from **Item B** and your knowledge, evaluate the contribution of feminist sociologists to our understanding of families and households today.*

For this question, as well as showing knowledge and understanding of relevant sociological theories, concepts and studies, you need to show the AO2 skill of Application and the AO3 skills of Analysis and Evaluation. You will also find it useful to study Box 36 *Using the Items*, because you have to apply material from the Item.

A level Paper 3

This paper covers Crime and Deviance, and Theory and Methods. It has four questions on Crime and Deviance, worth four, six, 10 and 30 marks, and two questions on Theory and Methods, worth 10 and 20 marks.

The A level Paper 3 topics are covered in Book Two.

Points to remember for essay questions

When answering AS or A level questions worth more than 10 marks, you should follow this advice:

- Read the question carefully until you understand it; then make a brief plan.
- Write a short introduction linking to key aspects of the question.
- Stick to the question. Don't write 'Everything I know about the family (or education, or methods)' answers.
- Discuss a range of concepts, explanations, theories, perspectives and/or methods, depending on the question. Use evidence from sociological studies.
- Use the Items when instructed to do so, and use examples.
- Write a brief separate conclusion that follows logically from the main points in your essay.
- Focus on showing the skills of Application, Analysis and Evaluation, rather than just description.

AS level practice papers

AS Paper 1 Education with Methods in Context

Answer all questions.
Time allowed: 1 hour 30 minutes

Item A

Since the late 1980s, the educational performance of both girls and boys has risen, but girls' improvement has been greater. Some sociologists argue that these gender differences in achievement are primarily the result of factors outside the school. Changes in the family and in wider society, especially in employment, may have caused girls to outperform boys.

Other sociologists disagree, claiming that schools play a more important part in creating gender differences in achievement.

Item B

Investigating teacher-pupil interactions

Most teaching and learning involves teacher-pupil interactions, mainly in the classroom and other learning contexts. Messages about pupils' abilities and attitudes are transmitted through such interactions and these often reflect differences in power between teachers and pupils. Many factors affect this interaction, including age, class, gender and ethnicity, and sociologists are interested in investigating the impact of each.

Sociologists may use covert participant observation to investigate teacher-pupil interactions. This can be very effective because the researcher is seeing what people actually do, rather than what they say they do. However, the mere presence of the researcher may itself affect teacher-pupil interaction. Maintaining one's covert role can also be difficult in a school setting.

Education

1 Define the term 'deferred gratification'. (2 marks)

2 Using **one** example, briefly explain how material deprivation may lead to underachievement. (2 marks)

3 Outline **three** policies that have created an education market in the United Kingdom. (6 marks)

4 Outline and explain **two** roles that functionalists see education as fulfilling for society. (10 marks)

5 Applying material from **Item A** and your knowledge, evaluate the view that gender differences in educational achievement are primarily the result of factors outside the school. (20 marks)

Methods in Context

6 Applying material from **Item B** and your knowledge of research methods, evaluate the strengths and limitations of covert participant observation for studying teacher-pupil interactions. (20 marks)

The examiner's advice can be found at the end of this chapter.

AS Paper 2 Research Methods with Families and Households

Answer all questions.
Time allowed: 1 hour 30 minutes

> Item A   Feminist sociologists see society as patriarchal and they see the family as a key social institution that plays a central role in reproducing patriarchy. For example, it subordinates women to men's power and maintains an unequal gender division of labour both in the home and in wider society. However, there are disagreements among feminists both about the underlying cause of women's oppression and exploitation, and about how this can be ended.

Research Methods

1 Outline **two** problems of using longitudinal studies.   (4 marks)
2 Evaluate the reasons why some sociologists choose to use official statistics when conducting their research.   (16 marks)

Families and Households

3 Define the term 'instrumental role'.   (2 marks)
4 Using **one** example, briefly explain how social policies may encourage family diversity.   (2 marks)
5 Outline **three** reasons why lone-parent families are usually headed by the mother.   (6 marks)
6 Outline and explain **two** reasons for the increase in the divorce rate since the 1960s.   (10 marks)
7 Applying material from **Item A** and your knowledge, evaluate the contributions of feminist sociologists to our understanding of families and households.   (20 marks)

> The examiner's advice can be found at the end of this chapter.

A level practice papers

The papers below test those parts of the two-year A level course that you should have completed by the end of year one. The timings of the papers reflect this.

A level Paper 1 Education with Methods in Context

Answer all questions.
Time allowed: 1 hour 45 minutes

Item A

Some teachers attach negative labels to pupils from certain ethnic backgrounds. These can reflect teachers' stereotypical views and may lead them to treat pupils differently. Sociologists have investigated the different ways in which pupils respond to these labels. For example, some responses involve pupils seeking to manage the contradictory demands of school and peer groups. Other responses are based on trying to avoid racism.

Item B

For Marxist sociologists, capitalism needs a workforce that is readily exploitable and willing to take low-paid working-class jobs. In their view, it is a key function of the education system to persuade the working class to accept their subordinate position. Some Marxists argue that working-class pupils passively accept ideologies such as the myth of meritocracy. However, others argue that the process also involves resistance to school and its ideology.

Item C

Investigating pupil anti-school subcultures

Some pupils, particularly those placed in lower streams, develop an anti-school subculture as an alternative way of gaining status among their peers. Pupils with anti-school attitudes are more likely to truant and be uncooperative with those in authority.

Sociologists may use unstructured interviews to investigate pupil anti-school subcultures. This method allows the researchers to establish rapport and gain the trust of the pupils. The presence of an interviewer can also be helpful in terms of prompting responses. However, the results from this method are often unrepresentative and difficult to quantify.

Education

1. Outline **two** reasons why boys and girls may opt to study different subjects when given the choice. (4 marks)
2. Outline **three** reasons why parents of working-class pupils may be less likely than parents of middle-class pupils to attend events at their children's school. (6 marks)
3. Applying material from **Item A**, analyse **two** responses by pupils from minority ethnic backgrounds to negative labelling by teachers. (10 marks)
4. Applying material from **Item B** and your knowledge, evaluate Marxist views of the role of the education system. (30 marks)

Methods in Context

5. Applying material from **Item C** and your knowledge of research methods, evaluate the strengths and limitations of unstructured interviews for studying pupil anti-school subcultures. (20 marks)

The examiner's advice can be found at the end of this chapter.

A level Paper 2 Families and Households

Answer all questions.
Time allowed: 1 hour

Item A

As a result of globalisation, more people now move across national boundaries, and they are more likely to move back and forth more often. Today's migrants are likely to differ both from the population of the society they leave and the society to which they migrate. Increased migration is also likely to have effects on both the country from which migrants come and the one to which they go.

Item B

Some sociologists and others argue that couple relationships in society today are increasingly unstable. For example, New Right commentators claim that today's high rates of cohabitation and divorce and low rate of first marriages indicate a lack of commitment on the part of many couples. From a different perspective, Giddens suggests that relationships in which individuals stay together only so long as it serves their self-interest are becoming the norm. Several sociologists point to women's increased independence as a destabilising factor.

---

1 Outline and explain **two** reasons why the position of children in the United Kingdom may be changing.   (10 marks)
2 Applying material from **Item A**, analyse **two** effects of patterns of migration since 2000.   (10 marks)
3 Applying material from **Item B** and your knowledge, evaluate sociological arguments and evidence for the view that couple relationships in society today are increasingly unstable.   (20 marks)

A level Paper 3 Theory and Methods

Answer both questions.
Time allowed: 45 minutes

> The examiner's advice can be found at the end of this chapter.

Item A

All research methods can be judged in terms of how far they produce valid, reliable and representative data. For example, some sociologists claim that what participant observation gains in validity, it loses in reliability and representativeness. While it may offer insight, it can only be used to study small groups and it is hard for others to check the findings. Some critics go further, arguing that participant observation may not even produce valid data.

---

1 Outline and explain two ethical problems that sociologists may experience when conducting research.   (10 marks)
2 Applying material from Item A and your knowledge, evaluate the claim that what participant observation gains in validity, it loses in reliability and representativeness.   (20 marks)

> The examiner's advice can be found at the end of this chapter.

The Examiner's Advice

This section contains advice on how to tackle the AS and A level practice papers in this chapter and the *Examining* questions that you will find at the end of Chapters 2, 3 and 4.

Examining education

The following advice is for the *Examining* questions on education that you will find on page 86.

AS question 4

Spend about 15 minutes on this question. Divide your time fairly equally between each factor. You don't need a separate introduction; just start on your first factor. Possible factors include the impact of feminism, changes in family structure, legal changes, employment opportunities, girls' changed ambitions, globalisation and the decline of traditional men's jobs, and development of laddish subcultures.

Describe each factor in some detail, explaining how it leads to gender differences in achievement. Do this by creating a chain of reasoning (see page 248). For example, equal opportunities legislation has increased job opportunities for women, enabling some women to break through the 'glass ceiling'. This raises girls' ambitions and gives them role models, encouraging them to work harder. This in turn is likely to lead to better exam performance. Use concepts such as those above and studies such as McRobbie, Sharpe, Francis and Epstein.

AS question 5

Spend about 30 minutes on this question. Identify the social groups concerned – class, gender and ethnicity. Refer to all three of these in your answer. Distinguish between the different internal factors that affect achievement, including labelling, self-fulfilling prophecy, streaming, the curriculum, and pupil identities and subcultures. Explain how each may affect achievement.

Do this by creating a chain of reasoning (see page 248). For example, teacher labelling of pupils from a particular class can create a self-fulfilling prophecy in which pupils internalise the label and, if it is negative, lose self-esteem and work less hard, resulting in underachievement.

Use evidence from studies such as Becker, Gillborn and Youdell, Sewell, Fuller, Ball, Francis and Archer, and develop the points noted in Item A. Evaluate the importance of these factors, making criticisms of each factor as you go, rather than separately at the end. Identify the connections between external and internal factors. For example, racism in school may mirror racism in wider society.

A level question 3

Spend about 15 minutes on this question. Divide your time fairly equally between the two processes. You don't need a separate introduction; just start on your first process. It's essential to take two points from the Item and show through a chain of reasoning (see page 248) how each leads to ethnic differences in achievement. (It's a good idea to quote from the Item for each factor.)

You could use role of parents, how far education is valued by families and community, or disadvantage resulting from racism. For example, some ethnic groups value educational success and encourage their children to respect teachers and work hard. This encourages positive responses from teachers, creating a cycle of success.

Use concepts such as racism in wider society, cultural deprivation, material deprivation and family structure, and studies such as Gillborn and Youdell, Sewell, Mirza and Flaherty. Include some brief evaluation, e.g. some explanations seem to simply reflect stereotypical images of different ethnic groups.

Examining research methods

The following advice is for the *Examining* question on research methods that you will find on page 160.

AS question 2

Spend about 25 minutes on this question. Keep the focus on unstructured interviews; avoid drifting into structured interviews. The question requires you to evaluate the reasons why some sociologists use unstructured interviews, so your main focus should be on their strengths.

These include rapport, sensitivity, insight, depth, flexibility, interviewees being able to set the agenda, checking understanding, opening up new topic areas, reducing power inequalities between interviewer and interviewee and greater validity. Ethical strengths may come from the closer rapport with trust and confidentiality being established. Use concepts such as those above and examples of studies such as Labov and Dean and Taylor-Gooby. Explain why interpretivists and feminists tend to see unstructured interviews as having many advantages.

Evaluate these strengths as you go through each one rather than offer a list of limitations in a separate section at the end. For example, when discussing the flexibility of unstructured interviews, evaluate this by explaining that flexibility can result in lack of reliability.

Examining families and households

The following advice is for the *Examining* questions on families and households that you will find on page 242.

AS question 4

Spend about 15 minutes on this question. Divide your time fairly equally between the two functions. You don't need a separate introduction; just start on your first function. These could include reproduction, stable satisfaction of the sex drive, unit of production or consumption, primary socialisation, stabilisation of adult personalities etc.

Describe each function in some detail. Explain how each may benefit society and/or individual family members. Do this by creating a chain of reasoning (see page 248). For example, the nuclear family is a small, compact unit containing only one adult worker. This means it can be geographically mobile, which is important in meeting the needs of a modern economy where industry is constantly relocating.

Use concepts and issues such as value consensus, norms, social stability, social integration, social and geographical mobility, pre-industrial and industrial society etc.

AS question 5

Spend about 30 minutes on this question. You need to deal with a range of issues. These should include not just roles in the domestic division of labour (both housework and childcare) but also power relationships (including domestic violence, decision-making and control over resources).

Develop points from Item A, e.g. on the impact of women's paid work (both full- and part-time), as well as power. Use concepts and issues such as who takes responsibility for and who performs domestic tasks, whether tasks themselves are gendered, patriarchy, dual burden, triple shift, 'quality time', background fathers, same-sex couples and gender scripts.

Use evidence from studies such as Ansley, Boulton, Braun et al, Crompton and Lyonette, Dex and Ward, Dunne, Nyman, Smart, Southerton, Sullivan, Vogler etc. You need to evaluate the view, e.g. by examining how well the evidence on these issues fits different approaches (e.g. march of progress and feminist). Also consider material versus cultural explanations of the division of labour and power relationships.

A level question 1

Spend about 15 minutes on this question. Divide your time fairly equally between the two ways. You don't need a separate introduction; just start on your first way. These could include ways in which laws and policies affect the position of men, women, children, the elderly etc.

Describe each way in some detail. Explain how each may affect family roles and/or relationships. Do this by creating a chain of reasoning (see page 248). For example, the availability of retirement pensions for the elderly may make them economically independent. This also means that their adult children have greater disposable income because they do not have to support ageing parents.

Use concepts and issues such as patriarchy, age patriarchy, structured dependency, burden of dependency, retirement pensions, child benefit, childcare, compulsory schooling, maternity and paternity leave, domestic violence, divorce laws etc.

A level question 2

Spend about 15 minutes on this question. Divide your time fairly equally between the two reasons. You don't need a separate introduction; just start on your first reason. These could include less stigma about being single, women's changing position, increased divorce, growing individualism etc.

To answer this question, it's essential that you take two points from the Item and show through a chain of reasoning (see page 248) how each reason explains a pattern. (It is a very good idea to quote from the Item when doing so.) You could use changes in attitudes, in education, in the labour market, in laws etc. For example, changed attitudes to same-sex relationships have led to changes in the laws of marriage. This means a fundamental change in marriage patterns, as gay marriages are now allowed.

Use concepts and issues such as higher education expansion, women's career opportunities, the pure relationship, secularisation, living apart together, singletons, fears of divorce etc.

AS Practice Paper 1

The following advice is for questions on the AS Practice Paper 1 that you will find earlier in this chapter.

Question 4

Spend about 15 minutes on this question. Divide your time fairly equally between each role. Don't write a separate introduction; just start on your first role. Possible functions include social solidarity, specialist skills, meritocracy, bridge between family and wider society, and role allocation.

Describe each role in some detail, explaining how functionalists see it benefiting society. Do this by creating a chain of reasoning (see page 248). For example, within the family, a child is judged on particularistic standards but in society by universalistic standards. School acts as a bridge between the two, introducing pupils to the idea of achieved status. This enables pupils to adjust to society's demands.

Use concepts such as social solidarity, meritocracy, shared culture, value consensus, skills, society in miniature, ascribed and achieved status, human capital theory and role allocation, and studies such as Durkheim, Parsons, Davis and Moore, and Blau and Duncan.

Question 5

Spend about 30 minutes on this question. Briefly identify the patterns of gender differences in achievement. Explain a range of factors outside schools that affect gender and achievement, such as feminist ideas, changes in the family, employment patterns and girls' changing ambitions, globalisation and changes to men's traditional jobs.

Explain how each factor may affect achievement. Do this by creating a chain of reasoning (see page 248). For example, legal changes have improved women's career opportunities, enabling some to break through the 'glass ceiling'. This has encouraged girls to see careers outside the home as possible and desirable. These career ambitions increase their motivation to gain qualifications.

Use evidence from studies such as McRobbie, Sharpe, Francis, Sewell, Jones, and Epstein, and develop the points noted in Item A. Evaluate these factors, making criticisms of each as you go, rather than in a separate section at the end. For example, discuss whether factors inside school, e.g. more positive role models, are more important than external factors.

Question 6

Spend about 30 minutes on this question. You must apply your knowledge of covert participant observation (CPO) to the study of the particular issue of teacher-pupil interactions. It is not enough simply to discuss CPO in general.

Use Item B to help you. For example, it suggests that one research characteristic of teacher-pupil interactions is that they are affected by many factors. This complexity thus makes it difficult for a single observer to see how each factor is affecting interactions – all while trying to maintain a covert role. The observer may thus miss or misinterpret interactions, reducing the research's validity.

Link other research characteristics of teacher-pupil interactions to the strengths and limitations of CPO. For example, the small-scale nature of the classroom means interactions are easier to observe, but it makes maintaining a covert role difficult. Other issues include peer pressure, teachers being overworked, access and consent, pupils' vulnerability etc. Link these to particular strengths or limitations of the method.

AS Practice Paper 2

The following advice is for questions on the AS Practice Paper 2 that you will find earlier in this chapter.

Question 2

Spend about 25 minutes on this question. Focus on evaluating the advantages of official statistics. Explain practical strengths, e.g. that governments regularly collect and publish statistics for free on a wide range of issues of sociological interest, enabling comparisons between groups and over time.

Ethically, a major advantage is that they do not identify individuals and the data already exists in the public domain. Examine the theoretical strengths of representativeness and reliability. Distinguish between 'hard' and 'soft' statistics and consider which might be more useful. Explain why positivists favour official statistics.

Evaluate these strengths as you consider each one in turn, rather than offering a list of limitations separately at the end. For example, explain that while official statistics may be reliable, their social construction creates a major problem with validity.

Question 6

Spend about 15 minutes on this question. Divide your time fairly equally between each reason. Don't write a separate introduction; just start on your first reason. Possible reasons include changes in the law, secularisation, rising expectations of marriage, changes in women's position, growing individualisation etc.

Describe each reason in some detail, explaining how it results in a higher divorce rate. Do this by creating a chain of reasoning (see page 248). For example, secularisation means that religion exerts less influence over people, so that religious opposition to divorce carries less weight and couples no longer feel prevented from divorcing. Secularisation also means some churches have softened their views on divorce and this makes divorce more acceptable for their own members.

Use concepts such as declining stigma, widening grounds for divorce, the dual burden, women's independence, the ideology of romantic love and the pure relationship.

Question 7

Spend about 30 minutes on this question. Cover a range of issues that feminists focus on. Develop points from Item A, e.g. by explaining feminist views about inequalities in the division of labour, decision making and power, and bring together different feminist views on the family. Use key concepts such as patriarchy, the dual burden, triple shift, gender scripts, non-heterosexual couples, different forms of control over resources, domestic violence, separatism, legislation, reproduction of the labour force etc.

Explain what different types of feminism (e.g. liberal, Marxist, radical and difference) see as the cause of and solution to women's oppression. Use evidence from a range of studies such as Crompton and Lyonette, Sullivan, Kan, Dex and Ward, Southerton, Dunne, Pahl, Smart, Dobash and Dobash, or Ansley.

Evaluate the importance of feminist contributions by using other perspectives (e.g. march of progress, functionalism, Marxism, the personal life perspective) or debates between feminists. Make criticisms as you go, rather than putting them in a separate section at the end.

A level Practice Paper 1

The following advice is for questions on the A level Practice Paper 1 that you will find earlier in this chapter.

Question 3

Spend about 15 minutes on this question. Divide your time fairly equally between each response. Don't write a separate introduction; just start on the first response. You must take two points from Item A – e.g. different ways pupils seek to avoid teachers' racism, or how they seek to achieve success while maintaining friendships with peers. Quote from the Item for each response.

Explain each response through a chain of reasoning (see page 248). For example, pupils who seek success may accept the school's educational goals while not appearing to work hard. This means they can achieve success without losing the friendship of less successful pupils.

Use concepts such as retreatism, rebellion, conformism, innovation, self-fulfilling prophecy, subculture, street culture, pupil identities. Use studies such as Sewell, Mirza, Fuller, Mac an Ghaill, Archer, Gillborn and Youdell. Include some brief evaluation, e.g. that the self-fulfilling prophecy explanation of pupils' responses to labelling is too deterministic.

Question 4

Spend about 45 minutes on this question. Examine the different functions Marxists see education performing, especially reproduction of inequality and legitimation of inequality. Be clear what these terms mean; deal with each separately.

Create chains of reasoning (page 248) to explain how each one serves capitalism. For example, the myth of meritocracy says everyone has an equal chance of success. Thus, when the system fails working-class pupils, they assume it is their own fault. This means they accept lower rewards, thus perpetuating class inequality.

Evaluate Marxist views via a debate between Willis and Bowles and Gintis, and between Marxists and non-Marxists. Use concepts such as ideology, ISAs, myth of meritocracy, resistance, determinism, reproduction, legitimation, Fordism, post-Fordism, correspondence principle, hidden curriculum. Use studies such as Althusser, Bowles and Gintis, and

Willis, as well as non-Marxists (e.g. functionalists, feminists, Morrow and Torres) and develop the points noted in Item B.

Question 5

Spend about 30 minutes on this question. You must apply your knowledge of unstructured interviews to the study of the particular issue of anti-school subcultures. It's not enough simply to discuss unstructured interviews in general.

Use Item C to help you. For example, it suggests that one research characteristic of such subcultures is that pupils are less likely to cooperate with those in authority. Thus, because they may see the researcher as an authority figure, they may refuse to cooperate. Interviews need pupils to participate in discussion, but they may be unwilling to do so.

Link other research characteristics of anti-school subcultures to the strengths and limitations of the method. For example, peer group pressure may inhibit individuals from speaking honestly if the interview is conducted in a group. Other characteristics include the pupils' greater vulnerability, higher levels of truancy, poorer linguistic skills, school selection of participants etc. Link these to particular strengths or limitations of the method.

A level Practice Paper 2

The following advice is for questions on the A level Practice Paper 2 that you will find earlier in this chapter.

Question 1

Spend about 15 minutes on this. Divide your time fairly equally between each reason. Don't write a separate introduction; just start on your first reason. Possible reasons include the impact of the media, consumerism, moral panics/risk society, legislation on children's rights/protection, changes in education etc.

Describe each reason in some detail, explaining how it may be changing the position of children. Do this by creating a chain of reasoning (see page 248). For example, the growing importance of the media and children's access to it means that knowledge once kept secret from children is now accessible to both young and old. This means childhood may be disappearing as a separate age-status.

Use concepts and issues such as social construction, the march of progress view, changes in family structure, toxic childhood, corporal punishment, child abuse, extension of compulsory schooling, etc, and studies such as Jenks, Postman, Mayall, Cunningham, Palmer.

Question 2

Spend about 15 minutes on this. Divide your time fairly equally between each effect. Don't write a separate introduction; just start on your first effect. You must take two points from Item A and show through a chain of reasoning (see page 248) the effect of each. Quote from the Item for each reason.

You could use differences between migrants and 'host' population (e.g. age, fertility rates), effects on migrants' identities, policy effects etc. For example, the younger age of migrants lowers the dependency ratio, meaning more tax revenue is available to support the old. Use concepts such as age structure, burden of dependency, demand for services, ethnic super-diversity, transnational identities, assimilationist versus multicultural policies, scapegoating, divided working class etc. Use studies such as Castles, Vertovec, Cohen, Eriksen, Ehrenreich and Hochschild.

Include some brief evaluation, e.g. while migration lowers the average age, it may increase the burden of dependency because migrants are of childbearing age.

Question 3

Spend about 30 minutes on this. Start by describing briefly some of the trends in couple relationships, e.g. divorce, first marriage, re-marriage and cohabitation rates. Deal with views that see increased instability, e.g. the New Right, postmodernism, feminism, the individualisation thesis.

Use concepts such as the biological division of labour, dependency culture, risk society, the negotiated family, individualism, choice, the pure relationship, women's independence, consumerism, the 'zombie family', secularisation etc. Use evidence from studies such as Benson, Patricia Morgan, Cheal, Stacey, Beck, Giddens, Beck and Beck-Gernsheim, Smart, Budgeon and May, and develop the points noted in Item B.

Evaluate the view by considering alternative interpretations such as the connectedness thesis, and evidence for stability, e.g. levelling out of divorce rates, gay marriage, high rates of re-marriage, cohabitation becoming more like marriage etc.

A level Practice Paper 3

The following advice is for the questions on the A level Practice Paper 3 that you will find earlier in this chapter.

Question 1

Spend about 15 minutes on this question. Divide your time fairly equally between each problem. Don't write a separate introduction; just start on your first problem. Possible problems include informed consent, confidentiality, privacy, psychological or physical harm to participants, involvement in immoral or illegal acts, etc.

Describe each problem in some detail, explaining how it may arise in research. Do this by creating a chain of reasoning (see page 248). For example, in covert research participants are unaware of being studied. This means they cannot give informed consent, since this would defeat the purpose of the research by changing participants' behaviour.

Use concepts and issues such as anonymity, deception, covert observation, field experiments, public interest, vulnerable groups, validity, the Hawthorne Effect etc, and studies such as Patrick, Humphreys, Festinger, Ditton, Milgram or Mayo.

Question 2

Spend about 30 minutes on this question. Be clear about definitions of validity, reliability and representativeness. Use the debate between positivism and interpretivism as a context for your answer. Explain why interpretivists see participant observation (PO) as producing valid data, e.g. by allowing the researcher to experience the actors' world by joining in it. Explain why positivists value reliability and representativeness, and why they feel PO fails to deliver these features.

Evaluate the view, e.g. by considering why PO might not even produce valid data because researchers are free to ignore data that doesn't fit their preconceptions. Evaluate how far overt and covert PO each produce valid data.

Use concepts and issues such as quantitative and qualitative data, generalisation, sociology as a science, 'going native', verstehen, objectivity and subjectivity. Use studies such as Griffin, Whyte and Punch, and develop points noted in Item A.

Key Concepts

The following is an alphabetical list of some of the key concepts you need to know for AS and A level Sociology. You can use the list as:

- **a handy reference** to find a quick definition of a term you're not sure of
- **a revision aid** to ensure you know and understand important sociological ideas.

When you look up a concept in the list, you may find other terms in the explanation printed *in italics*. This means you will find a separate entry for these terms elsewhere in the list. You will also find that a lot of entries give you a 'see also' reference. Following these up will show you some of the links between concepts and broaden your understanding of them.

A* to C Economy: a system in which schools concentrate their efforts on those pupils they see as most likely to gain five A*-C grades at GCSE and so boost the school's league table position. *See also* **educational triage.**

age patriarchy: *see* patriarchy.

ageism: the negative stereotyping of people on the basis of their age; e.g. the old are often portrayed as vulnerable, incompetent or irrational, and as a burden to society.

alienation: where an individual or group feels socially isolated and estranged because they lack the power to control their lives and realise their true potential. Marx describes workers in capitalist society as alienated because they are exploited and lack control of the production process. *See also* **Marxism.**

assimilationism: an approach to immigration policy that believes immigrants should adopt the language, values and customs of the 'host community' or country in which they settle.

banding: a form of streaming.

beanpole family: a family that is vertically extended but not horizontally extended, e.g. grandparents, parents and children, but not aunts, uncles and cousins.

birth rate: the number of live births per thousand of the population per year. *See also* **infant mortality rate**.

bourgeoisie: a Marxist term for the capitalist class, the owners of the means of production (factories, machinery, raw materials, land etc). Marx argues that the bourgeoisie's ownership of the means of production also gives them political and ideological power. *See also* **exploitation; ideology; Marxism; proletariat.**

capitalism: *see* **Marxism.**

case study: research that examines a single case or example, such as a single school, family or workplace, often using several methods or sources.

childhood: a socially defined age-status. There are major differences in how childhood is defined, both historically and between cultures. Western societies today define children as vulnerable and segregate them from the adult world, but in the past they were part of adult society from an early age. These differences show that childhood is a social construction. *See also* **patriarchy**.

civil partnership: the 2004 Civil Partnership Act gave same-sex couples similar legal rights to married couples in respect of pensions, inheritance, tenancies and property.

class: *See* **social class.**

closed-ended questions: questions used in a social survey that allow only a limited choice of answers from a pre-set list. They produce quantitative data and the answers are often pre-coded for ease of analysis. An example is 'Will you vote in the next election?' where the choices are Yes, No, Don't know. *See also* **open-ended questions**.

comparative method: a research method that compares two social groups that are alike apart from one factor. For example, Durkheim compared two groups that were identical apart from their religion in order to find out the effect of religion on suicide rates. The method is often used as an alternative to experiments.

compensatory education: government education policies such as Operation Headstart in the USA that seek to tackle the problem of under-achievement by providing extra support and funding to schools and families in deprived areas. *See also* **cultural deprivation.**

comprehensive system: a non-selective education system where all children attend the same type of secondary school. It was introduced in England and Wales from 1965. *See also* **tripartite system.**

conjugal roles: the roles played by husband and wife. Segregated conjugal roles are where the husband is breadwinner and the wife is homemaker, with leisure spent separately. In joint conjugal roles, husband and wife each perform both roles and spend their leisure time together. *See also* **symmetrical family**.

connectedness thesis: *see* **individualisation thesis.**

content analysis: a method of analysing the content of documents and media output to find out how often and in what ways different types of people or events appear. For example, the Glasgow University Media Group (1976) used content analysis to reveal bias in how television news reported strikes.

control group: in *experiments*, scientists compare a control group and an experimental group that are identical in all respects. Unlike the experimental group, the control group is not exposed to the variable under investigation and

Key Concepts

so provides a baseline against which any changes in the experimental group can be compared.

correlation: when two or more factors or *variables* vary together; e.g. there is a correlation between low social class and low educational achievement. However, the existence of a correlation between two variables does not necessarily prove that one causes the other. It may simply be coincidence. *See also* **experiments**.

correspondence principle: Bowles and Gintis' concept describing the way that the organisation and control of schools mirrors or 'corresponds to' the workplace in capitalist society. For example, the control teachers exert over pupils mirrors the control managers exert over workers. *See also* **reproduction**.

covert participant observation: *see* **participant observation**.

critical race theory (CRT): CRT sees racism as a deep-seated feature of society resulting not merely from the attitudes of individuals but from *institutional racism*. CRT identifies several ways in which the educational system is institutionally racist, including selection, the ethnocentric curriculum and assessment. CRT argues that racism cannot be removed merely by passing laws against it but requires direct action by oppressed groups. **See also institutional racism.**

cultural capital: the knowledge, attitudes, values, language, tastes and abilities that the middle class transmit to their children. Bourdieu argues that educational success is largely based on possession of cultural capital, thus giving middle-class children an advantage. *See also* **reproduction; speech codes**.

cultural deprivation: the theory that many working-class and black children are inadequately socialised and therefore lack the 'right' culture needed for educational success; e.g. their families do not instil the value of *deferred gratification*. *See also* **compensatory education**.

culture: all those things that are learnt and shared by a society or group of people and transmitted from generation to generation through socialisation. It includes shared norms, values, knowledge, beliefs and skills. *See also* **subculture**.

curriculum: those things taught or learnt in educational institutions. The overt or official curriculum includes the subjects, courses etc offered (e.g. the National Curriculum), while the hidden curriculum includes all those things learnt without being formally taught and often acquired simply through the everyday workings of the school, such as attitudes of obedience, conformity and competitiveness. *See also* **ethnocentric**.

death rate: the number of deaths per thousand of the population per year.

deferred gratification: postponing immediate rewards or pleasures, generally with the aim of producing a greater

reward at a later date, e.g. staying in to revise rather than going out with friends, which will bring success in exams. It is seen as a characteristic of middle-class *culture*. *See also* **immediate gratification; values**.

demography: the study of population, including birth, death, fertility and infant mortality rates, immigration and emigration, and age structure, as well as the reasons for changes in these.

dependency culture: where people assume that the state will support them, rather than relying on their own efforts and taking responsibility for their families. The *New Right* see *the welfare state* as over-generous, encouraging people to remain unemployed and dependent on benefits, and as responsible for the growing number of lone-parent families and rising crime rate. *See also* **underclass**.

dependency ratio: the relationship between the size of the working population and the non-working or dependent population.

deviance: behaviour that does not conform to the *norms* of a society or group. Deviance is a *social construction* (defined or created by social groups). Deviance is relative: what counts as deviant varies between groups and cultures and over time.

differentiation: distinguishing or creating differences between individuals or groups. In education, *streaming* is a form of differentiation that distinguishes between pupils on the basis of ability. In the study of *stratification*, differentiation refers to the process of distinguishing between people on the basis of class, gender, ethnic, age etc differences. *See also* **labelling**.

discrimination: treating people differently, whether negatively (disadvantaging them) or positively (advantaging them), usually because they are members of a particular social group. It can occur on grounds of *gender*, *ethnicity*, age, disability, *sexuality*, religion etc. *See also* **racism; sexism; ageism**.

documents: are of two types. Public documents are produced by organisations such as governments, schools, media etc. They include Acts of Parliament, school prospectuses, newspaper articles etc. Personal documents are created by individuals and often provide first-person accounts of events and experiences. They include diaries, letters, autobiographies etc. Both types are used as secondary sources of qualitative data in sociological research.

domestic labour: work performed in the home, such as childcare, cooking, and cleaning. Functionalists see it as part of the *expressive role* performed by women, while feminists regard it as a major source of women's oppression. *See also* **dual burden**.

dual burden: when a person is responsible for two jobs. Usually applied to women who are in paid work but also responsible for *domestic labour*. *See also* **emotion work**.

educational triage: the process whereby schools sort pupils into 'hopeless cases', 'those who will pass anyway', and 'those with potential to pass', and then concentrate their efforts on the last of these groups as a way to boost the school's exam league table position. Sorting may be based on stereotypical ideas about pupils' ability. *See also* **selection**.

emotion work: the work involved in meeting the emotional needs of other people, e.g. looking after a sick child involves responding to emotional as well as physical needs. Some sociologists argue that women carry a triple burden of housework, paid work and emotion work. *See also* **dual burden**.

empathy: an understanding of how another person thinks, feels or acts, achieved by putting oneself in their place. Interactionists advocate the use of qualitative methods such as participant observation as a way of achieving empathy and obtaining data high in *validity*. *See also* **interactionism; objectivity; subjectivity**.

empty shell marriage: a marriage in name only, where a couple continues to live under the same roof but as separate individuals. It may occur where divorce is difficult for legal, religious or financial reasons, or where a couple decides to stay together for the sake of the children.

ethics: issues of right and wrong; moral principles or guidelines. There are ethical objections to research that deceives or harms its participants or fails to obtain their *informed consent*.

ethnic group: people who share the same heritage, culture and identity, often including the same language and religion, and who see themselves as a distinct group, e.g. the Bangladeshi community in Britain. As well as having ethnic minority groups, societies such as Britain have an ethnic majority. *See also* **culture; racism; stratification**.

ethnocentric: seeing or judging things in a biased way from the viewpoint of one particular culture; e.g. the National Curriculum has been described as an ethnocentric curriculum since it tends to value white, western music, literature, languages, history, religion etc and disregards or does not value black and Asian cultures.

exchange theory: the idea that people create, maintain or break off relationships depending on the costs and benefits of doing so; e.g. a person may provide a relative with accommodation (cost) in return for help with childcare (benefit).

experiments: a laboratory experiment is a test carried out in controlled conditions in an artificial setting (a laboratory) to establish a cause-and-effect relationship between two or more variables. A field experiment has the same aim but is carried out in a natural setting (e.g. a street or workplace) not a laboratory. *See also* **control group; positivism**.

experimental group: see **control group**.

exploitation: paying workers less than the value of their labour. According to Marxists, it is the process whereby the *bourgeoisie* extract surplus value or profit from the labour of the *proletariat*. Feminists see men as exploiting the *domestic labour* of women. *See also* **Marxism; feminism**.

expressive role: the caring, nurturing, 'homemaker' role in the family. Functionalists argue that women are biologically suited to performing this role, but feminists reject this. *See also* **instrumental role**.

extended family: any group of kin (people related by blood, marriage or adoption) extended beyond the *nuclear family*. The family may be extended vertically (e.g. grandparents), horizontally (e.g. aunts, uncles, cousins), or both. *See also* **family structure**.

family diversity: the idea that there is a range of different family types, rather than a single dominant one (such as the nuclear family). It is associated with the postmodernist idea that in today's society, increasing choice about relationships is creating greater family diversity.

family practices: the routine actions through which we create our sense of 'being a family member', such as doing the shopping or the DIY. Morgan prefers the term to that of *family structure* because it conveys the idea that families are not 'things', but what their members actually do.

family structure: the composition of a group of people who live together as a family unit. Structures include the *nuclear family*, *extended family*, *reconstituted family*, lone-parent and same-sex families.

families of choice: (also called chosen families) people who are not necessarily related by blood or marriage but who feel a sense of belonging together and who choose to define themselves as a family. For example, gay and lesbian people have created support networks of friends, relatives and so on who they regard as family.

fertility rate: the total fertility rate (TFR) is the average number of children women will have during their fertile years. For statistical purposes, this is defined as age 15-44.

feminism: a sociological perspective and political movement that focuses on women's oppression and the struggle to end it. Feminists argue that sociology has traditionally taken a 'malestream' viewpoint that ignores women. Instead, they examine women's experiences and study society from a female perspective. There are different strands of feminism, including Marxist, radical, liberal and difference feminism. *See also* **patriarchy**.

Fordism: a type of industrial production based on a detailed division of labour, using closely supervised, low-skilled workers and assembly-line technology to mass-produce standardised goods. Named after the car manufacturing techniques first introduced by the Ford Motor Company in the early 20th century. *See also* **alienation; post-Fordism**.

Key Concepts

function: the contribution that a part of society makes to the stability or well-being of society as a whole. For example, according to Durkheim, one function of religion is to give individuals a sense of belonging to something greater than themselves and so integrate them into society. *See also* **functionalism**.

functional fit: Parsons' theory that, with *industrialisation*, the structure of the family becomes nuclear to fit the needs of industrial society for a geographically and socially mobile labour force. *See also* **functionalism; mobility**.

functionalism: a consensus perspective in sociology that sees society as based on shared values into which members are socialised. It sees society as like an organism, each part performing functions to maintain the system as a whole; e.g. the family and education system perform *socialisation* functions. *See also* **function; value consensus**.

gender: the social and cultural characteristics of men and women. Unlike sex differences, which are biological and inborn, gender differences in behaviour are cultural in origin and learned through gender role *socialisation*. Definitions of masculinity and femininity are socially constructed and vary between cultures and social groups. *See also* **feminism; patriarchy**.

gender domains: the tasks and activities that boys and girls see as the 'territory' of their respective genders; e.g. mending a car is seen as within the male gender domain. Children's beliefs about gender domains are shaped by their early experiences and adults' expectations.

globalisation: the idea that the world is becoming increasingly interconnected and barriers are disappearing, e.g. as a result of instantaneous communication systems, deregulation of trade, the creation of global markets, and global media and culture. Many see it as creating new risks, uncertainties and choices, and an increased rate of social change.

habitus: a concept introduced by Bourdieu. It refers to the learned, taken-for-granted ways of thinking, acting and being shared by a particular social class or group. It includes preferences for particular lifestyles and consumption patterns, and beliefs about what is realistic for members of that group to aim for. *See also* **cultural capital.**

Hawthorne Effect: where the subjects of a research study know they are being studied and begin to behave differently as a result, thereby undermining the study's *validity*. The term comes from Elton Mayo's studies at the Hawthorne electrical plant.

hidden curriculum: see **curriculum**.

hierarchy: an organisation or social structure based on a 'pyramid' of senior and junior positions and top-down control; e.g. an army with its different ranks and command from above. *See also* **stratification**.

household: a group of people who live together and share things such as meals, bills, facilities or chores, or one person living alone.

hypothesis: an untested theory or explanation, expressed as a statement. Sociologists seek to prove or disprove hypotheses by testing them against the evidence. *See also* **experiments**.

ideal pupil: an image held by teachers of the kind of pupil they prefer to teach: bright, hardworking, cooperative and so on. Teachers are likely to see white, middle-class pupils as closest to this ideal. Reay found that high-achieving girls had to adopt a desexualised ideal *female* pupil identity.

identity: the individual's sense of self, influenced by *socialisation* and interactions with others; a sense of belonging to a community. Postmodernists see identity as a choice that individuals make from among different sources of identity, such as *gender, ethnic group,* religion, *sexuality,* leisure interests, nationality etc. *See also* **postmodernism**.

ideology: originally a Marxist idea meaning a set of beliefs that serve the interests of a dominant social group by justifying their privileged position. The term usually implies that the beliefs are false or only partially true; e.g. Bowles and Gintis argue that meritocracy is a 'myth', i.e. untrue. *See also* **legitimation; Marxism**.

immediate gratification: a preference for immediate pleasure or reward, without regard for the longer-term consequences; e.g. going out with friends instead of doing one's homework. *Cultural deprivation* theorists argue that working-class children are socialised into the value of immediate gratification and that this explains their educational failure. *See also* **deferred gratification; values**.

impression management: involves manipulating the impression of ourselves that we give to others. Erving Goffman compares performing a social role with acting on stage. We act differently when we are 'front of stage', consciously playing the part (e.g. a teacher in front of the class) from when we are 'backstage' (e.g. the teacher relaxing in the staffroom).

industrialisation: the shift from an agricultural economy to one based on factory production. In Britain, industrialisation occurred from about the late 18th to the mid-19th centuries. Industrialisation often occurs along with *urbanisation*.

individualisation thesis: this argues that as a result of the weakening of the influence of traditional structures and norms (such as those governing personal relationships), individuals are now freer to make their own life choices. This is leading to more family diversity, risk and instability. By contrast, the *connectedness thesis* argues that we are not simply isolated individuals: social structures such as class and gender still limit choice and diversity. *See also* **pure relationship.**

individualism: the belief that the individual is more important than the group or community. In modern and postmodern society, individualism becomes more important than in traditional society and individuals' actions are influenced more by calculations of their own self-interest than by a sense of obligation to others.

infant mortality rate: the number of infants who die before their first birthday, per thousand live births per year. *See also* **birth rate; death rate**.

informed consent: where those taking part in a study have agreed to do so and understand the purpose of the study, the uses to which its findings may be put, and its possible effects. *See also* **ethics**.

institutional racism: discrimination that is built into the everyday workings of institutions such as schools and colleges. This discrimination may be unconscious rather than deliberate, but is a deeply ingrained, taken-for-granted part of the institution's culture. *See also* **critical race theory**.

instrumental role: the breadwinner or provider role in the family. Functionalists see this as the man's role. *See also* **expressive role**.

interactionism: a sociological perspective that focuses on small-scale (micro-level) interactions between individuals and groups, rather than on the large-scale workings of society. Interactionists seek to understand the meanings that social actors give to actions and situations, usually by using qualitative research methods. *See also* **interpretivism; labelling; self-fulfilling prophecy**.

interpretivism: a term covering a range of perspectives including *interactionism*. Interpretivists focus on how we construct our social worlds through the meanings we create and attach to events, actions and situations. They favour qualitative methods and see human beings as fundamentally different from the natural phenomena studied by scientists, in that we have free will, consciousness and choice. *See also* **positivism; subjectivity**.

interview schedule: the list of questions to be asked in an interview. It is useful because it allows some standardisation of the interviewing process, since all interviewers will use the same schedule of questions.

interviews: a method of gathering information by asking questions orally, either face-to-face or by telephone. Structured (or formal) interviews use pre-set, standardised, usually *closed-ended questions* producing *quantitative data*. Unstructured (informal or depth) interviews are more like a guided conversation and use *open-ended questions* producing *qualitative data*. Semi-structured interviews include both types of question. *See also* **questionnaires**.

labelling: the process of attaching a definition or meaning to an individual or group; e.g. teachers may label a pupil as a 'trouble maker'. Often the label is a stereotype that defines all members of a group in the same way. The concept is widely used in the study of *deviance*, mental illness and education. *See also* **self-fulfilling prophecy**.

legitimation: justifying something by making it seem fair and natural. This is the main function of *ideology*. Marxists argue that institutions in capitalist society such as education, the media and religion are 'ideological state apparatuses' whose function is to legitimate inequality. *See also* **meritocracy**.

life chances: the chances that different social groups have of obtaining those things society regards as desirable (e.g. educational qualifications) or of suffering those things regarded as undesirable (e.g. low income). Statistics on education, health, income etc show that such opportunities vary by *class, gender* and *ethnic group*. *See also* **stratification**.

life course analysis: an approach focusing on the meanings family members give to life events and choices, e.g. deciding to leave home, get divorced etc. It uses unstructured interviews to uncover these meanings and understand people's choices about relationships and how these may lead to family diversity.

life expectancy: how long on average people who are born in a given year can expect to live.

living apart together ('LATs'): couples who are in a significant relationship, but not married or cohabiting. Some sociologists suggest that LATs may reflect a trend towards less formalised relationships.

longitudinal study: study of a *sample* of people (sometimes called a panel) in which information is collected at regular intervals over an extended period of time; e.g. the National Child Development Study has been running since 1958. These studies usually use *questionnaires or interviews*, but other methods may also be employed.

macro-level: theories such as *functionalism* and *Marxism* that focus on the large scale, i.e. on the social structure as a whole or on the relationships between social institutions like the education system and the economy. These theories see the individual as shaped by society. *See also* **micro-level; positivism**.

marketisation: the policy of introducing market forces of supply and demand into areas run by the state, such as education and the National Health Service. The 1988 Education Reform Act began the marketisation of education by encouraging competition between schools and choice for parents. *See also* **New Right**.

Marxism: a conflict perspective based on the ideas of Karl Marx (1818-83). It sees society as divided into two opposed classes, one of which exploits the labour of the other. In capitalist society, the *bourgeoisie* exploits the *proletariat*. Marx predicted the proletariat would unite to overthrow capitalism and create a classless society. Marxist sociologists argue that institutions such as education

Key Concepts

and the media function to maintain capitalism. *See also* **alienation; exploitation; ideology; modernism; polarisation; reproduction.**

material deprivation: poverty; a lack of basic necessities such as adequate diet, housing, clothing or the money to buy these things. In education, material deprivation theory explains working-class under-achievement as the result of the lack of such resources; e.g. parents are unable to afford educational aids, overcrowding deprives children of a quiet study area etc.

means of production: *see* **bourgeoisie.**

meritocracy: an educational or social system where everyone has an equal opportunity to succeed and where individuals' rewards and status are achieved by their own efforts rather than ascribed by their *gender, class* or *ethnic group. See also* **myth of meritocracy.**

micro-level: theories such as interactionism that focus on small-scale, face-to-face interaction, e.g. between teacher and pupils in a classroom. These theories see individuals constructing society through their interactions. *See also* **interpretivism; macro-level.**

migration: involves the movement of people from place to place. It can be internal, within a given society, or transnational, crossing national frontiers. Migrants may settle permanently in a new place, stay temporarily, or move to and fro between places (circular migration).

mobility: movement; change of position. Sociologists distinguish between geographical mobility, in which people move from one place to another (e.g. in search of work), and social mobility, in which they change position or status in a *hierarchy* or *stratification* system. Functionalists argue that the geographical and social mobility of the *nuclear family* enable it to meet the needs of industrial society. *See also* **industrialisation.**

model minorities: a term used to describe minority ethnic groups, such as Chinese and Indian pupils, who achieve above average results. Gillborn argues that the achievements of model minorities are wrongly used to justify the claim that the education system cannot be institutionally racist.

modernism: modernist perspectives (e.g. *functionalism, Marxism* and *positivism*) believe that society has a fairly clear-cut, predictable structure and that it is possible to gain true and certain scientific knowledge of how society functions. This knowledge can be used to achieve progress to a better society. *See also* **postmodernism.**

moral panic: an over-reaction to a perceived problem where a group is labelled as a threat to society's values or 'folk devil'. The media play an important part by exaggerating the scale of the problem and channelling demands that something be done about it. However, steps taken to deal with the problem may 'amplify' it.

multicultural: a society or institution that recognises and gives value to different cultures and/or ethnic groups; e.g. multi-cultural education teaches children about the cultures of other groups, not just the dominant or majority *culture.*

myth of meritocracy: Functionalists argue that the education system is meritocratic, but Bowles and Gintis claim that meritocracy is an *ideology* legitimating inequality by falsely claiming that everyone has equal opportunity and that unequal rewards are the 'natural' result of unequal ability. *See also* **legitimation; meritocracy.**

natural change: the difference between the number of births and the number of deaths in a population, resulting in either a natural increase or a natural decrease.

net migration: the difference between the number of immigrants entering a country and the number of emigrants leaving it.

neo-liberalism: the theory that competition, choice and *privatisation* are the most efficient way to run the economy, free from state regulation. It favours low taxation and reduced state spending on education, healthcare etc. Individuals are seen as consumers who are free to make their own choices (e.g. about choice of school, or whether to apply to university) and obliged to live with the consequences. *See also* **marketisation; New Right; parentocracy; privatisation.**

New Right: a conservative political perspective whose supporters believe in self-reliance and individual choice, rather than dependence on the state. They believe in applying free market principles, e.g. the *marketisation* of education, and argue that generous welfare benefits encourage the growth of an *underclass.*

new vocationalism: the idea that education should be primarily about meeting the needs of the economy, especially by equipping young people with the knowledge, skills, attitudes and *values* needed to prepare them for work. Since the 1970s it has given rise to educational initiatives such as the Youth Training Scheme, BTEC and vocational GCSEs.

non-participant observation: a primary research method where the observer records events without taking part in them; e.g. a sociologist might observe and record how gender roles influence children's play without taking part. In sociology, *participant observation* is used much more often.

norms: social rules, expectations or standards that govern the behaviour expected in particular situations. Norms may be formal (e.g. written laws or rules) or informal (e.g. rules of politeness). Each *culture* has detailed norms governing every aspect of behaviour. *See also* **values.**

nuclear family: a two-generation family of a man and woman and their dependent children, own or adopted. *See also* **family structure.**

objectivity: the absence of bias or preconceived ideas. It implies that we can look at things as they really are, without our opinions or *values* getting in the way (and thus we can get at the truth). Positivists believe sociology can achieve objectivity by modelling itself on the natural sciences, using methods that keep sociologists detached from their research subjects. *See also* **positivism; subjectivity**.

official statistics: *quantitative data* collected by the government. They can be gathered either by registration (e.g. the law requires parents to register births) or by official surveys (e.g. the ten-yearly Census of the entire population).

open-ended questions: questions in a *social survey* that allow respondents to answer as they wish, in their own words (e.g. 'How did you feel about being excluded from school?'). Answers are harder to analyse because they cannot be pre-coded. *See also* **closed-ended questions**.

operationalisation: the process of turning a sociological concept or theory into something measurable. For example, a sociologist studying the effect of *social class* on educational achievement might use parental occupation to measure the concept 'social class'.

overt participant observation: *see* **participant observation**.

parentocracy: literally, 'rule by parents'. The concept is associated with marketised education systems, which are based on an ideology of parental choice of school. Middle-class parents may benefit from parentocracy because they have more economic and *cultural capital* and are better placed to exercise choice. *See also* **marketisation**.

participant observation: a primary research method in which the sociologist studies a group by taking a role within it and participating in its activities. It may be overt, where other participants are aware of the researcher's true identity and motive. Alternatively, it may be covert ('undercover'), where the sociologist's identity and purpose are kept secret.

patriarchy: literally, rule by the father. Feminists use the term to describe a society based on male domination; a system or *ideology* of male power over women. Child liberationists argue that children are victims of 'age patriarchy' – the domination of fathers, or adults generally. *See also* **feminism**.

pilot study: a small-scale trial run, usually of a social survey, conducted before the main study. Its basic aim is to iron out any problems, clarify questions and their wording, give interviewers practice etc, so that any necessary changes can be made before the main study is carried out.

polarisation: a process that results in the creation of two opposite extremes, e.g. pupils' responses to *labelling* and *streaming* in schools can create a pro-school and an anti-school *pupil subculture*. In the study of *stratification*, Marx describes how in capitalist society the class structure becomes polarised into a wealthy bourgeoisie and impoverished proletariat. *See also* **differentiation;**

self-fulfilling prophecy; Marxism.

population: in a *social survey*, the population (sometimes called the 'survey population') is all the members of the group that the researcher is interested in; e.g. in a study of political opinions, the population may be the entire electorate. *See also* **demography; sampling frame**.

positivism: the belief that society is made up of 'social facts' that can be studied scientifically to discover laws of cause and effect. Durkheim took *official statistics* on suicide as social facts and tried to produce a law explaining why suicide rates vary between groups. With such knowledge, sociologists would be able to find solutions to social problems. *See also* **comparative method; experiments; interpretivism; objectivity**.

post-Fordism: a type of industrial production. A highly skilled, adaptable workforce, combined with computerised technology, means that production takes the form of 'flexible specialisation', able to respond swiftly to changing consumer demands and to produce for a variety of small, customised 'niche' markets. *See also* **Fordism**.

postmodernism: a perspective that rejects the modernists' belief in progress and their view that we can have certain, true knowledge of society that will enable us to improve it. Society has become so unstable and diverse that it is now impossible to produce any absolute explanations. No one theory is 'truer' than any other; theories such as *Marxism* and *functionalism* are merely viewpoints. Instead, sociology should concentrate on reflecting and celebrating social diversity. *See also* **modernism**.

primary data: information collected first hand by sociologists themselves for their own research purposes. Methods such as *participant observation*, *social surveys* and *experiments* are sources of primary data. *See also* **secondary data**.

privatisation: the transfer of industries or services previously owned by the state (the public sector) to ownership by private businesses (the private sector), who run them to make a profit; e.g. the privatisation of parts of the education system, such as the building and running of schools. *See also* **neo-liberalism**.

proletariat: the working class in capitalist society They own no means of production and are 'wage slaves', forced to sell their labour-power to the *bourgeoisie* in order to survive. *See also* **exploitation; Marxism**.

pure relationship: one which exists solely to meet each partner's needs. Couples stay together for love, happiness or sexual attraction, rather than because of tradition or duty, or for the sake of the children. According to Giddens, it is increasingly regarded as the only acceptable basis for a relationship.

qualitative data: information, usually expressed in words, about people's thoughts, feelings, motivations, attitudes,

Key Concepts

values etc. It is obtained from qualitative methods and sources such as *participant observation, unstructured interviews*, diaries and letters. It aims to give an insight into what it is like to be in another person's 'shoes'. *See also* **empathy; interactionism**.

quantitative data: information in numerical form (percentages, tables, graphs etc). *Official statistics* and the results of *social surveys* are two important sources of quantitative data. See also **closed-ended questions; positivism**.

questionnaires: lists of questions. Written or self-completion questionnaires are widely used in large-scale social surveys, where they may be sent out and returned by post. Questionnaires tend to use mainly *closed-ended questions* with pre-coded answers for ease of analysis. *See also* **quantitative data; response rate**.

racism: a system of beliefs that defines people as superior or inferior, and justifies their unequal treatment, on the basis of biological differences such as skin colour. Individual racism refers to the prejudiced views and discriminatory behaviour of individuals. Institutional racism exists when the routine ways an organisation operates have racist outcomes regardless of the intentions of the individuals within it.

reconstituted family: a stepfamily, in which one or both partners has children from a previous relationship. *See also* **family structure**.

reliability: a piece of research is reliable if it produces exactly the same results (a replica) when repeated using identical methods and procedures. In general, quantitative methods such as *experiments* and *questionnaires* are more reliable than qualitative methods because they use standardised procedures that are easier to replicate; e.g. a questionnaire asking all respondents the same set of questions.

representative: typical; a cross-section. A researcher may choose to study a sample of a larger group. If the sample is representative, those in it will be typical of the larger group. This will allow the findings to be generalised, i.e. applied to all members of the group, not just those in the *sample*.

reproduction: the re-creation or continuation of something into future generations; e.g. Marxists argue that schooling reproduces the class structure by failing working-class pupils so that they take working-class jobs. *See also* **correspondence principle; Marxism**.

reserve army of labour: a Marxist concept describing groups who can be brought into the workforce when there is a labour shortage as the capitalist economy expands during a boom, and discarded when it contracts. Women were used as a reserve army of labour during the two world wars, returning afterwards to their primary domestic role. *See also* **Marxism**.

response rate: the proportion of those people included in a social survey who actually reply or respond to the questions

asked. A high response rate is important to help ensure that findings are *representative*.

role: how someone who occupies a particular *status* is expected to act; e.g. someone playing the role of bus driver is expected to drive safely, stop for passengers, charge the correct fare etc.

sample: a smaller group selected from the larger survey *population* to take part in a study. It may be too costly or time-consuming to study the whole population in which we are interested, so we choose a sample to study instead. *See also* **sampling; sampling frame**.

sampling: the process of selecting a *sample*. The aim of sampling is usually to select a sample that is representative of the wider survey *population*, so as to allow the study's findings to be generalised. There are several types of sampling, e.g. random, stratified random, quota and snowball sampling. *See also* **sampling frame**.

sampling frame: the list of people from which a *sample* for a *social survey* is selected, e.g. a school roll could be the sampling frame for a survey of pupils. It should list all the members of the survey *population* that the sociologist is interested in studying, though this is not always possible; e.g. there is no complete list of all criminals (since some are not caught).

sanctions: *see* **social control**.

secondary data: information collected not by sociologists themselves for their own research purposes, but by other people or organisations for non-sociological purposes. Sociologists make extensive use of this 'second hand' information because it is often free or cheap, readily available and covers large numbers. Secondary sources of data include *official statistics*, the media and *personal documents*. *See also* **primary data**.

secularisation: the decline of religion; the process whereby religious beliefs, practices and institutions lose their importance or influence; e.g. fewer couples now marry in church and many people disregard religious teachings on issues like divorce, homosexuality etc.

selection: in education, the process of choosing and allocating pupils to a particular school, class, stream etc; e.g. in the *tripartite system* after 1944, the 11-plus exam selected pupils supposedly on the basis of ability for either grammar or secondary modern school. *See also* **educational triage**.

self-fulfilling prophecy: where a prediction made about a person or group comes true simply because it has been made. For example, in predicting that some pupils will do badly, teachers treat them in line with these lower expectations. This will discourage the pupils from trying and make the prediction come true. The prediction is a form of *labelling*. It works by changing the individual's self-image to bring it in line with the expectations that others have of him/her. *See also* **interactionism; streaming**.

separatism: a radical feminist idea that women should live independently of men as the only way to free themselves from the patriarchal oppression of the heterosexual family.

sexism: prejudice and *discrimination* on the grounds of sex; e.g. seeing girls as better suited for courses in 'caring' subjects. *See also* **patriarchy**.

sexuality: sexual orientation; a person's sexual preference; e.g. heterosexual, homosexual (gay or lesbian).

social action theories: see individuals as having free will and choice, and the power to create society through their actions and interactions, rather than being shaped by society. *Interactionism* is the best-known theory of this type, *postmodernism* also has certain features in common with social action theories. *See also* **structural theories**.

social class: social groupings or hierarchy based on differences in wealth, income or occupation. Marx identified two opposed classes in capitalist society, the *bourgeoisie* and *proletariat*. Many sociologists use occupation to distinguish between a manual working class and a non-manual middle class. Some also identify an *underclass* beneath the working class. *See also* **life chances; Marxism**.

social construction: where something is created by social processes, rather than simply occurring naturally. For example, interpretivists argue that official crime statistics are socially constructed through the interactions of police and suspects. When something is socially constructed, it is likely to vary historically and between cultures. Sociologists see *childhood, gender, identity* etc as social constructs.

social control: the means by which society tries to ensure that its members behave as others expect them to. Control can be formal (e.g. the law) or informal (e.g. peer pressure). Negative sanctions (punishments) may be threatened or positive sanctions (rewards) offered to encourage individuals to conform to society's *norms* and *values*.

social policy: the actions, plans and programmes of government bodies and agencies that aim to deal with a problem or achieve a goal, e.g. raising levels of educational attainment. Policies are often based on laws that provide the framework within which these agencies operate. *See also* **welfare state**.

social survey: any research method that involves systematically collecting information from a group of people (either a *sample* or the whole target *population*, e.g. the Census) by asking them questions. Usually, this involves using written *questionnaires* or structured *interviews* and the questions are standardised.

socialisation: the process by which an individual learns or internalises the *culture* of society. Primary socialisation occurs largely within the family and involves acquiring basic

skills and *values*, while much secondary socialisation takes place within educational institutions and includes acquisition of knowledge and skills needed for work. Other agencies of socialisation include peer groups, the mass media and religion.

speech codes: patterns or ways of using language. Bernstein argues that the working class use only the context-bound restricted code, with short, grammatically simple sentences and limited vocabulary. The middle class use the context-free elaborated code, with complex sentences and which is able to describe abstract ideas. This code is used in education, giving middle-class children an advantage. *See also* **cultural capital**.

stabilisation of adult personalities: according to Parsons, one of the two functions of the nuclear family along with primary *socialisation*. It is a place where adults can relax and release tensions, enabling them to return to the workplace ready to meet its demands. This is functional for the efficiency of the economy.

status: a position in society. Ascribed status occurs where our position in society is determined by fixed characteristics that we are born with and cannot normally change, e.g. *gender*, ethnicity or family of origin. Achieved status occurs where an individual's position is the result of their effort and ability, e.g. getting into university. *See also* **meritocracy**.

stereotype: a simplified, one-sided and often negative image of a group or individual which assumes that all members of that group share the same characteristics; e.g. the image that all black boys are disruptive and unruly. *See also* **labelling**.

stigma: a negative label or mark of disapproval, discredit or shame attached to a person, group or characteristic. The stigma is used to justify the exclusion of the individual from normal social interaction; e.g. in the past, divorcees were often stigmatised and excluded from 'respectable' company. *See also* **labelling**.

stratification: the division of society into a hierarchy of unequal groups. The inequalities may be of wealth, power and/or status. Stratification systems may be based on differences in *social class, ethnic group*, age, *gender*, religion etc. Members of different groups usually have different *life chances*.

streaming: where children are separated into different ability groups or classes ('streams') and then each ability group is taught separately from the others for all subjects; the opposite of mixed-ability teaching. *See also* **differentiation; self-fulfilling prophecy**.

structural theories: see individuals as entirely shaped by the way society is structured or organised; e.g. *functionalism* sees society as socialising individuals into shared norms and values that dictate how they will behave. *Marxism* and most types of *feminism* are usually regarded as structural theories. *See also* **social action theories**.

Key Concepts

subculture: a group of people within society who share *norms*, *values*, beliefs and attitudes that are in some ways different from or opposed to the mainstream *culture*; e.g. an anti-school subculture formed by pupils in lower streams.

subjectivity: bias, lack of *objectivity*, where the individual's own viewpoint influences their perception or judgement. Interpretivists believe sociology is inevitably subjective, since it involves understanding other humans by seeing the world through their eyes. *See also* **empathy; interpretivism**.

survey: *see* **social survey**.

symbolic capital: a concept introduced by Bourdieu. It refers to the status, recognition and sense of worth we are able to obtain from others, especially those of a similar class position to us. Archer et al found that working-class girls gained symbolic capital from their peers by performing a hyper-heterosexual feminine, 'Nike' identity, but that this brought conflict with the school's middle-class ethos. *See also* **symbolic violence; habitus.**

symbolic violence: a concept introduced by Bourdieu. It refers to the harm done by denying someone *symbolic capital* (status and value), e.g. by defining their culture as worthless. Archer et al found that schools devalue working-class pupils' style preferences as tasteless. *See also* **symbolic capital; habitus.**

symmetrical family: a nuclear family with more equal and *joint conjugal roles*, in which husbands participate in domestic labour as well as being breadwinners, and wives go out to work as well as being homemakers. The couple spend their leisure time together and are more home-centred.

triangulation: the use of two or more different methods or sources of data so that they complement each other, the strengths of one countering the weaknesses of the other and vice versa; e.g. using both a qualitative method such as *participant observation* and a quantitative method such as structured *interviews*.

tripartite system: the system of secondary education created by the 1944 Education Act, based on three types of school. The 11+ exam was used to identify pupils' aptitudes and abilities. Those identified as having academic ability (mainly middle-class) went to grammar schools; most working-class children went to secondary modern schools. Although replaced in most areas after 1965, the tripartite system still continues in some. *See also* **comprehensive system**.

triple shift; triple burden: *see* **emotion work**.

underclass: those at the lowest level of the class structure; a class below the working class with a separate, deviant *subculture* and lifestyle, including a high rate of lone-parent families, male unemployment and criminality. *See also* **dependency culture; New Right**.

unit of consumption: unlike the pre-industrial family, the modern family no longer works together, but still consumes together as a single unit or group the income that its members earn, e.g. on food, housing and leisure activities. *See also* **unit of production**.

unit of production: where family members work together as economic producers, said to be more common in pre-industrial society; e.g. *an extended family* that works together on a farm. *See also* **unit of consumption**.

urbanisation: the process of change from a rural society where the majority of the population lives in the countryside to an urban society where most people live in towns and cities. It often occurs along with *industrialisation*.

validity: the capacity of a research method to measure what it sets out to measure; a true or genuine picture of what something is really like. A valid method is thus one that gives a truthful picture. Methods such as participant observation that produce *qualitative data* are usually seen as high in validity. *See also* **empathy; interactionism**.

value consensus: agreement among society's members about what values are important; a shared culture. According to functionalists, it integrates individuals into society by giving them a sense of solidarity or 'fellow feeling' with others and enables them to agree on goals and cooperate harmoniously. *See also* **functionalism**.

values: ideas or beliefs about general principles or goals. They tell society's members what is good or important in life and what to aim for, and they underlie more detailed *norms* of conduct. Functionalists see shared values as vital in holding society together. *See also* **functionalism; value consensus**.

variables: any factor that can change or vary; such as age, gender, occupation or income. Sociologists seek to discover *correlations* between variables; e.g. between *social class* and educational achievement. Laboratory *experiments* are occasionally used to control variables and measure their effect.

vocational: connected to a career. Vocational education and training transmits knowledge, skills and attitudes needed to pursue particular careers, e.g. courses in IT or hairdressing.
See also **new vocationalism**.

welfare state: where the government or state takes responsibility for people's well being, especially their basic minimum needs. In Britain, today's welfare state was created largely in the late 1940s. It includes various benefits to provide a minimum income, as well as the NHS, state education and council housing. *See also* **dependency culture; underclass**.

Bibliography

Abbott P and Wallace C (1992) *The Family and the New Right,* Pluto

Adonis A and Pollard S (1998) *A Class Act*, Penguin

Age Concern (2004) www.ageuk.org.uk

Allan G (1985) *Family Life*, Blackwell

Allan G (1996) *Kinship and Friendship in Modern Britain*, Oxford University Press

Allan G and Crow G (2001) *Families, Households and Society*, Palgrave

Almond B (2006) *The Fragmenting Family,* Oxford University Press

Althusser L (1971) *Lenin and Philosophy and Other Essays*, New Left Books

Amato P (2000) 'The consequences of divorce for adults and children', *Journal of Marriage and Family*

Anderson M (1980) *Approaches to the History of the Western Family*, Macmillan

Ansara D and Hindin M (2011) 'Psychosocial consequences of intimate partner violence for women and men in Canada', Journal of Interpersonal Violence

Ansley F (1972) cited in Bernard J (1976)

Arber S and Ginn J (1995) 'The Mirage of Gender Equality', British Journal of Sociology

Archer L, Hollingworth S and Mendick H (2010) *Urban Youth and Schooling,* Open University Press

Ariès P (1960) *Centuries of Childhood*, Penguin

Arnot C (2004) 'Where White Liberals Fear to Tread', The Guardian

Askew S and Ross C (1988) *Boys Don't Cry*, Open University

Atkinson M (1971) 'Societal Reactions to Suicide', in Cohen S (ed) *Images of Deviance*, Penguin

Ball S J (1981) *Beachside Comprehensive*, Open University

Ball S J (1993) in Burgess R *The Research Process in Educational Settings: Ten Case Studies,* Falmer

Ball S J (1994) *Education Reform*, Open University

Ball S J (2007) *Education plc*, Routledge

Ball S J (2008) *The Education Debate*, The Policy Press

Ball S J, Bowe R and Gewirtz S (1994), 'Market forces and parental choice', in Tomlinson S (ed), *Education Reform and its Consequences*, IPPR/Rivers Oram Press

Ballard R (1982) 'South Asian Families', in Rapoport R and Rapoport R (ed) *Families in Britain*, RKP

Barrett M and McIntosh M (1991) *The Anti-Social Family*, Verso

Bartlett W (1993) 'Quasi-Markets and Educational Reform', in Le Grand J et al (ed) *Quasi-Markets and Social Policy*, Macmillan

BBC (2006), 'Schools "too feminine for boys"', 13 June, www.bbc.co.uk

Beaujouan E and Bhroclain M (2011) 'Cohabitation and marriage in Britain since the 1970s', Population Trends

Beck U (1992) *Risk Society*, Sage

Beck U and Beck-Gernsheim E (1995) *The Normal Chaos of Love*, Polity

Becker H et al (1961) *Boys in White*, University of Chicago Press

Becker H (1971) 'Social Class Variations in the Teacher-Pupil Relationship', in Cosin B et al (ed) *Education Structure and Society*, Penguin

Beijin A (1985) *Western Sexuality*, Blackwell

Bell C (1968) *Middle Class Families*, RKP

Benedict R (1934) *Patterns of Culture*, Houghton Mifflin

Benson H (2006) *The conflation of marriage and cohabitation in government statistics – a denial of difference rendered untenable by an analysis of outcomes*, Bristol Community Family Trust

Bentley D (1987) 'Interviewing in the context of non-verbal research' in Powney J and Watts M *Interviewing in Educational Research.* Routledge and Kegan Paul

Bereiter C and Engelmann S (1966) *Teaching Disadvantaged Children in Pre-school,* Prentice Hall

Bernard J (1976) *The Future of Marriage*, Penguin

Bernstein B (1975) *Class, Codes and Control*, Schocken

Bernstein B (1976) 'Education Cannot Compensate for Society', in Butterworth E et al (ed) *The Sociology of Modern Britain*, Fontana

Bernstein B and Young D (1967) 'Differences in Conceptions on the Use of Toys', Sociology

Best L (1993) '"Dragons, dinner ladies and ferrets": sex roles in children's books', *Sociology Review*

Beynon J and Atkinson P (1984) '"Sussing out" teachers: pupils as data gatherers' in Hammersley M and Woods P (eds) *Life in School: the sociology of pupil culture*, Open University

Bhatti G (1999) *Asian Children at Home and at School: an Ethnographic Study*, Routledge

Black D et al (1980; 1992) 'The Black Report', in Whitehead M et al (ed) *Inequalities in Health,* Penguin

Blackstone T and Mortimore I (1994) 'Cultural factors in child-rearing and attitudes to education', in Moore B and Mayes AS (ed) *Teaching and Learning in the Secondary School,* Routledge

Blanden J and Machin S (2007) *Recent Changes in Intergenerational Mobility in the UK,* Sutton Trust

Blau P and Duncan O (1978) *The American Occupational Structure*, Free Press

Blauner R (1964) *Alienation and Freedom*, University of Chicago Press

Boaler J (1998) 'Mathematical Equity', in Epstein D et al (ed) *Failing Boys?* Open University

Bonke J (1999) 'Children's household work: is there a difference between girls and boys?' Working Paper, Danish National Institute of Social Research.

Bott E (1957) *Family and Social Network*, Tavistock

Boulton M (1983) *On Being a Mother*, Tavistock

Bourdieu P (1984) *Distinction,* Routledge

Bibliography

Bourdieu P and Wacquant L (1992) *An Invitation to Reflexive Sociology,* Polity

Bourne J (1994) *Outcast England*, Institute of Race Relations

Bowles S and Gintis H (1976) *Schooling in Capitalist America*, RKP

Brannen J (2003) 'The Age of Beanpole Families', Sociology Review

Brannen J et al (1994) *Young People, Health and Family Life*, Open University

Brass W and Kabir M (1978) 'Regional Variations in Fertility and Child Mortality during the Demographic Transition in England and Wales' in Hobcraft J and Rees P (eds) *Regional Demographic Development*, Croom Helm

Braun A, Vincent C and Ball S (2011) 'Working-class fathers and childcare', Community, Work and Family

British Crime Survey (2000; 2002; 2011) www.homeoffice.gov.uk

British Household Panel Survey (1998) www.iser.essex.ac.uk/bhps

British Social Attitudes (2000) www.esds.ac.uk

British Social Attitudes (2013) www.natcen.ac.uk

Browne J (2012) *The Impact of Austerity Measures on Families with Children,* Institute for Fiscal Studies

Browne N and Ross C (1991) 'Girls' Stuff, Boys' Stuff', in Browne N (ed) *Science and Technology in the Early Years*, Open University

Budgeon S (2011) *Third Wave Feminism and the Politics of Gender in Late Modernity,* Palgrave Macmillan

Bull D (1980) *What Price Free Education?* Child Poverty Action Group

Burn E (2001) 'Battling Through The System', International Journal of Inclusive Education

Byrne E (1979) *Women and Education*, Routledge

Callender C and Jackson J (2005) 'Fear of debt and higher education participation', Journal of Social Policy

Cameron M (1964) *The Booster and the Snitch*, Free Press

Carmichael S and Hamilton C (1967) *Black Power: The Politics of Liberation in America,* Random House

Cashmore E (1985) *Having to. The World of One Parent Families*, Allen and Unwin

Castles S (2000) *Ethnicity and Globalisation,* Sage

Castles S and Kosack G (1973) *Immigrant Workers and Class Structure in Western Europe,* Oxford University Press

Castles S, de Haas H and Miller M (2013) *Migration: International Population Movements in the Modern World,* Palgrave Macmillan

Centre for Longitudinal Studies (2007) *Disadvantaged children up to a year behind by the age of three,* Institute of Education

Chaikin A, Sigler E and Derlega V (1975) 'Non-verbal mediators of teacher expectancy effects', *Journal of Personality and Social Psychology*

Chamberlain M (1999) 'Brothers and Sisters, Uncles and Aunts', in Silva et al (ed) *The New Family?* Sage

Charles N, Davies C and Harris C (2008) *Families in Transition,* Policy Press

Cheal D (1991) *Family and the State of Theory*, Harvester

Cheal D (1993) 'Unity and Difference in Postmodern Families', *Journal of Family Issues*

Cheal D (2002) *Sociology of Family Life*, Palgrave Macmillan

Chester R (1985) 'The Rise of the Neo-Conventional Family', *New Society*

Chubb J and Moe T (1990) *Politics, Markets and America's Schools*, Brookings

Clarke A (2006) *Referrals, assessments and children and young people on child protection registers, England (First Release),* DfES

Cicourel A (1968) *The Social Organisation of Juvenile Justice*, Wiley

Claiborn W (1969) *'Expectancy effect in the classroom'*, Journal of Educational Psychology

Coard B (1971) *How the West Indian Child is Made Educationally Subnormal in the British School System*, New Beacon

Coard B (2005) 'Why I wrote the ESN Book", The Guardian, 5 February

Coast E (2006) 'Currently cohabiting: relationship attitudes, intentions and behaviour' *Royal Geographical Society annual conference*

Cockburn C (1987) *Two Track Training*, Macmillan

Cohen R (2006) *Migration and its Enemies,* Ashgate

Coleman K, Jansson K, Kaiza P and Reed E (2007) *Homicides, Firearm Offences and Intimate Violence 2005/06 (Supplementary volume 1 to Crime in England and Wales 2005/06)* Home Office Statistical Bulletin 02/07

Coleman K and Osborne S (2010) 'Homicide', in Smith K et al (ed) Homicides, *Firearm offences and intimate violence,* Home Office

Colley A (1998) 'Gender and Subject Choice in Secondary Education', in Radford J (ed) *Gender and Choice in Education and Occupation*, Routledge

Commission for Racial Equality (1992) *Set to Fail*, CRE

Commission for Racial Equality (1993) *Draft Circular on Admission Arrangements*, CRE

Condry R (2007) 'Families Shamed', *LSE Magazine,* Winter

Connell RW (1995), *Masculinities*, Polity

Connolly P (1988) *Racism, Gender Identities and Young Children*, Routledge

Connolly P (2006) 'The effects of social class and ethnicity on gender differences in GCSE attainment: a secondary analysis of the Youth Cohort Study of England and Wales 1997-2001', *British Educational Research Journal*

Connor H and Dewson S (2001) *Social Class and HE*, DfES Research Report

Cooke L and Gash V (2010) 'Wives' part time employment and marital stability in Great Britain, West Germany and the United States', Sociology

Crime Survey for England and Wales (2013) www.crimesurvey.co.uk

Crompton R (1997) *Women and Work in Modern Britain*, Oxford University Press

Crompton R and Lyonette C (2008) 'Who does the housework?' in Park A et al *British Social Attitudes: the 24th Report,* Sage

Crown Prosecution Service (2013) 'Violence against women and girls crime report', www.cps.gov.uk

Crystal D (2003) *The Cambridge Encyclopaedia of Language,* Cambridge University Press

Cunningham H (2007) 'Social constructions of childhood', *Sociology Review*

Currie D, Kelly D and Pomerantz S (2007) 'The Power to Squash People', British Journal of Sociology of Education

Curtis P (2007), 'Private schools prepare to face tests on keeping their charity tax breaks', The Guardian, 29 October

Dar A (2013) *Domestic violence statistics,* House of Commons Library

David M (1993) *Parents, Gender and Education Reform,* Polity

Davis K and Moore W (1945; 1967) 'Some Principles of Social Stratification', in Bendix and Lipset (ed) *Class Status and Power*, RKP

De Mause L (1974) *The History of Childhood,* Psychohistory Press

Dean H and Taylor-Gooby P (1992) *Dependency Culture,* Wheatsheaf

Delamont S (1976) *Interaction in the Classroom,* Methuen

Dex S and Ward K (2007) *Parental Care and Employment in Early Childhood,* Equal Opportunities Commission

Devine F and Heath S (1999) *Sociological Research Methods in Context*, Macmillan

Dewar A (1990) 'Oppression and Privilege in Physical Education', in Kirk D et al (ed) *Physical Education, Curriculum and Culture*, Falmer

Department for Education and Skills (2005) *Ethnicity and education*, DfES

Department for Education and Skills (2006), *School Workforce in England data*, DfES

Department for Education and Skills (2007) *Gender and education: the evidence on pupils in England,* DfES

DfE (2012) *Deprivation: what you need to know,* www.education.gov.uk

Ditton J (1977) *Part-time Crime*, Macmillan

Dobash R and Dobash R (1979) *Violence against Wives*, Open Books

Dobash R and Dobash R (2007) 'Violence against women', in O'Toole L and Schiffman J (ed) *Gender Violence,* New York University Press

Donzelot J (1977) *The Policing of Families*, Hutchinson

Douglas J (1964) *The Home and the School*, Penguin

Downes D and Rock P (1989) *Understanding Deviance*, Oxford University Press

Drew E et al (1995) *Families, Labour Markets and Gender Roles*, www.eurofound.eu.int

Driver G (1977) *Cultural Power, Social Power and School Achievement*, New Community

Duncombe J and Marsden D (1995) 'Women's Triple Shift', Sociology Review

Dunne G (1999) 'A Passion for Sameness', in Silva E et al (ed) *The New Family?* Sage

Dunne M and Gazeley L (2008) 'Teachers, social class and underachievement', British Journal of Sociology of Education

Durkheim E (1893; 1985) *The Division of Labour in Society*, Penguin

Durkheim E (1897; 2002) *Suicide*, Routledge

Durkheim E (1903; 2002) *Moral Education,* Dover

Economic and Social Research Council (2007) 'Men's housework could reduce divorce' *Britain in 2008,* ESRC

Edgell S (1980) *Middle Class Couples*, Allen and Unwin

Ehrenreich B and Hochschild A (2003) *Global Woman: Nannies, maids and sex workers in the new economy,* Granta

Elwood J and Murphy P (1998) 'Gendered Learning Outside and Inside School', in Epstein D et al (ed) *Failing Boys?* Open University

Elwood J (2005), 'Gender and achievement: what have exams got to do with it?' *Oxford Review of Education*

Engels F (1978) *Origin of the Family, Private Property and the State*, Foreign Languages Press, Peking

Epstein D et al (1998) 'Boys' Underachievement in Context', in Epstein D et al (ed) *Failing Boys?* Open University

Eriksen T (2007) 'Ernest Gellner and the multicultural mess', in Malesevic S and Haugaard M (ed) *Ernest Gellner and Contemporary Social Thought,* Cambridge University Press

Evans G (2006) *Educational Failure and Working Class White Children in Britain*, Palgrave Macmillan

Evans S (2009) 'In a Different Place', Sociology

Fairhurst E (1977) 'On Being a Patient in an Orthopaedic Ward', in Horobin G et al (ed) *Medical Encounters*, Croom Helm

Feinstein L (1998) 'Which Children Succeed and Why?', New Economy

Feinstein L (2003) 'Inequality in the early cognitive development of British children in the 1970 cohort', Economica

Feinstein L, Duckworth K and Sabates R (2008) *Education and the Family: Passing Success across the Generations,* Routledge

Ferri E and Smith K (1996) *Parenting in the 1990s*, Family Policy Studies Centre

Ferri E and Smith K (1998) *Step-parenting in the l990s*, Family Policy Studies Centre

Festinger L et al (1956) *When Prophecy Fails*, Harper and Row

Field J (n.d.) 'An interview survey of teenagers and parents', quoted in Powney J and Watts M (1987)

Finch J (1983) *Married to the Job*, Allen and Unwin

Finch J and Mason J (1989) *Family Obligations and Social Change,* Polity

Bibliography

Finch J and Mason J (1993) *Negotiating Family Responsibilities*, Routledge

Finn D (1984) 'Leaving School and Growing Up', in Bates I et al (ed) *Schooling for the Dole*, Macmillan

Firestone S (1970) *The Dialectics of Sex*, Paladin

Firestone S (1979) 'Down with Childhood', in Hoyles M (ed) *Changing Childhood*, Writers and Readers

Firth R (1970) *Rank and Religion in Tikopia*, Routledge

Fitz J et al (1997) 'Opting into the Past?' in Glatter P et al (ed) *Choice and Diversity in Schooling*, Routledge

Flaherty J et al (2004) *Poverty – the Facts*, 5th edition, CPAG

Flanders NA (1970) *Analysing Teacher Behaviour*, Addison Wesley

Fletcher R (1966) *The Family and Marriage in Britain*, Penguin

Flew A (1984) *Education, Race and Revolution*, Centre for Policy Studies

Foster P (1990) *Policy and Practice in Multicultural and Anti-Racist Education*, Routledge

Foucault M (1976) *The Birth of the Clinic*, Routledge

Francis B (2010) 'Girls' achievement', in Jackson C, Paechter C and Renold E (ed) *Girls and Education*, Open University

Francis B (2001), *Boys, Girls and Achievement: Addressing the Classroom Issues*, Routledge/Falmer

Francis B et al (2006) 'A Perfect Match? Pupils' and Teachers' Views of the Impact of Matching Educators and Learners By Gender', *Research Papers in Education Journal*

Frank A (1965) *The Diary of Anne Frank*, Pan

French J and French P (1993) 'Gender Imbalances in the Primary Classroom', in Woods P et al (ed) *Gender and Ethnicity in Schools*, Routledge

Fuller C (2011) *Sociology, Gender and Educational Aspirations*, Continuum

Fuller M (1984) 'Black Girls in a London Comprehensive School', in Deem R (ed) *Schooling for Women's Work*, RKP

Furlong J (1984) 'Interaction Sets in the Classroom', in Hammersley M et al (ed) *Life in Schools*, Open University

Future Foundation (2000) *Complicated Lives*, John Wiley & Sons

Gatrell C (2005) *Hard Labour: The Sociology of Parenthood*, Open University Press

Gershuny J et al (1994) 'The Domestic Labour Revolution', in Anderson M et al (ed) *The Social and Political Economy of the Household*, Oxford University Press

Gewirtz S et al (1995) *Markets, Choice and Equity in Education*, Open University

Gewirtz S and Cribb A (2009) *Understanding Education*, Polity

Giddens A (1992) *The Transformation of Intimacy*, Polity

Gill R (1988) 'Altered Images', Social Studies Review

Gill R and Scharff C (2013) *New Feminities: Postfeminism, Neoliberalism and Subjectivity*, Palgrave Macmillan

Gillborn D (1990) *Race, Ethnicity and Education*, Unwin Hyman

Gillborn D (1997) 'Race and Ethnicity in Education 14-19', in Tomlinson S (ed) *Education 14-19 Critical Perspectives*, Athorne

Gillborn D (2008) *Racism and Education: Coincidence or Conspiracy?* Routledge

Gillborn D and Mirza H S (2000) *Educational Inequality: Mapping Race, Gender and Class: a Synthesis of Research*, Ofsted

Gillborn D and Youdell D (2000) *Rationing Education: Policy, Practice, Reform and Equity,* Open University

Gittins D (1998) *The Child in Question*, Macmillan

Glasgow University Media Group (1976) *Bad News*, RKP

Graham H (1983) 'Do Her Answers Fit His Questions?', in Gamarnikow E et al (ed) *The Public and the Private*, Heinemann

Graham H (1984) *Women, Health and the Family*, Prentice Hall

Greene S and Hogan D (2005) *Researching Children's Experiences: Approaches and Methods,* Sage

Greer G (2000) *The Whole Woman*, Anchor

Gregson N and Lowe M (1994) *Servicing the Middle Classes*, Routledge

Greig A et al (2007) *Doing Educational Research*, Sage

Griffin J (1962) *Black Like Me*, Collins

Griffiths R (1988) *Community Care: Agenda for Action*, HMSO

Haase M (2008) 'I don't do the mothering role that lots of female teachers do', British Journal of Sociology of Education

Hardill I et al (1997) 'Who Decides What?', Work, Employment and Society

Hareven T (1999) *Families, History and Social Change*, Westview

Hargreaves D (1967) *Social Relations in a Secondary School*, RKP

Harper S and Hamblin K (2014) *International Handbook on Ageing and Public Policy,* Edward Elgar

Harvey D and Slatin G (1976) 'The relationships between child's SES and teacher expectations, *Social Forces*

Hastings S (2006) 'White underachievement', Times Educational Supplement, 28 April

Hatcher R et al (1996) *Racial Equality and the Local Management of Schools*, Warwick Papers on Education Policy

Hayton R (2010) 'Conservative Party modernisation and David Cameron's politics of the family', Political Quarterly

Haywood C and Mac an Ghaill M (1996) 'Schooling Masculinities', in Mac an Ghaill M (ed) *Understanding Masculinities*, Open University

HEFCE (2010) *Trends in Young Participation in Higher Education*, www.hefce.ac.uk

Hempel-Jorgensen A (2009) 'The construction of the ideal pupil and pupils' perceptions of misbehaviour and discipline', British Journal of Sociology of Education

Hey V (1997) *The Company She Keeps: an ethnography of girls' friendship*, Open University Press

Hillman M (1993) *Children, Transport and the Quality of Life*, Policy Studies Institute

Hirsch D (2005) 'Paying for ourselves as we get older: rethinking resource allocation', Institute of Actuaries

Hite S (1991) *The Hite Report on Love, Passion and Emotional Violence*, Penguin

Hochschild A (1983) *The Managed Heart*, University of California Press

Hochschild A (1997) *The Time Bind*, Metropolitan Books

Hochschild A (2013) *So How's the Family?* University of California Press

Hockey J and James A (1993) *Growing Up and Growing Old*, Sage

Holdsworth C and Morgan D (2005) *Transitions in Context: Leaving Home, Independence and Adulthood*, Open University Press

Holmes L (1974) *Samoan Village*, Thompson

Holt J (1974) *Escape from Childhood*, Penguin

House of Commons (2013) *Women in the Workplace,* The Stationery Office

Howard M et al (2001) *Poverty the Facts*, Child Poverty Action Group

Hugo R (1982) *The Hitler Diaries*, William Morrow

Humphreys C and Thiara R (2002) *Routes to Safety,* Women's Aid Federation

Humphreys L (1970) *The Tea Room Trade*, Duckworth

Hunt S (2005) *Life Course: a Sociological Introduction,* Palgrave Macmillan

Ingram N (2009) 'Working-class boys, educational success and the misrecognition of working-class culture', British Journal of Sociology of Education

Institute of Physics (2012) *It's different for girls: the influence of schools,* www.iop.org

Irvine J (1987) *Demystifying Social Statistics*, Pluto

Jackson D (1998) 'Breaking the Binary Trap', in Epstein et al (ed) *Failing Boys?* Open University

Jenkins R (1986) *Racism and Recruitment*, Cambridge University Press

Jenks C (2005) *Childhood,* Routledge

Jones D (2006) 'The "Right kind of man"', Sex Education 6

Kan M-Y (2001) 'Gender Asymmetry in the Division of Domestic Labour', *BHPS 2001 conference*, Institute for Social and Economic Research

Katz C (1993) *Growing up Global*, University of Minnesota Press

Keddie N (1973) *Tinker, Tailor: the Myth of Cultural Deprivation*, Penguin

Kelly A (1987) *Science for Girls*, Open University

Kempson E et al (1994) *Hard Times?,* Family Policy Studies Centre

Kendal Project (2004) www.lancs.ac.uk

King R (1984) 'The Man in the Wendy House', in Burgess R *The Research Process in Educational Settings*: *Ten Case Studies',* Falmer

Kinsey A et al (1953) *Sexual Behaviour in the Human Female*, WB Saunders

Labov W (1973) 'The Logic of Nonstandard English', in Keddie N (ed) *Tinker, Tailor: the Myth of Cultural Deprivation*, Penguin

Lacey C (1970) *Hightown Grammar*, Manchester University Press

Land H (1978) 'Who Cares for the Family?' Journal of Social Policy

Laslett P (1972) *Household and Family in Past Time*, Cambridge University Press

Laurie H and Gershuny J (2000) 'Couples, work and money', in Berthoud R and Gershuny J (ed) *Seven Years in the Lives of British Families,* Policy Press

Lawrence E (1982) 'The Sociology of Black Pathology', in CCCS (ed) *The Empire Strikes Back*, Hutchinson

Lawson T and Garrod J (2000) *The Complete A to Z Sociology Handbook*, Hodder

Leach E (1967) *Runaway World?* BBC

Lees S (1986) *Losing Out*, Hutchinson

Lees S (1993) *Sugar and Spice*, Penguin

Leonard D (1978) 'The Regulation of Marriage', in Littlejohn G et al (ed) *Power and the State*, Croom Helm

Leonard D (2006) 'Single-sex schooling', in Francis B et al (eds) *Handbook of Gender And Education,* Sage

Liebow E (1967) *Tally's Corner*, Little Brown

Liverpool Victoria (2014) *Annual 'Cost of a Child' survey 2014*, www.lv.com

Lobban G (1974) 'Data Report on British Reading Schemes', Times Educational Supplement

Lupton R (2004) "Schools in Disadvantaged Areas", Centre for Analysis of Social Exclusion

Lyotard J (1984) *The Postmodern Condition*, Manchester University Press

Mac an Ghaill M (1994) *The Making of Men*, Open University

MacDonald M (1980) 'Socio-cultural Reproduction and Women's Education', in Deem R (ed) *Schooling for Women's Work*, RKP

Maguire M (1997) 'Missing links: working-class women of Irish descent', in Mahoney P and Zmroczek C (ed) *Class Matters,* Taylor and Francis

Madge N (2006) *Children These Days,* Policy Press

Malinowski B (1957) *The Sexual Life of Savages*, RKP

Margo J and Dixon M (2006) *Freedom's Orphans,,* IPPR

Marx K (1848; 2002) *The Communist Manifesto*, Penguin

Mason D (1995) *Race and Ethnicity in Modern Britain*, Oxford University Press

Mason E J (1973) 'Teachers' observations of boys and girls as influenced by biased psychological reports and knowledge of the effects of bias', Journal of Educational Research

Bibliography

May V (2013) *Connecting Self to Society*, Palgrave Macmillan

Mayo E (1927; 2003) *Human Problems of an Industrial Civilisation*, Routledge

McKeown T et al (1972) 'An Interpretation of the Modern Rise in Population in Europe', *Population Studies*

McRobbie A (1978) 'Working-Class Girls and the Culture of Femininity', in Hall S et al (ed) *Resistance Through Ritual*, Hutchison

McRobbie A (1994) *Postmodernism and Popular Culture*, Routledge

McVeigh T (2001) 'Boys Lagging in Class for Years', The Observer

Mead M (1943) *Coming of Age in Samoa*, Penguin

Meighan R (1981) *A Sociology of Educating*, Cassell Education

Merton R (1949) *Social Theory and Social Structure*, Free Press

Milgram S (1974) *Obedience and Authority*, Harper Collins

Millett K (1970) *Sexual Politics*, Doubleday

Mirza H (1992) *Young Female and Black*, Routledge

Mirza H (1997) *Black British Feminism*, Routledge

Mirza H (2005) 'The more things change, the more they stay the same', in Richardson B (ed) *Tell It Like It Is*, Bookmarks Publications and Trentham Books

Mitchell J and Goody J (1997) 'Feminism, Fatherhood and the Family in Britain', in Oakley A and Mitchell J (ed) *Who's Afraid of Feminism*, Penguin

Mitsos E and Browne K (1998) 'Gender Differences in Education', Sociology Review

Modood T (2004) 'Capitals, ethnic identity and education qualifications', Cultural Trends

Moore D and Davenport S (1990) 'Choice: the New Improved Sorting Machine', in Boyd W et al (ed) *Choice in Education*, McCutchan

Morgan D (1996) *Family Connections*, Polity

Morgan D (1997) 'Risk and Family Practices', in Silva E et al (ed) *The New Family*, Sage

Morgan D (2007) *Passing Acquaintances*, Open University Press

Morgan P (2003) 'The Family Today', in Holborn M (ed) *Developments in Sociology*, Causeway Press

MORI (2004) *Schools Omnibus 2004: A Research Study Among 11-16 Year Olds on behalf of The Sutton Trust*, www.suttontrust.com

Morrow R and Torres C (1998) 'Education and the Reproduction of Class, Gender and Race', in Torres C et al (ed) *Sociology of Education: Emerging Perspectives*, University of New York Press

Mortimore P and Whitty G (1997) *Can School Improvement Overcome the Effects of Disadvantage?* Institute of Education

Moynihan D (1965) *The Negro Family*, US Department of Labor

Murdock G P (1949) *Social Structure*, Macmillan

Murphy P (1991) 'Gender Differences in Pupils' Reactions to Practical Work', in Woolnough B (ed) *Practical Science*, Open University

Murray C (1984) *Losing Ground*, Basic Books

Murray C (1990) *The Making of the British Underclass*, Institute of Economic Affairs

Myhill D and Jones S (2006) 'She Doesn't Shout at No Girls, *Cambridge Journal of Education*

National Audit Office (2002) www.nao.gov.uk

Nazroo J (1997) *The Health of Britain's Ethnic Minorities*, Policy Studies Institute

Noon M (1993) 'Racial Discrimination in Speculative Applications', Human Resources Management Journal

Nordqvist P and Smart C (2014) Relative Strangers: *Family Life, Genes and Donor Conception*, Palgrave Macmillan

Norman F et al (1988) 'Look, Jane, Look', in Weiner G (ed) *Just a Bunch of Girls*, Open University

NUS-HSBC (2010) *Student Experience Full Report: Finance and Debt*, www.nus.org.uk

Nyman C (2003) 'The social nature of money', Women's Studies International Forum

Oakley A (1973) *Sex, Gender and Society*, Temple Smith

Oakley A (1974) *The Sociology of Housework*, Martin Robertson

Oakley A (1982) *Subject Women*, Penguin

Oakley A (1997) 'A Brief History of Gender', in Oakley A and Mitchell J (ed) *Who's Afraid of Feminism*, Penguin

Opie I (1993) *The People in the Playground*, Oxford University Press

Osler A (2006) 'Excluded girls: interpersonal, institutional and structural violence in schooling', Gender and Education

Osler A, Watling R, Busher H, Cole T and White A (2001) *Reasons for exclusion from school*, DfEE Research Brief

Paechter C (1998) *Educating the Other*, Falmer

Pahl J and Vogler C (1993) 'Social and Economic Change and the Organisation of Money within Marriage', Work, Employment and Society

Palmer G (2012) *The Poverty Site*, www.poverty.org.uk

Palmer S (2007) *Toxic Childhood*, Orion

Palmer S (2010) *Twenty-first Century Boys*, Orion

Parker A (1996) 'Sporting Masculinities', in Mac an Ghaill M (ed) *Understanding Masculinities*, Open University

Parker H et al (1998) *Illegal Leisure*, Routledge

Parsons T (1955) 'The American Family', in Parsons T and Bales R (ed) *Family Socialisation and Interaction Process*, Free Press

Parsons T (1961) 'The School Class as a Social System', in Halsey A et al (ed) *Education, Economy and Society*, Free Press

Patrick J (1973) *A Glasgow Gang Observed*, Methuen

Phillipson C (1982) *Capitalism and the Construction of Old Age*, Macmillan

Pilcher J (1995) *Age and Generation in Modern Britain*, Oxford University Press

Pollock L (1983) *Forgotten Children*, Cambridge University Press

Polsky N (1971) *Hustlers, Beats and Others*, Penguin

Postman N (1994) *The Disappearance of Childhood*, Vintage

Powney J and Watts M (1987) *Interviewing in Educational Research*, Routledge and Kegan Paul

Pryce K (1979) *Endless Pressure*, Penguin

Punch M (1979) *Policing the Inner City*, Macmillan

Punch S (2001) 'Negotiating autonomy: childhoods in rural Bolivia' in L. Alanen and B. Mayall (eds) *Conceptualising Child-Adult Relations*, Routledge Falmer

Ramos X (2003) 'Domestic Work Time and Gender Differentials in Great Britain 1992-1998' *BHPS 2003 conference*, Institute for Social and Economic Research

Rapoport R and Rapoport R (1982) *Families in Britain*, RKP

Read B (2008) 'The world must stop when I'm talking', British Journal of Sociology of Education

Reay D (2001) 'Spice girls, nice girls, girlies and tom boys', Gender and Education

Reay D, Davies J, David M and Ball S (2001) 'Choices of Degree or Degrees of Choice?' Sociology

Reay, D, Davies J, David M and Ball SJ (2005) *Degrees of Choice*, Trentham Books

Redman P and Mac an Ghaill M (1997) 'Educating Peter', in Steinberg D et al (ed) *Border Patrols*, Cassell

Renvoize J (1985) *Going Solo*, Routledge

Rex J (1986) *Race and Ethnicity*, Open University

Reynolds T (2010) 'Mis-representing the Black Super-woman', in Mirza S (ed) *Black British Feminism*, Routledge

Ribbens McCarthy J et al (2003) *Making Families: Moral Tales of Parenting and Step-Parenting*, Sociology Press

Rich J (1968) *Interviewing Children and Adolescents*, Macmillan

Ridge T (2002), *Childhood Poverty and Social Exclusion: from a child's perspective*, The Bailey Press

Ringrose J (2013) *Postfeminist Education?* Routledge

Rist R (1970) 'Student Social Class and Teacher Expectations', Harvard Educational Review

Robertson Elliot F (1996) *Gender, Family and Society*, Macmillan

Robinson P (1997) *Literacy, Numeracy and Economic Performance*, London School of Economics

Roithmayr D (2003) 'Locked-in inequality: the persistence of discrimination', Michigan Journal of Race and Law

Rosenhan D (1973) 'On Being Sane in Insane Places', Science

Rosenthal R and Jacobson L (1968) *Pygmalion in the Classroom*, Holt Rinehart and Winston

Roulstone A (1998) 'Researching a Disabling Society', in Shakespeare T (ed) *The Disability Reader*, Cassell

Rutter M et al (1979) *Fifteen Thousand Hours*, Open Books

Sanders W and Horn S (1995) 'Educational assessment reassessed', Education Policy Archives

Sayer A (2002) 'What are you worth? Why class is an embarrassing subject', Sociological Research Online

Schofield M (1965) *The Sexual Behaviour of Young People*, Longman

School Census (2010), Department for Education

Scott J (1990) *A Matter of Record*, Polity

Scruton R (1986) 'The Myth of Cultural Relativism', in O'Keefe D (ed) *Anti-Racism: an Assault on Education and Value*, Sherwood

Sewell T (1998) 'Loose Cannons', in Epstein D et al (ed) *Failing Boys?* Open University

Sewell T (2009) *Generating Genius,* Trentham Books

Shain F (2003) *The Schooling and Identity of Asian Girls,* Trentham Books

Sharpe S (1994) *Just Like a Girl*, Penguin

Shaw C (1930) *The Jack-Roller*, University of Chicago Press

Shelton B and John D (1993) 'Does Marital Status Make a Difference?', Journal of Family Issues

Shipman M (1997) *Limitations of Social Research*, Longman

Shorter E (1975) *The Making of the Modern Family*, Fontana

Shutes I (2011) *Social Care for Older People and Demand for Migrant Workers,* Migration Observatory, www. migrationobservatory.ox.ac.uk

Silva E and Smart C (1999) 'The new practices and policies of family life', in Silva E and Smart C (ed) *The New Family?* Sage

Skeggs B (1997) *Formations of Class and Gender*, Sage

Slee R (1998) 'High Reliability Organisations and Liability Students', in Slee R et al (ed) *School Effectiveness for Whom?* Falmer

Smart C (2007) *Personal Life,* Polity

Smart C (2011) 'Children's Personal lives', in May V *Sociology of Personal Life,* Palgrave Macmillan

Smart C (2011) 'Close Relationships and Personal Life', in May V *Sociology of Personal Life,* Palgrave Macmillan

Smith T and Noble M (1995) *Education Divides: Poverty and Schooling in the 1990s,* CPAG

Somerville J (2000) *Feminism and the Family*, Macmillan

Southerton D (2011) 'Are we running out of time?' in May V (ed) *Sociology of Personal Life,* Palgrave Macmillan

Stacey J (1998) *Brave New Families*, University of California Press

Stone M (1981) *The Education of the Black Child in Britain*, Fontana

Strand S (2010) 'Do some schools narrow the gap?' School Effectiveness and School Improvement

Strand S (2012) 'The White British-Black Caribbean achievement gap', British Educational Research Journal

Sugarman B (1970) 'Social Class Values and Behaviour in Schools', in Craft M (ed) *Family Class and Education*, Longman

Sullivan A (2001) 'Cultural capital and educational attainment',

Bibliography

Sociology

Sullivan O (2000) 'The Division of Domestic Labour: Twenty Years of Change?' *Sociology*

Swann J and Graddol D (1994) 'Gender inequalities in classroom talk', in Graddol et al (eds) *Researching Language and Literacy in Social Contexts*, Clevedon

Swann J (1998) 'Language and Gender', in Epstein D et al (ed) *Failing Boys?* Open University

Tanner E et al (2003) *The Costs of Education*, Child Poverty Action Group

The Home Office (2013), www.gov.uk

The Sutton Trust (2011) *Degrees of Success: University chances by individual school,* www.suttontrust.com

Thomas W and Znaniecki F (1919; 1995) *The Polish Peasant in Europe and America*, University of Illinois Press

Thornton S (1995) *Club Cultures*, Polity

Tipper B (2011) 'Pets and Personal Life', in May V (2011) *Sociology of Personal Life,* Palgrave Macmillan

Tranter NL (1996) *British Population in the Twentieth Century,* Macmillan

Troyna B and Williams J (1986) *Racism, Education and the State*, Croom Helm

Tuchman G (1978) *Hearth and Home*, Oxford University Press

Tuckett D (2001) *An Introduction to Medical Sociology*, Routledge

Tumin M (1967) *Social Stratification*, Prentice Hall

UCAS (2011), www.ucas.com

UNICEF (2013) *Child Well-being in Developed Societies*, UNICEF

Vertovec S (2007) *New Complexities of Cohesion in Britain,* Commission on Integration and Cohesion

Vogler C (1994) 'Money in the Household', in Anderson M et al (ed) *The Social and Political Economy of the Household*, Oxford University Press

Vogler C, Brockmann M and Wiggins R (2007) 'Managing money in new heterosexual forms of intimate relationships', Journal of Socio-Economics

Walby S and Allen J (2004) *Domestic Violence, Sexual Assault and Stalking,* Home Office

Wagg S (1992) 'I Blame the Parents', Sociology Review

Walker A (2011) 'Living longer still seen as a problem', in *Britain in 2011,* ESRC

Warde A and Hetherington K (1993) 'A Changing Domestic Division of Labour?" Work, Economy and Society

Weber M (1905; 2002) *The Protestant Ethic and the Spirit of Capitalism*, Routledge

Weeks J (2000) *Making Sexual History*, Polity

Weeks J et al (1999) 'Everyday Experiments', in Silva E et al (ed) *The New Family?,* Sage

Weeks J, Heaphy B and Donovan C (2001) *Same Sex Intimacies,* Routledge

Weiner G (1993) 'Shell-shock or Sisterhood', in Arnot M et al (ed) *Feminism and Social Justice in Education*, Falmer

Weiner G et al (1995) *Equal Opportunities in Colleges and Universities*, Open University

Weston K (1992) 'The Politics of Gay Families', in Thorne B and Yallom M (ed) *Rethinking the Family*, Northeastern University Press

Whitty G et al (1998) *Devolution and Choice in Education*, Open University

Whyte W (1955) *Street Corner Society*, University of Chicago Press

Wilkinson R and Pickett K (2010) *The Spirit Level: Why Equality is better for Everyone,* Penguin

Willis P (1977) *Learning to Labour*, Saxon House

Willmott P (1988) *The Evolution of a Community*, Routledge

Women's' Aid Federation (2014), www.womensaid.org.uk

Wood M, Hales J, Purdon S, Sejersen T and Hayllar O (2010) *A test for racial discrimination in recruitment practice in British cities,* DWP

Woods P (1979) *The Divided School*, RKP

Wright C (1992) 'Early Education', in Gill D et al (ed) *Racism in Education*, Sage

Wrong D (1961) 'The Oversocialised Conception of Man', *American Sociological Review*

Yablonsky L (1973) *The Violent Gang*, Penguin

Yearnshire S (1997) 'Analysis of Cohort', in Bewley et al (ed) *Violence Against Women*, RCOG Press

Youdell D (2001) 'Engineering school markets, constituting schools and subjectivating students', *Journal of Educational Policy*

Youdell D (2006) *Impossible Bodies, Impossible Selves,* Springer

Yougov (2007), 'Primary School Kids', www.yougov.com

Young M and Willmott P (1962) *Family and Kinship in East London*, Penguin

Young M and Willmott P (1973) *The Symmetrical Family*, Penguin

Zaretsky E (1976) *Capitalism, The Family and Personal Life*, Pluto Press

Index

Index

Index

Index

Index